THE

PIATKUS

DICTIONARY

of

MIND, BODY
AND SPIRIT

About the Author

Paula Byerly Croxon, RawDip., ITEC, AOC, practises as an alternative therapist in addition to working as a journalist and editor. She obtained diplomas in Holistic Aromatherapy and Holistic Reflexology from the internationally respected Raworth Centre College for Sports Therapy and Natural Medicine in Dorking, Surrey. She has been MBS consultant to various publications and businesses including *Health and Fitness*, *Cosmopolitan*, *Financial Times* and Waterstone's, and has acted as a literary commentator on all matters MBS on radio and television in the UK and the US. She lives in Kent.

THE
PIATKUS
DICTIONARY
of
MIND, BODY
AND SPIRIT

PAULA BYERLY CROXON

PIATKUS

Copyright © 2003 by Paula Byerly Croxon

First published in 2003 by
Judy Piatkus (Publishers) Limited
5 Windmill Street
London W1T 2JA

First paperback edition 2003

e-mail: info@piatkus.co.uk

The moral right of the author has been asserted

A catalogue record for this book is available from the British Library

ISBN 0 7499 2430 6 (HB)
ISBN 0 7499 2417 9 (PB)

Edited by Alice Wood
Text design by Tracy Timson

This book has been printed on paper manufactured
with respect for the environment using wood from
managed sustainable resources

Typeset by Wyvern 21 Ltd, Bristol

Printed and bound in Great Britain by MPG Books Ltd, Bodmin, Cornwall

Contents

Acknowledgements

Like any author, I am deeply indebted to a large number of people who have made this work possible. First, I would like to thank my editors, Anna Crago, Gill Bailey, Alice Wood and, of course, Judy Piatkus, who had the idea in the first place. I would also like to thank Ginny Surtees and Kay Gale for their contributions to this project.

I'd also like to acknowledge the contributions of the following authors whose books were particular sources of information and inspiration: Cassandra Eason, Jonathan Cainer, Kristin Olsen, Eileen Campbell and J.H. Brennan.

I was fortunate enough to have the following network of individuals who provided invaluable references, advice and encouragement or just plain friendship in the midst of my writing haze: Philippa Nice, Judith Stead, Martin Latham, Jo Scrimshaw, Elspeth Moore, Liesl Malan, Stephen Scott, Travis Elborough, Nick Rennison, Claire Milburn, Steve Davis, Jennifer Boone, Pat Dickinson, Eunice Weekes, Carole Bayliss, Sue Lacey, Helen Bareham, Richard Detrano, Penny Davies, and Vicki Gardner. Thanks y'all – I couldn't have done it without you.

Finally I'd like to thank my mother, Marion Byerly, and my sisters Becky Byerly-Adams, Robin Byerly and Wendy Byerly-Purdy, for their love and support this past year. You are a blessing to me, and to the world.

Abominable Snowman see Yeti

Abracadabra A magical incantation, renowned for its healing properties and for protection against evil. Abracadabra is a word derived from the Gnostic deity Abraxas, whose name means 'hurt me not'. When the word is arranged in a charm or chanted it is said to possess the magical power to guard against illness. The charm is a triangle formed from writing the word ten times centred each time on a new line, leaving the final letter off each time until you are only left with the letter 'a'. The charm triangle is often worn or carried for nine days, then taken off and discarded in a river or stream running east (towards the land where Abraxas lived). See also: **Magic**, **Sorcery**.

Abracadabra
Abracadabr
Abracadab
Abracada
Abracad
Abraca
Abrac
Abra
Abr
Ab
A

The abracadabra charm

Absent Healing, Distant Healing A situation where the patient is not in the same location as the healer, or the object of healing is the focus of prayer or visualisation by a distant person or persons. How this is accomplished remains a mystery, but a growing body of evidence supports the belief that physical and emotional healing does take place under these conditions. American doctor Larry Dossey has conducted several double-blind studies where a group of patients was subdivided into two separate sets. One set was the focus of a group of meditators, who prayed for their health and healing; the others were not the objects of any prayer. The patient group which had been prayed over showed greater improvement in their health conditions than the control group.

Absent healing does not seem so unlikely when you consider that most spiritual healing is based on rebalancing the energies within the sick body. Energy can be directed from afar, and many **psychics**, reiki practitioners and

medical intuitives can do distance healing at will. When spiritual healers exercise their gift this way, they carry it out either by speaking the name of the sick person or by focusing on a photograph, an appropriately coloured candle or a doll (which represents the person). The healing energies are then directed to wherever they are needed. Spiritual healers and reiki practitioners prefer the term 'distant healing' over 'absent healing', as they say the person is not 'absent' once you have made the connection with the intended recipient and sent the healing energy to them. See also: **Candle Magic**.

Acupressure A general term used to describe different massage techniques derived from **Traditional Chinese Medicine** that stimulate energy pathways on the body. These pathways, called **meridians**, circulate bioelectric energy (**chi**) throughout the body along specific channels. When the flow of chi becomes imbalanced through blockage, illness can result. Acupressure works by pressing down on meridians to free up this bioelectric flow. It is related in theory to **acupuncture**, but is a gentler, non-invasive therapy that uses manual pressure alone on meridian points. **Shiatsu** (finger pressure massage) and **tui na** (soft tissue massage) are two variations of acupressure.

The three most common massage techniques used in this therapy are: finger-tapping (which arouses sluggish muscles and improves nerve function); brisk rubbing (which stimulates the blood and lymphatic system); and steady finger pressure (which helps relieve pain and relaxes the nervous system).

An acupressure treatment usually has three distinct stages. First, the practitioner will do an overall energy balancing of the patient, followed by work on specifically blocked meridians. Finally the therapist will perform a closing massage routine that will both seal in the energy work as well as gently end the session.

Acupressure is recommended as a treatment for chronic pain (especially of the back) and for general relaxation and stress reduction.

Acupuncture (Latin *acus*, 'needle', + *punctura*, 'puncture', originally from Chinese, *zhen*, 'metal that bites', + *jiu*, 'fire') A **Traditional Chinese Medicine** technique of treating ill-health and maintaining wellness in which fine needles are inserted into the skin at specific points along pathways of energy called **meridians**. In health, this energy, called **chi** or qi, flows freely through the meridian channels. When disease or injury occurs, chi becomes blocked and does not flow. Acupuncture needles, **moxibustion** or **acupressure** used at precise locations along meridians release these blockages by stimulating the trapped chi in the same way breaking up a dam on a river releases the water's flow. Chi may also flow either too quickly or too slowly, in which case acupuncture is used to regulate the stream of energy.

There is a total of 365 different acupuncture points scattered across the exterior surface of the body, arranged in a series of 14 main meridians.

Acupuncture has been practised in China for at least 4,000 years, with acupuncture needles found in archaeology digs of the late Shang Dynasty (c.1000 BC) and discussed in detail in **Yellow Emperor's Inner Classic**, a fourth-century AD Chinese medical text. There are three types of acupuncture: five element; traditional yin/yang theory; and medical, or Western acupuncture. All three use similar diagnostic methods and the same system of acupuncture points, but take a different philosophical approach to underlying causes of illness and treatment.

Practitioners of five element acupuncture (see **five element cycle**), believe that each human being has a tiny weakness in one of the organs of a particular element. Illness is also believed to be the product of emotional distress as much as of any physical cause. Acupuncture points are treated along obstructed meridians that correspond with the affected **element**. As the emphasis is on treating the underlying cause of an illness, a complete recovery, while possible, can be slow in coming.

Traditional yin/yang theory focuses on restoring the overall balance of **yin** and **yang** in the body. Acupuncture points are stimulated along several different meridians and therefore affect more than one element at a time.

Medical, or Western acupuncture, focuses on acute, short-term treatment, combining Eastern and Western medical techniques. There are two subtypes of medical acupuncture: anaesthetic acupuncture, which is used in surgical and dental procedures, and symptomatic or first-aid acupuncture, which is used to bring temporary analgesic relief from pain and illness without diagnosing the underlying cause. This is also known as the **Barefoot Doctor** approach to acupuncture. Other variations of acupuncture include electro-acupuncture, where meridian points are stimulated using a mild electrical current with either special needles or equipment; and ear acupuncture, or **auriculotherapy**, where only points on the ear corresponding to parts of the body are treated.

Reputable medical research has found acupuncture to be effective in treating depression, allergies, asthma, arthritis, infertility, gynaecological disorders, migraines and high blood pressure. Like many **energy medicines**, acupuncture is most effective for treating either chronic conditions that do not respond to conventional medicines, or in handling ailments related to a person's lifestyle. See also: **Complementary Medicine**.

Adept A master of the occult arts, who has gained magic and power through study and initiation into an esoteric cult like the **Golden Dawn**, or **Theosophy**.

Adi Granath, also **Gurn Granth Sahib** (Punjabi, 'original or first book') Sacred holy book of **Sikhism**, which was compiled by Guru Arjun Dev in 1604. It expresses Sikh belief about the nature of God and contains an important and oft-quoted recital (a Sikh Lord's Prayer) from the founder of the religion, Guru Nanak. The *Adi Granath* forms an important part of Sikh ritual, as it is ceremonially opened each morning in Sikh temples, and closed and wrapped in the evening. During high holy days and special festivals, the book is actually paraded about in processions through the streets, with continuous readings of scripture taking place in the temples.

Aeromancy (Greek *aero*, 'air', + *manteia*, 'divination'). A form of **divination**, (predicting future events) from observing air, sky and atmospheric phenomena. Cloud shapes, comets and falling stars have all been used to interpret the future – examples include the star over Bethlehem foretelling when and where Jesus Christ would be born, and the appearance of Halley's Comet around the time of the Battle of Hastings that supposedly foretold William the Conqueror's victory. See also: **Astromancy, Austromancy**.

Aesculapius The Greek god of healing and medicine, whose staff, intertwined with a snake, is a symbol for the art of healing or medicine. Aesculapius was the son of the sun god **Apollo**, but was raised by the centaur **Chiron**. His healing skills grew so great that he was able to restore life to the dead, prompting **Hades**, the god of the underworld, to ask head god **Zeus** to kill him. At the request of Apollo, he was placed among the stars. His daughter was Hygieia, goddess of health.

Age of Aquarius Term used to describe a **new age** of thinking in Western culture, based on the astrological theory of the 'Procession of the Equinoxes'. Western **Astrology** holds that for the past 2,000 years or so, our world has been in the Age of Pisces.

Where our solar system was located in the zodiac was determined by the Greek astrologer and philosopher Hipparchus. He used measurements of star movements taken on the eve of the spring **equinox** to determine our place in the galaxy. The procession causes the fixed stars to appear to move 'backwards' in the zodiac – thus placing (at his time) the world in the constellations of the sign **Aries**. Sometime around 60 BC the world lurched into the Age of

Pisces and it is about to move backwards into the Age of Aquarius (estimated to start sometime between AD 2060 and 2100).

Each age is characterised by cultural changes in society, thought and religion and everything that has been happening over the last 30 years points to us thinking in 'Aquarian' ways. The meteoric pace of technological innovation, the rise of interest in spirituality, divination and other esoteric knowledge; all of these concepts are associated with the sign of **Aquarius** and the dawn of the 'new age'.

Agrimony A flower essence made from the agrimony blossom. This tincture is one of the **Bach Flower Remedies**. Dr Bach said that this is recommended for 'those who hide their feelings behind a cheerful face'.

Air Element 1. One of the four natural elements harnessed in **pagan** rituals of **magic** and religious worship. In **Wicca**, an air **elemental** is one of the four spirits that energise a spell and bring its wishes into being. Air symbolises communication and intellectual pursuits as well as new beginnings. It represents the masculine principles often embodied in sky gods and deities, who are invoked at the start of new ventures. The magical tool associated with the air element is the **athame**, or ritual knife. Air colour is yellow, and air is associated with the **zodiac** signs of **Aquarius**, **Gemini** and **Libra**. 2. One of the five elements in Indian philosophy and medicine. In ayurvedic medicine it is known as rayu and is associated with touch, thought and breath, with the elemental qualities of movement, electricity and flow. It combines with ether to form the vata dosha.

Akasha (Sanskrit, 'luminous essence') A mystical entity containing stored occult and other esoteric knowledge past, present and future, which can only be accessed on the astral plain, according to **theosophy**. Akasha is also the term for one of the five Hindu natural elements, better known as **ether**, or space. See also: **Akashic Record**, **Hinduism**.

Akashic Record Astral realm in which the memory of all events, actions, thoughts and feelings past and present is recorded, according to **theosophy**. This cosmic memory bank comes courtesy of **akasha**, an astral entity or substance containing stored occult and other esoteric knowledge. Psychics can access these records for spiritual insights including clairvoyance, prophecy and information on past lives. See also: **Collective Unconscious**.

Albertus Magnus A thirteenth-century alchemist and theologian who claimed to have discovered the **Philosopher's Stone**. He also believed he had magical powers and could control the weather, although he is best known for being the teacher of Christian philosopher Thomas Aquinas, and the author of several **grimoires** of magic. See also: **Alchemy**.

Alchemy (Greek *chyma*, 'casting of metals') An ancient practice that sought to transform matter, combining elements of mysticism, philosophy and science, and is now considered the forerunner of modern chemistry. It was most concerned with trying to find the **Philosopher's Stone** (a formula to convert base metals into gold or silver). Alchemists also sought to discover the 'elixir of life' that would grant immortality to the drinker. The prime three ingredients they used were **sulphur**, which represented the spirit; quicksilver, a symbol of the soul, and salt, the body.

Although we are most familiar with medieval alchemists like Nicholas Flamel and Paracelsus, alchemy was first practised in ancient Egypt. Hermes Trismegistus, a first-century BC Egyptian sorcerer, is credited with inventing alchemy. He wrote all of his occult secrets down on an 'Emerald Tablet', which was supposedly discovered years later by Alexander the Great and brought to Europe.

The transmutation of metals was not the only occupation of the medieval alchemist. Deeply religious men, they sought how to transform themselves and believed the success of their chemical experiments depended upon the clear thoughts and pure intentions they themselves held.

It is alchemy's focus on perfection of the soul that made psychologist **Carl Jung** believe it was the link between ancient **Gnosticism** and modern psychology. Jung held that there was a four-stage 'alchemical process' which a person's psyche went through to reach maturity, and he felt that the highly symbolic language of alchemy was handy for describing **archetypes** from the **collective unconscious**. See also: **Hermeticism**.

Alectryomancy, also **Alectormancy**, **Alectoromancy** (Greek *alectruon*, 'cock', + *manteia*, 'divination') **Divination** (fortune-telling) through the action of a cock or hen. The bird is placed in a circle of grain around which are placed letters of the alphabet. The diviner interprets the patterns of the remaining grains and the letters they point to, after the bird has had its fill. For yes or no questions, two piles of grains are used and the most-pecked grain pile left is the answer.

A famous example of alectryomancy involved the Roman emperor Valens, who wanted to know the name of his successor so he could launch a pre-emptive strike against the usurper. Using this method, the cock spelled out 'THEOD' and so Valens duly killed all those with the name 'Theodorus', only to miss out on 'Theodosius', who actually succeeded him. See also: **Ornithomancy**.

Aleuromancy (Greek *aleuron*, 'flour', + *manteia*, 'divination') An archaic form of **divination** (fortune-telling) by either dropping cakes made of flour into water and interpreting the result, or inserting messages into a ball of flour and distributing them to those seeking information. Used mainly by the ancient Greeks, it is seldom practised today, although modern-day fortune-cookies still carry on the tradition.

Alexander Technique A method of improving body posture and movement to reduce physical and mental tension. Working in conjunction with a teacher, a person goes through a series of exercises to re-educate the body to stand and move in different ways.

Frederick Matthias Alexander (1869–1955), an Australian actor, created the technique when he noticed a connection between losing his voice (a tragedy for a performer) and his habitual posture. By changing the way he stood and how he held his neck and head, he was able to regain full use of his strained vocal cords permanently and noticed the side benefit of greatly improved health and coordination.

He went on to found a training school for his technique in London in 1931, which still functions today.

The theory and practice behind Alexander's work are simple, although it takes a number of one-to-one sessions with a teacher to retrain the body to stand and react in healthier ways. At the first session, your trainer evaluates your stance, and then helps you to align your body, head and neck into new postures. To start with, it feels unnatural, but you gain immediate benefits from the first session. It can take up to 30 sessions to complete your posture changes for good, but this commitment of time and energy has lasting beneficial effects, especially in improving physical performance. Other benefits include improved coordination, reduction of neck, back and head aches, and greater self-esteem as a result of a more positive way of moving through life.

Allah (Arabic, 'God') The Islamic name for **God**. Used in preference to the word God to indicate a single deity, which is not associated with either masculine or feminine characteristics.

Allopathic (Greek *allo*, 'other', + *pathos*, 'suffering', 'disease') A phrase that describes conventional medical approaches to ailments where the emphasis is on treating the symptoms of an illness rather than the underlying cause. **Samuel Hahnemann** (1755–1843), the founder of **homeopathy**, coined the phrase to describe the harsh medical practices of his day that influenced his studies into homeopathic principles. Many alternative and complementary medical disciplines now use it to describe the 'medical establishment', especially in cases of aggressive interventionist treatments like radical surgery and toxic pharmaceuticals.

Giving a person 'allopathic treatment' involves inducing an opposite effect to that produced by a disease, illness or injury. For example, taking an anti-inflammatory to reduce pain in swollen, arthritic hands seeks to alter body chemistry by reducing the 'pain' chemical. A complementary medical approach might involve change of lifestyle including diet, and/or supplements that concentrate on the body chemical producing swelling in the first place. Despite the inclination of some alternative therapists to treat all ailments with complementary rather than conventional medicine, at times allopathic treatment is the best way to go, especially in cases involving life-threatening trauma and disease.

Aloe Vera A plant, *Aloe barbadensis*, of the spiky cactus lily family, whose sap is used for a variety of healing purposes. This sticky gel is taken from the insides of the leaves. Aloe vera is one of the most versatile plants used in **herbalism**. The soothing, healing juice can be used externally on skin problems including wounds, rashes and burns (which is why you see it in many sunburn remedies). It can also be diluted and taken internally to help ease the pain from ulcers, arthritis and other inflammatory conditions. It is also an excellent bowel tonic, although care should be taken not to overindulge in drinking aloe vera juice as it can also be used as a laxative.

Alphitomancy (Greek *alphiton*, 'barley', + *manteia*, 'divination') An ancient method of separating out the guilty from the innocent. Either a leaf of barley or a specially prepared barley cake would be given to a group of the accused. Those innocent of any crime would suffer no ill effect from eating the barley but the guilty party would either find the barley distasteful, or suffer from grave indigestion. This negative reaction on the part of the culprit was interpreted as a sign of guilt as opposed to a delicate stomach.

Alternative Therapy Any form of standardised therapeutic technique that seeks to promote healing in the body using methods not accepted in scientific and orthodox medicine circles. Often, alternative therapies are **holistic**, seeking to treat the root causes of a person's illness or complaint (whether physical, mental or spiritual) instead of just relieving topical symptoms. Alternative therapists believe that there is a bioelectric flow of energy throughout our body, also known as **life force**, **prana** or **chi**, that becomes blocked or imbalanced in disease and ill-health. When these energies are unblocked or harmoniously rebalanced, the mind, body and spirit of a person are able to heal.

This phrase is at times used interchangeably with the term **complementary medicine**, with good reasons behind the confusion. Whether or not a therapy can be considered 'alternative' or 'complementary' depends on the way it is practised. Consulting a trained, qualified homeopath for a chronic ailment that your regular doctor cannot treat would be an example of 'complementary' use. Self-medicating with homeopathic remedies bought from the chemists would be 'alternative'. See also: **Allopathic**.

Amethyst (Greek *amethystos*, 'non-intoxicating') The most valuable form of quartz **crystal**, with significant healing and cleansing abilities. The ancient Greeks and Romans thought that it could prevent drunkenness and dropped it into their wine before drinking. In ancient Egypt, hearts carved from amethyst were placed with the bodies of the dead as a protection against evil in the afterlife. Amethyst is used to cleanse other crystals before their use in healing and **divination** and is called the 'psychic crystal' for its use in enhancing intuition and **ESP**. In magic, wearing an amethyst or using one in a spell will keep evil away.

Amidism   see Buddhism

Amoroli   see Urine Therapy

Amulet   A **charm**, either carried on the body or displayed in a house, that offers protection against magic, danger and illness. Unlike **talismans**, which actively seek out good fortune for their owners, an amulet is passive, almost like a wall between its wearer and outside harm. It is thought that jewellery originated as amulets of health and healing, rather than mere adornment.

Analytical Psychology   see Jungian Psychology

Ananda Yoga   see Yoga, Hatha

Anemoscopy   see Austromancy

Angels (Greek *angelos*, 'messenger') 1. An immortal spiritual being who acts as a messenger of **God**, according to Christian, Muslim, Zoroastrian and Jewish faiths. According to the **Bible**, there is a ninefold hierarchy of angels. At the top are **seraphim**, followed by **cherubim**, thrones, dominations, virtues, powers, principalities, **archangels** and angels. The first three are closest to the Lord in heaven, the second three are angelic governors of different realms and the final three work closely with the earth. These various spirits have different duties to God and serve as his intermediary with his mortal children, humankind.

2. Advanced spiritual entities that act to aid and guide us in life. Some believe that personal angels are externalised forms of our higher self; others that they are beings from a different plane of existence who choose to interact with us. Most angels are androgynous spirits whose guardianship and advice can be requested through certain meditative and **magical** rituals. Angels also have specific associations with the months of the year, astrological signs and the planets. See also: **Christianity**, **Islam**, **Judaism**, **Kabbalah**.

Anima, Animus The anima is the unconscious inner feminine side of a man, and the animus is the unconscious inner masculine side of a woman. Psychoanalyst **Carl Jung** formulated the theory that these **archetypes** of the human **psyche** help to regulate individual behaviour. By understanding this aspect of our personality, 'getting in touch with our inner woman or man', we can help overcome psychological problems, or unacceptable forms of behaviour.

To men, the anima appears in dreams as figures like the seductress, the maiden or the goddess. She represents a man's feeling nature, and he must accept this part of himself to be psychologically balanced.

To women, the animus represents the thinking, logical part of her psyche, and appears in dreams as heroes, poets, wise sages and so on. She must accept this part of herself to be psychologically whole. See also: **Collective Unconscious**.

Animal Magnetism see Mesmerism

Animism (Latin *anima*, 'spirit or soul') 1. The belief that there is an 'animating' spirit or soul in every aspect of nature, including animals, plants, trees, mountains, rocks and rivers. Individual spirits are called **elementals**, because they represent the consciousness of a particular natural element. This was a concept common to many different world religions and cultures, and is still a key element of **paganism**. The supernatural power of nature comes about from the **life force** that flows throughout all matter in the universe, which, it is believed, can be accessed through certain magical rites and worship practices. 2. In **Gaian theory**, the belief that the world has a single soul animating all matter, which possesses spiritual awareness.

Ankh An ancient Egyptian symbol resembling a cross with a loop at the top. The ankh is widely used as a symbol of life, love and reincarnation, and every major god and goddess of Egyptian mythology is depicted in works of art carrying it. In **witchcraft** it is also known as the *crux ansata*, used in health and fertility spells.

The ankh

Anodyne Necklace A famous quack remedy of eighteenth-century England. The anodyne necklace supposedly imparted great healing to the wearer, especially babies and small children. It claimed to do so by helping infants 'cut their teeth', as the popular conception at the time held that infant mortality was caused by stress resulting from the growth of the infant's first set of teeth.

Anthropomancy (Greek *anthropos*, 'man', + *manteia*, 'divination') The archaic, barbaric rite of divining the future by examining human entrails, usually those of virgin women or young children. It is mentioned in classical literature and was used in ancient Egypt as well as Greece and Rome. Thankfully, a practice no longer in fashion.

Anthroposophy (Greek *anthropos*, 'man', + *sophia*, 'wisdom') The study of human spiritual nature, founded by Austrian mystic **Rudolf Steiner** in 1909. Originally a member of the **Theosophical Society**, Steiner founded the Anthroposophical Society after he disagreed with the theosophists, although the basic tenets and beliefs of both schools of thought are virtually identical. Anthroposophists believe that reality is essentially spiritual, and that you can train yourself to overcome the material world by accessing different planes of knowledge and existence through occult means.

Anthroposophy is a blend of traditions from a number of religions, including Buddhism and Hinduism, as well as esoteric practices involving **spiritualism** and magic rituals. See also: **Theosophy**.

Anubis, also **Anpu, Ienpw, Yinepu** The ancient Egyptian god of death, who is depicted as half-man, half-canine (either jackal or wild dog according to myth). His name has one of two meanings – either 'royal child' or 'to putrefy'. Both are appropriate to this funerary deity. His unusual appearance was drawn from the observation that jackals and wild dogs often haunted the edges of cemeteries. The myths do not agree on his parentage. In one tradition he was the son of **Osiris**; in others the offspring of **Nepthys** and **Ra**, the sun god. In the earliest period of Egypt's history, Anubis held the position of lord of the afterlife, one that the god **Osiris** would later command. When Osiris attained the status of ruler of the dead, Anubis became the divine undertaker, symbolically performing the act of embalming on the bodies of the deceased, in preparation for their existence in the afterlife.

His main role in the Egyptian pantheon was to escort the souls of the dead into the Hall of Osiris, to await final judgement.

Anusara Yoga see **Yoga, Hatha**

Aphrodite, also **Venus** The Greek goddess of love and beauty, known as **Venus** in Roman myth. She was one of the Olympiad, the 12 chief gods and goddesses of Greek legend who lived on Mt Olympus.

Apollo, also **Helios, Helius, Hyperion, Phoebus Apollo** The Greek god of the sun, fine arts and music. He was the son of Leto and the god **Zeus**, who courted Leto in the guise of a swan. His twin sister, **Artemis**, was his counterpart, the goddess of the moon. He was one of the Olympiad, the 12 chief gods and goddesses of Greek legend who lived on Mt Olympus.

Apport A solid object materialising from nowhere, during a spiritualist meeting like a **séance** or in the presence of a magic practitioner like an **adept**. This object is often a flower or piece of jewellery that is transported into the room by **supernatural** means. See also: **Spiritualism, Teleportation**.

Aquarius The eleventh sign of the **zodiac** in Western **astrology**, and the **sun sign** for those born between 21 January and 19 February. The symbol of Aquarius is the Water Carrier and the ruling planets are **Saturn** and **Uranus**. Aquarians are a **fixed sign** influenced by the **air** element, with 'idealism' the best single word to define them. Those born under Aquarius tend to be independent and intellectual, but occasionally eccentric and unpredictable. They can be generous, altruistic individuals but perversely emotionally detached at the same time.

Aquarians love to experiment with new recipes and dishes but enjoy the novelty of food more than eating itself – they would rather go hungry than eat a boring meal. In health, Aquarians may be prone to circulatory problems, especially in the legs, and sometimes suffer from an excess of nerves. Soothing, cooling tisanes and herbs help balance the spirit of this excitable soul.

Aradia Italian **Wiccan** goddess of magic, who is the daughter of the moon goddess **Diana** and Lucifer, the sun god of light. Diana and Lucifer (Artemis and Apollo in Greek mythology) were also brother and sister, and the divine provenance of Aradia indicates that she comes from both the sun and the moon. She is known as the 'Queen of the Witches' and Wiccas call on her to channel the elemental powers of darkness and light. She is at her strongest when the moon is full, so magical rites performed at that time are especially powerful and sacred. In **pagan** worship, she is often depicted as the quintessential young and beautiful earth goddess, counterpart to the horned god **Cernunnos**. The witch's **sabbat** of **Beltane** is especially dedicated to her.

Legends of Aradia have been present in Italy for centuries (including an incarnation as a semi-Christian medieval saint) but she is best known from Charles Leland's book *Aradia*, first published in 1899 and still in use today by Wiccan practitioners. See also: **Horned God, Witchcraft**.

Arcana (Latin *arcanus*, 'to shut up', from *arca*, 'chest') Term used to refer to the cards in **tarot** and in **Kabbalistic** practices. The 78 cards of a tarot pack are divided into 'major' and 'minor' arcana. The 22 cards of the major arcana (also called the 'trump' cards) represent all the main **archetypes** of human experience (like the fool, the trickster, the maiden, death, the moon, etc.) and allegedly come from the Thoth religion of ancient Egypt. The minor arcana are more like regular playing cards, with cards numbered one to ten in suits, and 16 court cards (the Jack takes on two aspects, the Page and the Knight, so there are more court cards in a tarot deck than in a playing deck). Instead of hearts, spades, diamonds and clubs, the suits are Cups, Pentacles, Swords and Wands. Each suit is associated with one of the four natural **elements** – **earth** (Pentacles), **water** (Cups), **fire** (Wands) and **air** (Swords).

The cards of the major arcana are considered of greater import than those of the minor arcana, and have more significance when they come up in a tarot spread. Each trump card has a roman number, a picture and a title: 0 The Fool; I The Magician; II The High Priestess; III The Empress; IV The Emperor; V The High Priest; VI The Lovers; VII The Chariot; VIII Justice; IX The Hermit; X The Wheel of Fortune; XI Fortitude (Strength); XII The Hanged Man; XIII Death;

XIV Temperance; XV The Devil; XVI The Tower; XVII The Star; XVIII The Moon; XIX The Sun; XX Judgement; and XXI The World. Each card has a dual interpretative meaning, depending upon where they fall in a tarot spread. See also: **Kabbalah**.

Arcane (Latin *arcanus*, 'to shut up', from *arca*, 'chest') Anything that is understood by few, seen as mysterious, and which may require a secret code or key to decipher it. This is the root word for **arcana**, cards used in **tarot** and **Kabbalah**.

Archangels (Greek *arkhi*, 'chief', + *angelos*, 'messenger') A special class of angels mentioned in Jewish, Christian and Islamic scriptures, and heavily featured in the Jewish mystical practice of **Kabbalah**. According to the Christian **Bible**, there are seven archangels who rule the seven heavens. They are: Michael, Gabriel, Raphael, Uriel, Jophiel, Zadkiel and Samael. Islam recognises only four: Gabriel, Michael, Azrael and Israfil. In Kabbalistic lore there are ten, each associated with a different branch on the **Tree of Life**: Metratron/Kether; Ratziel/Chokmah; Rzaphqiel/Bonah; Tzadquiel/Chesed; Kamael/Geburah; Raphael/Tiphareth; Haniel/Netzach; Michael/Hod; Gabriel/Yesod; and Sandalphon/Malkuth. Each of these archangels has different magical properties and divine force associated with it, and calling on its name in Kabbalistic rituals allows you to access its power.

Archetype A recurring image or pattern of thinking which manifests itself through our dreams, ideas and behaviours, according to psychoanalyst **Carl Jung**. These significant symbols appear to us in the form of mythological figures like the hero, the maiden, the wise man, the joker, etc., and serve an important purpose in helping us to resolve psychological problems. Archetypes arise spontaneously in the mind, especially in times of crisis, to reveal some deep truth hidden from our ordinary consciousness. They are located in the **collective unconscious**, a communal psychic realm we all share. Archetypes work by reminding us first that many experiences – confronting death, choosing a mate, giving birth – are common to all of human existence. You then are able to meditate on the archetypal figure's tale, and how they resolved their problem, helping you to make a decision about your own choices and behaviours.

They also serve as symbols in different belief systems, like the **goddess** archetype in **paganism**, for mysterious elements that cannot be answered by the rational, scientific mind. Jung claimed that archetypes were not drawn from mythology, legends and fairy tales, but that these stories were composed to explain their appearance in the collective psychic memory of humankind. That is why myths always follow the same types of pattern (like the **hero's journey**). You only need to compare the storylines of *Star Wars* or *The Lord of the Rings*, with the Greek myth of Theseus, to understand this concept.

Ares, also **Mars** The Greek god of war, known as **Mars** in Roman myth. He was the son of the god **Zeus** and the goddess **Hera**, and was notoriously the lover of the goddess **Aphrodite**. He also was one of the Olympiad, the 12 chief gods and goddesses of Greek legend who lived on Mt Olympus.

Argent. Nit. One of the 15 major **polychrests**, or major remedies in **homeopathy**. It is also a **constitutional type**, which is a way homeopaths have of classifying different patient profiles. The fitting constitutional remedy acts preventatively and curatively on its matching personality type – for example, a person with an Argent. Nit. constitution will respond well to the Argent. Nit. remedy almost regardless of the illness they are suffering from. Argent. Nit. people are extroverts, usually cheerful and are often found in high-pressure jobs. They tend to suffer from anxiety and stress-related conditions (especially digestive complaints), and are very sensitive to heat.

Arhat, also **Arahant**, **Arahat** (Sanskrit, 'enlightened disciple' or 'worthy one') Buddhist term or title for one who has achieved the highest level of enlightenment, which allows the individual to escape the need to be reborn. An arhat is then entitled to enter **nirvana** after his/her time on this plane of existence has finished, i.e. after death. See also: **Buddha, Buddhism, Eightfold Path, Samsara**.

Arianrhod (Welsh, 'silver wheel') In Celtic mythology, a Welsh goddess of time and destiny, who is associated with the star constellation *corona borealis*, the Crown of the North. Arianrhod is worshipped during the full moon, and rules over Caer Feddwidd (Fort of Carousa), the second realm of the Welsh underworld. See also: **Paganism**.

Aries The first sign of the **zodiac** in Western **astrology**, and the **sun sign** for those born between 21 March and 20 April. The symbol of Aries is the ram, and the ruling planet is **Mars**. Arians are a **cardinal sign** influenced by the **fire element**, with 'assertiveness' the best single word to define them. Those born under Aries are innovative, enterprising free spirits, quick, impulsive and confident; but they can be bossy, opinionated and excitable. Arians do not beat around the bush and they have extremely warm hearts. They tend to hurry and can be accused of impatience.

The ideal Arian meal is hot and spicy, and fast – instant coffee instead of brewed and soft-boiled eggs over hard because they are quicker to prepare. In health, Arians tend to suffer from headaches and feverish complaints, and can be prone to high blood pressure. Arians benefit from nutrition and herbs for relaxation and relief from mental exhaustion.

Arithmancy, also **Arithmomancy** (Greek *arithmos*, 'number', + *manteia*, 'divination') **Divination** (predicting the future) using numbers. The father of arithmancy was Pythagoras, he of the famous theorem. He thought there were connections between gods, men and numbers that could be codified and used to foretell the fate of a person, or future events, when certain number patterns appeared.

Ancient Greeks examined the numbers and value of letters between two combatants to predict the victorious party. In the Trojan War, diviners supposedly used this method to predict that Achilles would defeat Hector. The Chaldeans divided their alphabet into three parts, each with seven letters attributed to the then-known seven planets of the solar system. Through this method they made astrological predictions based on the number patterns of the planets. Arithmancy is an early form of **numerology**, and is similar to certain number aspects used in the Jewish mystical religion **Kabbalah**.

Aromatherapy (French origin, literally 'fragrant remedy') The therapeutic use of plant **essential oils** to promote health and well-being. Although this branch of **herbalism** has been known and used since ancient times (mentioned both in the Bible and in the Indian scriptures, the **Vedas**), the modern phrase was coined by French chemist René-Maurice Gattefosse in his 1928 paper 'Aromathérapie'. Gattefosse, a cosmetic research scientist, suffered third-degree burns on his arm in a laboratory accident and instinctively plunged his hand into a vat of lavender essential oil. To his surprise, the pain stopped immediately and his arm and hand healed quickly with minimal scarring.

In this **holistic** health therapy, the oils are absorbed through the skin and carried throughout the body by the lymph and circulatory system, through three primary methods: **massage**, bathing or inhalation. The most effective route is through massage, as the oils are absorbed more quickly into the bloodstream via pressure on the skin (and it provides additional physical benefits). For the sensitive and frail, bathing in water that has had essential oil sprinkled into it can be just as effective. In inhalation, either the oils are diluted in water and heated, or a specialised vaporiser is used that allows their scent to diffuse throughout the room. Inhalation methods are especially effective in sickrooms either to ease breathing or to help disinfect the air.

Whatever the use, essential oils should always be used diluted, with a few notable exceptions. Lavender oil is safe to use undiluted in small quantities, as is tea tree oil. Most, however, are too concentrated to be used neat. Some countries, most notably France, also advocate the internal use of these essences. See also: **Alternative Therapies, Herbalism**.

Arsen. Alb. One of the 15 major **polychrests**, or major remedies in **homeopathy**. It is also a **constitutional type**, which is a way homeopaths have of classifying different patient profiles. The fitting constitutional remedy acts preventatively and curatively on its matching personality type – for example, a person with an Arsen. Alb. constitution will respond well to the Arsen. Alb. remedy almost regardless of the illness they are suffering from. Arsen. Alb. people are perfectionists and are extremely ambitious. They are always on the go, tend to be hypochondriacs, and often suffer anxieties about their lifestyle and health. They are susceptible to headaches and breathing difficulties.

Artemis, also **Diana** The Greek virgin goddess of the moon, and hunting. She was the daughter of Leto and the god **Zeus**, who courted Leto in the guise of a swan. Her twin brother, **Apollo**, was her counterpart, the god of the sun. She was one of the Olympiad, the 12 chief gods and goddesses of Greek legend who lived on Mt Olympus, but is better known in some traditions as **Diana**, a powerful **goddess** figure of many ancient mystery ceremonies. See also: **Eleusinian Mysteries**.

Arthur, King The historical and quasi-mythic ruler of ancient Britain, best known for the legends surrounding his court. The real Arthur's reign occurred shortly after Britain's separation from the Roman Empire, c. AD 410–542, and he was located in and around Cornwall and Wales. By all accounts, he was a just and wise king and fought bravely against the Saxon invaders threatening his lands.

His legends, set in the same area, are much more colourful than the historical record. Born of Uther Pendragon and Ywaine with the help of the wizard **Merlin**, Arthur came to power when he pulled a magical sword from a stone, an act that proclaimed his royal heritage. He married the beautiful, adulterous **Guinevere**, and started an order of good and virtuous knights he called the Knights of the Round Table. His wife betrayed him with his best friend, **Lancelot du Lac**, and in a subsequent battle for his throne he was mortally wounded by his treacherous nephew Mordred. He is said to be buried on the mythical isle of **Avalon**, where he will rise again at Britain's greatest hour of need. See also: **Arthurian Legends**.

Arthurian Legends A body of literature surrounding the mythical reign of Britain's **King Arthur**, set sometime between the Roman withdrawal from its borders and the Anglo-Saxon invasion of England. The best-known tales involve Arthur's birth and upbringing, the Knights of the Round Table, Queen **Guinevere's** adulterous affair with **Lancelot du Lac**, and the Quest for the **Holy Grail**. The basis for most of the legends comes from the writings of Geoffrey of Monmouth, which were later used as a source for the fifteenth-century *Morte D'Arthur* by Thomas Malory and the modern work *The Once and Future King* by T.H.White.

There was a historic Arthur who ruled somewhere in Cornwall and/or Wales in the fifth to sixth century AD but why his life and reign were blown up into such fantastic legend remains a mystery. Some believe Arthur represents a break between the emerging Saxon culture and older Celtic beliefs about power and society (especially in the clash between **Christianity** and the older, pagan religion of **Druidry**). Others view it as a metaphor for Welsh history and culture, or a convenient vehicle to convey medieval courtly standards of chivalry and romance.

Asana (Sanskrit, 'posture' from *as*, 'to stay, be, sit') The physical postures or poses in **yoga**, designed to stretch and strengthen muscles, as well as stimulate nerve centres and internal organs. Asanas are one of the 'eight limbs' or **ashtangas** that are mentioned in the earliest writings on yoga, the **Yoga Sutras** of Patanjali, and are the first step towards meditation and the spiritual discovery that is the ultimate goal of yoga. Through asana practice you awaken the subtle connections between the mental and physical, and allow your **prana**, or life energy, to flow in a balanced manner throughout your body. Asanas each have their own name (like *tadasana*, 'mountain pose', or *vrksasana*, 'tree pose'), and a specific effect that the posture should have on the mind and body. In general, asana postures improve digestion, elimination and breathing, and they tone, detoxify and strengthen the body's systems.

Ascendant In **astrology**, the constellation rising over the horizon at the moment of your birth, according to your **horoscope**. It is also known as your 'rising sign'. Your ascendant sign determines how people perceive you, as well as the position of the **houses** in your birth chart, i.e. the rising sign is always in your first house. Your ascendant will be the same as your **sun sign** if you are born at sunrise, as the sun spends two hours in each sign. The ascendant is considered more important than your birth sign in **natal astrology**.

Ashram (Sanskrit *asrama*, 'hermitage') A Hindu monastic community or retreat, where a **guru** participates in teaching spiritual concepts to a group of devotees.

Ashtanga Yoga see Yoga

Aspects In **astrology**, the angular distance between two celestial planets, or points, and the earth. It also determines the nature of the relationships between the planets and our horoscopes.

Aspects are calculated looking at the wheel of the **zodiac**. Your starting point for figuring out the aspect is your own **sun sign** and where the planets were located when you were born. From this, there are five different aspects to be found: some positive and some negative. The first is *opposite* – when a planet is in the opposite sun sign from your birth sign. This signifies a tug-of-war between the two, and is not very positive. The second is *conjunction* – when a planet is next door to your sun sign. This aspect can be positive (if the two planets get along) or negative (if they do not). Third is *sextile* – when a planet is next door but one to your sun sign. Harmony rules in this aspect. Fourth is *squares* – next door but two (negative – tension) and finally is *trine* – next door but three (positive – very easy going).

The planets in the sky today are making aspects with other planets in your horoscope. Astrologers read these aspects to find out what is going on in your life. When astrology is used to predict the likely outcome in a romantic relationship, each person's aspects put together are used to determine whether it will be peaceful sailing or stormy seas, metaphorically speaking (also known as **synastry**).

Aspen A flower essence made from the blossom of the aspen tree. This emotionally healing tincture is one of the **Bach Flower Remedies**. Dr Bach said that this is indicated for 'those with vague, unknown feelings that cause apprehension and anxious anticipation'.

Astarte, also **Ashtar**, **Astoreth** Caananite and Phoenician **goddess** of the moon, who symbolised the power of fertility and reproduction. Astarte was the sister and co-consort of the god Baal. The Babylonian and Assyrian counterpart of Astarte was Ishtar.

Astragalomancy (Greek *astragalos*, 'dice', or 'knucklebone', + *manteia*, 'divination') **Divination** or predicting the future from the throw of small bones or bits of wood, or dice, which were originally made from bones. The bones would be marked with letters and mystical symbols. In the case of dice, numbers were associated with letters to form words pertinent to the matter being asked. The diviner would then ask a question before throwing the dice or bones, interpreting the subsequent patterns to obtain an answer. Divination specifically using dice or black and white beans is called **cleromancy**.

Astral Body The spirit self, which is part of our **aura**, that forms our consciousness and which animates our carnal selves. Every living thing has two bodies: the physical body and the spiritual 'auric' body upon which the physical body is imposed. If a person dies, or has an out-of-body experience like **astral travel**, the body that goes walkabout is the astral body. An astral body is often referred to as an 'etheric body', because it travels through the element of **ether**, also known as **akasha**, which holds the memory of all events, actions, thoughts and feelings past and present. The idea that astral travel is possible, even desirable, is an integral part of many different world religions and cultures, including **Hinduism**, **paganism**, the beliefs of the ancient Egyptians and those of advanced practitioners of **Yoga**.

In order to be able to return once the travels are done, the astral body stays linked to the physical body by what is known as a 'silver cord' – sort of an ethereal umbilical cord. In death, the silver cord is severed from the body, so the body decomposes.

Astral Plane An alternate dimension of reality inhabited by spirits or higher beings. It is also the place that our **astral body** (spirit self) visits during an out-of-body experience.

Astral Projection, Astral Travel The deliberate separation of a person's spirit or **astral body** from their physical body, in order to alter their consciousness and travel in a different plane of existence. Astral projection is a type of **out-of-body experience**, where an astral body can fly or float about, visiting other people, places and even dreams.

People use a variety of different routines to accomplish the separation of astral self from physical self, from a self-induced trance state to relaxation and visualisation techniques.

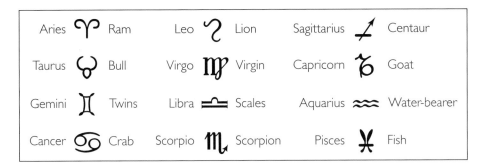

Aries ♈ Ram		Leo ♌ Lion		Sagittarius ♐ Centaur				
Taurus ♉ Bull		Virgo ♍ Virgin		Capricorn ♑ Goat				
Gemini ♊ Twins		Libra ♎ Scales		Aquarius ♒ Water-bearer				
Cancer ♋ Crab		Scorpio ♏ Scorpion		Pisces ♓ Fish				

Astrological symbols

Astrology (Greek *astro*, 'star', + *logos*, 'word, study') A predictive system based on the idea that the movements of the stars, planets and other heavenly bodies have an influence on our lives. Astrology is an ancient practice and one found in all cultures, with the first recorded instances occuring in Babylonia c. 500 BC. It was once indistinguishable from astronomy and in fact many scientific findings about the stars and planets came from medieval astrologers. Astrology practised in the West is known as a 'tropical' system because it is based on the turning of the constellations as fixed in the zodiac. Vedic astrology, as practised on the Indian sub-continent, is known as a 'sidereal' system as it is based on the actual stellar constellations in the sky.

In astrology, everything starts with your **horoscope** – a map of the heavens at the time of your birth. From this your **zodiac** signs can be determined, and what **aspects** are important to you. This allows an interpretation of what type of person you are (or will be) as well as what is likely to happen in your future.

Each world culture has different star signs but they use several different methods to make predictions. The two main types are: **horary** (making predictions for a specific action at a precise time) and **mundane** (focusing on large-scale events). In addition there are different branches of astrology that focus on particular elements of your horoscope: **electional** (the right moment to begin a venture); **medical** (your health); and **natal** (aspects of the sky at your exact moment of birth). See also: **Chinese Astrology, Esoteric Astrology, Sidereal Astrology, Vedic Astrology.**

Astrology, Chinese A predictive system specific to Chinese culture, based on the idea that the movements of the stars, planets and other heavenly bodies have an influence on our lives. As in Western astrology there are 12 signs of the **zodiac**, but they are applied to years, not months, and change at the Chinese New Year, sometime between late January and late February (the exact date varies each year). The signs of the zodiac are named after animals featured in an old Chinese folktale involving either **Buddha** (if you are a Buddhist) or the great sage **Lao Tzu** (if you are a Taoist). The story goes that either lord decided to give a party for his favourite animals, some of whom were friends with each other, and others who were enemies. In order to guarantee that they would all come despite their conflicts, he decreed that he would name the years after the first 12 animals to arrive, in order of their arrival.

The signal honour of having a year named after you was enough to spur the animals' attendance at this ultimate A-list party. The highest prize, the first year, was named after **the Rat**, who hitched a ride on animal number two, **the Ox**, and then scurried ahead of him at the last minute and nabbed the honour. After these two, the other ten that arrived (in order) were: **the Tiger, the Hare, the Dragon, the Snake, the Horse, the Sheep** (also, known as **the Goat** or the **Ram**), **the Monkey, the Rooster, the Dog** and finally **the Pig**.

Each Chinese year is associated with a different natural **element** (which changes each 12-year rotation), and has either a **yin** (passive) or **yang** (active) quality assigned to it. In addition, each monthly moon cycle has one of the 12 animals assigned to it, and even the day can be divided into two-hour chunks and named for one of the animals.

All of this detail allows a Chinese horoscope to be as precise as a Western astrology horoscope. Let us say you were born on 23 June 1960 at 5.30 a.m. You are a yang metal Rat, your animal moon is the Sheep, and your animal hour is the Tiger. That means your primary character is a Rat personality, but you have also got plenty of Sheep characteristics and a touch of Tiger. The yang metal aspect will also influence you. Finally, it means that your **birth chart** will be as accurate as those used in Western astrology.

Astrology, Electional A branch of **astrology** used to calculate the most favourable time to begin a business venture, or stage an important event like a marriage or major journey. Dr **John Dee**, Queen Elizabeth I's court astrologer, used electional astrology to determine the best moment for her coronation.

Astrology, Esoteric A school of **astrology** that combines elements of occult beliefs about **chakra** energies with more general astrological method. Estoteric astrologers believe there are seven personal energy 'rays' that need to be defined and put into your horoscope, and then meditated upon.

Astrology, Horary A method of **astrology** focused on making predictions for a specific action at a precise time, usually just for one individual. It then advises the best course of action considering the circumstances. It is one of the most common used in Western astrology, and the one at play when we read our daily **horoscopes**.

Astrology, Medical A branch of **astrology** that deals with matters of health and disease, and how they correlate to someone's sign of the **zodiac**. Each **sun sign** is prone to particular health problems, both physical and emotional, with specific foods and medicines beneficial for one or some signs over others. The seventeenth-century English herbalist **Nicholas Culpeper** assigned each of the plants in his herbal as remedies for the various astrological signs, and medieval feasts often featured special dishes prepared for each guest based on their star sign.

Astrology, Mundane A method of **astrology** that focuses on making predictions about large-scale events. As opposed to **horary astrology** or **natal astrology**, which usually looks at an individual's horoscope and future, mundane astrology is based on the belief that the heavens affect large groups of people and the physical structure of our world. This is the type of astrology used when predicting a country's future, and is much less accurate because of the large scale involved.

Astrology, Natal A branch of **astrology** that focuses specifically on a person's birth **horoscope**. Rather than the birth or **sun sign**, the ascendant (constellation rising over the horizon at the moment of birth) is seen as the most important **aspect**.

Astrology, Sidereal A school of **astrology** that uses fixed star constellations in conjunction with planets, to determine your **horoscope**. It is based on the true celestial position of the constellations, taking into account the procession of the equinoxes. Because of this, everyone's birth sign moves back a month (Arians become Pisceans, etc.). Sidereal astrologers believe that the standard sun signs and aspects give a person's general tendencies, but fixed constellations supply the particular, peculiar details and qualities of a person's character.

Astromancy, also **Rodomancy** (Greek *astron*, 'star', + *manteia*, 'divination') **Divination** or predicting the future by the stars. Astromancy differs from **astrology** in that it is concerned only with the physical patterns of stars as they appear in the sky, and does not seek to interpret meaning based on specific stars and planets. Astromancy can be further split into various subdivisions like meteoromancy (divination by meteors and falling stars) and cometomancy (divination by omens taken from comets), although astromancy itself is a form of **aeromancy**, fortune-telling by observing clouds, sky and other atmospheric phenomena.

Athame   A ritual sword or knife used in witchcraft. Traditionally, the athame was a ceremonial sword, long and shaped like a sabre, with a double-edged blade. Inscribed on the handle and blade were magical and astrological symbols. The knife should either be made of silver, representing the moon, or have a black wooden handle (signifying darkness) and a sharp steel blade (illumination).

Wiccans believe the athame represents **air**, and it is held high above the head to utilise the energies of this **element** to control the power of spells, At the climax of the ritual, it is brought swiftly down in a cutting action to 'sever' the harnessed energy and end the spell. This sword also appears in **tarot** cards as the air suit symbol, and plays a role in Kabbalistic rituals. See also: **Kabbalah, Wicca.**

Athena, also **Minerva, Pallas Athena**   The Greek goddess of wisdom, skills and warfare. She sprang fully grown from the head of her father, **Zeus**, and her beloved city Athens was the seat of her worship. She was one of the Olympiad, the 12 chief gods and goddesses of Greek legend who lived on Mt Olympus.

Atlantis   The mythical lost continent, said to have sunk beneath the ocean surface after a cataclysmic natural event. The main source of Atlantean legend comes from the writings of the Greek philosopher Plato (427–347 BC). In *Timaeus* and *Criteas*, he records tales of an island 'larger than Libya and Asia put together' located in the Atlantic somewhere beyond the Straits of Gibraltar. This island empire (c. 1500–900 BC) of military might had visions of conquering both Egypt and Greece, but suffered such a violent series of earthquakes and floods that the island itself sank and its vast army was lost. The natural disaster was of such magnitude that Atlantis was lost within the space of one day and night, and the Atlantic Ocean itself was impassable for some time due to mud and debris.

Plato's myth was later underscored by the visions of **Madame Blatvatsky** and **Edgar Cayce** in the early twentieth century. Since that time, a popular belief is that the Atlantis myth may have described the fall of the Minoan civilisation on the island of Crete. In its heyday, according to Plato, this empire controlled most of the Mediterranean and surrounding ocean waters, but was reduced to rubble by the volcanic eruption on the island of Thera, now known as Santorini, 70 miles north of Crete. Thera erupted sometime around 1500 BC, which matches the timings of the Atlantis legends. Modern historians, however, tend to dispute this account.

Atman (Sanskrit, 'self') Term for the essential self according to Hindi religion and thought. This self is also the part of us that is part of the larger universe, a sort of 'cosmic consciousness'.

Atum (Egyptian, 'the all' or 'the complete') The Supreme Being in ancient Egyptian myth, and an aspect of the great sun god **Ra**. His name and persona were often combined with Ra's to form 'Ra-Atum' or 'Atum-Ra', a dual god. Atum was considered to be the creator of the world. He represented the setting sun, and was the first divine entity to crawl from Nun, the primeval waters of pre-existence. Because of his self-creative ability, he was able to form the other gods – the first two, **Shu** and **Tefnet** (air and moisture), he either created by masturbating, or he 'sneezed out Shu and spat out Tefnet'.

Atum was the head of the **Ennead**, the pantheon of nine gods who were worshipped in the ancient Egyptian city of Heliopolis. His divine symbol was a black bull which bore the sun disk between its horns.

Augury (Latin *augurium*, 'interpretation of omens') A school of **divination** applying to interpretations of the future based on various omens and signs, mostly related to the appearance and behaviour of animals. Augury has been practised throughout the world, but became part of official religion in ancient Rome; a special job role, the augur, was created to oversee the practice in the temples. Although many different methods were used to predict the future, most augurs used birds and bird behaviour to make their interpretations.

Aumakua (Hawaiian) The spirit of a dead person who stays in contact with their living descendants in the guise of a protector, teacher or guardian. Through prayer and ritual, these spirits could be called upon for advice and healing, appearing in the shape of an animal that was significant to the family (often a lizard or a shark). See also: **Spirit Guides**.

Auras The invisible, psychic energy field surrounding both animate and inanimate objects. Every living thing has two bodies: the physical body and the spiritual 'auric' one upon which the physical body is imposed. If a person dies, or has an out-of body experience like **astral travel**, the body that goes walkabout is the auric body.

Auras can be perceived by the psychic, or through **Kirlian photography**, to emanate out from the average body by a few inches. The more spiritual or enlightened you are, the bigger your aura. According to his original disciples, Buddha supposedly had a personal energy field extending approximately 200 miles out from his body.

Like **chakras**, auras have associations with particular colours and energetic properties; each corresponding to one of seven layers.

The first auric layer is the etheric layer, the one closest to the body (almost like a second skin) and associated with the colour red and physical illness. The second layer is the emotional body. This orange layer deals with both our own and others' emotions. The mental layer is next, is associated with the colour yellow, and is where thoughts and ideas are seated. Out from this is the green astral layer, which marks the boundary between the physical and spiritual and is associated with all our relationships. The fifth auric layer is the etheric template, which is a copy of the physical body on a higher level. It is either clear or navy-blue in colour. The sixth layer, the celestial body, is the emotional body on the spiritual plane. This indigo or purple-hued layer is where we communicate with spirits. Finally comes the ketheric template, which is white or gold in colour. It is the most holy layer, which is why you see halos of white or gold depicted around the divine.

If a person becomes ill or depressed, this can affect their aura. A number of alternative therapies help to correct imbalances of the aura, most notably **colour therapy**. By doing so, healing in the physical body can take place.

Aura-Soma Therapy A form of **colour therapy** that uses trademarked bottles of coloured oils. These 'Equilibrium Bottles' are clear glass into which is poured a combination of **essential oils**, spring water and plant dyes, to produce gem-like vials in a range of bright hues.

Vicky Hall, an English herbalist and pharmacist who went blind from medical complications in early adulthood, started to experiment with the theories of Aura-Soma in the late 1980s and early 1990s. In 1993, she published her ideas and founded Aura-Soma. She formulated the oils in a series of meditative visions that she said matched the colours of a person's **aura** (personal bioelectric field). In an Aura-Soma session, you choose the four bottles that most attract you. Theoretically, these bottles help to rebalance your aura using the contrasting vibrational energy of colour.

Each bottle has a specific meaning. The first bottle represents your personality and inherited traits, the second the area of your life that requires change, the third the present and the fourth the future. You change your energy over several sessions by choosing different bottles, of which there are over 100. Gradually your energy is balanced and the therapy is complete.

Auriculotherapy A variation of traditional acupuncture based on the belief that the ear is the map of the bodily organs, similar to **reflexology**. Acupuncture points on the ear are stimulated by finger pressure, or by inserting needles, pointed studs or staples that correspond to the part of the body requiring treatment. The advantage of these is that they can be left in place for a specified time period (days, weeks) and the patient can stimulate the acupressure point themselves by pressing on the ear when symptoms arise. Very popular for treating conditions requiring lifestyle changes, like weight loss or smoking. See also: **Acupuncture**, **Traditional Chinese Medicine**.

Austromancy (Latin *australis*, 'south', + Greek *manteia*, 'divination') **Divination** or predicting the future by means of interpreting the winds and cloud shapes. This archaic form of fortune-telling, first practised in ancient Greece, paid special attention to the intensity and direction of the wind, with certain qualities ascribed to different points of the compass. The south wind, 'auster', was considered destructive to flowers and health, hence the origin of the phrase 'an ill wind that blows nobody any good'. Austromancy, a form of **aeromancy**, is itself divided into anemoscopy (divination solely by winds) and nephomancy (divination solely by clouds).

Autogenic Therapy, also **Autogenic Training** (Greek, 'generated from within') A structured series of mental exercises designed to gain deep relaxation and to trigger the body's self-healing mechanisms. German neurologist and psychiatrist Dr Johannes Schultz developed the technique in the early twentieth century based on studies of the body's 'fight-or flight' reaction at times of stress. He found that consciously relaxing specific parts of the body decreased the amount of stress hormones in the blood. This in turn triggered a flood of 'feelgood' endorphins throughout the body, which reduced the heartbeat, respiration and muscle tension of the subject.

Each exercise in the autogenic training session focuses on a different part of the body, and the sensations associated with relaxation, and a trainer monitors your progress in a log or diary. You are directed to passively concentrate on a particular colour or object in an almost meditative state while you perform your exercise. You move from specific concentration on an object onto an abstract idea or affirmation. Somewhere along the way, the body relaxes.

This 'relaxation response' (coined by Harvard professor Dr Herbert Benson in the 1970s) has many positive benefits beyond the physical. Writers, artists and musicians report enhanced creativity and imagination, and airline flight crews say it can help jet lag. It is also recommended as a supportive therapy for chronic health conditions like migraine headaches, hypertension, gastrointestinal disorders and diabetes.

Automatic Writing The practice of receiving written messages from the spirit world or higher realms, often thought to come from the ghost of a departed loved one. A **medium** or other psychic is the usual channel for these writings while they are in a **trance** state, with the handwriting on the page not that of the medium, but of the dead person or higher being. People who engage in this practice report a tingling in the arms or hand just before the message is received, and the actual speed of writing is much faster than is normally thought possible.

Avalon The enchanted isle where legendary British **King Arthur**'s sword **Excalibur** was forged, and Arthur's final resting place. Avalon was associated with the English town of Glastonbury, due to its surrounding swamp, and the discovery of the graves in 1190 of two bodies identified as the historical King Arthur and Queen Guinevere. The bodies were later interred on the grounds of Glastonbury Abbey. The mystical King Arthur sleeps in a cave on the island, awaiting the day when Britain needs him, when he will arise again. See also: **Arthurian Legends**.

Avatar (Hindi, 'one who descends') An incarnation, or representation, of a returned deity or holy man. In **Buddhism**, it could be the **Buddha** or other past spiritual masters. In **Hinduism** it is one of the forms of the god **Vishnu**. The phrase is used more generally in occultist beliefs to indicate the return of any holy or divine entity. See also: **Reincarnation**.

Ayurveda, Ayurvedic Medicine (Sanskrit *ayu*, 'life', + *veda*, 'science or knowledge') The traditional medical system of India that claims well-being is only possible through a balance between body, mind and spirit. Ayurvedic principles are grounded in Hindu holy texts, the **Vedas**, written sometime between the eighth and seventh centuries BC. Ayurveda is similar in philosophical nature to **Traditional Chinese Medicine**, in that it believes in the importance of the flow of life energy, or **prana**, to maintain physical and mental health. Ayurveda also seeks to treat the whole person, focusing on the root causes of illness rather than merely its symptoms.

If prana is at the top of a triangle, next comes the division of this universal energy into two polarities – **shiva** and **shakti** (similar to **yin** and **yang** in Chinese tradition). These two divide into the five natural **elements** of the universe: **ether** (also known as **akasha**); **air** (vayu); **fire** (tejas); **water** (jala); and **earth** (prithvi). Body types, called **prakriti**, are determined by the combination of the elemental energies that govern our physical constitution, intellect and personality, called **doshas** (also known as tridosha, because there are three). When an ayurvedic practitioner treats a patient, he looks at the proportion of the three doshas, with the aim of equally balancing these energies, to stimulate healing in the body and mind and, ultimately, restore health.

The three doshas are: **vata**, which is a combination of ether and air energies; **pitta**, a combination of fire and water; and **kapha**, water and earth.

Ayurvedic treatments are mostly dietary and herbal, with a strong emphasis on detoxification of the body through supplements, massage and steam baths. In certain cases, an ayurvedic practitioner might suggest *panchakarma*, a rigorous system of physical and mental cleansing and purging that includes enemas, laxatives, therapeutic vomiting and nasal rinsings. A convalescent, rejuvenating course of yoga, meditation and massage follows this extreme routine. These methods should always be carried out under strict guidance from a qualified ayurvedic doctor.

Ayurvedic treatment has been found to be extremely effective on all medical conditions (it is the national health system of India, after all) but has the highest rate of success with chronic ailments and with conditions associated with unhealthy lifestyles. Fully qualified ayurvedic physicians must complete a five-year degree course at an accredited college or university, and are strictly regulated by several professional and governmental bodies.

Bach Flower Remedies A set of healing tinctures created by British homeopathic physician Dr Edward Bach in 1930. He discovered that soaking a flower in water and exposing the preparation to sunlight or heat imparted the essential energies of the plant into the water. The water is then strained and preserved in alcohol (usually brandy).

These essences have been shown to have beneficial effects on a person's mental state, and help to restore their emotional equilibrium. Bach Flower Remedies are particularly good for those suffering from shock, bereavement or other forms of psychic trauma. There are 38 different remedies to choose from, each associated with a particular mood, emotion or personality type (Dr Bach wrote succinct descriptions to match the type of person with the required remedy, still in use today). The best-known remedy is **Rescue Remedy**, a combination of five different flower essences.

A small amount (one to five drops) of the tincture chosen is taken either neat or in a glass of water, and repeated at half-hour intervals as needed. The Rescue Remedy can be taken every half hour in times of stress or trauma.

Bach, Dr Edward English homeopathic physician (1886–1936) who wrote about and developed in the 1930s the formulas for a series of 38 flower essences. These flower formulas were based on his realisation that blossoms infused in water imparted their healing energies. See also: **Bach Flower Remedies**.

Baha'i Religion established in 1863 by Iranian Mirza Husayn Ali, who renamed himself 'Baha'u'allah', the 'Glory of God'. Followers of Baha'I believe that Mirza was a prophet, in the line of Abraham, Moses, Buddha, Zoroaster, Jesus Christ and Muhammad. Baha'u'allah preached that there was but a single god, and that some day all religions would be one, through continuing revelations from other prophets and spiritual masters.

This peace-loving faith also believes that humanity is one single race and that the time has come for unification into one great global society. Baha'i's followers work to bring this about by abandoning all forms of prejudice, ensuring sexual equality and opportunity, eliminating the extremes of poverty and health, and providing universal education. There is no formal church ritual, and there are Baha'I faith centres all over the world, with approximately three million believers.

Bane (Old English *bana*, 'causing death, poison') Something that causes great distress or death, like a **curse** or poison. Used only in dark magics.

Banshee (Gaelic *bean shith*) A wailing spirit of ill-omen or death, nicknamed 'The Washer of the Clothes of the Dead', according to Irish or Scottish folklore. The banshee, usually the red-eyed, weeping ghost of a woman, would appear to a person in the guise of an ethereal washerwoman, wailing their name. You could then ask three wishes of the banshee, but in the time-honoured tradition of such apparently tempting offers these wishes did not always turn out so well. In fact, the person who got their wishes granted usually died soon thereafter.

Bardo Plane (Tibetan *bar*, 'between', + *do*, 'two') Tibetan Buddhist term for the period between death and rebirth, usually reckoned to be 49 days. During this time, the soul passes through a series of visions that relive the good and bad deeds and actions of their life, prior to **reincarnation** (unless they have been lucky enough to achieve **nirvana** this time around). See also: **Astral Plane**.

Bardo Thodol (Sanskrit/Tibetan, 'Book of the Between Two') See also: **Tibetan Book of the Dead**.

Barefoot Doctor In **Traditional Chinese Medicine**, a doctor who brings temporary relief from pain and illness without diagnosing the underlying cause. A Chinese doctor traditionally was only paid when the patient stayed healthy; therefore, when he became ill, the doctor would have to give treatment free. Oftentimes it fell to the local village practitioner to treat short-term illnesses; he made little money from the practice and theoretically could not afford to buy shoes. In Taoist folklore, the barefoot doctor was also considered a merry sage, travelling from village to village administering healing potions, teaching meditation and marital arts, and playing music on a bamboo flute. Barefoot Doctor is also the public persona of Stephen Russell, a British Taoist journalist and wellness expert best known for his advice on being an 'Urban Warrior'. See also: **Taoism**.

Basilisk (Greek *basiliskos*, 'little king') A mythical winged creature with the head and body of a reptile and a fantastic three-pointed tail. The head had small bony bumps sticking out in the shape of a crown, hence its name. The basilisk, which supposedly originated from the head of Medusa (the mythological Greek monster) was a deadly creature whose gaze could turn you to stone. If you're familiar with the Harry Potter books, you will know it was the basilisk that wreaked such havoc in Hogwarts. The basilisk's breath was also poisonous and the only way you could kill the creature was to show its reflection to itself – without looking at it yourself, of course.

Bastet, also **Bast**, **Bat** The cat-headed goddess in Egyptian mythology, who represents the gentle, pacifist side of the female **archetype**. She was often paired with her sister, the lion goddess **Sakhmet**. Bastet was one of the 'Daughters of **Ra**', the sun god, and the cat was her sacred animal. In a number of excavated temples dedicated to her, hundreds of mummified holy cats were found laid on the altars of the dead. For the most part, Egyptian women considered her as the protector of the family home. Like any guardian of the hearth, she could be merciless to those who attacked her loved ones. As one of the 'Eyes of Ra', she was forced to become an avenging spirit to lay waste to the enemies of Egypt. She was traditionally considered one of the solar deities, but after Greek cultural mythology started to influence Egypt's own legends, she became identified with **Artemis**, the goddess of the moon. Bastet is still revered in certain modern traditions of **witchcraft** and magic.

Bates Method A self-help way of improving your eyesight without lenses or surgery. Dr William H. Bates (1860–1931), a New York eye specialist, devised this method after observing many thousands of people with eye problems. He found out that many vision problems had less to do with eye lens malfunction than with the results of injury, underlying health conditions or bad habits learned in childhood. Bates took a holistic approach to his work; he believed that we do not see with our eyes alone but with our entire selves – mind, body and spirit. He devised a series of exercises for his patients that combined physical and isometric movement and mental relaxation techniques. He thought that if his patients could change the way they perceived the world both physically and mentally, their vision would improve. He wrote a book describing his techniques, *Better Eyesight Without Glasses*, which is still available today. The Bates method, which is not suitable for everyone, can allegedly help stop your eyesight deteriorating as you age. Even if you cannot throw away your glasses or contact lenses you can use this method to improve your sight to some degree.

Bau Gua, also **Baugua Pa-kwa, Pa'Kua** An eight-sided compass used in **feng shui** to determine the location of different sorts of **chi** energies in a building. It is also known as the 'eight **trigrams**' because each side of the octagon shows one of the three-lined pictograms from the **I Ching** representing the elemental qualities of life. Each side of the Bau-Gua also indicates the areas of your house where particular types of chi are found. These types can roughly be divided into the following categories: health, career, finances, relationships, education, fertility, fame and spirituality. Improving the arrangement of objects in that particular corner of the bau-gua will also improve the flow of energy to that area of life.

BCE Abbreviation for Before Common Era. A non-Christian alternative for the term BC, Before Christ.

Beech A flower essence made from the blossom of the beech tree. This emotionally healing tincture is one of the **Bach Flower Remedies**. Dr Bach said that this is indicated for 'those who find it hard to tolerate or understand other people's methods of doing things, and are therefore critical and easily irritated'.

Bell, Book and Candle The three implements used in the excommunication ritual in the Roman Catholic Church. After relaying this dread message to the miscreant, the priest closes his Bible, throws the candle on the ground and rings the bell. The book represents the heavenly 'book of life' where the excommunicant's name no longer appears, the extinguished candle the soul which is no longer seen by God or the Church, and the bell is tolled as if for a dead person.

Beltane, also **May Day**, **Walpurgis** (Gaelic, from *Belanus*, Celtic god of fire) The pagan celebration of spring that is one of the two high holy days in the **Celtic wheel of the year**. The name comes from the tradition of lighting 'bel fires' on hilltops to celebrate the return of spring and fertility to the earth. The best-known symbol of Beltane is the maypole – a phallic pole planted deep into the receptive earth. Beltane celebrates the coming of summer and the flowering of life, and is therefore one of the best nights of the year to practise fertility magic. Ceremonial rites portraying the union of the goddess **Aradia**, quintessential young and beautiful earth goddess, with the quintessential male, the horned god **Cernunnos**, are re-enacted by eager participants.

Beltane is the second most important **sabbat** of the year for **witches** (the first being **Samhain**), and celebrating it is an important way of tapping into the magical powers of nature. See also: **Paganism, Wicca**.

Bermuda Triangle A triangular area in the Atlantic Ocean that lies between Bermuda, Puerto Rico and the tip of Southern Florida. This area is infamous as a place where people, ships and planes have mysteriously vanished, never to be found. The Bermuda Triangle (also known as the 'Devil's Triangle') got its reputation in 1945 soon after six US Navy planes vanished in the area. Some think these disappearances might be the work of extraterrestrial aliens, or that the area is a mystical vortex that sucks people and things into an alternate dimension. Regardless of the cause, and in the face of scientific scorn, the belief persists that this is not the place you would want to go to on a leisurely cruise.

Besom A broom or broomstick used by witches and Wiccans in their magic ceremonies. Contrary to popular belief and the Harry Potter novels, broomsticks do not actually fly. They originally got this reputation because witches, practising sympathetic magic (which works on the basic principle that like produces like), would straddle their brooms and jump up and down in order to show their crops how high to grow. In current witchcraft practice, a besom is used to sweep away negative energies from a place, and to provide protection, particularly for someone's house, against evil. As the door is the most vulnerable point of entry for these negative energies, it is considered especially important to sweep a threshold clean, and hang the broom near the door for easy access.

The besom is also used during folk and pagan wedding ceremonies. The couple 'jump the besom' to symbolise their common-law union, and to draw in fertility blessings on their marriage.

Bhagavad Gita (Sanskrit, 'Song of the Blessed One') The fifth book of the epic Indian poem, the **Mahabharata**, written during the sixth century BC by the mythic author Vyasa. It takes the form of a dialogue between the Hindu god **Krishna** and Prince Arjuna, who is both his son and pupil. Arjuna questions the necessity of going to war, especially as he is pitted against former teachers, friends and relatives that he is likely to kill. Krisha answers by saying, 'When a man sees that the God in himself is the same God in all that is, he hurts not himself by hurting others: then he goes to the highest Path.' In other words, making the right efforts will lead you to enlightenment, or **nirvana**, because the battle is for the kingdom of the soul, not the kingdom of the land.

The three main themes covered in the *Bhagavad Gita* are **jnana**, 'the light of knowledge'; **bhakti**, 'love and devotion'; and **karma**, the right action. These themes, incidently, constitute three of the four paths to enlightenment through **yoga** (the fourth yogic path, **raja**, is mentioned but not in detail).

Another major theme is the importance of contemplation as a path to higher truth and bliss. Again and again Krishna tells Arjuna that only through self-control, humility, selflessness and devotion to others can the path to nirvana can be found. Many of the themes in this spiritual poem formed the basis for the later religions **Hinduism**, **Buddhism** and **Jainism**, and for the philosophical elements of yoga.

Bhakti (Sanskrit, 'devotion') One of the three aims of **Hinduism**, bhakti is devoting yourself to the service of others, in the service of the supreme being.

Performing bhakti, along with seeking **jnana** (knowledge) and changing your **karma** (actions), will allow you to attain **moksha**, the ultimately blissful goal of liberation from endless death and rebirth. See also: **Yoga**.

Bhakti Yoga   see Yoga, Bhakti

Bible   (Semitic/Greek *biblios*, 'book, papyrus, or scroll') The holy text of **Christianity**, and one of the revered books of **Islam**. The Bible comprises two books – the Old Testament (the Jewish Tanakh and Apocrypha) and the New Testament (four gospels of Jesus' life and letters/teachings of his apostles). All of these writings are considered sacred scripture, and form the basis of belief, morality and conduct of all Christians and religious traditions descended from Christianity.

Bibliomancy   (Greek *biblion*, 'book', + *manteia*, 'divination') 1. **Divination** or seeking spiritual insight by selecting a random passage from a holy book such as **I Ching**, the **Bible** or the **Koran**. It is a form of **stichomancy**, which involves selecting a random passage from any type of book. 2. A method used in medieval and Puritan times to discover if a person was innocent of witchcraft and sorcery. The accused was weighed against the great Bible in the local church. If the subject weighed less than the Bible, they were innocent.

Bikram Yoga   see Yoga

Bilocation   The ability to appear in two places at the same time (one a physical body, the other a spirit double) through mystical or supernatural means like **astral travel** or an **out-of-body experience**.

Bindi, also **Bindiya**, **Bottu**, **Kumkum**, **Tilaka**   The coloured dot worn in the middle of the forehead indicating to others that the wearer follows the Hindu religion. It is worn over the **third eye**, and symbolises piety. Both men and women wear it, although it is going out of fashion with young men. It used to be that unmarried women wore black marks, whereas married women wore red marks. Now, most women wear bindis that match the colour of their saris. See also: **Mehndi**.

Bioenergetics   A therapeutic bodywork technique based on the work of psychoanalyst **Wilhelm Reich**. Specific combinations of massage, breathing and movement exercises are designed to break through 'body armouring' that impedes a patient's functioning. This somewhat controversial therapy, developed in the mid-twentieth century, works on the idea that focusing on body awareness, especially in sexuality, will help to heal physical and emotional traumas and even treat psychiatric illness. In ill-health, the life force or 'bioenergy' gets trapped in muscles. This bioenergy is a measurable physical phenomenon (according to Reich) and can be moved throughout the body via physical stresses and exercise.

Altough no longer widely practised, advocates of bioenergetic therapy say that it is an effective treatment for those suffering from psychosomatic health disorders, or for those who feel emotionally or physically stressed. See also: **Orgone Energy**.

Biofeedback A technique for learning to monitor and control involuntary body mechanisms, through information gained from computer-based probes or electrodes. These probes produce signals that 'feed back' body information, such as heart rate, respiration rate and skin temperature, which you can interpret and then learn to control through various methods. Biofeedback developed from US-based research on sleep and dreaming in the late 1950s and early 1960s and takes its name from the radio industry. 'Feedback' is an information loop set up to feed back activity results for evaluation and adjustment.

In a biofeedback session, you are first hooked up to the monitoring equipment and your body's baseline ratings are taken. Your personal monitor or trainer gives you this information and then asks you to use a relaxation technique like **visualisation** or **meditation** to consciously relax the stressed area of the body. You become more efficient at biofeedback through repetition; the more sessions you do, the more adept you become at controlling your body's involuntary functions.

Athletes, and people suffering from incontinence, back and neck pain, high blood pressure, migraine headaches or other stress-related illnesses, find biofeedback to be particularly effective in improving performance or helping to return the body to health.

Biorhythms Cyclic patterns of our physical, emotional and intellectual cycles, which begin at birth and then have highs and lows throughout our lives. Unlike **circadian rhythms**, which only focus on 24-hour sleeping/waking patterns, biorhythm cycles are grouped into periods of 23 days (for physical matters), 28 days (emotional), or 33 days (intellectual). By charting out where you are on the scale of each of these, you can predict what kind of day you are likely to have. In general, the more positive a cycle is at any given point in time, the better you are able to interact in that arena. If a cycle is charted out negative, it does not mean you cannot succeed in that particular area; just that it will be harder to do well.

Biorhythm theory originated in the late nineteenth century with Dr Wilhelm Fliess, an advocate of **numerology**, and was developed further by Dr Hermann Swoboda and Dr Alfred Teltscher in the early years of the twentieth century. They discovered that the cycles begin at birth, set to zero. Using your date of birth as a reference point, where you are in your personal biorhythm cycles can be determined for today's date, or for any given date in the future.

In recent years, a greater number of cycles has been added: the 38-day intuition cycle, the 43-day *aesthetic* cycle and the 53-day *spiritual* cycle. All of these cycles can be charted out and followed, much like a horoscope, to alert you to the most 'positive' or 'negative' times to take action in a particular arena.

Birth Chart In **astrology**, a map of the heavens at the time of one's birth which details the exact positioning of the planets in the **zodiac** signs and **houses**. The chart uses the person's place, date and time of birth as reference points for the planetary diagram. See also: **Horoscope**.

Black Madonna One of the faces of the **Virgin Mary**, who represents the earth mother **goddess** in Christian mythology. As opposed to Mary, her alter ego, the incorruptible and immaculately conceived icon of worship, the Black Madonna is fertile and sensual, the personification of Mother Nature, and all life emanates from her. The rise of the Black Madonna probably occurred when earlier images of mother goddesses were combined with the Catholic cult of the Virgin Mary, sometime in the early medieval period (AD 1100–1300).

Images of her are found throughout Europe, famously in Chartres Cathedral, France, in Częstochowa, Poland and in Monserrat, Spain, but there are countless statues of her in and near small grottos and caves in France, Spain and Italy. There are strong connections between the cult of the Black Madonna and **pagan** goddesses like **Isis**, **Gaia**, **Ceres** and **Diana**. She is believed to have profound healing powers, and some say if you pray at one of her shrines you will awaken that ability in yourself. See also: **Eleusinian Mysteries**, **Golden Bough**.

Bladder Meridian A channel or **meridian** of **chi** energy running through the body that penetrates the bladder, according to **Traditional Chinese Medicine**. It is associated with the water element, has **yang** energetic properties and is partnered with the **kidney meridian**, which is **yin**. Bladder meridian energy affects the spinal cord, nerves and back, and bears the brunt of physical and emotional tension. Chi is strongest in this channel between 3 and 5 p.m., and conversely the weakest between 3 and 5 a.m. Both left and right sides of the body have this meridian, which roughly begins at the inner eye then runs down the head, neck, spine and legs to end at the edge of the little toenail.

Blavatsky, Madame Helena Petrovna (1831–91) Founder of the esoteric religion **theosophy**, Madame Blavatsky was a Russian **medium** who wrote many of the key texts used in that belief system, including *Isis Unveiled*, *The Key to Theosophy* and *The Secret Doctrine*. After a rakish childhood and early adult life travelling throughout the world, she claimed to have been initiated by Indian holy men into the secrets of occult **mysticism**. Along with others, she started the Theosophical Society in 1875 to study world religions and their mystic traditions; this later grew into the sect she is associated with today.

Blessed Be A traditional greeting of **Wiccans** to each other, 'blessed be' also has multiple meanings to Wiccan practitioners. Initially, 'blessed be' was used only as a ritual phrase or ritual abbreviation, and not outside a coven's circle. In recent years that has changed so now it is a generic **pagan** salutation. 'Blessed be' comes from the ritual initiation of the fivefold kiss. As the text of the ritual goes, 'Blessed be thy feet, which have brought thee in these ways,' etc., it was shortened to the bare phrase that still conveys the best wishes of the speaker. Now 'blessed be' appears as a greeting and as a farewell, often abbreviated to 'BB' on e-mails. Some use 'BB' to mean bright blessings, as they still consider 'blessed be' a ritual-only term.

Blood In **Traditional Chinese Medicine (TCM)**, blood is both the red liquid that circulates through the body, and a force that houses **shen**, the mind-spirit, in a person. As in Western medicine, blood which is responsible for providing nourishment, physical and mental, to all parts of the body, has a special relationship with three organs of the body – the heart (which 'rules the blood'), liver (which 'stores the blood') and spleen (which 'governs the blood'). Blood vessels are sometimes referred to as 'Jing Mei', which lends a certain irony to the name of a doctor Jing Mei in the popular US television drama ER. TCM practitioners use a variety of methods to determine if blood essence is 'deficient' or in 'excess' and treat a patient accordingly. See also: **Acupuncture**, **Shen**, **Jing**.

Bodhi Tree (Sanskrit, 'awakening to the way') The tree (*Fiscus religiosa*) under which the **Buddha** was sitting when he realised **enlightenment**. It is known as the tree of wisdom and is usually present in Buddhist temples. The leaf of

Leaf from the Bodhi tree

the Bodhi tree is used as a symbol of wisdom and enlightenment and is often depicted in Buddhist artwork. 'Bringing forth the Bodhi resolve' means generating a true intention in your mind to become enlightened. That intention is a seed that can grow to create a Buddha. See also: **Buddhism**.

Bodhisattava, also **Bodhisatta** (Sanskrit, 'a wisdom being') In **Buddhism**, Bodhisattava is a **theravada** Buddhist term for an individual working towards enlightenment, one who is on the way to becoming a **Buddha**. In **mayahan Buddhism** a Bodhisatta's emphasis is more on practising Buddhism to eliminate the suffering of all sentient beings. They postpone their own final attainment of **nirvana** in order to help others.

Bodywork A general term to describe therapies that work on the body to produce better physical, psychological and spiritual health. The key idea in bodywork is that even though you only work on the body, you affect the whole person, because any sort of trauma – psychic, spiritual, mental – is stored in body tissues and can be released through various methods. This theory is based on the work of psychoanalyst **Wilhelm Reich**, although bodywork ideas are now accepted in many disciplines unconnected to him. See also: **Cellular Memory, Holistic Therapy**.

Boggart (Medieval English, Northern Counties) A general term for any supernatural being which deliberately frightened people. These spirits could be quite malevolent, or merely mischievous. Boggarts were often tied to one specific residence or family (a **poltergeist** is a form of boggart) and had shape-shifting powers. They would employ these powers in the form that would be most likely to scare their chosen target.

Bolline A ritual white-handled knife used in **witchcraft**. As opposed to the **athame**, which is not used for physical cutting, a bolline is used to trace out magic circles and other diagrams on the ground, inscribe candles and cut herbs and plants for use in spells and herbal remedies.

Book of Changes see I Ching

Book of Shadows   A **witch's** book of spells, rituals and magical lore, better known as a **grimoire**. The phrase 'Book of Shadows' reflects that other world beyond the veil of life that abounds with spirits, **elementals** and other magical creations. To any witch, then, this life can only be a shadow in comparison to those wonders. It is commonly abbreviated as BOS. See also: **Wicca**.

Book of the Dead   see Egyptian Book of the Dead

Book of the Way   see Tao

Bowen Technique, also **Bowen Therapy**   A healing system of soft-tissue bodywork targeted at reducing pain from injury or chronic health problems. This technique, also known as 'Bowtech', aims to balance and stimulate energy flows by relaxing the body. Practitioners use a specifically designed set of rolling massage movements (with thumb and fingers) on precise points in the body. These low-pressure, delicate movements are interspersed with frequent pauses to give the body time to respond and benefit.

   Bowtech gets its name from Australian founder Thomas A. Bowen (1916–82). After serving in World War II, he noticed that certain moves on the body had particular pain-relieving effects. Although he was not a trained masseur, professionals in massage therapy have carried his ideas forwards. Bowtech can be effective on a host of musculo-skeletal problems like back pain and sports injuries, when used in conjunction with other therapies.

Brahma   The creator god in **Hinduism**, who is sometimes depicted as the top of the **trimurti**, a triad of deities that includes **Vishnu** and **Shiva**. Brahma is considered a god still engaged in creating new realities, who is simultaneously one with the universe as well as transcendent of it.

Brahman   The 'One', the supreme reality of **Hinduism**, who is the absolute and ultimate truth in the universe. He is technically beyond description, but the three most important manifestations of Brahman are the triad of gods **Brahma** (creator), **Vishnu** (preserver of the universe) and **Shiva** (destroyer of evil). They represent some of the qualities of Brahman, who continues to evolve as reality changes.

Breathanarism, also **Inedia**   The alleged ability to live on light and air alone for indefinite periods. The technical term for this is 'inedia' and various saints throughout history have reported such phenomena. The best-known proponent of breathanarism is Australian Ellen Greve, who is also known as

Jasmuheen. She claims to have stopped eating in 1993 and to have survived on life force or **prana** alone, although she does admit to the occasional 'taste orgasm' of chocolate or ice cream.

Brigid, also **Bride** (Gaelic, 'High One') In Celtic mythology, the Irish archetypal mother goddess, seen as three daughters of the god **Dagda**, the Divine Father. Brigid also represents the three generations of the goddess – maiden, mother and crone – and is sometimes known as **Danu**. She is patron of smiths, healers and poets, and an important fertility goddess, who signalled the coming of spring in the festival **Imbolc**. When **Christianity** came to Ireland, Brigid became St Brigit of Kildare, said to be the midwife of Christ and the Mary of the Gaels. See also: **Celtic Wheel, Paganism**.

Buddha (Sanskrit *budh*, 'to understand or be awakened') Term in Buddhist religion to denote a person who has reached **enlightenment** and therefore attained **nirvana**. Particularly used to refer to the first person, **Siddartha Gautama**, to reach enlightenment. Buddhists believe that in the future another master, **Maitreya Buddha**, will be revealed who will lead all living beings to enlightenment. Buddha statues or pictures are always present in Buddhist temples as a focus of teaching and contemplation, and depicted on **mandalas** and other religious artwork.

In **feng shui**, a statue of Mi Lo Foh, the 'Laughing Buddha', is considered to bring good luck and wealth, so is often placed in an auspicious corner of a home or business. See also: **Buddhism**.

Buddhism (Sanskrit *budh*, 'to understand or be awakened') The Asian religion or philosophy based on the fifth-century BC teachings of **Siddartha Gautama**, 'Shakyamuni **Buddha**'. There is no god or supreme being in Buddhism; rather it teaches that everyone is caught up in a cycle of birth, life, disease, old age, death and rebecoming or rebirth by **reincarnation**, caused by greed, hatred and ignorance. This concept of **samsara** is fully explained in the doctrine of the **Four Noble Truths**. Your circumstances in this life depend on your **karma**, formed in previous lives. **Enlightenment** must be achieved in order to escape this endless cycle, made possible by following the **eightfold path**. Once enlightenment is achieved then the cycle ends and **nirvana** is attained, thereby ending a soul's existence.

Buddhism can be roughly divided into six different schools although this number is disputed even among Buddhists. They are: the Teachings school, the Vinaya school, the Vajrayana or Tantric school, the Chan or Zen school, the Pure Land school and Tibetan Buddhism. The Teachings school includes the oldest forms of practice, most notably the **Mahayana** and **Hinayana** sects, of which **Theravada** Buddhism is a sub-sect. All schools of Buddhism follow the basic tenets of Buddhist belief in order to attain enlightenment but argue ferociously over how to go about it.

It is not the promise of rebirth and nirvana as much as the actual practice of Buddhism that has led to the religion's exponential growth and popularity in the West. Buddhists believe in the denial of self in service to others, and in peaceful, meditative practices that seek to uncover wisdom and compassion. The goal is to take the 'Middle Way', to become the sort of wise person who recognises the relativity of things and therefore shuns all extremist views. Ultimately, possessions and even worry about the future and regrets about the past become unimportant, because the present moment is the most important; 'living in the now' is the ultimate goal. You focus on what you can do now to help someone else, you change your behaviour now to try and change your **karma**. In some ways, these beliefs diametrically oppose the culture of materialism and individualism running rampant through Western societies. Living a Buddhist lifestyle, especially with its emphasis on **meditation**, has also been shown to improve a person's health and state of mind.

Bunyip, also **Dongus**, **Kine Pratie**, **Wowee Wowee** Mythical Australian swamp-dwelling water monster. These grotesque creatures have many different aspects, but the face is always hideous and the feet turned backwards. Aboriginals greatly feared the bunyips, who supposedly fancied them as tasty snacks.

Butterfly Effect The principle that the flapping of a butterfly's wings might, through a series of events involving weather, environment and location, cause a massive storm on the other side of a globe. The butterfly effect was discovered by accident in 1961 by meterologist Edward Lorenz using computer models of weather prediction, and is often cited as a prime example of **chaos theory**.

Buzan, Tony An English psychology lecturer and memory expert who in the late 1960s developed the learning technique **mind maps**.

Caduceus (Greek *karukeion*, 'herald') The golden staff with serpents intertwined on top, carried by the Greek messenger god **Hermes** (also known as **Mercury** in Roman mythology). Legend has it that Hermes acquired it from Apollo, in a trade for the musical instrument, the lyre, which Hermes invented. The caduceus is also the astrological symbol for the planet Mercury, and is often mixed up with the staff of **Aesculapius**, which only has one snake.

Cailleach In Celtic mythology, the bone goddess (goddess of death) who is also known as the 'Grey Hag of Winter', the 'Veiled One' and the 'Dark Wise Woman'. Cailleach is connected to nature's cycle of death and life, is reborn at the start of each year (in the Celtic calendar that is **Samhain** or **Halloween**) and in the threefold **archetype** of the **goddess** represents the Crone. Cailleach is associated with cairns and **menhirs**, the ancient standing stones that dot Ireland's landscape. She sometimes appears in the guise of **the Morrigan**, the goddess of battle. See also: **Celtic Wheel, Paganism**.

Calc. Carb. One of the 15 major **polychrests**, or major remedies in **homeopathy**. It is also a **constitutional type**, which is a way homeopaths have of classifying different patient profiles. The fitting constitutional remedy acts preventatively and curatively on its matching personality type – for example, a person with a Calc. Carb. constitution will respond well to the Calc. Carb. remedy almost regardless of the illness they are suffering from. Calc. Carb. individuals tend to be overweight, quiet and cautious. They are somewhat obsessive and tend to suffer from circulation and perspiration problems. They are also susceptible to constipation, joint and dental pain, and in women, gynaecological ailments.

Camelot, also **Caerleon, Camlann** The seat of **King Arthur**'s kingdom, the location of the Knights of the Round Table, and the departure point for the **Grail Quest**. Some Anglo-Saxon historians believe the legends of Camelot were based on the seat of the historical King Arthur, thought by many to be located in or near the modern town of Cadbury. See also: **Arthurian Legends**.

Campbell, Joseph (1904–87) American professor of comparative literature and religion, and one of the foremost authorities on mythology and legends. Joseph Campbell is best known for the idea of the 'monomyth' – the **hero's journey**, which states that all stories, but especially those of a mythic nature, are essentially the same tale of a hero's rite of passage through a quest or journey.

His interest in mythology and folklore began at an early age. He was an avid reader of Native American legend as a child, and came back to this body of literature when studying for his master's degrees in English and comparative literature. He did postgraduate work in Europe on Arthurian romances, and was struck by the similarity between these tales and those of the folklore he had read as a youth. This led Campbell to search for the common elements, which he found in the work of German anthropologist Adolph Bastian (1826–1905) and Swiss psychoanalyst **Carl Jung**.

Bastian proposed the idea that myths from all over the world seem to be built from the same 'elementary ideas'. This fitted into Jung's theory of the **collective unconscious** where dwelled **archetypes**, images and figures which represented the entirety of human experience. Campbell took the concept of archetypes and grafted it onto the 'elementary ideas', arguing that all myths deal with the same issues of personal discovery through a quest or journey. He published his ideas in the 1948 book *The Hero With a Thousand Faces*.

He continued his research on comparative myths and religions, and published a number of articles and papers on the subject over the years. In 1959 he published the first of four volumes of his magnum opus, *The Masks of God*, titled *Primitive Mythology*. Volume Two, *Oriental Mythology*, came out in 1962, followed by Volume Three, *Occidental Mythology*, in 1964 and Volume Four, *Creative Mythology* in 1968. He was always well known in literary and academic circles, but came to the attention of the wider world through a 1986 US public television series *The Power of Myth*, with Bill Moyers. The programme, a series of conversations with Moyers on the role myth plays in our life, popularised Campbell's body of work.

He died in 1987 after a brief illness.

Campbell's work continues to be an important influence on popular culture. Film-maker George Lucas credits Campbell's idea of the hero's journey as a major inspiration for his *Star Wars* movie series.

Cancer The fourth sign of the **zodiac** in Western **astrology**, and the **sun sign** for those born between 22 June and 22 July. The symbol of Cancer is the crab, and the ruling planet is the **moon**. Cancerians are a **cardinal sign** influenced by the **water element**, with 'sensitivity' the best single word to define them. Those born under Cancer are home-loving, empathetic and nurturing, but secretive and prone to oversensitivity. Cancerians crave security in their relationships and finances, but have a streak of loony, lunar-influenced humour that pops up at unexpected times.

The ideal meal for the Cancerian is home-cooked or plain home-style fare at a cosy restaurant, and in generous portions (they do love their food). In health, Cancerians tend to suffer from digestive disorders as well as excess of worry. They benefit from herbs meant to calm the stomach and the soul, and from relaxing forms of exercise like swimming and yoga.

Candle Magic The use of candles in performing **spells** and rituals for wish-granting, protection against evil or illness, or constructing **charms** or curses. Candle magic is also a form of **pyromancy**, divination using fire and flame. Candle magic has been utilised since prehistory, with the ancient Egyptians using it to interpret dreams, medieval farmers using candles blessed by the Church to ward misfortune off their livestock, and all of us asking for a wish to be granted every year when we blow out our birthday-cake candles.

Different types and colours of candle have different magical meanings. For wishes and needs, the following colours should be used: white for new beginnings and energy; red for change and courage; orange for happiness, health and balance; yellow for communication, learning and travel; green for love, healing and the natural world; blue for power, justice and career; violet and indigo for psychic development and spirituality; pink for love, reconciliation, children and family; brown for house and home, money and possessions; grey for secrets and compromise; silver for secret desires; gold for wealth and prosperity; and black for endings and banishing guilt. Black is also the colour used in candle curses.

Most people believe that it is best to use a 'virgin' (unused) candle in your spell. You prepare it by rubbing it with natural oils, which also infuses the candle with your psychic energies.

To activate the magical qualities of candles, you either write your wish or desire on a piece of paper and burn it in the flame, or engrave a symbol for the desired object, person or event on the candle with a pin or awl. You may also light your desired candle and focus all your intention on your wish as you gaze at the flame. See also: **Witchcraft**.

Capnomancy, also **Libanomancy** (Greek *capno*, 'smoke', + *manteia*, 'divination') A form of **divination** or fortune-telling, using smoke obtained by the burning of sacred plants, incense or sacrificial offerings, practised by many ancient cultures. The shapes in the smoke and the direction of the smoke were taken into consideration. If the smoke quickly ascended, it was considered a good **omen**. It was thought to be an ill portent if it hung about, refusing to clear the area. Poppy seeds or other hallucinogenic plants were often cast upon the fire and the smoke inhaled, with the subsequent visions considered to be the truth from the smoke. See also: **Pyromancy**.

Capra, Fritjof (b. 1939) Quantum physicist and modern philosopher, who in 1969 noticed the similarities between the movement of subatomic particles and the Hindu mystic concept of the Dance of **Shiva**. After this insight he left his more traditional research projects to explore his theory that there were connections between modern physics and ancient mystical beliefs about the world. He published the results of his study in the groundbreaking 1983 work *The Tao of Physics*. Since that date, work on quantum mechanics and **chaos theory** has supported his initial findings.

Capricorn The tenth sign of the **zodiac** in Western **astrology**, and the **sun sign** for those born between 22 December and 20 January. The symbol of Capricorn is the goat, and the ruling planet is **Saturn**. Capricorns are a **cardinal sign** influenced by the **earth element**, with 'prudence' the best single word to define them. Those born under Capricorn are cautious, persistent individuals, who are very self-disciplined, ambitious and good at establishing structure. They can be a touch mean and inflexible upon occasion, but underneath a steady, stable exterior they have a soft centre of emotions you can reach if you know how to appeal to it.

The ideal meal for a Capricorn is one of wholesome, simple foods. They do have cosmopolitan tastes but are not easily impressed. In health, they are prone to skin complaints and dodgy knees. They also suffer from stiff muscles and jaws, and benefit from general tonic herbs and deep relaxation techniques like yoga and meditation.

Cardinal Signs In Western **astrology**, the four signs of the **zodiac** (**Aries**, **Cancer**, **Libra** and **Capricorn**) that share a desire to initiate and take command of people and situations. They are called 'cardinal' or 'initiating' because when the sun moves into their signs, it marks the start of a new season.

Cartomancy (Old French *carte*, 'cards', + Greek *manteia*, 'divination') The art of predicting the future with playing cards. This might be through using a special deck like the **tarot**, or just ordinary playing cards. A tarot deck has particular meanings ascribed to each of its 78 cards (see **arcana**). Each of the suits in a 54-card playing deck also has a symbolic meaning that can be interpreted when using these ordinary cards. The clubs suit deals with business affairs and other practical matters. Diamonds link to money, status, fame and influence. Hearts are associated with (surprise) matters of the heart, especially love and romance. Finally, spades are the problem cards, indicating obstacles and challenges to be overcome. The numbered cards refer to situations, events and changing circumstances, and the court or face cards represent people and their thoughts. See also: **Divination**.

Castaneda, Carlos (1925–98) Anthropologist and author who explored Native North and South American **shamanism** through becoming apprentice to an old Yaqui Indian named Don Juan Matus. Don Juan, a *brujo* (magical healer), taught Castaneda sorcerous rituals that involved ingesting copious amounts of hallucinogenic drugs, most notably peyote cactus, jimson weed and mushrooms. While in the grip of a psychedelic vision he met the peyote god Mescalito, and experienced many **astral travels** in the form of a crow. He wrote tales of his apprenticeship and magical journeys in a series of spiritually well-received books including *The Teachings of Don Juan, Journey to Ixtlan,* and *A Separate Reality.* See also: **Peyotism**.

Caste System A controversial aspect of **Hinduism**, officially abolished in India in 1949, where all followers are separated into one of four *varnas* or social castes, plus a fifth group called the 'untouchables'. All believers once belonged to one of thousands of 'jats', or communities, and these jats were in turn divided between *Brahmins* (the priests and academics), *Kshatriyas* (the rulers and military), *Vaishyas* (farmers, landlords and merchants) and *Sudras* (peasants, servants and workers in non-polluting jobs). If you did not belong to one of these castes, you were *Dalit*, 'unclean and untouchable'. In some areas of India, even to come into contact with the shadow of a *Dalit* was enough to pollute you.

The caste system's lingering effects can still be felt in that society. One of the most significant is the mass emigration of *Dalit* from India, as well as mass conversions to **Buddhism** and **Christianity**.

One of the few remaining reminders of the caste system is the **bindi**, the coloured dot worn in the middle of forehead, signifying piety. Both men and women wear it, although the practice among men is gradually going out of style.

Cathars An offshoot sect of **Gnosticism** that flourished in twelfth- and thirteenth-century Europe, mostly in southern France and northern Italy. It grew so strong as a religion that Pope Innocent III declared a Catholic crusade against it that only ended in 1229 with the Treaty of Meaux. Cathars still continued to be persecuted as heretics for years afterwards.

Cathars believed that God (or good) was not all-powerful, and that while evil (known as the 'monster of chaos') was weaker than God, the outcome of the final battle of the world was not known – mostly because Satan was God's first son. The second son, Jesus, was created to rectify the sins of the firstborn. They also believed that Jesus was not crucified; instead the crucifixion was a hoax created so that Jesus could move to another **astral plane** and continue his teachings there.

Catoptromancy (Greek *katoptron*, 'mirror', + *manteia*, 'divination') A form of **divination** or fortune-telling using mirrors, reflective glass or a polished metal disc. First practised in ancient Egypt and Greece, it was a common form of divining the future used extensively in Late Medieval and Early Renaissance Europe following innovations in mirror and glassmaking techniques. The reflection in the mirror would reflect the truth of a situation. A mirror was said to show the shadow, or soul, of a person, which is why **vampires** (who have no soul) have no reflection in a mirror.

The mirror was never gazed upon directly; instead it was set at an angle, either to reflect the rays of the moon or to be able to see more of the environment and background of the mirror-gazer. If the gazer concentrated hard enough, they could open a line of communication to the after-world and communicate with the spirits of the dead. See also: **Scrying**.

Cauldron (Latin *caldus*, 'hot') A large kettle with a rounded bottom and three legs used in **witchcraft** and **magic**. The shape of a cauldron represents Mother Nature, in which all things are contained, and the three legs symbolise the three aspects of the **goddess** archetype. Witches use a cauldron to cook up **potions** and herbal medicines, scent the air with vapours and, of course, make soup.

Cauldron of Inspiration, also **Ceridwen's Cauldron** The magical cauldron of **Ceridwen**, Celtic Welsh moon goddess and sorceress associated with wisdom and inspiration. If someone partook of Ceridwen's potion, they would be granted wisdom. In legend her kitchen boy, Gwion, either by accident or design, consumed some of this brew and was granted knowledge intended for Ceridwen's son Afagddu. After a wild chase, Ceridwen swallowed up Gwion in an attempt to regain this lost wisdom. Instead, nine months later, she gave birth to **Taliesin**, the mythic Welsh bard and poet.

Cayce, Edgar (1877–1967) Famous American psychic who was given the nickname 'the Sleeping Prophet' because he uttered his predictions and medical advice while in a trance state. From a very early age he showed signs of **ESP** abilities, but in his life he was known primarily as a healer and seer. His best-known predictions were those of the 1929 Wall Street Crash and the outbreak of World War II. Despite a lifetime of other prophetic visions, his accuracy rate was lamentable. One of his most famous predictions gone wrong was his expectation that part of **Atlantis** would resurface in the 1960s, destroying most of the West Coast of California as well as Japan and parts of Northern Europe.

CE Abbreviation for Common Era. A non-Christian alternative for the term AD, *Anno Domini*, 'In the Year of Our Lord'.

Cellular Memory The concept that every cell in our bodies contains a blueprint of our personalities, tastes and life histories. This is possible because all matter (including cellular) is held together by energy and energy flows through all cells. Whatever becomes stored and then saturated in one cell – likes, dislikes, trauma, good and bad memories – is passed on by psychic osmosis to the next cell.

Cellular memory can explain why universal, shared archetypes from the **collective unconscious** pass down through generations of man. Paul Pearsall expands this concept in his book *The Heart's Code*. According to him, 'the heart has a coded subtle knowledge connecting us to everything and everyone around us. That aggregate knowledge is our spirit and soul…The heart is a sentient, thinking, feeling, communicating organ.'

The idea of cellular memory has gained popularity from the many accounts of tissue-transplant recipients who suddenly take on the persona or characteristics of the original donor. It also accounts for the rise in anxiety concerning animal to human organ transplants.

Celtic Spirituality Umbrella term for the **pagan** tradition of nature- and goddess-worship using the deities and practices of ancient Ireland, Scotland, Cornwall and Wales. Many of the gods and goddesses, rites and rituals associated with this school of thought have influenced paganism as a whole, and been subsumed into Christian celebrations and practices. Chief among these influences is the **Celtic wheel**, also known as the 'wheel of the year', which divides the year into eight seasons, each with a major pagan festival associated with it. There is also a panoply of deities and spirit beings with magical powers, like **fairies** and goddesses such as **Ceridwen, Aradia, Brigid** and **Cailleach**, whose powers are invoked in **Wiccan** practice.

Celtic spirituality today often focuses on bringing the ancient arts and crafts methods back into common use. This is most clearly seen in Celtic knotwork, which is incorporated into many decorative arts. It is symbolic of Celtic attitudes, because all existence is linked in a constant and flowing pattern, much as the way a Celtic knot intertwines in one sinuous, continuing line.

Celtic Wheel, also **Wheel of the Year** The calendar of the seasonal year, according to **Celtic spirituality**. It was constructed according to the **moon**, queen of the night, because the Celtic day started at nightfall. In keeping with

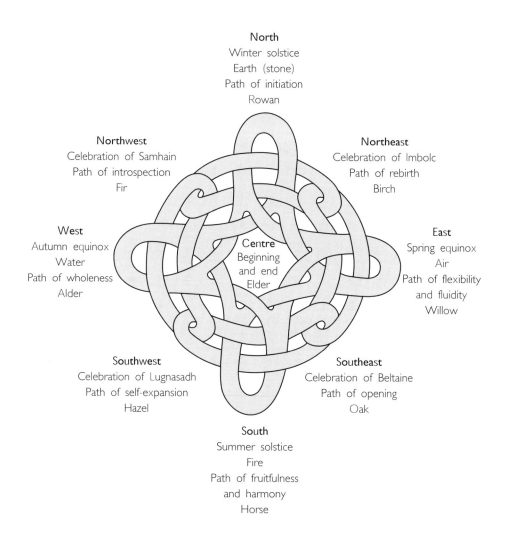

North
Winter solstice
Earth (stone)
Path of initiation
Rowan

Northwest
Celebration of Samhain
Path of introspection
Fir

Northeast
Celebration of Imbolc
Path of rebirth
Birch

West
Autumn equinox
Water
Path of wholeness
Alder

Centre
Beginning
and end
Elder

East
Spring equinox
Air
Path of flexibility
and fluidity
Willow

Southwest
Celebration of Lugnasadh
Path of self-expansion
Hazel

Southeast
Celebration of Beltaine
Path of opening
Oak

South
Summer solstice
Fire
Path of fruitfulness
and harmony
Horse

Celtic wheel

this tradition, the new year in the Celtic calendar starts at another time of gathering darkness, **Samhain**, also known as **Halloween** (31 October). The seasonal cycle is often depicted as a wheel with eight spokes or segments, with each segment defined by the great festival held during that time period.

These celebrations, the **sabbats**, are divided into four major and four minor festivals. The four main sabbats, **Samhain/Halloween**, **Imbolc/Candlemas** (2 February), **Beltane/May Day** (30 April) and **Lagnasad/Lammas** (31 July), are aligned with the four most important seasonal changes in the year. They are a time for cleansing the old and welcoming the new, by lighting great 'bane' or 'bone' fires (made from rubbish and old bones). The four minor sabbats, **Yule** (22 December), **Eoastre** (21 March), **Midsummer** (22 June) and **Michaelmas** (21 September), coincide with the winter and summer **solstices** and the spring and autumn **equinoxes**.

Time is also marked by the **esbats**, the monthly moon cycles. As the lunar calendar has 13 months, there are usually 13 esbats per year, each with its own moon name and qualities associated with it. Esbats are less solemn than sabbats, comparable to the difference between a cocktail party and a black-tie affair in **Wiccan** and **pagan** practice.

Centaury A flower essence made from the centaury blossom. This emotionally healing tincture is one of the **Bach Flower Remedies**. Dr Bach said that this is indicated for 'those who are kind and eager to please, but find their good nature easily imposed upon and exploited by those with more dominant personalities'.

Cerato A flower essence made from the cerato blossom. This emotionally healing tincture is one of the **Bach Flower Remedies**. Dr Bach said that this is indicated for 'those who seek the reassurance of others as they do not trust their own decisions, judgement or intuition'.

Ceridwen, also **Caridwen**, **Cerridwen**, **Kerridwyn** Celtic Welsh moon goddess and sorceress associated with wisdom and inspiration, she is best known for the **cauldron of inspiration**. If someone partook of Ceridwen's potion, they would be granted wisdom. Her symbol was a white, corpse-eating sow, and in **Wicca** she represents, like the **moon**, the cycle of life: death, fertility, regeneration. She is also associated with magic, astrology, herbs, poetry and spells; her special plants are vervain and acorns.

Ceridwen is loosely associated with the Arthurian cycle and the **Mabinogion**, the great epic of Welsh poetry and folklore, credits her role in the mythical life of the Welsh bard **Taliesin**. Wife of the giant Tegid, she had two children – Crearwy, a daughter, whose name means 'light' or 'beautiful'; and a son, Afagddu, meaning 'dark' or 'ugly'. To compensate the boy for his unfortunate appearance, Ceridwen brewed a magical potion called *greal* that would make him wise. The potion required boiling for a year and a day for the magic to develop and she foolishly left her kitchen boy, Gwion, in charge of the brew. Towards the end of the year, Gwion (either by accident or on purpose) licked off three drops of liquid that had fallen onto his hand – and assimilated all the wisdom intended for Afagddu. Furious, Ceridwen chased Gwion across Wales in a wild, shape-shifting hunt: first he became a hare and she a greyhound, then he a fish and she an otter, then he a rabbit and she a hawk. Finally he became a grain of corn and she a hen, and she ate him. This did not end the magic, as Ceridwen became pregnant and nine months later gave birth to Taliesin. Because of this association, Welsh bards call themselves 'sons of Ceridwen'.

Cernunnos (Gaelic, 'horned one') One of the gods of Celtic mythology, used as a generic term for the various horned gods of Irish tradition. Cernunnos was Lord of winter, the hunt, animals, death and male fertility, and god of the underworld. He is sometimes portrayed as a triple or trefoil god (youth, maturity, old age) the same way that **goddesses** are portrayed as maid, mother, crone. Because of this threefold nature, he is associated with the shamrock, which was assimilated by St Patrick after **Christianity** came to the Irish isles. See also: **Celtic Wheel, Herne the Hunter, Paganism**.

Chakras (Sanskrit, 'wheel') Seven major energy centres found in the human body. According to many different Eastern philosophies including **Hinduism**, **Tibetan Buddhism**, and **yoga**, spiritual energy flows through these vortexes and each has a profound effect on the mind and body of a person. They exist on the subtle level but have a precise physical location on the body, vertically aligned either on or just in front of the spine. There are also smaller vortexes located in the hands and feet but they are not as significant as the main seven.

Each of the seven chakras has particular qualities, element, animal symbol and colour associated with it.

The *root* or *base* chakra (known as *muladhara* in Sanskrit) is located at the base of the spine, is related to the **earth element**, and the colour red, and has as its symbol the bull. This is where the energy of our animal strength and survival instinct lives.

Next is the *sacral* (*svadhisthana*) chakra, located in the groin and associated with the moon, the **water element**, and the colour orange. Its symbol is the fish and this is the home of desire: physical, mental and sexual.

Third is the *solar plexus (manipura)* chakra, seated around the navel. Known as the sun or power chakra, its colour is yellow, its element **fire** and symbol the ram. The solar plexus rules personal power, will and independence.

Fourth is the *heart (anahata)* chakra, situated in the centre of the chest. It is associated with the **air element**, and the colour green; its symbol is the dove. This chakra controls love and emotions.

Next is the *throat (vishuddha)* chakra, also known as the chakra of time and space. Its colour is blue; its element sound and symbol the elephant. The throat chakra 'speaks the truth' and is associated with communication of all kind.

The *brow (ajna)* chakra is also known as the **Third Eye** and is located in the centre of the forehead. Its colour is indigo; its element light and symbol the cobra. Psychic visions, dreams and brain functions are associated with this chakra.

Last is the *crown (sahasrara)* chakra, situated on the top and centre of the head. Associated with the colour of violet fading to white and then eternity, this chakra's element is thought and its symbol the serpent. It connects a person to the higher self and, ultimately, to divinity.

Like any energetic body system, chakras can become weakened or strengthened by lifestyle and practice. Different disciplines have evolved, like **ayurveda** or **yoga**, which help to balance out chakra energies, and there is a

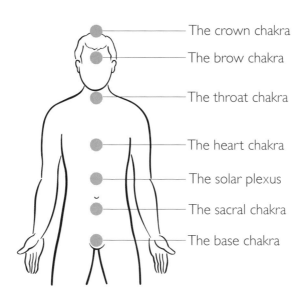

The crown chakra

The brow chakra

The throat chakra

The heart chakra

The solar plexus

The sacral chakra

The base chakra

Chakra locations

number of therapies that will have a beneficial effect on chakras as well. See also: **Colour Therapy.**

Chan Buddhism see Zen Buddhism

Changeling According to traditional Celtic folklore, a changeling is a baby left by **fairies** in place of a human child, after an elf or fairy abducted the human youngster. Due to the glamour spells cast over them, changelings appeared to be identical to the missing offspring but often seemed precocious or abnormally advanced for their age in intellect or physique.

It could also be a wizened, misshapen baby who was always crying, always ravenous but never satisfied.

There was a number of ways to get the changeling to reveal its origin and, by doing so, get your own child returned to you. You could make the unhappy changeling laugh, and that would break the enchantment. Or there was the harsher option of trying to whip the child until the fairy mother appeared. This latter method was unfortunately the more common technique, particularly during the medieval period.

Defining a child as a changeling was one way for parents to explain away a socially unacceptable child, especially one with birth defects or genetic disorders, which is why the phrase 'he's away with the fairies' came into existence.

Channelling The process whereby a **medium** or willing person serves as a 'channel' for a spirit or other **discarnate entity**, for the purposes of receiving information of some sort. The spirit speaks through the channeller, who is temporarily possessed by this entity and has no memory of what has been said. Messages are communicated through the channeller in the entity's voice or through **automatic writing**, and are often thought to contain wisdom of great portent. See also: **Spiritualism.**

Chaos Theory A principle in quantum physics that chaos, the apparent lack of order in a system, nevertheless obeys particular laws or rules, and only appears to be random. The theory, first mooted in the 1970s, was based on the work surrounding the **butterfly effect**, discovered by Edward Lorenz in 1961, and on Benoit Mandelbrot's study of computer fractals. This idea blew up the traditional principles of Newtonian laws of physics, which state that unseen effects can be predicted through precise measurements. Instead, work on the chaos theory showed that even very tiny errors in initial measurements would yield enormous unpredictability, far out of proportion to what would be expected mathematically. In effect what chaos theory means is that anything is capable of affecting anything else – a prime tenet of **new age** and **holistic** thinking. See also: **Fritjof Capra**.

Chardin, Pierre Teilhard de (1881–1956) A Jesuit priest and mystic philosopher who believed that humanity was on the verge of a leap of consciousness that would dramatically alter our lives and lead to spiritual enlightenment. This change would be effected by a network of thought he called the noosphere surrounding the globe and connecting all humanity. He came up with a series of phrases to describe the distinct layers of the earth and how it related to this living network. The earth's core is called the barysphere, the earth's crust the lithosphere, followed by our atmosphere. On the boundary between the lithosphere and atmosphere is the biosphere, the domain of all organic life.

The noosphere is the next phase in the earth's evolution and will have an effect on all the other realms of the planet. See also: **Gaian Theory**.

Charms (Latin *carmen*, 'song') A magical object or spell that has supernatural powers to ward off evil and bring good luck. See also: **Amulet**, **Horseshoes**, **Talisman**.

Chavutti Thirumal (Sanskrit, 'massage by foot') A form of **massage** where the therapist uses their feet, instead of hands. It combines elements of dance, yoga and ayurvedic medicine in the treatment, and can be quite a vigorous, detoxifying experience. The main goal of chavutti thirumal is to stimulate 'marma' energy points on the body (similar to **acupuncture**) to ensure a balanced flow of **prana** (life force) throughout the body.

During a treatment, the masseur will apply pressure to the body, one foot at a time, while holding onto a rope suspended over the patient at head level across the room. This helps the therapist to give a smooth, even massage all over.

People with back problems, especially posture-related ones, can benefit from this form of massage, as it will stretch and realign the spine, as well as alleviate aches and pains. Chavutti thirumal also boosts oxygen uptake to the muscles and helps the body cleanse the system of toxins, both physical and emotional. See also: **Ayurveda**.

Chela (Sanskrit, 'pupil') Term used to describe a pupil of a spiritual teacher, or **guru**, according to Hindu thought. Chelas often have complex and interdependent relationships with gurus, whereby they submit themselves to harrowing tests and questioning of their self-image, in order to reach **enlightenment**.

Chelation Therapy (Greek *chele*, 'claw') A controversial alternative medical therapy involving a set of slow-drip intravenous injections of a synthetic amino acid called EDTA. Chelation therapy allegedly removes plaque and calcium deposits from arteries and veins. The name of the therapy arises from the 'claw-like' structure of the EDTA (ethylenediaminetetraacetic) molecule, first synthesised in 1930s Germany. EDTA is effective in removing toxic metals like mercury from the blood but it is still unproven to be effective against atherosclerosis and coronary heart disease. Proponents of the therapy argue that there is evidence but the medical establishment has suppressed it. Despite its advocates, it is not recognised by hospitals and insurance companies as a valid method of treating illness.

Cherry Plum A flower essence made from the cherry plum blossom. This emotionally healing tincture is one of the **Bach Flower Remedies**. Dr Bach said that this is indicated for 'irrational thoughts and fear of the mind giving way'.

Cherub (plural **Cherubim**) (Arabic *kerabya*, 'like a child') A winged **angel** that in appearance resembles a small, chubby child. In the hierarchy of the Christian **heaven**, cherubim are located in the second highest of the ninefold celestial angel order. The **Bible**'s Book of Revelation represents cherubim as lions or bulls with eagles' wings and human faces. See also: **Seraphim**.

Chestnut Bud A flower essence made from the blossom of the chestnut tree. This emotionally healing tincture is one of the **Bach Flower Remedies**. Dr Bach said that this is indicated for 'those who make the same mistake time and again, learning little from past experience'.

Chi, also **Ch'i**, **Qi** (Chinese, 'life force') Vital energy of the universe that animates all existence and permeates all things. Although this Chinese phrase is one of the best-known, many other cultures have a name for this metaphysical energy. In Japan it is called ki, in India **prana**, in Tibet rlun. The idea of chi forms the bedrock for all Chinese philosophies, most notably in **feng shui** and **Traditional Chinese Medicine**. Central to the concept of both is viewing chi as a 'river flow' of energy, cyclical in nature (particularly in health), and the optimal state of chi as being in balance – with nature and surroundings, or harmony within the body. When this flow is disrupted the energy can become blocked, or be made to veer off into destructive channels. Remedies such as **acupuncture**, or feng shui solutions like clearing clutter and realigning furniture and other possessions, are intended to redirect chi back into harmonious patterns.

Chi is divided into two aspects, **yin** (negative) and **yang** (positive). These two aspects are always in dynamic interaction, as they both oppose and depend upon one another. This is why the **yin/yang** symbol is known as the 'Great Polarity'. Yin and yang can be further subdivided into the **five elements** of water, wood, fire, earth and metal. **Traditional Chinese Medicine** further defines chi as the body's personal energy system, which runs through a series of channels called **meridians**; their disruption leads to ill health. Chinese medicine categorises a person's chi in three main ways: parental chi, acquired chi and inherited chi. Parental chi is the basic health you are given at the moment of conception and depends upon how healthy your mother and father were at that specific point in time. Acquired chi is the energy derived from our nourishment after birth – food, fluids and air. Inherited chi, also known as **jing essence**, is genetic in nature. This inherited energy determines how robust our constitution will be throughout life. The amount of jing at birth is the quantity we have for the rest of our life and can only be diminished, never replenished.

Chi flows in a 24-hour cycle similar to our own body clock and is broken up into 12 two-hour chunks, each relating to a specific organ and meridian. When chi is in the time zone of a corresponding organ, like the heart or kidneys, the energy is strongest. Twelve hours later, when chi is directly opposed, the energy will be weakest in the organ. Chinese medical practitioners treat a person according to how strong chi is in each particular organ/meridian in the body.

Other alternative therapies, such as **therapeutic touch, reflexology, shiatsu** and **reiki**, use the Chinese concept of chi in diagnosing and treating ailments. See also: **Orgone Energy, Prana**.

Chicory   A flower essence made from the chicory blossom. This emotionally healing tincture is one of the **Bach Flower Remedies**. Dr Bach said that this is indicated for 'those inclined to impose their love on others in a selfish or possessive way, blind to their need for independence and social freedom, and who are easily hurt when snubbed'.

Chi Kung, also **Quigong** (Chinese chi, 'energy', + kung, 'cultivation, practice') An ancient Chinese system of working with energy, '**chi**', to promote health and well-being, although the phrase has only been in common use since the 1950s. Chi kung is the blanket term used to describe a broad category of physical exercises, martial arts, healthcare and meditation that all seek to cultivate a person's chi. Chi kung improves health and vitality by teaching a person how to recognise and control their own personal energy. By restoring a balance to your chi, you encourage self-healing processes in your body. It is recommended as a discipline for stress-related conditions, fatigue, high blood pressure and heart disease, as well as for easing the aches and pains of arthritis, old age and everyday life. Breathing, postures and meditation exercises are an integral part of chi kung discipline, and are very similar in nature to **yoga**.

Chimera (Greek *cheimon*, 'winter') A fierce fire-breathing monster of Greek myth, who had the head and front body of a lion, and a tail end of a dragon. She also had three heads – goat, lion and dragon. The chimera is best known for her ability to present the face most needed in a fight, which is why people who present false fronts and hide their true selves, or people who fabricate a reality to suit their beliefs, are also known as chimeras.

Chimera

Chinese Astrology see Astrology, Chinese

Chinese Facial Analysis A comprehensive Chinese method of reading fortunes and characters in people's faces, which is also known as **physiognomy**. This art has been in use for well over 2,000 years, and there are texts from the second century BC that are still used today in reading people's faces. Skilled practitioners can interpret a person's past behaviour and health, if they are likely to be rich or poor, have children, be trustworthy in business and be lucky in love, as well as what is likely to happen in the future, by a number of specific facial elements. These elements include: the shape of the face; eye shape and colour; the shape and slope of the nose, eyebrows, lips and chin, as well as distinguishing wrinkles, moles and other marks. All of these characteristics indicate which one of the **five element** types a person is – wood, water, metal, earth or fire. From that, strengths and weaknesses about a person's character, as well as what areas of their health they should safeguard, can be determined. See also: **Chinese Hand Analysis**, **Iridology**.

Chinese Hand Analysis A comprehensive Chinese method of reading fortunes and characters in people's hands, very similar in nature to the Western art of **palmistry**. Hand analysis has been practised for well over 2,000 years, and as with facial analysis Chinese texts from the second century BC are still used today in reading people's hands. Skilled practitioners can interpret a person's past behaviour and health, if they are likely to be rich or poor, have children, be trustworthy in business, be lucky in love and much more, as well as what is likely to happen in the future, using this art. The size and shape of the hand and fingers, fingernails, specific lines and marks, colour, temperature and such factors as bony or fleshy hands, are all considered in making a diagnosis. According to Chinese palmistry, a woman's right hand and a man's left hand reflect their actions, thoughts, aspirations and fortune. The opposite hand – in women the left and in men the right – is the one influenced by family and inherited tendencies. To get the fullest picture about a person's past, present and future, therefore, you should take a reading from a woman's right hand and a man's left hand. As in **Chinese facial analysis**, people can be classified into one of five character 'types' – wood, water, metal, earth or fire – based on the **five element cycle**. From that, strengths and weaknesses about a person's character, as well as what areas of their health they should safeguard, can be determined.

Chinese Herbal Medicine A branch of **Traditional Chinese Medicine** that utilises herbs to treat illness and increase vitality. Chinese herbalism differs from Western herbal traditions in that herbs are rarely used on their own, but instead in formulas that are designed to treat specific 'patterns of disharmony'.

Chinese herbal prescriptions have four main components: Emperor Herb, the main herb for the condition; Minister Herb, which assists in easing symptoms and secondary health problems arising from the main ailment; Assistant or Adjutant Herb, to help balance out the mixture; and Messenger Herb, which carries other herbs in the prescription to the affected area. What herb is used depends upon what energetic quality it has (hot, cold, damp or dry) and its taste (sweet, sour, bitter, salt, pungent).

When a Chinese practitioner examines a patient, he will discover the energetic quality of whatever ailment exists, and mix his herbs to counterbalance the illness. Herbal formulas are made from all parts of the plant – roots, stems, bark, leaves, seeds or flowers – with different parts of the same plant having different medicinal properties depending upon the plant material used. The herbs are dried before use and the mixed formulas are usually taken as teas, or in the form of pills or tinctures. Some complaints require months of treatment, while others respond after one or two doses.

Chinese herbal medicine came into widespread use in Western culture in the 1970s, and is most commonly used in the West to treat skin and gynaecological ailments, allergies, digestive complaints, respiratory complaints and immune system illnesses, although in China it is used for nearly all health conditions and is considered more important than **acupuncture**. See also: **Five Element Cycle, Herbalism**.

Chirognomy, also **Chirology** (Greek *kheir*, 'hand', + *manteia*, 'divination') A form of **divination** or fortune-telling based solely on the shape of the hand. The size of the hand, the shape of the fingers and fingernails, skin textures, colour and temperature are all taken into consideration. It is a subset of **chiromancy** (also known as **palmistry**), a form of divination that interprets all aspects of the hand. See also: **Chinese Hand Analysis**.

Chirographology (Greek *kheir*, 'hand', + *graphe*, 'writing' + *logos*, 'word, study') Study of hands and handwriting for the purposes of predicting character and behaviour. It is closely related to **graphology**, or handwriting analysis. See also: **Chinese Hand Analysis, Chirognomy**.

Chirology see Chirognomy

Chiromancy, also **Cheiromancy** (Greek *kheir*, 'hand', + *manteia*, 'divination') **Divination** by interpreting the lines, shapes and markings of a person's hand. See also: **Palmistry**.

Chiron The wisest of the centaurs in Greek mythology and the teacher of the semi-divine physician **Aesculapius**. It is also the name of a large asteroid discovered in 1977, with a fixed orbit between **Saturn** and **Uranus**. Chiron's appearance in the galaxy excited astrologers as well as astronomers, as they pondered the symbolism of this new astral body. In Western **astrology**, there is a tradition of interpreting a new planet's meaning according to world events that coincide with the time of the planet's discovery. Several new ideologies about government and healing came to fruition in around 1977 – so in astrology Chiron symbolises a person's healing ability as well as the maverick, rebel spirit in society. As it is a fairly new astrological factor, its full effects on a person's **horoscope** are not yet known.

Chiropractic (Greek *kheir*, 'hand', + *praktos*, 'doing') A method of diagnosing and treating disorders of the nervous system through manual manipulation of bones. A chiropractor will examine, both manually and through X-rays, the alignment of the spine and joints, and will then make a decision on how best to alleviate symptoms such as back pain and other nerve disorders. Chiropractors focus mainly on 'realigning' and 'adjusting' the spine along a straight vertical axis, to improve nerve function. The spine is the main structural support and 'telephone line' of the body, and any damage there, particularly to nerves, affects the rest of the body. These adjustments to the spine and other joints, tendons, muscles and ligaments not only relieve pain in tender areas, but also have beneficial effects on other problems like digestive upsets or menstrual disorders.

Chiropractic is often confused with **osteopathy** and there are some similarities. The main difference is that chiropractors use X-rays more in treatment and focus only on joint and vertebrae movement, while osteopaths are less likely to use X-rays, instead focusing on muscle and joint movement, as well as spinal alignment and manipulation.

In a typical session, the chiropractor will take a full medical history, often followed by X-rays and a test to discover your physical range of movement. The therapist then places your body in a particular posture (it could be standing, sitting or lying on a couch) and, using pressure, takes the vertebrae or joint to the end of their normal range of movement. Then the vertebrae or joint are given a sharp tap, which allow them to spring back into position. The force for this motion is not painful, but is often accompanied by a loud popping noise or 'click'. This scary sound is actually harmless, as it signifies the gas bubble between joints popping when there is a change of pressure between the two bones.

Chiropractic treatment is highly recommended for pain in the back, neck, shoulders, arms and legs, especially pain caused by accidents, injuries and poor posture. It also benefits headache sufferers as well as helping stressed-out individuals to relax.

David Daniel Palmer, a Canadian osteopath, developed chiropractic technique in late nineteenth-century America. The practice has only recently gained legitimacy in medical circles and, in 1994, UK chiropractors were granted statutory regulation, similar to doctors, dentists and physiotherapists, which means you cannot call yourself a chiropractor unless you are properly licensed. Chiropractic is now the Western world's third largest health-care profession, after medicine and dentistry.

Chirosophy see **Chiromancy**

Christian Science, also **Church of Christian Scientist** A religion founded in the latter part of the nineteenth century by Mary Baker Eddy, who was inspired to investigate the power of mind over body after seeing displays of **mesmerism**. In 1875 she published *Science and Health, with Key to the Scriptures*, which remains the canonical text of the religion.

Christian Scientists believe that disease is caused by negative emotions, specifically fear, and can be healed by the mind if the person seeks the truth of reality and the divine. Reality to a Christian Scientist is a reinterpretation of conventional **Christianity**, except evil and matter are not real. If you live in the divine spirit (that is, do not smoke, drink, take drugs or even think about being ill) you will not get sick. Christian Scientists refuse medical treatment, because to acknowledge illness is to make it real, to acknowledge that you are in a state of sin.

An easier guide to this school of thought can be found in the novels written for children by devout believer Frances Hodgson Burnett (*The Little Princess, The Secret Garden, Little Lord Fauntleroy*), whose characters at times spout almost verbatim from *Science and Health*.

Christianity (Greek *khristos*, 'anointed one' translating Hebrew *masiah*, 'messiah') The largest religion in the world and a dominant force in Western civilisation. Believers are called Christians and they follow the teachings of **Jesus Christ** (Yeshua in Hebrew), an itinerant Jewish preacher who lived around 2,000 years ago in the Judean province of the Roman Empire, the modern-day region of Palestine in the Middle East. It is sometimes termed an 'Abramic religion' as it arose out of the covenant that the Jewish prophet Abraham made with the Lord, for his descendants to inherit a great land and nation state, in return for solely worshipping God. Christians believe that Jesus is the Son of **God**, born of a virgin (**Virgin Mary**), that he was crucified and died on the cross for our sins, that he rose from the dead after three days and later ascended to **heaven**. His life on this earth was for the purpose of showing the way to salvation for all people, who have mortal bodies but immortal souls that (depending on the path you take in life) reside after death either in paradise or in **hell**.

Jesus is part of the 'Holy Trinity' – the teaching that God is experienced in three distinct ways – which places God at the apex of the triangle, the creator of the world and universe and 'Father' to all people. Jesus, 'the Son', is next, who sacrificed his life to save others and will some day return ('at the end of days') to save the earth. Finally there is the Holy Spirit, who dwells inside a true believer and continues to guide them throughout this life.

Christians believe that while God created the world as a good and holy place, it has become corrupted by evil and sin. Man is therefore born sinful, but can be saved by believing in Christ and repenting of his sins. The only way to get to heaven in Christianity is to believe in Jesus' divinity, which is significantly different from what is taught in Judaism (which Christianity is based on). In the Jewish faith, you must obey the law and scriptures and it is by your actions that you will reside with God in the afterlife. In Christianity, it is faith, not works, which will save your immortal soul.

Christian morality and conduct are based on the information contained in their holy text, the **Bible**, which comprises two books – the Old Testament (the Jewish Tanakh and Apocrypha) and the New Testament (the four gospels of Jesus' life and letters/teachings of his apostles). Jesus' teachings can be summed up in two commandments: love God, and love (meaning show care and concern for) others.

The Orthodox Christian tradition began to differ from Western traditions early on in Christianity's history. In AD 313, the Christian Roman Emperor, Constantine, formally established freedom and toleration for Christianity in his Edict of Milan. He also decided to build a 'New Rome' on the site of the Greek city of Byzantium, which he named Constantinople (now Istanbul, Turkey). It became the centre of the new Christian empire, and eventually Church authority became concentrated in the five bishops or patriarchs located in Alexandria, Antioch, Constantinople, Jerusalem and Rome. In AD 381, Rome was given the lead position, followed by Constantinople (based on the secular status of the cities involved). Jealousies and quarrels led to a schism between the two that widened in subsequent centuries. Each faction began to develop different traditions and beliefs that continued to separate and alienate the two Church centres from one another. Finally, in AD 1054, the leaders of the Roman Catholic Church and Eastern Orthodox Churches excommunicated each other. Thereafter, Orthodox believers followed the teachings of Greek patriarch and scholars, while Western Christian tradition came to be dominated by the teachings of St Augustine of Hippo (AD 354–386).

This schism extends to the calendar systems each tradition follows. The Orthodox Church follows the Julian calendar, first devised by pagan Roman priests circa 50 BC for Julius Caesar. Unfortunately, this calendar is too long by 11 minutes and 14 seconds each year, or one day every 128 years. By the late sixteenth century, this led to an error of 10 days, so the Roman Catholic pope Gregory XIII commissioned the creation of a more accurate calendar system, the 'Gregorian Calendar', which is the one that Western Christianity, and most of the world, follow today. The Orthodox Church refused to accept this calendar, so to this day, they celebrate Christian holidays approximately 11 days and 14 seconds later than the Western Christian Church.

There are many different sects and divisions of Christianity, depending upon where you are on the globe, and they all have different interpretations of what it means to be saved and how best to follow Christ's commandments. Orthodox Christianity roughly operates in eastern-hemisphere churches like those of Russia and Greece. Western Christianity is primarily located in the western hemisphere although neither tradition is geographically restricted.

In Western Christianity there are two main divisions: Roman Catholicism and Protestantism. The major points of contention between these two factions is that Catholics believe in the divinity of Jesus' mother, the Virgin Mary, and that the Pope in Rome is the head of the Church, the direct spiritual descendant of the first Pope, Jesus' disciple Peter. As such, the Pope has the final say on Church doctrine and belief. Catholics also believe that salvation comes from God but is channelled through the sacraments of the Church.

Protestants do not accept the Pope's supremacy; they believe salvation is dependent upon repentance of sins and acceptance of the Lord as saviour, and that while Jesus may have been born of a virgin, Mary is not actually the Mother of God.

All Christians celebrate the three significant festivals of their faith: **Christmas** (25 December), which was fixed as the date of Jesus' birth in the fourth century AD; **Easter** (late March/early April), when Jesus rose from the dead; and Whitsun, also known as Pentecost (seven weeks after Easter).

Christmas One of the significant holidays of the **Christian** year, which celebrates the birth of their god, **Jesus Christ**. Although 25 December is Jesus' official birthday, this date was chosen and fixed in the fourth century AD to take advantage of the old traditions and rituals of **Yule**, the hitherto **pagan** celebration of the midwinter **solstice**.

How Christmas is celebrated varies from country to country, but nearly all cultures incorporate trees, decorations, feasting, gift-giving, goodwill, a Santa figure and displays of lights to chase away the winter's gloom and to commemorate the gift of Jesus to the world and his gifts to us.

Chromotherapy see Colour Therapy

Circadian Rhythms (Latin *circa* + *dia*, 'about a day') Body rhythms that recur in a 24-hour cycle, even in the absence of light. They are based on such things as our sensitivity to light and darkness and therefore our sleeping/waking patterns.

Circumambulation A fancy term used in **witchcraft** and other **magic** practices to describe walking around an object or person three times as part of a **spell** or ritual. The 'power of three' (an important concept of magnifying the power of a spell in witchcraft) is invoked by doing so. See also: **Wicca**.

Clairaudience (French, 'clear hearing') The ability to hear the voices of the spirits of the deceased, through either **ESP** or other paranormal means. The most famous examples of people possessing clairaudience are Joan of Arc (AD 1412–1431), who claimed to hear supernatural voices urging her to fight for France, and **Muhammad** (AD 570–632), who was dictated the contents of the **Koran** by the angel Gabriel. Clairaudience is often practised by **mediums** during their contact with the spirit world, where only they can hear the voices of the dead communicating with them.

Clairvoyance, Clairvoyant (French, 'clear seeing') The ability to look beyond the normal world and obtain information about a person, event or situations through **ESP** or other paranormal means. This may take the form of being able to predict the future, or being able to replay a scene from a past incident in the mind of the clairvoyant as though they were present on the scene. Clairvoyance is sometimes referred to as 'second sight' for this reason. Sometimes clairvoyants can perceive the presence of a ghost or other spirit, or the **aura** of a living person.

Citizens of ancient Egypt and India used to believe this power came from viewing the world through a **third eye**, located in the centre of the forehead, which corresponds with the seat of the brow **chakra**.

Cledonomancy An informal method of **divination**, or fortune telling, in which apparently random events and/or chance remarks are taken to be portents of the future.

Cleidomancy, also **Clidomancy** (Greek *kleis*, 'key' + *manteia*, 'divination') A form of **divination**, first practised in ancient Greece, using a key for fortune-telling purposes. Over time, the practise evolved and became widespread throughout Europe up to and including modern times. Several different methods were used, but the most common one involved the use of a suspended key. A question or the name of a person who required proof of innocence would be inscribed on the key and then hung either from a Bible or the finger of a virgin who chanted ritualistic words. The key would turn and the direction of this rotation would determine the answer, or the guilt/innocence of the person.

Clematis A flower essence made from the clematis blossom. This emotionally healing tincture is one of the **Bach Flower Remedies**. Dr Bach said that this is indicated for 'those who are dreamy, living in the future, day-dreaming, absent-minded, and need to have something to look forward to'.

Cleromancy (Greek, 'divination by casting dice') **Divination** or predicting the future from the casting of dice into lots. Black and white beans, small bones or stones were also used – the important thing was their ability to be cast into lots. Whichever dice were thrown, or objects selected, were considered to be chosen by the gods. This method of divination was common in ancient Egypt as well as Rome, whose citizens believed that the practice was sacred to the god **Mercury**. See also: **Sortilege**.

Cloud of Unknowing A Christian mystical work of the fourteenth century, whose author is unknown. It teaches that the 'Cloud of Unknowing' separating us from **God** cannot be overcome through the intellect. Instead, we must strive to bridge this gap through love, which is the only thing that will connect the individual to the divine. See also: **Christianity**.

Cognitive Behaviour Therapy A school of psychotherapy based on the idea that unconscious distress caused by learned behaviour, thoughts or experiences of the past can be unlearned through a conscious process. Our thoughts control a large part of our behaviours and emotions, so altering the way we think can result in positive changes in the way we act and feel. This is done through the patient and therapist working together to change the negative beliefs and learn new patterns of behaviour.

If the patient is sincerely interested in overcoming neuroses and unhealthy lifestyle choices, then cognitive behaviour therapy has been proved very effective. It is now psychiatry's 'treatment of choice' for anxiety, obsessive-compulsive disorders and depression, as well as eating disorders, panic attacks and chronic pain syndrome.

Collective Unconscious Psychic realm shared by everyone where all the elements of human experience are stored. The realm of the collective unconscious is a sort of 'group mind' that operates under the level of our own individual unconscious.

Carl Jung, who formulated this idea, said 'the collective unconscious contains the whole spiritual heritage of mankind's evolution, born anew in the brain structure of every individual'. He felt that the collective unconscious was the only way to explain why different symbols of our existence,

archetypes, would appear in times of psychological crisis. The spontaneous welling-up of archetypes would provide you with answers to some of life's deepest questions, and give you a way to deal with things all people must face – like the death of a loved one, the desire to find a mate, the longing for a child, the search for meaning.

Dreams, crises, fevers, psychoses and synchronicity are all gateways to the collective unconscious, which is ready to restore the individual psyche to health with its insights. See also: **Anima, Jungian Psychology, Psyche, Shadow, Synchronicity.**

Colonics, also **Colonic Hydrotherapy, Colonic Irrigation, Colon Lavage**
The irrigation of the large intestine with water under pressure to rid it of stagnated faecal material and other toxic substances. It differs from an enema in that it goes much deeper into the intestine, and afterwards seeks to create an ideal environment for beneficial gut flora.

Although colonics as we now know it uses sophisticated machinery and modern techniques, the concept is an ancient one. It forms an important part of ayurvedic health practice, and was used by the ancient Egyptians and Greeks.

A colonic irrigation session is not complicated. A tube is inserted into the anus and the water infused into the colon. The direction of the water is then reversed and waste material is sucked out via the same channel. Sometimes a nutrient tonic like aloe vera, oxygen or wheatgrass will be added to the water to help heal the intestinal wall and encourage the growth of intestinal bacteria.

The first session or few sessions take longer because of the build-up of waste, and proponents of colonics say that once you are past your initial squeamishness and discomfort, it can become an emotionally cathartic experience. Once the colon has been cleared of build-up it functions more efficiently and also stimulates the rest of the body to eliminate toxins more effectively – as long as other healthy living practices like improved diet and exercise are undertaken.

As colonic therapies are not currently government regulated, it is important to find a reputable practitioner. The Colonic International Association in London keeps a register of such therapists. See also: **Ayurveda, Detox.**

Colour Therapy, also **Chromotherapy** An alternative therapy treatment that uses different shades of colour to stimulate our natural healing processes. Whether on its own or in combination with other disciplines, colour therapy can have a profound effect on physical and emotional health.

When pure white light is refracted through a prism, it splits into a dizzying array of colours. As light is composed of energy particles, colour therefore has energetic properties, both physical and mental. According to Eastern philosophy, each of the seven energy centres of the body, **chakras**, has a different colour associated with it. Because of illness or some other imbalance in your life (stress, depression, or even just a bad hair day) the energy in one of your chakras may become weak. By using the appropriate colour to balance out the suffering chakra (through light, crystals, oils, environment, clothes or even coloured cards) the energy is boosted and healing occurs. This same therapy works on your **aura** (personal energy field), because each energetic layer of your aura also has a colour associated with it.

Although it is hard to say exactly which exact hue or tint will be of most benefit to a person, in general the following colours have the following healing properties.

Indigo/dark blue acts as a sedative and has a soothing effect on the ears and eyes. It also helps to reduce fatigue. Purple strengthens the mind and enhances the immune system. It can help calm the mind and is the colour most associated with psychic powers. Light blue cools and calms; it slows down and retards growth. It is an excellent colour for meditation rooms, and helps the throat area, whether in colds or in talking. Green is excellent for weak eyes, and has very soothing, healing effects on the stressed and ill (which is why it is so often found painted on the walls of hospital and therapy rooms). Yellow is uplifting in mood and smartens the reflexes, and also helps the digestive system. Red is warming and stimulating to the blood and nerves, and helps stimulate the appetite, which is why you often see red walls and furnishings in a successful restaurant. See also: **Aura-Soma Therapy, Crystal Healing**.

Cometomancy see Astromancy

Complementary Medicine Therapies and healing systems that do not conform to Western theories of medicine, but which have achieved a certain degree of respectability in these orthodox and scientific circles. The British Medical Association introduced the term in 1993 because it acknowledged that there were benefits to be had from **alternative therapies** but thought them too risky to be used without medical supervision or approval. As the name suggests, treatments from these systems tend to enhance or 'complement' ongoing therapy of a more traditional sort, although they can be used on their own. Examples of complementary medicine include **naturopathy, Traditional Chinese Medicine, osteopathy, chiropractic, homeopathy, acupuncture** and **herbalism**.

This phrase is at times used interchangeably with the term **Alternative Therapy**, with good reasons behind the confusion. Whether or not a therapy can be considered 'alternative' or 'complementary' depends on the way it is practised. Consulting a trained, qualified homeopath for a chronic ailment that your regular doctor cannot treat would be an example of 'complementary' use. Self-medicating with homeopathic remedies from your chemist would be 'alternative'. See also: **Allopathic**, **Holism**.

Confucius, Confucianism An ethical code of behaviour based on the teaching and writings of the Chinese philosopher Confucius (551–479 BC). He was a sage much concerned with proper conduct in public life, especially in politics and business, which no doubt derived from his own experiences as a local government official.

Confucius taught that in every relationship – between parent and child, husband and wife, peasant and emperor – people have responsibilities and obligations to each other. If these responsibilities are honoured, then society will be just and harmonious. He felt that although evil existed in the world, man was intrinsically good and if he acted in accordance with his nature, life could be made better for all. Part of this ethic involved accepting your place in the world, and deferring to those in power or wisdom above you.

Confucius is also credited with writing the interpretive **hexagram** meanings in the divinatory text **I Ching**, although that is a matter of fierce debate in some circles.

Later in life, Confucius left his official post and travelled throughout the country preaching his ethical philosophy. A band of students dutifully recorded all of his teachings and condensed them into a book of sayings, which still has great relevance to Chinese culture. See also: **Taoism**.

Coning see **Thermoauricular Therapy**

Conjunction In **astrology**, when two planets appear to move next to each other in the heavens, in some cases appearing as a single object. This is considered to be a favourable omen because the energies of the planets are working together. The 'Star of Bethlehem' present at **Jesus'** birth was actually the conjunction of Jupiter (said to be the planet of kings) and Saturn (said to rule the Jews).

Constitutional Type In **homeopathy**, the classification system for discovering what distinctive physical, mental and emotional traits a person has, which defines the type of constitution they have. This is important, because a homeopath needs to correctly match a homeopathic remedy with a constitutional type, or the cure will be ineffective. The main 15 homeopathic remedies (called **polychrests**) give their names to the different constitutional types. It is inaccurate to say that a person will always be just one type – most people are a combination of any number of types, although one personality profile will stand out. In general, the fitting polychrest acts preventatively and curatively on its matching personality type – for example, a person with a Calc. Carb. constitution will respond well to the Calc. Carb. remedy almost regardless of the illness they are suffering from. There are 15 types: **Argent. Nit.**; **Arsen. Alb.**; **Calc. Carb.**; **Graphites**; **Ignatia**; **Lachesis**; **Lycopodium**; **Merc. Sol.**; **Natrum Mur.**; **Nux Vomica**; **Phosphorus**; **Pulsatilla**; **Sepia**; **Silica** and **Sulphur**.

Cosmology (Greek *kosmos*, 'universe', + *logos*, 'study') Blanket term used to describe the study of the universe and all its parts, including time, space, and eternity. It is also used to describe the study of gods and goddesses, and their part in the **creation myths** of the world.

Coven A group of **witches**, usually numbering 13, who work together in an organised fashion to perform magical rites or ceremonies. A coven can be smaller than 13, but that is the optimum number as there are 13 full moons in the year. A full moon is a source of great power and wisdom to a witch, allowing her to call down the magical abilities of the archetypal lunar goddess.

Crab Apple A flower essence made from the crab apple blossom. This emotionally healing tincture is one of the **Bach Flower Remedies**. Dr Bach said that this is 'the cleansing remedy for those who dislike themselves or feel unclean, diseased, or ugly'.

Craft, The Insider slang term for **Wicca**. Used by Wiccans to denote their religious devotion to white magic and goddess worship.

Craniosacral Therapy, also **Cranial Osteopathy**, **Craniopathy** A very gentle and subtle form of treatment that originally grew from osteopathy, it focuses on manipulation of the skull bones and the sacrum to relieve pain and a variety of other ailments.

Dr William Garner Sutherland, an American osteopath, developed the technique in the 1930s. He discovered that, contrary to popular belief, the bones in the head were not rigidly fused but did make tiny movements, as did the bones of the sacrum (which we know as the tailbone). Experimenting on himself, he found that cranial and sacral bones could be manipulated the same way as larger muscles and joints.

Unlike regular **osteopathy**, which uses physical force to move a malfunctioning joint or muscle back into proper position, craniosacral therapy works on balancing cerebrospinal fluids and connective tissues through a series of fingertip movements and 'head-cradling' holds. Practitioners believe that cerebrospinal fluid pulses through the body in a precise rhythm of 6–15 times per minute. This 'cranial rhythmic impulse' (CRI) works separately from other body systems, and is called the 'breath of life'; it affects every cell in the body (much like **chi** or **prana** does in Oriental medical theory). Accidents, injury and other pressures in the head, neck and spine can adversely affect CRI flow. Freeing up CRI flow can help improve your health, relax your body and, surprisingly, affect your emotional state. People who have undergone craniosacral therapy often report feeling a surge of emotions during or after treatment.

Although the medical establishment has its doubts about craniosacral therapy, it is extremely safe and is often used on newborn infants. It relieves pressures in the neck following difficult labour and birth and is supposed to be absolutely brilliant at calming tense, colicky babies. It is important, however, to find a practitioner who is first a qualified osteopath, as many who call themselves 'craniosacral therapists' have not undergone proper osteopathic training.

Creation Myths   Any mythology or tale in different cultures or religions that describes how the world was created. They range from the biblical tale of God and his seven-day creation cycle to the Scandinavian traditions of **northern paganists**, who believed the universe was an immense ash tree, Yggdrasil, that sprang from the body of a giant.

Crop Circles   Oval and near-circular patterns that appear in the middle of fields of grain like wheat, oats and barley, when the crop is high. These intricate and complex geometric figures often appear suddenly, and can only be fully appreciated from a height. Most crop circles have been found in the southeast of England, but some have been reported in other countries of Europe, and in the United States.

Crop circles are certainly artificially created, but by whom is a continuing mystery. Some circles are hoaxes, created by pranksters who have subsequently come forward. Not all can be explained by those means and some people claim that they are either created by **extraterrestrial** visitors as an opening conversational gambit, or that the patterns are a result of bioelectric and magnetic forces either below the surface of the soil, or present in the atmosphere above the field.

Circles have ranged in size from a few centimetres across to hundreds of metres in diameter. The crop itself is not damaged by radiation or other toxins, and can be harvested for later consumption.

Crowley, Aleister (1875–1947) Notorious occultist and best known as a practitioner of sex magic, his drug excesses and his belief that he was the Antichrist, 'The Beast'. He did not start out that way. Crowley was raised in a strict Plymouth Brethren home, but came to be fascinated by magic and the occult while at university. He was a member of the Hermetic Order of the **Golden Dawn**, but grew disillusioned with it and started his own magic order, Argenteum Astrum, claiming to have exclusive access to an ancient Egyptian magical force.

Crowley was a prolific writer of esoteric magic texts like *The Book of Thoth, Magick in Theory and Practice*, and *Qabalah of Aleister Crowley*; despite his associations with black magic he is responsible for several **Wiccan** mottos including 'Do what thou wilt shall be the whole of the law; love is the law, love under will'. See also: **Theosophy, Witchcraft**.

Cryptozoology (Greek, 'puzzle animals') Branch of zoological research that studies unusual, theoretically extinct and unknown, possibly mythological creatures. The best examples of cryptozoology at work are the search for the legendary **yeti**, or abominable snowman of the Tibetan Himalayas; and the ongoing hunt for Nessie, the **Loch Ness Monster**.

Crystal Gazing, Crystallomancy (Greek *krystallos* from *krysos*, 'icy cold', + *manteia*, 'divination') A form of **divination** using crystals and gemstones to predict the future. There are two main ways – gazing into a crystal ball, also called **scrying**, or crystals can be cast down and interpreted like dice or **runes**. Crystals are particularly effective in focusing the mind and providing a gateway to the altered consciousness required to correctly divine the truth about the future, or a past matter.

Crystal Healing A system using **crystals** to bring about healing by stimulating and balancing the body's inherent energies. This energy, also known as **life force** or **chi**, needs to flow evenly throughout the body to maintain health. Because of the ability crystals have to retain and focus electromagnetic energy, they are ideal tools to assist in restoring this balance.

There are two main methods of crystal healing. The first works with the body's seven energy centres, the **chakras**. A crystal is chosen, with properties that match or enhance the energies of the ailing chakra. This helps to unblock the flow of body energy through this chakra. The second method of crystal healing is to choose a stone that has the protective, healing qualities you desire. For example, rose quartz is said to speed up healing, garnet is considered beneficial for depression and skin complaints, and malachite helps with toothache and asthma. Very occasionally, a crystal will be crushed and distilled into a gem essence, which can be ingested to obtain the energetic properties required.

Crystals (Greek *krystallos* from *krysos*, 'icy cold') A rock or stone with a faceted, crystalline structure that has potent healing, protective and decorative properties. The ancient Greeks thought they were made of ice that never melted, hence the origin of the name. Crystals have been known and used by man since prehistoric times: worn as protection against evil, ground up to make medicines and cosmetics, used as a focus for meditation and healing, cast into patterns to answer questions, gazed into to foretell the future, polished and worn as jewellery, placed on computers to soak up stray radiation, traded as currency, dissolved into alchemical potions and used in most magical traditions as an aid to working spells.

The reason for their effectiveness in these areas has to do with their crystalline structure. Crystals can absorb, channel and transmit subtle electromagnetic energies, depending upon their mineral structure. That is why different crystals have different properties. They can repel bad energies, or attract good ones.

In order to most effectively use crystals, you will need to be very selective about the stones you use. Most people who work with crystals believe the stone chooses who to work with, not the other way around. Once selected, crystals should be 'programmed' by attuning them to your particular energies. There is also a particular way to cleanse a crystal, to keep its inherent vibrational energies fresh and effective. The best method is to run your crystal under cold, running water and as you do so, visualise the bad energies collected therein being washed away and dissipated with the water. Another method is to use a piece of **amethyst** crystal to cleanse the other stones of negative energy.

The two best-known methods of using crystals are in **divination** and **healing**. Gazing into a crystal ball to foretell the future is known as **scrying**, and is very popular in **gypsy magic**. General fortune-telling with crystals is known as **crystallomancy**. **Crystal healing** is a system that works with the body's energy centres, the **chakras**, to bring about a harmonious balance and restore health.

Culpeper, Nicholas (1616–54) Seventeenth-century English herbalist and astrologer, who wrote *Culpeper's Herbal*, still used as a reference book in **herbalism**. His medical and herbal practices were revolutionary for his time, as he consciously tried to follow the medical values and principles of the ancient Greek physicians Galen and **Hippocrates**, whose philosophies are the foundation for Western medicine today.

He was particularly interested in Hippocrates' idea of **holism** – treating the body, mind and spirit of a person to bring about healing, and did extensive work on the **Doctrine of Signatures**, which is one of the basic principles of **homeopathy**.

Cupping 1. The use of small glass or bamboo jars heated and placed on the skin to induce a vacuum suction. Used extensively in **Traditional Chinese Medicine** as a means of dispersing localised congestion beneath the cup and extracting bad **chi**, especially around joints and areas of injury. Cupping eases pain and draws inflammation away from deep parts of the body to the surface for dispersal by the skin's blood and lymph vessels. This method was also used by Native Americans and throughout the classical world, and is still in use today in many Mediterranean cultures. Cupping was a common treatment during the Middle Ages, designed to pull out and balance a person's 'humours', often extracting blood in the process.

2. In **Swedish massage**, one of the six classical massage movements. Cupping is a percussion movement that creates a suction on the surface of skin that stimulates deep muscle, but not the skin itself. Performed with cupped hands, it can be used on large muscles in legs, buttocks and back. It increases blood flow to the skin's surface and to the lungs, as well as loosening mucus in the lungs. It also helps to soften and break down fatty deposits.

Curse A deliberately malevolent oath or invocation of spirits directed towards another person by magical means. This could be via a spell or incantation, or by sending an object of symbolic evil. Curses are associated with black magic and are intended to harm someone.

Cusp In **astrology**, the day the sun (or moon) changes from one sign or house of the **zodiac** to another. It functions almost as an invisible line between each sign; a person 'born on the cusp' shares characteristics of both signs in their personality and temperament. See also: **Horoscope, Sun Signs**.

Dactylomancy, also **Dactyliomancy** (Greek *dakterlios*, 'finger ring', + *manteia*, 'divination') A form of **divination**, or foretelling the future with the aid of rings. The ring was either tied to a string and used as a **pendulum**, or dropped into a bowl of water with its position at the bottom determining the response to the question asked. Wedding rings were considered to be ideal for this purpose. See also: **Dowsing**.

Daemon (Greek *daimon*, 'spirit') A spirit of evil, better known as a demon. Daemon is also used to describe someone or something halfway between human and godlike, with the status of inspiration or genius. Philip Pullman, in his trilogy *His Dark Materials*, uses the word daemon to describe the inner conscience, the innate instinctive part of us that serves both as mentor and as companion. His concept of the daemon is similar to either the **spirit guide** of **shamanism**, or a witch's **familiar**.

Dagda In Celtic mythology, a god known as *Eochaid Ollathair* ('Father of All') and *Ruadh Rofessa* (the Red One of Knowledge). Dagda was the first king of the *Tuatha de Danaan*, the **fairy** realm, before being deposed by **Lugh**, the harvest god. He does not have as much importance as the mother goddess **Brigid**, but he is the primary fertility god, the 'Good Father' in Irish legend, and considered lord of life and death. See also: **Celtic Wheel**, **Paganism**.

Dalai Lama Spiritual leader of Tibetan Buddhism, who is an acknowledged reincarnation of the previous holder of the position. The current Dalai Lama is His Holiness the Dalai Lama Tenzin Gyatso, regarded by most as the political leader of Tibet since the Chinese invasion of that country in 1950 and His Holiness' subsequent exile in 1959.

He was born Lhamo Dhondrub on 6 July 1935, in a small village called Taktser in northeast Tibet. He was recognised at the age of two as the reincarnation of his predecessor the thirteenth Dalai Lama. He is fourteenth in a succession of recognised reincarnations or **rinpoches**, which began with Gendun Drup in 1391, and is considered to be the manifestation of the **Bodhisattva** of compassion, who chose to reincarnate to serve the people.

His Holiness was awarded the 1989 Nobel Peace Prize for his efforts to bring peace and liberation to Tibet, and continues to write and travel the globe on that mission.

Danu Earth mother goddess in Celtic spirituality and legend. See also: **Brigid**.

Daphnomancy (Greek *daphne*, 'laurel', + *manteia*, 'divination') A form of **divination** practised in ancient Greece that foretold the future by burning a branch of laurel in an open fire. It was considered a good omen if the laurel burned with a great crackling sound. If the laurel burned quietly, the prognosis was bleak. Daphnomancy is a form of **pyromancy**, divinatory methods using fire.

Darshan (Sanskrit, 'sight, vision') In Hindu belief, a type of energy blessing that can be conveyed from a **guru** merely through his gaze. Just by catching a darshan you can partake of the spiritual qualities that the guru has attained, and most importantly his power. The guru can also see into your soul, just by you being in his presence. See also: **Hinduism**.

Dead Sea Scrolls A collection of Jewish mystical texts discovered between 1947 and 1953 in the caves above the Jordanian city of Qumran. Carbon-dated to the time around the life of **Jesus Christ** (50 BC–AD 68), these scrolls revealed the beliefs of the **Essenes**, a pacifist Messianic sect of Judaism. The Essene religion mirrors very closely many practices considered to be exclusive to the Bible's New Testament, leading many to believe that Jesus may have been influenced by their teachings.

Dee, John (1527–1608) Queen Elizabeth I's official court astrologer and transcriber of the angelic **Enochian** alphabet of **alchemy** and magic. Dee was responsible for setting the date of Elizabeth's coronation by casting her horoscope to find the most auspicious day and time. He wrote extensive accounts of his alchemical experiments that attracted the attention of psychic huckster Edward Kelley. Kelley, who may have had genuine powers as a medium, was reportedly the channel vessel for magical formulas from the angel Enoch. In a trance state, he babbled out the numeric magic alphabet, which Dee duly recorded. Dee is also associated with the divinatory art of **scrying** (crystal-gazing). He felt it was a way of attaining levels of wisdom and knowledge not available from more conventional sources of study.

Kelley persuaded him to leave his position at court to concentrate on alchemically producing gold. When this failed, the Queen took pity on him and reinstated him as rector of a small college, but he was never to attain his earlier prestige and died in obscurity. It is thought that Shakespeare used Dee for his model of the magician Prospero, in *The Tempest*.

Déjà-vu (French, 'already seen')The sensation of recognising a place you have never seen before, or finding familiar-seeming events happening for the first time. The phenomenon is thought to be a psychological process where the unconscious mind is stimulated to recall past events of a similar nature that somehow get associated with the present event. Some also feel that it is evidence of **reincarnation**, when for a brief moment memories of a past life intrude into your present existence.

Demeter, also **Ceres** Greek goddess of agriculture and the harvest, known as Ceres in Roman myth. Demeter was one of the daughters of Chronos (Time) and Rhea (Earth), and one of the Olympiad, the 12 chief gods and goddesses of Greek legend who lived on Mt Olympus. She is best known as the mother of the goddess **Persephone**, who was abducted by **Hades**, the god of the underworld, and taken to his dark realm to be his queen. Demeter pined away at the sudden, unknown loss of her daughter and, in her grief, neglected the land and harvest and humankind started to die. She found out from the goddess **Hecate** of Hades' treachery and threatened to curse the earth permanently if her daughter was not returned.

She persuaded **Zeus** to allow Persephone to come back, but as the unfortunate girl had eaten six pomegranate seeds she was doomed to be Hades' queen for six months of the year. This myth reflects the origin of the four seasons of the year – autumn is when Demeter says goodbye to Persephone, who takes her place at Hades' side throughout winter. When spring arrives, Persephone is reunited with her mother and summer arrives.

This ritual was important in the secret rites of the **Eleusinian mysteries**, which were conducted each year to invoke the **goddess** back to the land.

Demon, Demonology (Greek *daimon*, 'spirit'; *daimon*, 'spirit', + *logos*, 'word, study') Evil spirits or spirit beings, traditionally thought to be fallen **angels** and servants of **Satan**. Demonology is the study of demons and the rituals attached to them. Like the Devil, demons were kicked out of heaven for rebelling against **God**'s authority, and work in league with Old Nick to tempt mankind into damnation.

In other religious traditions outside the Judaeo-Christian/Islamic structure, demons are considered more an intrinsic part of the light/dark axis of the world, or as dispossessed older brothers of mankind. This is particularly true in **Hinduism**, where deities often possess two faces, one good and one evil.

In many **occult** traditions, demons can be called from the underworld to assist in black magic rituals, usually at great risk to the sorcerer. **Demonancy**, as it is known, would help the summoner make predictions about the future.

Demonancy, also **Necyomancy** (Greek *daimon*, 'deity, genius', + *manteia*, 'divination') A form of **divination** that calls on demons or spirits to reveal the truth of a matter, or of future events. This is done through oracles or by summoning spirits via occult magic. Demonancy is considered to be highly unreliable, as demons are reputedly vain and inclined to lie. More malevolent types are also hard to control and, if they fought free of the constraints placed on them by the summoner, could take over the body and soul of the hapless magician.

Detox, Detoxification Specific mental and physical actions undertaken to rid the body of toxins and cleanse the system. Detoxification rituals form part of many different religions and healthcare systems, most notably **ayurveda**. The concept of 'detox' is also central to many **holistic** healing programmes, and is often recommended for chronic ailments caused or aggravated by the wrong sort of lifestyle.

Detox can take place internally or externally. External methods include saunas, steam rooms, salt scrubs, mud treatments, body wraps, skin-scraping, dry-brush skin treatments, facial treatments, **thalassotherapy**, **massage**, baths and showers. Internal methods include fasting, purgatives, laxatives, ingesting herbs and vitamin supplements, increased water intake, enemas, and **colonic hydrotherapy**.

Mental detox rituals involve a host of psychotherapeutic techniques across many different disciplines but, as with physical detox, the intent is to permanently rid yourself of the effects of the toxins reducing your quality of life.

Devas (Sanskrit, 'shining ones') Higher nature spirits considered members of the angelic realm. They are known as *adhibautas* in Sanskrit, and are minor deities in **Hinduism**. They appear human in form but are etheric in nature, only inhabiting the **astral plane**. They communicate with people through psychic means, like **channelling** or **ESP**, and are capable of great powers over the stars, tides and earth. The channelled wisdom of devas was responsible for the location of the **Findhorn** community in Scotland, and devas are in charge of **elementals**, spirits of **air**, **water**, **fire** and **earth**.

Devil's Mark A mark on the body of a **witch** that supposedly meant she was in league with the Devil. In the height of the Anglo-American witch-hunts of the late sixteenth and early seventeenth centuries, witchfinders and other inquisitors would search the accused for such marks, which they believed would prove her guilt. For those accused of witchcraft, confessions were often forced from the hapless individuals through sleep deprivation and torture. In Scotland, where witchcraft was declared illegal in 1563, 3,500 people (the majority of them poor single or widowed women) were accused of witchcraft, of whom 1,500 were later executed. In England 513 people were charged with witchcraft, of whom 200 were convicted and 109 hanged. See also: **Witchcraft**.

Dharana (Sanskrit, 'concentration') The practice of concentration to reach total union of mind, body and spirit, in **yoga**. Dharana is the first of three stages of the 'inner path' of yoga, and its aim is learning to sit and focus your entire attention on the moment. It is one of the 'eight limbs' or **ashtangas** mentioned in the **Yoga Sutras** of Patanjali, whose practice will lead to enlightenment.

Dharma, also **Dhamma** (Sanskrit, 'universal law'; 'ultimate truth') 1. In **Buddhism**, the spiritual teachings of a **Buddha** or an enlightened being that come from his or her direct personal experience of reality. Dharma is the law, which explains the true nature of everything that exists, both physical and non-physical, and is the true basis of reality. It is both teaching and a practice of the **eightfold path**, which leads to the end of suffering, as well as the cessation of life itself.

2. One of the four aims of **Hinduism**, seen as righteousness in your religion. The concept of dharma (also known as duty) is applied to such aspects of life as family, caste and life stages. Each person has a duty to fulfil their destiny in society, and to accept a responsibility to care for all living things.

Dharmapada, also **Dhammapada** Famous Buddhist scripture of 423 verses. See also: **Buddhism, Dharma**.

Dhyana (Sanskrit, 'meditation') The practice of **meditation** to reach total union of mind, body and spirit, in **yoga**. Dhyana, the second stage of the 'inner path' of yoga, is the point of unwavering stillness, where the mind cannot be distracted. It is one of the 'eight limbs' or **ashtangas** that are mentioned in the **Yoga Sutras** of Patanjali, whose practice will lead to enlightenment.

Dhyana Yoga see Yoga, Dhyana.

Diana Ancient **goddess** figure in many cultural traditions including Greek and Roman mythology, paganism, and Christian reveries of the **Virgin Mary**. In Greek legend she was known as Artemis, the virginal moon goddess, and in Roman mythology Diana held the same role. She was merged with the figure of the Virgin Mary and worshipped in the great temple at Ephesus in Turkey. No man was allowed to enter her temples and her followers were devoted to chastity.

Diana was also an earth mother goddess of fertility in many European and Mediterranean cultures. She is often depicted with multiple breasts, symbolising the fertility of the earth. The ancient witches of Italy (c. 500 BC) worshipped Diana, and this tradition has carried through to modern **Wiccan** practice, where she is honoured as the queen of the witches and daughter of Wicca's chief goddess, **Aradia**.

Discarnate Entity (Latin dis, 'without', + carne, 'flesh') A spirit – the **ghost** of a dead person – contacted during a **séance** or other sitting by a **medium**. Because they previously had an earthly body, they had an 'incarnate' existence. Now that they are just spirit, they have become 'discarnate'. This is in contrast to other entities, which may never have lived on this earth, just in the spirit realm. These are also known as 'disembodied spirits'.

Disembodied Spirit see Discarnate Entity

Diwali (Sanskrit, 'rows of diyas') A holiday in the Hindu and Sikh religious calendars. It is known as the 'festival of lights', because it commemorates the return of Lord Rama from exile (see **Ramayana**). When he returned to his kingdom, the people set out rows of diyas, or oil lamps made of clay, to light his way home. Celebrated in late October/early November, it is a family-orientated holiday, symbolising the victory of righteousness and the lifting of spiritual darkness. Relatives and friends gather together to offer prayers, celebrate and distribute sweets to the less fortunate. See also: **Hinduism, Sikhism**.

Divination (Latin divinare, 'predict') The art or practice that seeks to foresee or foretell future events, discover hidden knowledge, find the lost or uncover the guilty by the interpretation of omens or by the aid of intuition or supernatural powers. There are hundreds of variations on divination, but they can all be classified as belonging to one of two types: either a system, like the tarot or dice, or communication with a spiritual agency, like the ghosts of the dead, through mediums or ritual sacrifice. Both methods accomplish the same thing – they put the practitioner, or 'diviner', into contact with the gods of a higher spirit realm. When you select a card or cast dice, the randomness of your action allows the deity or spirit to affect the outcome, and give you a message through the result.

Divination has been known since earliest times and is mentioned in ancient literature from all world cultures. Early Chinese tombs from 5,000 years ago have been discovered with bone **I Ching** fortune-telling markers and the ancient Greeks made historic decisions based on cryptic utterances from the **oracle** at Delphi. Native American **shamans** and Celtic **Druids** regularly contacted **spirit guides** for wisdom and advice, which was accepted as divine law in their culture.

Divinatory methods range from the widely accepted (tarot, palmistry) to the esoteric (bronchiomancy – divination by studying the lungs of sacrificed white llamas) and downright bizarre (uromancy – divination by reading bubbles made by urinating into a pot). Most terms associated with divination end either in 'mancy', from the ancient Greek *manteia* (divination) or 'scopy', from the Greek *skopein* (to look into, to behold). See also: **Augury**.

Divine Farmer's Classic of Herbal Medicine, also Shen Nong Ben Cao **Jing** (Chinese *shen*, 'divine', + *nong*, 'farmer', + *ben*, 'tree roots', + *cao*, 'grasses or herbs', + *jing*, 'blood') A first-century BC classic text that laid out the principles of **herbalism** still used today in **Traditional Chinese Medicine**. The apocryphal Shen Nong (divine farmer) is said to have taught mankind how to grow foods and herbs. He possessed a magical ability to work out the properties of plants and herbs, which he would then test by eating the plants (including poisonous ones) himself. One day, however, he overstretched his body's ability to neutralise these toxins and he died. The results of his studies were collected in this treatise, a list of all the important herbs and their properties. The book also mentions the flavours (sour, salty, sweet, bitter and acrid) and temperature (cold, warm, hot and cool) of each. These correlate to the different energetic properties of the **five element cycle** and are vital in treating illnesses and imbalances in the body, according to Chinese medical philosophy. See also: **Chinese Herbal Medicine**.

Djinn, also **Jinn** (Persian, 'elementals') Fierce spirits in Arabian myth and folklore who are frequently portrayed as **demons**. The djinn (likely source for the word genii) supposedly lived on the earth prior to man. Created from fire, the djinn were vicious and corrupt and were eventually driven from the fertile areas of the world to live in the harsh, unforgiving fringes of existence. Because of their unrepentant behaviour, the djinn were made subject to man and, if ever a person could capture them, could be commanded to do their master's will.

Doctrine of Signatures The ancient Greek medical concept that the external appearance of a plant is God's signature. Because of this 'signature' the healing powers of the plant will treat the part of the human body it most resembles. An example of this is the herb eyebright, whose bright white and yellow flowers resemble inflamed eyes. Remedies made from this plant do indeed help ease the stinging and pain of eye infections and inflammation.

This idea was revived in the sixteenth century by Swiss physician **Paracelsus**, and further developed by English herbalist **Nicholas Culpeper** in the seventeenth century. When the father of **homeopathy**, **Dr Samuel Hahnemann**, first began to formulate his theories, he used the Doctrine of Signatures as a stepping stone to developing his philosophy of medicine. See also: **Herbalism, Law of Similars**.

Dog, The In **Chinese astrology**, the eleventh sign of the **zodiac**. You are a Dog if you were or will be born in the years 1934, 1946, 1958, 1970, 1982, 1994, 2006 or 2018. The Dog is the sign of loyalty in Chinese mythology, symbolising fidelity and wisdom. Those born under this sign are faithful and loyal in all relationships in their lives, in their families and in their careers. They believe in justice and fair play but have a tendency to sacrifice their own best interests to suit others. Their Western zodiac equivalent is **Libra** and their ruling planet is **Venus**.

Dogen (1200–1253) Founder of the Soto (Tsaotung) **Zen** tradition in Japan and one of the most important Buddhist figures in that country. Dogen wrote 'Instruction for the Tenzo' (head cook), which is still followed in temples all over Japan. Dogen emphasised simplicity and quiet meditation, '**zazen**', as the path to **enlightenment**. See also: **Zen Buddhism**.

Dogon Tribe in the African country of Mali, whose members still practise pagan and magical rituals in their religion. They claim these came from **extraterrestrial** visitors from the Sirius star system a millennium ago, long before Sirius was discovered by astronomers in 1844. A study conducted in 1970 found the Dogon to have an unusual level of scientifically accurate astronomical information about star and planetary systems that would not normally be known in such a pre-industrial society.

Dolmen (Breton, 'table of stone') A prehistoric stone table, consisting of a large, unhewn stone resting on two or more uprights, found mostly in Britain and France. See also: **Megaliths**.

Doppelgänger (German, 'double walker') The appearance of a double of a living person, thought to be the **astral body** of someone having an **out-of-body experience**.

Doshas The three fundamental energies that make up different body types, according to **ayurvedic medicine**. Doshas are different combinations of the five natural **elements** of the universe, and govern our physical constitution, intellect and personality. When an ayurvedic practitioner treats a patient, he looks at the proportion of the three doshas, with the aim of equally balancing these energies to stimulate healing in the body and mind and, ultimately, restore health.

The three doshas are: **vata**, which is a combination of ether and air energies; **pitta**, a combination of fire and water; and **kapha**, water and earth. Everyone has all three present in their body, but one type prevails, which characterises who you are and what you need to do and have to improve or maintain health.

In the body, doshas govern all of our physical and psychological processes. When in balance, you are happy and healthy. When doshas become imbalanced through disease, stress or improper living habits, we become ill in either mind or body.

Downshifting see Voluntary Simplicity

Dowsing, also **Divining, Rhabdomancy, Water Witching** (Dowsing: Old Cornish *dewsys*, 'goddess'; Rhabdomancy: Greek *rhabdos*, 'rod' + *manteia*, 'divination') A form of **divination** performed by using a forked stick, pendulum or rods to seek out hidden things, particularly underground water, minerals or oil deep in the ground. Dowsing can also be used to locate lost objects, missing persons and sources of **geopathic stress**, and to diagnose illness.

Dowsing is an ancient skill. A cave drawing of a man holding a forked stick in his hands was recently found in southern Algeria, and dated back at least 6,000 years. Archaeological finds confirm that people in both ancient China and Egypt practised dowsing, especially in the search for precious gems and metals.

There are two main ways of dowsing, either of the physical site of a search, or by using a map or pictorial representation. Physical searches require the use of a dowsing rod, of which there are plenty. There is the classic rod in the shape of a fork or 'Y', which will dip downwards over its target; and a wand or 'bobber', a flexible wire or twig usually weighted at one end. The wand bobs up and down or from side to side to signify an affirmative response. Angle rods, also known as 'L-rods', 'wishing rods' or 'Swiss rods', look like two wires bent into the shape of a letter L. A dowser walks forwards holding the two rods at waist level, pointed in front like two pistols. When the desired object is intuited, the rods swivel inwards and cross, or swivel outwards and diverge (depends upon the individual dowser).

If dowsing is done over a map or picture, or for diagnosing illness, a pendulum is used as a pointer, giving the precise location of the object or disease.

It is still not known precisely why dowsing works, but it seems to be connected with our intuitive ability to sense vibrational energies, either in the magneto–electric fields transmitted by water, minerals and other substances, or in people's personal energy fields. When we locate what we are looking for, our intuition responds by vibrating in sympathy with the found energy field, causing small involuntary muscle contractions to occur. These contractions move the diving rod or pendulum. It is also common for a dowser to feel a tingling sensation, chills, shivering or trembling when the desired object is located.

Dowsing is still practised today by officials in law enforcement and emergency management, as well as individuals and major businesses. Dowsers have located people lost in avalanches, buried landmines, unexploded shells on land and in sea, and (regrettably) the remains of murder victims. Not widely known is the fact that some of the world's leading petrochemical companies also employ dowsers to confirm underground sources of oil and natural gases indicated by geological analysis, with great success.

See also: **Geomancy**, **Radiesthesia**, **Virgula Furcata**.

Dragon (Greek *drakon*, 'to see, watch over') A mythological creature, which figures in the legends of most of the world's cultures. Dragons are ferocious lizard- or serpent-like creatures, with long necks and scaly hides. Often they have the ability to fly, and some even breathe fire. Dragons can be either malevolent or beneficial, depending upon which country you are visiting. In China, dragons (called *lung*) are celestial symbols of power, representing the spirit of the earth and sky. In the past the use of the dragon's image was restricted to the imperial house, because Chinese emperors believed themselves descended from them. Dragons represent prosperity and happiness, and are powerful guardians of the home.

In Indo-European cultures, the dragon does not have as good a reputation. Although they are still considered powerful guardians, and are popular heraldic symbols, there are many tales of vindictive, bloodthirsty dragons guarding treasure they do not deserve and eating pure young maidens, who have to be rescued by stalwart knights like England's St George. This negative image may be connected to the way they are depicted in the **Bible** – in the Book of Revelations, St Michael casts a horrific dragon, symbolising evil, out of heaven.

What is puzzling is how a supposedly fictitious creature has permeated so many cultures. Many believe the dragon to have been the last of the dinosaurs, which survived into historic times in the dark swamps of Africa and Indonesia. Natives in those regions do still have to contend with such beasties as the nine-foot long Komodo dragon, which lives on the Indonesian island of Komodo, and the *mokele mbembe*, believed to be a descendent of the sauropod dinosaurs, which lives in the Likoula swamp in Central Africa.

Dragon, The In **Chinese astrology**, the fifth sign of the **zodiac**. You are a Dragon if you were or will be born in the years 1940, 1952, 1964, 1976, 1988, 2000 or 2012. The Dragon is the sign of luck in Chinese mythology, symbolising destiny and the forces of nature. Those born under this sign are proud, stylish individuals, with dazzling, energetic personalities. Dragons can be promiscuous, but have a strong sense of honour. Their Western zodiac equivalent is **Aries** and their ruling planet is **Mars**.

Drawing Down the Moon A **Wiccan** ceremony performed to bring down the power of the moon **goddess**. The rite is performed by a high priestess during the full moon and is part of the opening ceremony of the **sabbats**, the holy festival days of a witch's year. See also: **Celtic Wheel, Paganism**.

Dreamcatcher A Native American device used theoretically to retain the fragments of good dreams and allow nightmares to disappear. In widespread use throughout many Native American cultures, it originated with the Lakota Sioux tribe, whose traditional territory is located in the present-day states of North and South Dakota. It is based on an old Lakota folktale about a legendary spiritual leader to whom the god Iktomi, the great trickster and teacher of wisdom, appeared in the form of a spider. Using the materials from the spiritual elder (including feathers, horse hair and beads), Iktomi began to spin a web as he gave advice about the cycles of life and how we move from infancy to old age. Along the way, Iktomi said, 'In each time of life there are many forces – some good and some bad. If you listen to the good forces, they will steer you in the right direction. But if you listen to the bad forces, they will hurt you and steer you in the wrong direction.' He went on to stress the importance of working in harmony with nature, and then presented the elder with the completed web – with a hole in the centre of the circle. Iktomi concluded: 'Use the web to help yourself and your people to reach your goals and make good use of your people's ideas, dreams and visions. If you believe in the great spirit, the web will catch your good ideas, and the bad ones will go through the hole.'

The Lakota elder passed on his vision to his people and now the dreamcatcher is hung above the bed to sift good from bad dreams and is used by modern-day spiritual seekers as a talisman to ensure restful sleep and productive dreaming.

Dreams, Interpretation and Divination Of   see Oneiromancy

Dreamtime   Australian aboriginal belief of a realm and time when their hero gods made human beings from plants, animals and natural features. The spirits of these different elements of nature then became guardian spirits for man, and can be accessed during trance states and at night, in dreams. Dreamtime is not separate from the real world; in fact it inhabits the part of our consciousness that we can access in meditation or sleeping. It is very similar to **Jung**'s concept of the **collective unconscious**, a psychic realm shared by everyone.

Each Aboriginal believes they come from the dreamtime to take human form. As the dreamtime realm is specific in geography for specific tribes, this means that an Aboriginal is tied to his ancestral lands, and that the land itself is sacred. This explains why Native Australians are upset by what they see as tourist sacrilege at some of their most holy monuments like Ayers Rock, which they call Uluru. Aboriginals also believe that all of life is spiritually interconnected; when a tree is cut down, a person shares its pain. See also: **Songlines**.

Druids, Druidry   (Greek *drus*, 'oak') The high priests and leaders of Celtic Britain and Ireland, who followed **pagan** traditions of nature and **goddess** worship, performed magical rituals and sacrifices, and possessed great knowledge of healing, astronomy and the **sacred geometry** of the earth. These wise men and women preserved in their writings and teachings their respect for trees and natural cycles form an important part of English folklore today. In fact, the name comes from the Greek word for oak, which was the Druids' sacred tree. The Celtic name for the oak tree was *duir*, and *wid* is 'to know or see'. Put together, the two words meant one who knows the wisdom of the oak, a long-lived tree. The reverence of tree wisdom in Druidry was even expressed in their alphabet, the **ogham**, which consisted of 25 different tree symbols, each embodying the elemental wisdom of the particular plant. There are modern Druids in the UK today.

Becoming a Druid means a lifetime of study, ascending through three levels to attain spiritual enlightenment. On the first level are the Bards, and working through this grade could take up to 12 years. Bards learn all the poems and songs of the tribe and compose their own poems. This is done so the Bard can understand the sacred power and creative force of sound, important in later magical work. The Bardic level is represented by the birch tree and associated with spring and dawn.

The second grade is that of the Ovate, where the student learns to open the doors of perception and to alter their consciousness, using **shamanistic** methods of shape-shifting and **astral travel**. The Ovate spends years learning about tree, plant and herb lore for healing purposes and for their mind-altering properties. The Ovate's sacred tree is the yew, and is associated with the seasons of autumn and winter.

The final grade is that of the Druid. By the time this level is achieved, the student is able to act as judge, philosopher, fortune-teller and teacher to those in the Bard and Ovate levels. He is considered the master of his craft, with the power to directly access the powers of nature and the earth. His tree, appropriately enough, is the slow-growing oak, and his season that of full summer.

As with most pagans, Druids follow the **Celtic wheel** of the year, celebrating the **sabbats** and **esbats** of the seasons. Contrary to popular belief, it is not now thought that human sacrifice was part of common Druidic tradition, although it is rumoured that there were breakaway sects which did practise this heinous procedure.

Duhkha, also **Dukkha** (Sanskrit, 'suffering, ill, imperfection') Buddhist term to describe the nature of existence. See also: **Buddhism, Four Noble Truths**.

Duk Rak Romany phrase for a self-created psychic shield from curses and other bad luck and energy drains. The duk rak is created through **visualisation**. See also: **Psychic Protection**.

Ear Candling see Thermoauricular Therapy

Earth Element 1. One of the four natural elements harnessed in **pagan** rituals of **magic** and religious worship. In **Wicca**, an earth **elemental** is one of the four spirits that energise a spell and bring its wishes into being. Earth symbolises order, both in nature and in society. It represents the female principle of **yin**, the nurturing and fertile aspect of Mother Nature, and also the material realm of money and business. The magical tool associated with earth is the bell. Earth colours are green or dark/brown, and earth is associated with the **zodiac** signs of **Taurus**, **Virgo** and **Capricorn**.

2. One of the **five elements** in Chinese philosophy and medicine that make up the 'building blocks' of the universe. In **Traditional Chinese Medicine**, earth is associated with the **spleen** and **stomach meridians**, and with the season of late summer. Earth represents stability and practicality, and is the element involved in personal transformation. Dampness, the colour yellow, worrying, sweet tastes and the sound of singing are also related to the earth element. Earth-type people are productive and fertile, with flabbiness and weight gain a potential problem. In the five element cycle, earth generates or gives birth to **metal** and controls **water** and in turn earth is given life by **fire** and controlled by **wood**.

This interdependent relationship to other elements has implications in health. If someone has weak earth energy they might have one of the following: digestive and bowel problems, eating disorders, yeast infections and food intolerances, poor memory and concentration. Left unchecked, this could then go on to weaken other elemental energies and lead to other health problems in the way that anorexia (weak earth energy) can lead to heart conditions (weak fire energy). See also: **Taoism**, **Yin**, **Yang**.

3. One of the **five elements** in Indian philosophy and medicine that defines the universe based on the spiritual concept of **prana**, or life energy. In **ayurveda**, the earth element, also known as prithvi, is associated with the nose and smells, sweet, sour and astringent tastes, and has the elemental qualities of being solid, heavy, stable and slow. In combination with the **water element**, earth forms the **dosha** (mind/body type) **kapha**. See also: **Hinduism**, **Tridosha**.

Easter One of the significant holidays of the **Christian** year that celebrates Jesus' resurrection from the dead. Christians lead up to it with an annual remembrance of the last week of his life and death, culminating in Maundy Thursday (the Last Supper, betrayal and arrest), Good Friday (the day of his crucifixion) and Easter Sunday (the day of his resurrection). Unlike **Christmas**, which is fixed on 25 December, the date of Easter fluctuates from year to year because the original events took place during the Jewish holiday of Passover. This was dated according to the moon's cycle, so Easter falls on the first Sunday after the first full moon after the **spring equinox** (21 March).

Although Easter is primarily a religious holiday, it has assimilated many of the folk rituals and practices of the pagan festival of fertility, **Eoastre**, which is held to coincide with the spring equinox. Easter comes from the name of Eoastre, the Anglo-Saxon goddess to whom the hare was sacred, explaining how the Easter Bunny came about.

Eckankar An international organisation and patented form of **astral travel**, devised by American 'guru' Paul Twitchell (1908–71). He claimed to have come into contact with 'Eck Masters' while travelling on the astral plane, and they gave him his techniques for travel in this etheric realm.

Ectoplasm (Greek *ektos*, 'outside or external', + *plasma*, 'mould, shape') A jelly-like, elastic substance that appears when a **ghost** or **spirit** makes a physical manifestation during a **séance** or other organised communication session. The phrase was coined in the late nineteenth century by French psychologist Charles Richet, who documented the phenomenon during his psychic research. Ectoplasm extrudes from the mouth, ears, nose and other orifices of the **medium** conducting the session. It often disappears spontaneously when the spirit leaves the room, or is gathered back into the medium's body in a painful process. Many believe this substance to be the matter that composes your **astral body**. See also: **Spiritualism**.

Effleurage The classic opening movement in Swedish and holistic **massage**, which the therapist uses to acclimatise their client's body for the treatment. Effleurage, characterised by smooth, flowing movements, is of light pressure, concentrating on the skin and the superficial level. The therapist also massages the body in the direction of venous blood and lymphatic flow, to get the blood circulation going and help in elimination of toxins. Effleurage has a soothing effect on nerve endings and forms a link between other parts of the massage treatment.

Ego (Latin, 'I') According to **Sigmund Freud**, the conscious part of the mind that represents the self, whose focus is to define our reality. It is practical and rational, making our decisions for us and organising our lives. The ego is without any energy and must borrow it from the primitive **id** by means of 'identification'. Through identification, the ego acts as intermediary between the unacceptable urges of the id and the over-conscious aspects of our higher mind, the **superego**.

According to **Carl Jung**, the ego was the conscious part of the **psyche** (mind, soul or spirit); the other part being the unconscious.

Egyptian Book of the Dead, also Book of the Dead A group of funerary writings from ancient Egypt that provides the only living record of their beliefs on death and the afterlife. The collections of writings were discovered carved on the walls of burial tombs dating from 1600 BC onwards. These ancient texts were commissioned by the deceased before their death and, in essence, were guides to happy living in the afterlife.

Egyptians believed that there were three worlds: Nut, the world above (heaven), Ta, the world below (earth) and Dwat, the world in between (underworld). The soul travels from the realm of Ta to the realm of Dwat and finally to the spiritual realm of Nut, where you are either reincarnated or granted eternal rest.

The Books of the Dead were meant to be read during the journey into the underworld and acted as a map so the soul would not lose its way to heaven.

Eighth House In **astrology**, the **house** or part of the heavens in your birth chart that describes your feelings and attitudes to sex, death and mortality. It is ruled by the sign **Scorpio** and the planets **Mars** and **Pluto**. See also: **Ascendant**, **Horoscope**.

Eightfold Path In **Buddhism**, the path, or mode of behaviour, that will lead to **enlightenment**. The eight elements are: Right Speech (abstention from lying, slander, harsh or abusive language); Right Thought (having only thoughts that are unselfish, loving and non-violent); Right Action (behaving in moral, peaceful and honourable ways); Right Livelihood (making one's living in a way that is not harmful to others); Right Mindfulness (being aware of one's actions); Right Concentration (developing focus through meditation); Right View (understanding the **four noble truths**); and Right Effort (staying enthusiastic and committed to the practice of faith).

Electronic Voice Phenomenon (EVP) Communications by the dead received through tape recorders and other electronic devices. The phenomenon was discovered by accident in 1959 by Russian-Swedish filmmaker Sir Friedrich Jurgenson when out recording birdsong. He discovered an unknown voice on the tape and, when he later went out to repeat the experiment, he recorded a message from his mother, who had been dead for four years.

EVP was further documented in the 1970s by electronic engineer Konstatin Raudive, who picked up unexplained voices in the background while recording other things. He then started to record in empty rooms, yet still picked up conversation, which it later became apparent contained messages from dead loved ones.

Interest in EVP apparently began in the late 1920s with the famous inventor Thomas Edison, who was an active pursuer of contact with the dead. Edison predicted that someday we would have a machine that would allow communication with spirits. Although this machine does not yet exist, there are many organisations around the world which regularly document this phenomenon and are convinced that a standard EVP instrument will soon be perfected. See also: **Spiritualism**.

Element (Latin *elementum*, 'principle, rudiment') A natural or spiritual substance regarded as one of the fundamental constituents of the universe, with inherent powers of energy and transformation. How many elements exist depends upon which culture or philosophy is consulted. In Taoism there are five elements: earth, metal, water, wood and fire; in Hinduism the elements are: earth, water, fire, air and ether; Western Classical and pagan traditions hold there are four elements: earth, water, air and fire. Many religions and belief systems have rituals and methods designed to harness elemental energies, either in magic, or in promoting and maintaining health. See also: **Astrology**, **Ayurveda**, **Five Element Cycle**, **Paganism**, **Traditional Chinese Medicine**, **Wicca**.

Elementals Nature spirits considered to be the manifestation of the four elements: **water**, **air**, **fire** and **earth**; elementals exist in the traditions of many world cultures, but are most strongly a part of Indo-European myth and religions. They occupy a place in the angelic order below **devas** (who rule over them), and are important entities in magical traditions like **Wicca**, where they are called 'Lords of the Watchtower'. Witches and other magical practitioners cast a magic circle divided into four quarters, each representing one of the four elements. In their rituals they call down elemental beings to occupy the relevant part of the circle to their rite, so that their spells may be charged with the power of nature. They then bring magical thoughts and desires into actual being. Elementals are also important in the practice of **alchemy**, and other magical traditions like the **Golden Dawn** and **Druidry**. See also: **Devas, Fairies, Paganism.**

Eleusinian Mysteries The most famous religious mysteries of the ancient world, which consisted of purifications, fasts, rites and drama concerning the tale of **Demeter** and **Persephone**. According to myth, Triptolemus, a mortal who was nearly made a god when Demeter roamed the earth looking for her daughter, started the mysteries.

The seat of the cult was Eleusis in Greece, and it was believed the rites would ensure happiness for the next year, and provide predictions about the future. Surprisingly, the ceremonies were open to both men and women. What initiates came away with was a sense of security in the afterlife, and a sense of bounty guaranteed in this world. Through the rituals the union of man with the goddess was celebrated and the mysteries were considered an intimate participation in the cycles of life.

Eleventh House In **astrology**, the **house** or part of the heavens in your birth chart that describes your social life, including friends and clubs/organisations you belong to. It is ruled by the sign **Aquarius** and the planets **Saturn** and **Uranus**. See also: **Ascendant, Horoscope.**

Elm A flower essence made from the blossom of the elm tree. This emotionally healing tincture is one of the **Bach Flower Remedies**. Dr Bach said that this is indicated for 'those who are normally confident but at times find the pressure and responsibility of life or work too much to cope with, and are then prone to undermine their confidence and become despondent'.

Emotional Intelligence The awareness of and ability to manage one's emotions in a healthy and productive manner. Emotional intelligence is best known from the popular 1995 book of the same name by psychologist Daniel Goleman, but the concept has been around since the 1920s. It has its roots in research conducted by American psychologist E.L. Thorndike, who in 1920 devised the theory of 'social intelligence'. He defined it as 'the ability to understand and manage men and women, boys and girls – to act wisely in human relations'. The concept of social intelligence continued in development for the next 70 years, when 'emotional intelligence' was given its own school of thought.

The work of psychologists Salovey and Mayer in 1990 categorised emotional intelligence into five domains: self-awareness – observing yourself and recognising a feeling as it happens; managing emotions – handling feelings so that they are appropriate, realising what is behind a feeling, and finding ways to handle fears and anxieties, anger and sadness; motivating oneself – channelling emotions in the service of a goal, showing emotional self-control and delaying gratification and stifling impulses; empathy – sensitivity to others' feelings and concerns and taking in their perspective, and appreciating the differences in how people feel about things; and handling relationships – managing emotions in others, your social competence and skills.

Daniel Goleman took this idea of emotional intelligence and applied it to the real world, especially interactions in the field of business and management. He discovered that the higher a person's 'emotional quotient' (EQ): that is, the ability to recognise and control one's own emotions, and to recognise them in others, the more successful at managing people and processes that person would be. He also rather surprisingly discovered that there was no gender bias towards women having higher EQs than men, because it was more about how emotions were handled than simply feeling free to express them. Since then, Goleman has gone on to apply his theories to the field of interpersonal relationships, with great success.

Energy Medicine Any branch of **alternative therapy** or **complementary medicine** whose methods involve working with our natural energy field, called the **life force**, to stimulate the body's own healing mechanism. These range from structured disciplines like **ayurveda, Traditional Chinese Medicine, acupuncture, homeopathy** and **reflexology** to less defined systems like **reiki** and **spiritual healing**.

Enlightenment The ultimate goal in **Hinduism** and **Buddhism**, necessary in order to achieve **nirvana**, or **moksha**. The enlightened person is in a totally awakened, illuminated state, characterised by omniscience and absolute wisdom. In Buddhism, Buddha taught that enlightenment is possible for all and that all beings will eventually attain it. You come to enlightenment by acknowledging the **four noble truths** and by following the **eightfold path** of behaviour. In Hinduism, you must follow the four paths to liberation: **dharma** (duty), **karma** (action), **bhakti** (devotion) and **jnana** (contemplation), in order to achieve moksha.

Ennead The pantheon of nine major deities in Egyptian mythology, who were worshipped in the legendary city of Heliopolis. These nine gods and goddesses – **Atum-Ra**, **Shu**, **Tefnet**, **Seb**, **Nut**, **Osiris**, **Isis**, **Seth** and **Nepthys** – were a divine ruling council, and considered the most important gods to honour. The Ennead is similar to **Mt Olympus** in Greek mythology.

Enneagram (Greek *enneas*, 'nine', + *gramma*, 'written') A nine-pointed diagram which forms the basis of a personality classification system. It formed part of esoteric practices in many Eastern mystic traditions, including **Sufism**. The occultist G.I. Gurdjieff brought it to the West in 1920 from Afghani Sufis, and the meanings of the diagramming symbols eventually made their way into mainstream spiritual circles.

In essence, an enneagram is used to determine what type out of nine personalities you are. These nine are split evenly into three 'triads' (groups): head-based types; heart-based types; and belly-based types. The three head-types are 'thinking' personalities and are called 'the observer', 'the questioner' and 'the epicure'. Heart-based personality types are all about emotion and relationships, and are called 'the giver', 'the performer' and 'the romantic'. Belly-based types are 'doers', and tend to operate on instinct. Those three are 'the perfectionist', 'the boss' and 'the mediator'.

Each of the personality types has very specific traits associated with it, and there is a somewhat complex formula involved in figuring out what the other types on the wheel and their associated numbers have to do with you.

Enneagrams are used to bring self-awareness to the user, and are increasingly used in some Jungian psychotherapies as a healing tool.

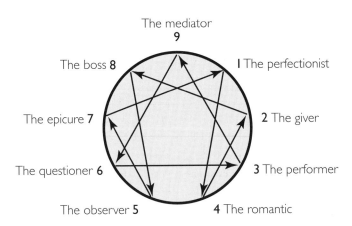

Enneagram

Enochian A system of magic that uses the numeric symbols and letters of the Enochian alphabet, received from the angel Enoch by Elizabethan court astrologer **John Dee**, and his psychic friend, Edward Kelley, who channelled the vision. This tradition of magic is similar to methods used in the **Kabbalah** to understand the **Tree of Life**, and used in the esoteric rituals of the **Golden Dawn**.

Eoastre, also Ostara   The pagan festival that surrounds the spring **equinox** (21 March) named after the Anglo-Saxon goddess of fertility. In the **Celtic wheel** of the year, Eoastre was the day when the god of light overcame the god of darkness, so marking the coming of days that were longer than the night. In Irish tradition, it is also the date that the goddess **Brigid** conceived a child, to be born at the winter **solstice** (thus neatly tying in this pagan deity to the **Virgin Mary** and Christian tradition). It is also one of the important **sabbats** of a witch's year, where bonfires are lit and rituals of renewal and new beginnings are performed.

Because this is the time of year that chickens start laying eggs again after winter, the first of these orbs were painted and offered on the shrine of Eoastre. The hare was a sacred animal to her and, as hares are notoriously fertile, they were taken to be a representation of the earth's fecundity. These early pagan symbols eventually evolved into our beloved Easter eggs and the Easter Bunny.

Ephemeris (plural **Ephemeredes**)   (Greek *ephemeros*, 'lasting only a day') An almanac used by astrologers which lists the sky positions of the planets and other astronomical data for a given time period. Details of latitude, longitude and declination for the sun, moon and planets are given for each day of the year. This reference work usually covers 100 years in total, and is vital for casting an accurate **horoscope**. See also: **Astrology**.

Equinox   (Latin *aequi-*, 'equal', + *nox*, 'night') The twice-yearly time that the sun crosses the equator, resulting in a day and night of equal length. In the northern hemisphere, the spring equinox usually occurs between 20 and 23 March, and the autumn equinox between 20 and 23 September. In the southern hemisphere the seasons are reversed. Equinoxes are significant in the **pagan** calendar of the year (also known as the **Celtic wheel** or **wheel of the year**), as festival days called **sabbats**. The spring celebration is known as Eoastre, and the autumn festival **Michaelmas**. See also: **Celtic Spirituality, Wicca, Witchcraft**.

Eros, also **Cupid**   The Greek god of passionate love, known as Cupid in Roman myth. He was the son of the goddess of love **Aphrodite** and **Hermes**, the messenger god. Often depicted as a small, chubby child with wings, he grew into a youth of incredible beauty and assisted his mother in passionate endeavours. He fell in love with a mortal woman, **Psyche**, who betrayed his trust. After many trials, she was reconciled with him and was granted immortality to live with her lover.

Esbat (Old French *s'ebattre*, 'to amuse oneself, to frolic') In **Wicca**, the non-festival celebrations that follow the monthly moon cycle of the **Celtic wheel of the year**. As the lunar calendar has 13 months, there are usually 13 esbats per year, each with its own moon name, seasonal attribute and quality association.

The Celtic year starts on **Samhain** (31 October) so the first moon is called the 'Hunter' or 'Blood Moon'. November is 'Snow Moon'; December 'Oak Moon'; January 'Ice Moon'; February 'Storm Moon'; March 'Chaste Moon' or 'Awakening Moon'; April 'Seed Moon' or 'Grass Moon'; May 'Hare Moon' or 'Planting Moon'; June 'Rose Moon' or 'Dyad Moon'; July 'Lightning Moon' or 'Mead Moon'; July/August 'Wort Moon' or 'First Fruits Moon'; and September 'Harvest Moon' or 'Wine Moon'. Esbats are akin to monthly membership meetings for Wiccans, and can be celebrated together in a **coven**, or on your own as a solitary practitioner. This is a time for healing ceremonies and for love magic, invoking the powers of the **goddess**, but also a great excuse for dancing, drinking and feasting. An esbat traditionally lasts from midnight to dawn and are less solemn than sabbats.

Esoteric (Greek *esoterikos*, 'within') Term used to describe ideas and concepts intended to be understood only by a selected few with specialised knowledge. It is usually applied to mysterious, occult teachings.

ESP, Extra-sensory Perception An umbrella term to describe the ability some people possess to perceive things beyond that which their five senses can tell them. J.B. Rhine coined the phrase in 1934 during his experiments into the phenomenon. Often these powers are **paranormal** in origin, like **clairvoyance**, **precognition**, **psychometry**, **telekinesis** or **telepathy**. If you possess these abilities, you are known as a **psychic**. In one case documented by The Society of Psychical Research, based in London, a woman driver on the M62 motorway near Irlam in Lancashire heard an inner voice cry 'Get out' and swerved dangerously into the fast lane. But by doing so, she avoided collision with a lorry that shed its load at that precise instant. Another case involves Maureen Blyth, wife of the long-distance yachtsman Chay Blyth. She was sitting in a restaurant when she was suddenly overcome with nausea. She knew, was absolutely convinced, that Chay was in trouble; she did not know how or why, but she was so distressed that she left the restaurant. It was later discovered that at that exact moment, Chay's catamaran had overturned in the freezing Atlantic Ocean, and he was trapped underneath for several hours before being rescued.

It is not only people who possess ESP; animals (particularly dogs, cats and horses) have been known to display it. One celebrated case of animal-human ESP connection took place during World War I. A dog named Prince lived with an Irish soldier and his wife in Hammersmith, London. Soon after the soldier left for the Western Front, Prince disappeared and the distraught wife was forced to write to her husband to inform him of the dog's disappearance. Much to her surprise, she received a return letter from her soldier spouse saying that Prince had found him in the heavily bombarded trenches at Armentières in northern France, having made his way from the crowded streets of London, across the Channel, and through nearly 100 kilometres of war-torn French countryside reeking of burst artillery shells and nerve gas.

Essenes A Jewish messianic sect which existed at the time of Jesus, and which is associated with Qumran, the ancient monastic settlement where the **Dead Sea Scrolls** were found. The discovery of these texts in the mid-twentieth century led many to think that Jesus may have been an Essene, so closely did their pacifist credo match New Testament belief and practice (including baptism, communion and the continued existence of the soul after death).

Essential Oils Natural aromatic essences or oils extracted from plants, and used in perfumes and **aromatherapy**. Essential oils are derived from many plants and many parts of plants, including flowers, leaves, bark, roots, stems and fruits. These oils may have been developed by the plant to keep away predators, or to attract pollinating insects and birds.

There is a variety of different chemical constituents in every essential oil and the pharmaceutical effects of these chemicals account for an oil's use in aromatherapy. Essential oil compounds have both physiological and psychological effects on the body, when absorbed into the bloodstream via massage, inhalation or digestion. Essential oils also carry the bioenergetic qualities of their particular plant, which affect a person's spirit as much as their body.

Ether (Greek *aither*, 'upper air') The substance that makes up the universe and all matter, according to occultist beliefs. It is also considered to be one of the five natural **elements**, according to **Hinduism**. Ether, also known as **akasha**, can roughly be considered 'space': space between every living cell, space as in outer space, space as the fluid that sound vibration and thought waves travel through and space as the place the spiritual or **astral** body inhabits (which is sometimes known as an 'etheric body'). This rarified element has particular properties and applications in ayurvedic medicine. Ether governs the ears and hearing, and has the elemental qualities of subtlety, sound and boundless light. Because it is closest to the universal consciousness, it is also considered the most pure of natural elements. See also: **Ayurveda**.

Evil Eye The belief that certain people can inflict bad luck, disease or death through their eyes. This negativity is transmitted to the victim through the gaze of a malevolent, envious person, often someone accused of witchcraft. During medieval times in Europe and until recent times in some non-European cultures, blue-eyed people were under particular suspicion. The superstition, which is unique to Indo-European cultures, was known as far back as fourth-century BC Babylonia and there are references to women in ancient Egypt painting their eyes and lips with cosmetics to keep the evil eye out. It is even mentioned in the **Koran** by the Prophet Muhammad, who said: 'No spell is to be used except for the evil eye, a snake bite, or a scorpion sting.' In English folklore, a person or thing afflicted by the evil eye was said to be 'overlooked' by a witch. For some reason, small children and cows seem to have been special targets of the evil eye, if you believe medieval parish records.

There were several methods of averting the evil eye. Because it was believed the evil eye was first brought down by overpraising the virtues of a person or thing, you could deflect it by denying or playing down the praise. Admired infants would be smeared with dirt before being taken out, or bells and **horse brasses** would be hung from a baby's pram or from horse carriages for general protection. Touching wood was another appeasement. One of the most effective means of averting the evil eye, however, was through the use of an **amulet** or **talisman**. Wearing blue beads or mystical symbols around the neck, hanging horseshoes above the door, or hanging **witch bottles** (protective charms directed against specific individuals) in windows were all believed to confuse a witch's gaze and thus deflect the bad luck away from the intended target.

Excalibur The magical sword of **King Arthur**, given to him by the Lady of the Lake. The name 'Excalibur' comes from the name Geoffrey of Monmouth gave to it, 'Caliburn', and is derived from the Latin word *chalybs*, or steel. At the end of Arthur's life as he lay mortally wounded by his nephew Mordred, he ordered one of the surviving Knights of the Round Table to cast Excalibur into the water. When he did so, a hand arose from the lake, caught it and sank back beneath the water's surface. See also: **Arthurian Legends, Avalon.**

Exorcism Ceremony where the satanic or evil entity possessing an unwilling human host or a location is banished. It is usually practised using Christian rituals, but there are other effective methods used in white witchcraft. Exorcism is a recognised ritual of the Catholic Church. See also: **Possession.**

Extraterrestrial A living being not of the earth. Specifically, the term refers to alien visitors from another world, whose existence has yet to be empirically proven. See also: **UFO.**

Fairies, Faeries (Latin *fata*, 'fate') Non-human, immortal earth spirits who have magical powers. These small creatures, who specialise in enchantments and glamorous illusions, can bring either good luck or ill-luck down on a person. Fairies are mainly associated with Northern European cultures, especially in the Celtic folklore of Ireland, Wales, Brittany and Cornwall. In Ireland, they are known as the *sidhe*, and their court the *daoine sidhe*; they are also known as *Tuatha de Danaan*. The *Tuatha* were supposedly responsible for building the **megaliths** of Ireland, which are still seen as gateways to the world of fairy.

There are several ideas about how fairies originated. The first is that they are descendants of the hidden children of the biblical Eve; the second that they are fallen angels not bad enough to be sent to hell, but not good enough to stay in heaven; a third one suggests they are the spirits of the restless, haunted dead.

Regardless of their origins, fairies were tricky folk with whom to get involved. A fairy might steal away your own baby and in its place leave a **changeling**, or they might curse your crops or household, leading to bad harvests or ill-health. If a fairy fell in love with you and spirited you away to their realm, it proved a decidedly mixed blessing – as long as you were there, you would be ageless and live a life of pleasurable enchantment. When you returned to the world, however, you might find all your friends and family long dead.

Fairies come in all shapes and sizes, and some, like leprechauns **or** brownies, are almost lovably cuddly. Others are fearsome, shining aristocratic creatures with great powers; they are best avoided.

Whatever their shape, fairies have a great affinity for the earth and all its wild places, and many consider them powerful **elemental** spirits of nature. See also: **Devas**.

Fairy Ring   A circle of inedible mushrooms, or of differently coloured grass, that was thought to be a magical place where **fairies** met and danced, sang and otherwise twisted the night away. You could run nine times around the outside of a fairy ring to see fairies, and sit in the middle of the circle on a full moon, and your wish would come true. The one thing you would never want to do is to interfere in any way with fairy revels and rituals, or you might become enchanted. Many believe that fairy rings also are connected to ceremonies performed by **elementals** (earth spirits) conducted on **Halloween** and **May Day** eves.

Fakir   (Arabic *faqir*, 'poor person') Originally a fakir was an initiate in a mendicant Sufi order, who gave up family life to live as a beggar, so that he might develop psychic powers. That meaning has been stretched to accommodate the less positive view that a fakir is a holy man of India who can perform allegedly impossible or miraculous acts. The classic image is the fakir lying on a bed of nails, or charming a snake through the power of his mind. This is in contrast to a **yogi**, a master of yoga who does have amazing powers of **levitation** and mind/body control.

Falun Gong, also **Falun Dafa**   (Chinese, 'the practice of the wheel of the Dharma') A Chinese spiritual movement that combines elements of **Taoism** and **Buddhism**, with exercise and physical discipline. Originally Falun Gong was just a set of five exercises combined with **yoga** postures done to music, and Falun Dafa was the faith that accompanied the routine. Increasingly, it is all referred to as Falun Gong.

None of the components of Falun Gong is new; in fact the founder, Li Hongzhi, claims that it is not a religion at all, but 'a network for transmitting information and practices, in which people may dip on an incidental basis.' Great emphasis is placed on cultivating personal energies through exercise and meditation, in order to reach a transcendent state of mind. The idea of cultivation is key, and followers are told, 'One literally cultivates their qualities like a garden, planting seeds of goodness and not letting that goodness be damaged by circumstances or events.'

Li, or 'Master Li' as he is known, registered Falun Gong with the **Chi Kung** Research Association of China in 1992 as a healing and exercise discipline. Its emphasis on guiding people to higher dimensions, however, tipped off the authorities as to its true identity as a spiritual belief system. Due to its growing popularity, the Chinese government began to persecute the movement and in 1996 Master Li emigrated to the US to escape imprisonment.

Considering the fact that Falun Gong has more followers in China than the Communist Party (it claims a membership of 70 million there and a further 30 million worldwide) it comes as no surprise that the movement has no legal protection or status.

Familiar A spirit companion, usually in animal form, of a witch or wizard. A familiar provides magical powers, as well as protection from danger, to their chosen one. The most common familiars are cats, followed by dogs, hares, birds, frogs and snakes. It was once thought that these spirits were the physical incarnation of **elementals** or demons. To bind a witch and a familiar together, the witch would put a drop of her blood into the animal's food, thereby creating a psychic bond between the two. At the height of Europe's witchcraft hysteria of the late sixteenth and early seventeenth centuries, a lone woman's mere possession of a cat (especially a black one) was enough to convict her of witchcraft in certain hysterical circles, especially in Scotland. Sometimes the poor offending cat would be sacrificed alongside the witch, as the only sure way of preventing the familiar from seeking out another magician.

Fates, The In Greek mythology, the three daughters of the god Zeus and of Themis (goddess of law) who determined the fate of all human life. They were portrayed as spinners and weavers, each with a particular duty. Clothos, the youngest, spun the thread of life, and presided over birth. Lachesis, the matron, was responsible for holding this thread and measuring out the length of life. Atropos, the crone, was death, who cut off the thread of life. The Roman fates were very similar, only this time it was three old women – Nona, Decuma and Morta – who performed the tasks.

Feldenkrais, Feldenkrais Method A type of bodywork therapy, developed by Moshe Feldenkrais in the mid-twentieth century, which teaches people to be aware how their movement affects their physical and mental condition. Feldenkrais is taught either in one-to-one sessions (called Functional Integration) or group sessions (called Awareness Through

Movement). The key to this method is awareness – of your body's skeleton and muscle system, of how you move and how you hold yourself in the space around you. You need to learn how to develop this state of awareness, and Feldenkrais classes focus on doing so through specific exercises.

In the early sessions, you actually start by lying on the floor and working on such simple movements as flexing your foot back and forth. You are then guided to think – how am I moving my foot? What happens to the rest of my body when I'm doing it? What happens when I get up?

This method is deceptively simple but very powerful. Feldenkrais uses repetition of movement and thought to retrain the body into new ways of working. It is particularly effective for people suffering from neuromuscular health problems like cerebral palsy and Parkinson's Disease, and for those with chronic pain and injury traumas.

Feng Shui (Chinese, 'wind and water') The ancient Chinese art of placement to enhance the flow of **chi** energy through your personal environment. It is a philosophy that determines how you can best position and structure items in your living and working places to enhance all areas of your life. Both natural and artificial features can either assist or block the flow of chi, and determining which is which, as well as applying other energetic solutions, is the goal of feng shui.

Originally, it was known as hum yue – the heavenly and earthly paths. The philosophy of hum yue was not written down until sometime during the Han Dynasty (206 BC–AD 220). These secret teachings were passed down through centuries, culminating in the writings of Yuen Kuen Chok (Tang Dynasty AD 618–906) and the scholar Wang Chi (Sung Dynasty AD 960–1279), which form the basis for modern feng shui theory.

There are two different approaches – the 'Form School' and the 'Compass School'. The Form School originated around the period AD 840–888 and is also known as the 'shape method'. It is an intuitive method of visually assessing the environment, instead of precisely measuring a building's dimensions and placement in the landscape. The placement of natural features – mountains and hills, rivers and streams – is also of prime importance.

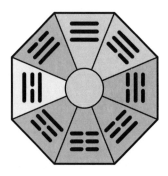

Feng shui bau-gua or pa-kwa

Finally the five natural elements are studied: **water, fire, earth, metal** and wood. Different elements suit different types and functions of buildings. Advice is then given for improving the flow of chi.

The Compass School is less intuitive, and therefore less subjective, than the Form School. It originated in the tenth century AD and involves precise measurements obtained by using an eight-sided compass called a **bau-gua**, or **pa-kwa**. It is this method of feng shui that is best known in the West.

Drawing out a floor plan of your house and overlaying the bau-gua on it is the best way to determine how to improve your surroundings. The bau-gua is also known as the 'eight **trigrams**' because each side of the octagon shows one of the three-lined pictograms from the **I Ching** that represents the elemental qualities of life. Each side of the bau-gua also indicates the areas of your house where particular types of chi are found.

These types can roughly be divided into the following areas: health, career, finances, relationships, education, fertility, fame and spirituality. Improving the arrangement of objects in that particular corner of the bau-gua will also improve the flow of energy to that area of life.

Feng shui is a form of **geomancy**, a practice that works with the natural magnetic and **life force** energies of the earth.

Fetch An Irish folklore phrase to describe the ghostly double of a living person. Seeing this fetch is a sure sign of your own (if the fetch is you) or a loved one's imminent death. See also: **Wraith**.

Fifth House In **astrology**, the **house** or part of the heavens in your birth chart that describes your attitude to fun, the creative arts, sports and pleasure. It is ruled by the sign **Leo** and the planet the **sun**. See also: **Ascendant**, **Horoscope**.

Findhorn A community in the north of Scotland established in 1962 by Eileen and Peter Caddy, and Dorothy MacLean. This community believes that behind the material world there lies a spiritual reality that permeates and unites all people, all life and all matter, similar to **akasha** and the **akashic record**. This community, which the founders claimed was chosen for them by spirit guides, specialises in educational seminars on spiritualism and personal transformation, and has many new-age businesses on its 'campus', including a publishing house.

Fire Element 1. One of the four natural elements harnessed in **pagan** rituals of **magic** and religious worship. In **Wicca**, a fire **elemental** is one of the four spirits that energise a spell and bring its wishes into being. Fire symbolises light, the sun, joy, ambitions and achievements. It represents the male principle of **yang**, which destroys that which is no longer needed. The magical tool associated with the fire element is the **wand**. Fire colours are gold and orange, and fire is associated with the **zodiac** signs of **Aries, Leo** and **Sagittarius**.

2. In Chinese philosophy and medicine one of the **five elements** that make up the 'building blocks' of the universe. In **Traditional Chinese Medicine**, fire is associated with the **heart, small intestine, pericardium** and **triple warmer meridians**, and with the season of summer. Fire represents joy and passion and is considered the seat of all emotions, in particular love. The colour red, heat, bitter tastes, the tongue and speech in general, the sound of laughter and a ruddy complexion are also associated with this element. Fire-type people make good leaders but they can also be restless and hyperactive.

In the five element cycle, fire generates or gives birth to **earth** and controls **metal** and in turn fire is given life by wood and controlled by **water**. This interdependent relationship with other elements has implications in health. If someone has weak fire energy they will be uneasy, anxious, hyperactive and most likely have disturbed sleep patterns and, ultimately, heart disease. Left unchecked, this could then go on to weaken other elemental energies and lead to other health problems in the way that congestive heart failure (weak fire energies) will lead to lung congestion (weak metal energies). See also: **Yang, Yin, Taoism**.

3. In Indian philosophy and medicine, one of the **five elements** that define the universe based on the spiritual concept of **prana**, or life energy. In **ayurveda**, the fire element, also known as tejas, is associated with the eyes and vision, as well as pungent, sour tastes; and has the elemental qualities of heat, activity, light, and acid. Fire alone makes up the **dosha** (mind/body type) **pitta**. See also: **Hinduism, Tridosha**.

Firewalking Walking through a bed of hot coals or fire without harm or burning to the feet or body. This technique has been practised for thousands of years and formed part of religious practice in India and some Polynesian cultures. Firewalking has been revived in recent years, first in the **human potential movement** and now as part of business and self-help seminars.

How it works is not entirely understood, but the person doing the walking will be in some sort of trance state (either self-induced or brought on by hypnotism) where they believe the fire will not burn them.

First House In astrology, the **house** or part of the heavens in your birth chart that describes your personality and self-image. It is commonly referred to as the 'house of self' because it is so closely associated with your own sun sign. It is ruled by the sign **Aries** and the planet **Mars**. See also: **Ascendant, Horoscope**.

Five Element Theory, also **Five Element Cycle** 1. Five categories, or elements, in the natural world, according to Chinese philosophy, which form the building blocks of the universe. They are: earth, metal, water, wood and fire. The principles of the five elements can be applied to everything – spirituality, health, survival – and are in a state of constant motion and change. In the Chinese universe, **chi**, or life energy, occupies the top of a pyramid. Chi is divided into two separate aspects, **yin** and **yang**, which can be further subdivided into the five elements. They are arranged in a five-point circle that explains their connections to each other and the influence they have either in creating or controlling the other elements in the cycle.

This theory was first formulated in China sometime between the Yin and Zhou Dynasties (1500s–221 BC) and derives from observing daily life. Water causes new plants to grow in spring to create wood, which in turn is destroyed by fire and returns to ashes and earth. Earth is the source of metal, which, being cold, causes condensation to appear as water. This is what is known as the **shen** or creation cycle, because one element generates the next in a never-ending circle (the Chinese also call this the 'mother-son' cycle, as one element 'gives birth' to the next).

Each element can also have a controlling effect on another element. Water will keep fire in check and fire makes metal usable. Metal cuts and tames wood and wood, through its roots, stabilises earth. Earth defines the boundaries of water. This is known as the **ke** or control cycle. Taken to extremes, as in dysfunctional health, it could also be called the 'destruction' cycle because water unchecked will douse fire, fire will melt metal, metal will destroy wood, lack of wood will make earth crumble or too much wood will become parasitic to earth, and without earth, water has no boundaries.

To maintain balance and health, either in the body or the world at large, it is imperative that all the elements live in harmony with each other. Each element is related to the world around it, to an affiliated set of qualities and to organs in the body. See also: **Earth Element, Fire Element, Metal Element, Taoism, Traditional Chinese Medicine, Water Element, Wood Element, Yang, Yin**.

2. In Indian philosophy, in particular **ayurveda**, five elements that hold all phenomena in the universe based on the spiritual concept of **prana**, or life energy. These five elements are: fire, earth, water, air and ether. In ayurvedic

| Earth | Metal | Water | Wood | Fire |

Chinese element symbols

philosophy, if prana occupies the top of a pyramid it is first divided into **Shiva** and **Shakti** and below that fall the five elements. The five elements then go on to form the basis of the 'three humours', or **tridosha**, that classify the world around us as well as the body types and temperaments of people in spirit and health. See also: **Air Element, Doshas, Earth Element, Ether Element, Fire Element, Hinduism, Kapha, Pitta, Vata, Water Element.**

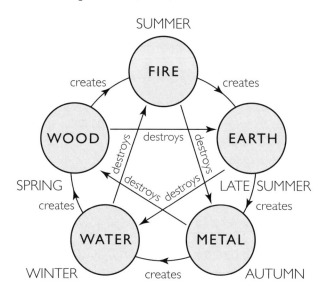

Chinese five element cycle

Five Pillars of Islam The five foundations of religious practice in **Islam**. All Muslims must perform the sacred duties of the pillars to be true to their religion. These form the framework of a Muslim's life, and are based on admonitions from the divine prophet **Muhammad**, in the holy book **Koran**. They are: **Shahadah**, the declaration of faith; **Salah**, the routine of daily prayers; **Sawm**, fasting during the holy month of **Ramadan; Zakah**, tithing a percentage of assets to charity; and **Hajj**, the pilgrimage to **Mecca**, which every Muslim who can afford it must make once in a lifetime.

Fixed Signs In Western **astrology**, the four signs of the **zodiac** (**Leo, Taurus, Aquarius** and **Scorpio**) that share a certain stubbornness, stability, and tendency to continue on a predetermined path. They are called 'fixed' because the sun enters their signs in the middle of a season.

Floromancy (Latin flos, flor, 'flower', + Greek manteia, 'divination') A form of **divination** using flowers, first practised in ancient Greece, but still in use today. Floromancy is based on the belief that flowers radiate vibrations and respond to sympathetic shocks in the environment around them. Because of this sensitivity, the appearance, smell, shape and form of particular plants (especially those with curative properties) can be interpreted to read the truth of a situation, or of an upcoming event. Flowers can also be used to cure disease, mental and physical, because of their power. See also: **Bach Flower Remedies**.

Flotation Therapy, also **Klimatherapy, Balneo-phytotherapy** A relaxation technique that uses sensory isolation and a specially constructed bath to bring about deep relaxation of the mind and body. Flotation therapy developed from the work of Dr John C. Lilly, an American neurophysiologist and psycho-analyst, in the mid 1950s. His experiments centred on the reaction of the human being to sensory deprivation.

He developed an 'isolation tank' (basically a bath with a lid) and filled it with water into which copious amounts of salt and other minerals were poured. These salts prevented a person from sinking when immersed in the tank. He then closed the lid, which made the bath light- and soundproof. Floating on the water also meant that any effects of gravity were removed. Lilly discovered that instead of his subjects going to sleep, in fact their minds became more active and increased their imaginative and problem-solving ability.

From these experimental beginnings has come a deeply relaxing way of releasing stress and tension, and improving mental and physical performance. Despite fears to the contrary and the highly imaginative film *Altered States* (based on Lilly's work) you will not revert to your earlier Cro-Magnon self if you indulge in flotation therapy. Instead, it is often compared to **meditation** in its focus on 'not-focusing' and has the same benefits as that Eastern discipline. Flotation therapy today makes sensory deprivation an option and has become seen as a sensually pleasurable spa treatment. It is particularly good for the highly stressed, and for those suffering from chronic back and other pain.

Flower Essences Healing tinctures created by soaking a flower in water and exposing the preparation to sunlight or heat. Doing this imparts the essential energies of the plant into the water. These essences have been shown to have beneficial effects on a person's mental state, and help to restore their emotional equilibrium. British physician Dr Edward Bach pioneered the technique in the 1930s with his eponymous set of flower remedies, but the field has grown to include flower essences from the United States, South America, Australia, India and Southeast Asia. See also: **Bach Flower Remedies**.

Food Combining, also **Hay Diet** A dietary regime that produces a beneficial chemical balance in the body through a specific combination of foods eaten at specific times. Dr William Howard Hay introduced the system in 1911 after discovering that many of his patients had higher than normal ph acid levels in the blood. Through experimentation, he discovered that the alkaline level in the blood could be raised to equalise ph levels, using dietary manipulation. He believed that the underlying cause of ill-health was the manufacture and accumulation of acid in the blood, from food digestion. This unhealthy chemical condition caused a build-up of toxins in the body.

Dr Hay classified foods into three types, according to their acid/alkaline balance. Alkali forming foods are fruits and vegetables; concentrated proteins like meat, game, fish, eggs and cheese are acid-forming, and the third group, concentrated carbohydrates or starch foods, are also acid-forming. Therefore, eating proteins and concentrated carbohydrates together at the same meal overloads the body with too much acid-forming food, so they should be eaten at different meals at least four hours apart.

Conventional medical nutritionists scoff at Hay's dietary theory, but there are many advocates of food combining who can directly attribute weight loss, improved digestion, enhanced energy and an increased sense of well-being to his method. See also: **Naturopathy, Nutritional Therapy**.

Force, The Filmmaker George Lucas' pop-cultural take on the concept of universal life energy, also known in various philosophical traditions as **chi**, **prana** or **vitalism**, as portrayed in his *Star Wars* film series. See also: **Life Force**.

Fortune-telling The art of predicting the future using a number of different forms of **divination**, including the **tarot**, **crystal-gazing** and **palmistry**. The phrase fortune-telling is particularly associated with the Romany people, also known as gypsies, who have a special word for it – *dukkerin*. See also: **Gypsy Magic**.

Four Humours   The idea in ancient Greek and medieval European medicine that the body contained four vital fluids connected to the four natural **elements** of the universe; these sustained life and were responsible for the type of person you were. These 'vital fluids' were: blood (linked to the **fire element** and responsible for passion), phlegm (linked to the **water element** and responsible for laziness), yellow bile or choler (linked to the **air element** and associated with anger), and black bile (linked to the **earth element** and associated with melancholy). As long as the four humours remained fairly balanced (individuals were always inclined towards one sort of humour), a person would remain healthy. If one or more of these humours became either too plentiful or too depleted, they would get sick. Medical treatment was based on trying to rebalance these 'vital fluids', which is why so many horrific practices like bloodletting and some truly disgusting lotions and potions existed. See also: **Four Temperaments**.

Four Noble Truths   The fundamental doctrine of **Buddhism**, which states the root causes of suffering and the way to emancipation from this condition. The truths are: that all conditions of existence entail suffering; that suffering is caused by ignorance which gives rise to desire, anger and illusion; that there is an end to suffering; that the way out of suffering is by following the **eightfold path**. These truths were the **Buddha**'s first teaching, given shortly after he attained **enlightenment** in 546 BC.

Four Temperaments   The four personality types, according to medieval philosophy and medicine. They were based on the **four humours** (the body fluids blood, phlegm, choler, bile) and whichever one of these humours was dominant in an individual determined what kind of person they were. Blood-dominant types were sanguine, considered hopeful and eager individuals. Then there were easy-going types, the phlegmatic. Third was the excitable or choleric, and fourth was the bile-dominant type, the sadly thoughtful melancholic. Medieval doctors believed that as long as you didn't become too imbalanced towards one humour at the expense of the other three, you would remain healthy. A good way to keep this balance was through food. Many medieval feasts and banquets concentrated on preparing dishes individually suited to the reveller's temperament.

Fourth House   In **astrology**, the **house** or part of the heavens in your birth chart that describes your feelings for family and home. It also refers to how you view your ancestry and your sense of emotional security. It is ruled by the sign **Cancer** and the planet the **moon**. See also: **Ascendant, Horoscope**.

Freemasonry, also **Masonic Order, Masons** An international fraternity organisation that started out as an **esoteric** society with secret initiation rituals, codes, ceremonies and (some say) a link to the order of the **Knights Templar**. It started out as a professional organisation of English stonemasons in 1717 but expanded into a general craftsman's guild, with one important difference – only men could belong to the freemasons and admission would be confined to a certain 'quality of membership' (i.e. rich, white, educated and no Catholics). The ruling ethos of the order was to help each other out through their members' influence, wealth and connections.

Lodges quickly grew throughout England and spread to North America and the rest of the English and non-English-speaking world, although the organisation is now banned in several countries, including Italy, Germany, Austria and China.

Freemasons will never stop anyone from applying for membership but exercise the right of refusal to those who do not fit their 'quality of membership'. In recent years there has been a conscious effort to become a more open and accepting organisation, but it does remain primarily the reserve of well-to-do, educated white Protestant men.

Freud, Sigmund (1856–1939) Austrian doctor and prolific writer who was the founder of the practice of psychoanalysis, and often referred to as the father of clinical psychology. Freud's ideas about the mind, personality and memory function have become the foundation for nearly all schools of psychology and self-help thought, and he coined many of the phrases we use today to describe our own or others' behaviour.

Key among his concepts was the idea of the unconscious and how it works. He theorised that most of our behaviours in life could be put down to motivations that we ourselves were unaware of. We are driven by several basic desires – sex, power, aggression, and the pleasure principle (which actually means avoiding pain) by the primitive part of our mind, the **id**. In order for us to function in society, however, we needed a controlling force to channel these primitive urges and tell us what is real and not real in the world – that is the part of our mind we call the **ego**. When it comes to making judgements about what is right and wrong, acceptable and taboo, our upper mind, or **superego**, monitors our behaviour.

All three parts of our mind are at constant war for supremacy, and which part of our personality dominates our character all depends upon a number of things, chief among which are our childhood experiences and relationship with our parents.

Freud was responsible for producing one of the seminal theories on childhood development. According to him, there were five stages of psychosexual development: oral (birth–one year) where the mouth is the prime source of pleasurable sensations; anal (one–three years), when the act of elimination becomes the focus of these sensations; phallic (three–five years), when the focus switches to the penis and clitoris; latency period (five–puberty), a rest period; and genital (puberty upwards), no explanation needed. If you got 'developmentally' stuck at any of these stages when growing up, this would be the explanation for any neuroses, psychoses or other ailments you had when you were an adult.

Freud felt that through psychoanalysis – analysing a patient's upbringing, interpreting their dreams, memories, current behaviours and ailments (mental or physical) – you could discover the root cause of a person's neurosis and enable them to heal the wounds of their past. He is also the author of the **parapraxis** theory, better known as the 'Freudian slip'.

During his lifetime and for decades after his death, Freud's theories dominated how psychotherapy and treatment were approached in psychiatric circles. He influenced several generations of great psychologists, including most notably his peer and former student, **Carl Jung**, but his theories have fallen into some disfavour because of their emphasis on sex as the root of all our problems and psychoses.

Freudian Slip see **Parapraxis**

Gabriel see **Archangel**

Gaia, also **Gaea**, **Ge**, **Tellus**, **Terra** In Greek mythology, she is Mother Earth, the most ancient of deities after Chaos, the universe. She bore **Uranus**, also known as the heavens, and then mated with him to bring forth the first generation of gods and goddesses, the Titans. She is one of the most important **goddess** archetypes and the inspiration for the **Gaia theory** of scientist James Lovelock.

Gaia Theory, also **Gaian Theory** The idea, formulated by British scientist James Lovelock, that the earth is not a dead rock of a planet, but instead a living, evolving organism. This idea was present in many ancient cultures and traditions including **hermeticism** and Greek mythology, but Lovelock was the first to present scientific evidence to support his 'living earth' thesis.

He came across his theory almost by accident. In the 1970s NASA had asked for his help in designing life-detecting probes for their unmanned Viking Mars missions. He first analysed the chemical constituents of Venus and Mars and then applied these same measures to the earth. He came across what he called the 'Goldilocks phenomenon'. This is a simple way of stating that Venus was too hot for life to exist, Mars too cold, and the earth just right. He came to realise that the earth appeared to be not so much a planet adorned with diverse life forms as a planet that had been transfigured and transformed by a self-evolving and self-regulating living system. In view of the nature of this activity, earth seemed to qualify as a living being in its own right.

Lovelock got the name for his theory while walking out in the country with his friend the author William Golding, who suggested the Greek goddess **Gaia** – the earth mother who drew life from chaos.

Galahad Son of **Lancelot du Lac**, and one of **King Arthur's** Knights of the Round Table. Galahad was reputed to be the only knight pure and virtuous enough to seek and find the **Holy Grail**, the cup used by Jesus Christ at his Last Supper, and hidden somewhere in the vicinity of **Glastonbury**. Galahad himself was often seen as a Christ-like figure in medieval eyes. See also: **Arthurian Legend, Grail Quest**.

Gall Bladder Meridian A channel or **meridian** of **chi** energy running through the body that penetrates the gall bladder, according to **Traditional Chinese Medicine**. It is associated with the **wood element**, has **yang** energetic qualities and is partnered with the **liver meridian**, which is **yin**. Gall bladder meridian energy is most involved in making decisions and affects hips and thighs, shoulders and head. Chi is strongest in this channel from 11 p.m. to 1 a.m. and conversely the weakest between 11 a.m. and 1 p.m. Both left and right sides of the body have this meridian, which roughly begins at the outer eye, circles on the forehead, then runs down the front of the body to end on the top of the foot at the fourth toenail.

Ganesha The elephant-headed god of **Hinduism**, who is one of the sons of **Shiva** and his wife, Parvati. He is considered god of wisdom, strength and literature, created from the dust and mist from his mother's body. Ganesha is the deity Hindus ask to remove obstacles, and prayers are offered to him specially when undertaking an important task.

Gargoyles (Greek *gargarizein*, 'gargle') Protective hideous creatures carved from stone or wood, and placed on churches and other sacred buildings to keep guard against evil spirits and influences. They are also known as 'grotesques', which means 'spirit of the grottos'. Gargoyles and grotesques are most likely pictorial representations of earth spirits who dwelled in grottos and small underground places, and whose misshapen, ugly facades belied their true purpose. The one constant in all gargoyles is a large mouth, leading to a large windpipe. It was thought these huge tracheas and lungs could suck in and trap magical power in the air – just the type of thing that could be found at a sacred place. When earth spirits used to communicate in their grotto lairs, this large throat would cause them to speak in gravelly voices, almost 'gargling' their words.

Garlic A plant, *Allium sativum*, and member of the onion family, whose roots have been used since ancient times as a folk remedy and cure-all. Recent medical studies have found that the oil in garlic, *allicin*, has antibacterial, antifungal and antiviral properties, and is able to lower blood cholesterol and blood sugar levels. It is one of the strongest natural antibiotics, and is excellent for a number of ailments including catarrh, coughs and colds and digestive complaints. It also helps to boost the immune system, and can be used as a topical treatment for surface wounds.

Gautama, Siddhartha, also **Gotama Siddhattha** The secular birth name of the **Buddha**, whose teachings are the groundwork for Buddhist belief. Gautama Siddhartha was an Indian prince born in Lumbini in North India (now Nepal) in 581 BC, who until the age of 29 lived a life of great comfort and luxury. He renounced the world and became a holy man and, at 35, while meditating under a **Bodhi tree** at Gayasisa, India (also known as Bodh Gaya, or Elephant Head Peak), he attained **enlightenment** and was therefore known after as 'Shakyamuni Buddha' or just Buddha, 'the awakened one'. He taught the truths he had realised for the rest of his life, founded the order of monks and nuns called the **Sangha**, and passed away at Kusinara in 501 BC when he was 80 years old. See also: **Buddhism**.

Gehenna The Jewish equivalent of **hell**. The name was derived from Ge Hinnom, a valley outside Jerusalem where the city's rubbish was burnt.

Gematria A branch of **Kabbalah** that transforms words or phrases into numerical equivalents. These occult numbers can then be compared to other words/phrases with the same number value, so a mystical connection can be inferred from the two concepts. An example of this is in the Book of Revelation where John the Baptist mentions the infamous number of the beast, '666'. Early Christians thought this referred to the Roman Emperor Nero, who violently persecuted Christians for their beliefs. The number equivalent of his name in Greek, *Nero Casaer*, totals 666. See also: **Numerology**.

Gemini The third sign of the **zodiac** in Western **astrology**, and the **sun sign** for those born between 22 May and 21 June. The symbol of Gemini is twins, and the ruling planet is **Mercury**. Geminis are a **mutable sign** influenced by the **air element**, with 'communication' the best single word to define them. Those born under Gemini are adaptable, inquisitive and intellectual, but at times restless and inconsistent. Geminis are fascinated by ideas, facts and fancies, and are known as the zodiac's perpetual children in their zest and quest for something new. This can make committing to one thing problematic, however.

The ideal Gemini meal would not be one at all unless it was at some dreadfully smart restaurant, with frightfully fashionable types dining out on gossip and refined air. In health, Geminis are prone to allergies, respiratory disorders and weak lungs. They worry a great deal and suffer from high-strung nerves. Herbs to help the immune system, especially with colds, are good for Geminis, as well as treatments to reduce anxiety.

Genethliaology see Astrology

Gentian A flower essence made from the gentian blossom. This emotionally healing tincture is one of the **Bach Flower Remedies**. Dr Bach said that this is indicated for 'depression of any known reason. For setbacks that cause discouragement or disappointment'.

Geomancy (Greek *ge*, 'earth' + *manteia*, 'divination') 1. A form of **divination** using the energies of the earth. Geomancers would throw down handfuls of pebbles, nuts or seed then predict the future from patterns made on the ground. Geomancy originated in Africa, but the Greek naturalist and writer Pliny the Elder (AD 23–79) is credited with coining the phrase after observing a group of diviners at work.

A grid composed of 12 squares would be drawn on the ground, and the fortune 'caster' would ask a question. Then, a stone marked with one dot on one side and two dots on the other was tossed down on the grid four times. A figure composed from those four throws and an interpretation of the pattern would indicate what was in store. 2. Term applied to any practices or beliefs like **feng shui, dowsing, sacred geometry** and **ley lines**, to indicate working with the natural magnetic and **life force** energies of the earth.

Geopathic Stress (Greek *ge*, 'earth', + *pathos*, 'suffer') Naturally occurring earth radiation that becomes distorted by underground water, certain mineral concentrations and man-made structures like buildings and power lines. The negative effects of these energies can be detrimental to structures and to people's health. The concept of geopathic stress explains events like radon gas leaking into homes, and 'sick building syndrome', which is thought to be caused by a combination of electromagnetic fields surrounding computers, lights and other office equipment, sealed buildings with inadequate or non-existent fresh air supply, plus radiation coming from blocked underground streams. Fortunately, there are measures that can be taken to relieve geopathic stress, some less radical than others.

Feng Shui cures, like bringing in house plants or rearranging furniture away from the focal points of stress (especially beds in a bedroom) is one solution. Using an ioniser, increasing the amount of outside light and ventilation in an office environment, or improving air quality and electromagnetic fields by bringing in plants and certain crystals, will improve geopathic stress in the workplace. In extreme cases, it may be necessary either to relocate structures away from sources of geopathic stress (particularly when radon gas is involved) or to invest in efficient, albeit expensive, specialist systems of ventilation. If neither is an option, those suffering the ill-effects of geopathic stress may well need to permanently move themselves away from the toxic location.

Gestalt Therapy (German, 'whole' or 'form') An approach to psychology that emphasises the awareness and understanding of your feelings. It originated in Germany in the 1920s with Fritz Perls, who trained as a Freudian psychoanalyst but soon felt that you could not analyse just part of a person's consciousness; in addition you had to take into consideration their entire body of sensory experiences – thoughts, feeling, emotions and sensuality. Gestalt psychologists were responsible for changing the way we view perception but, owing to the vagueness of the therapy's principles, it is not much practised today.

Ghosts (Old English *gast*, 'spirit, soul') General term for the apparition of a dead person, said to be the spiritual essence or **astral body** of the deceased. Ghosts are prone to haunt the place where they resided in life. They often are trapped souls caught between our world and the afterlife, who either do not realise they are dead, or cannot bear to leave their own home.

Ghouls (Arabic *gul*, 'terrifying demon') A particularly evil **ghost** or phantom, which is said to feed off the bodies of dead human beings. They also like to terrify the living. Ghouls are associated with particular places like forests, lonely places and cemeteries, where they like to dig up bodies for their dining pleasure.

Gibran, Khalil (1883–1931) Lebanese poet and artist best known for his inspirational work *The Prophet*, first published in 1923 and still one of the world's best-selling works of spiritual poetry.

Ginger A plant, *Zingiber officinale*, whose root is used in Western and oriental herbal medicine, **aromatherapy** and cooking. It is a core remedy in Chinese and ayurvedic medical practice, and was extensively used by Greek and Arab doctors, who even thought it an antidote to poison. It has a warming, antispasmodic effect on the body, particularly useful in quelling nausea, especially related to pregnancy and travel sickness. Ginger has a stimulating effect on the heart and circulation, creating a feeling of warmth especially during cold weather. Taken as a pill, powder, tea or merely eaten raw, ginger has the ability to neutralise excess acid in the stomach, and helps to reduce a fever and clear catarrh and colds. In aromatherapy, ginger **essential oil** increases blood flow to the surface of the skin, along with the other properties mentioned. See also: **Ayurveda, Herbalism, Traditional Chinese Medicine.**

Ginkgo, also **Ginkgo Biloba, Maidenhair Tree** A plant of the *Ginkgo biloba* genus, whose seeds and leaves are used in both Western and oriental herbal medicine. It is currently the best-selling herbal remedy in the world, as it is known as the 'memory tree' for its ability to improve a person's blood circulation and mental concentration. It is used both in **alternative medicine** to treat degenerative memory disorders orders associated with age and extensively in **Traditional Chinese Medicine** and **ayurveda** medical practices to treat asthma and chesty coughs associated with phlegm.

Ginkgo is often called a living fossil as it is the oldest living species of tree, having survived for 200 million years. One tree can live as long as 1,000 years, which is why its medicinal properties are associated with imparting longevity. Medical reseach has found its primary effect is to increase blood circulation throughout the body, but particularly to the brain. It is used as herbal remedy to treat arteriosclerosis, high blood pressure, heart attacks, varicose veins, ulcers – anything, in short, where it is beneficial to make 'sticky, thick' blood less viscous in arteries and veins. See also: **Herbalism**.

Ginseng   A plant, *Panax ginseng*, whose root is used in Western and oriental herbal medicine. Ginseng has a reputation as a rejuvenating tonic that is particularly effective for men in regaining their health and libido. Ginseng has been prized in Europe since the sixteenth century, when it was first introduced by a visiting delegation of the King of Siam to the French 'Sun King' Louis XIV.

It is used extensively in **Traditional Chinese Medicine** to treat a number of debilitating conditions, including insomnia, stress-related illnesses and post-viral infections. Because of its high level of antioxidants, ginseng also helps to delay the ageing process and has been shown to improve mental concentration and memory. It is one of the most useful herbs there is, acting as a stimulant as well as a sedative, depending on what is required. See also: **Herbalism**.

Glossolalia   see **Xenoglossisia**

Glyph   A symbol that represents a person's name and birth date, often used in **magic**. It is similar in construction to a **sigil**, where the sequence of letters and numbers is fashioned into a single picture. Because this symbol represents the heart of who a person is, it has protective powers and can be worn as a personal **amulet** or **talisman** to ward off misfortune and illness.

Gnomes   Ancient, mythological dwarf-like creatures, who are **elemental** spirits of the earth and dwell in dark forests or underground caves. Gnomes, like goblins, have an affinity for treasure and can often be found mining for precious gems and metals.

Gnosticism   (Greek *gnostos*, 'known') A school of mystic Christian thought that flourished in the early years of that religion. Gnosticism is based on the idea that there was more to **Christianity** than belief in **Jesus** and his message, that hidden spiritual knowledge was revealed in a visionary experience. It was this experience, this *gnosis*, which – so these Gnostics claimed – set the true follower of Christ apart from his fellows.

Gnostic practice was forbidden in later Church doctrine, and mostly died out until the mid-twentieth century. Then in 1947 the 'Gnostic Gospels' were discovered in Nag Hammadi, Egypt. This discovery supported the idea that Gnosticism was more a part of early Christian practice than had earlier been thought; in fact, there were other gospels written by Jesus' disciples that had been suppressed by later Church factions. Subsequently, there has been a revival of belief in Gnostic traditions of Christianity.

Gnosticism differs from more mainstream Christian beliefs in four areas. The first, previously mentioned, is the importance of the mystical visionary experience as a path to truly knowing God. The second tenet is that this experience leads to an 'awakening' of the godly soul within; in short, that while man is not God, he becomes 'godly' through this vision. Third is the acceptance of gospels and scriptures proscribed by the larger Church body and fourth (and most controversially) that God has a dual nature, that he is both masculine and feminine, with his female counterpart taking the form of **Sophia**, the divine wisdom. See also: **Nag Hammadi Library**.

Goblin, also **Orc** An earth spirit or **elemental**, known for its malicious tendencies and evil cunning. This earth-dwelling member of the **fairy** family shuns daylight, and delights in terrifying and harassing travellers and children. Goblins live in dark underground places and deep forests, and roam together in great bands, forcing other fairies and spirits to work as their slaves.

God, god 1. Big G: the Supreme Being, the sole creator and ruler of the universe and source of all wisdom, knowledge and moral authority, according to **Judaism**, **Christianity** and **Islam**. He has several names in these spiritual traditions (like Jehovah or Allah) but all relate to the same monotheistic concept.

2. Little g: a male deity, divine individual or supernatural being or spirit worshipped as having power over people and the world. A god may have the same authority as God in certain religions and belief systems. A female god is called a **goddess**.

Goddess Ancient archetype of divine feminine power, which represents the intuitive elements of life that cannot be explained using rational or scientific methods. Goddess is a generic term used for a female deity, but it also symbolises the three aspects of woman – maiden, mother, crone – using myths to depict the story of a woman's life cycle.

It is thought that before the rise of male-centred religions like **Judaism** and **Christianity**, the first deities to be worshipped were women. This was connected to women's procreative role; life came from her and she often outlived men and buried the dead.

There are goddesses worshipped throughout every world culture, and they remain an important part of many belief systems, including **paganism**, the cult of the **Virgin Mary** in Christianity and **Hinduism**. In the Judaeo-Christian Western world, many people are returning to goddess worship as a way of honouring the earth and preserving nature. It also allows many in our science-weary, technologically driven society a way of reconnecting to more intuitive ways of living.

Golden Bough, The A landmark in the study of comparative folklore, magic and religion, by James Frazer, published in 1922. It raised much controversy on its appearance for its thesis that Christianity may have evolved directly from earlier **pagan** religions, instead of being divine revelation.

It is a massive work of 69 chapters, detailing goddess myth, the principles of magic, primitive beliefs about nature and the elements, the festival cycle of the year (better known as the **Celtic wheel of the year)**, a number of ancient taboos and the source myths for these prohibitions, and most provocatively (and still hotly disputed by most pagans) the prevalence of human sacrifice in magic and pagan rituals.

Frazer's work had a huge impact on psychology and literature (**Jung** thought Frazer's work groundbreaking). He did have his detractors. One of the most persistent criticisms of Frazer was that he accepted as true many 'historical' and 'travelogue' accounts that were clearly questionable.

The Golden Bough (a reference to the goddess **Diana)** influenced an entire generation of thinkers, and was the source of inspiration for Robert Graves' work *The White Goddess*.

Golden Dawn, also **Hermetic Order of the Golden Dawn** A secret occult society whose most infamous member was **Aleister Crowley**. This magical order, which is still going strong, was founded in 1888 by a group of **freemasons** headed by Dr Wynn Westcott and Dr William Woodman. It attracted such followers as the poet W.B. Yeats, the author Bram Stoker and A.E. Waite, of the Waite **tarot** pack (the first set of cards mass-marketed to the public). Based on **Rosicrucian** writings, esoteric codes and myths from many ancient lands, and teachings of **Kabbalah**, the Golden Dawn practises rites of magic and **alchemy** that are supposedly grounded in the dark arts. The aim of the Golden Dawn is to develop and expand the borders of human consciousness through experimentation with **occultism**, **astral travel** and, some say, sexual rites.

Golden Mean see Sacred Geometry

Golem A Jewish creature of folklore, which took the shape of a human being and could be made to serve the magical master who conjured it into existence. The golem was little more than an automaton, however, as it had no animating spirit. This soulless creature could grow more powerful than its master, given enough time, so it was periodically reduced to dust by magic rituals to keep it in its place. See also: **Kabbalah**.

Gorse A flower essence made from the blossom of the gorse bush. This emotionally healing tincture is one of the **Bach Flower Remedies**. Dr Bach said that this is indicated for 'those who have lost hope of being well or of the subject of their hopelessness ever returning to normality. They are pessimistic and see only the negative outcome'.

Grail Quest The legendary quest for the **Holy Grail**, by King Arthur and his Knights of the Round Table. The Holy Grail was the cup used by Christ at the Last Supper and for that reason was considered a symbol of perfection and virtue. One of Jesus' followers, Joseph of Arimathea, supposedly brought the Grail to Britain and hid it somewhere in the vicinity of Glastonbury Tor, in Somerset, where he also founded a monastic order.

Graphites One of the 15 major **polychrests**, or major remedies in **homeopathy**. It is also a **constitutional type**, which is a way homeopaths have of classifying different patient profiles. The fitting constitutional remedy acts preventatively and curatively on its matching personality type – for example, a person with a Graphites constitution will respond well to the Graphites remedy almost regardless of the illness they are suffering from. Graphites people are habitually indecisive, and prefer action (even if wrong) to discussion. They can be lethargic and are prone to skin conditions. They also often suffer from headaches.

Graphology (Greek *graphe*, 'writing', + *logos*, 'word, study') The study of handwriting in order to analyse a person's character and temperament. Graphologists take a sample of handwriting, examine the minutiae of its construction and make deductions about a person based on the writing's size, shape and appearance. In order to carry out a proper analysis a sample of at least one page plus signature is required.

The different factors examined include letter loops, dotted 'I's' and crossed 'T's', letter spacing, slants, heights, ending strokes, general readability (messy?

neat?), whether the letters are joined together or separate, cursive or non-cursive, and upper or lower case.

There is great debate about the value of graphology; in countries like France, Germany, Switzerland and Austria, submitting a handwriting sample for analysis prior to a job interview is de rigueur, and graphology is considered a branch of psychology and studied at degree level. It does not have the same legitimacy in Britain or North America, where it is viewed as a party trick or quasi-scientific quackery of the highest sort.

Green Man The figure of a man whose face is composed of a 'foliate mask' – green leaves. He is a symbol of the greening of nature and the return of spring in English **pagan** folklore and ritual, who represents the spirit of plants, trees and vegetation. In his role as Jack-in-the-Green, he plays a part in May Day rites, where he symbolically mates with the great Earth Mother in her maiden form, ensuring fertility and fecundity for the land for the following year.

Prior to 1939, the figure of a 'Green Man' was depicted as a large, shaggy, bearded man with a club, and was thought to be the early version of the medieval Robin Hood and St George. In that year, the scholar Lady Raglan connected the 'foliate mask' with carvings found in medieval churches and monasteries and thereafter the Green Man was pictured as half-man, half-plant, with twigs and leaves for features. See also: **Celtic Spirituality, Herne the Hunter.**

Greenhouse Effect Atmospheric effect where carbon dioxide and other gases act as a barrier to prohibit the escape of radiant heat from the earth into outer space. As a consequence, the trapped heat causes the earth's mean temperature to rise, triggering massive climate change. In recent years, the amount of carbon dioxide in the atmosphere has radically increased, due to pollutants from fossil-burning fuels. If pollution levels are not decreased, the theory goes, the earth's temperature will continue to rise, causing catastrophic changes to our planet's weather and land.

Gremlin Earth spirit of the **fairy** realm who delights in tinkering with human tools and machinery, fouling them up in the process. These malevolent little folk were reportedly seen during World War II, on the wings of both German and British fighter planes. There are even alleged cases where they caused damage or terrified pilots by suddenly appearing in front of the windscreen. The reason for their enmity is unclear, but one theory suggests they once had the ability to fly and lost it, so resent humans who have that power (even if through machines). The second theory is that gremlins were once friendly with people, showing them how to make better, more efficient tools and inventions. When humans started to take credit for the gremlins' work, the relationship soured. So if anything goes wrong with tools, machinery or engines, you say 'There's a gremlin in the works.' Who knows, that might literally be true. See also: **Elementals**.

Griffin, also **Gryphons**, **Griffon** A mythical half-bird, half-mammal creature, with the wings, front legs and head of an eagle and the back end,

tail and ears of a lion. It was thought to be the result of a pairing between these two animals, and is featured in the legends of many Indo-European cultures (some think it is merely an extinct species). They have majestic, aloof characters and often are guardians of great treasure. Because of this connotation, they are popular heraldic symbols.

Griffin

Gri-gri, also **Gris-gris** Amulets to protect the wearer from the effects of **voodoo** curses and magical spells cast by **witch doctors**. They are commonly worn in African tribal communities and in certain areas of the Caribbean.

Grimoire A witch's personal book for recording spells, ritual information, formulae, magical properties of natural objects, incantations and brews, and herbal and incense recipes. Grimoires date back to ancient Jewish mystical practices, first described in the *Key of Solomon*, King Solomon's personal book of magic. Two other famous grimoires are the *Necronomicon*, written by an Arab, El Hazzared, and the *Sacred Book of Magic* by Abra-Melin the Mage, whose teachings are said to have been given to Moses by **God**. Traditionally a witch would copy bits from another witch's grimoire, resulting in a uniquely personal book. The term grimoire is often used interchangeably with **Book of Shadows**.

Guided Imagery A form of **visualisation** used in medicine to aid healing and increase a patient's quality of life. Practitioners in the growing field of psychoneuroimmunology, the study of the mind's effect on health and illness, have found it to be a particularly effective technique in fighting disease, especially in those individuals with compromised immunity, life-threatening illnesses and/or chronic degenerative conditions. The patient works with the doctor, or other healthcare individual, to construct a detailed, specific mental picture of their health condition. The patient then visualises overcoming the problem; imagines the actual body processes taking place inside them (example: a white blood cell devouring a cancer cell like a lion devouring meat). Guided by the doctor, the patient then imagines getting better. Guided imagery can be used by anyone to conquer any illness and to maintain wellness, and has expanded beyond medical circles to be used in psychological treatment to promote and improve self-esteem, and change negative patterns of behaviour and thought.

Guinevere, also **Ganhumara**, **Guenevere**, **Guenievre**, **Gwenhwyfar** The Queen of the legendary and historical ruler of ancient Britain, **King Arthur**. Best known for her role in Arthurian romances, she betrayed her husband with the knight **Lancelot du Lac**, who was also Arthur's best friend. When their long-standing affair came into the open, Arthur reluctantly sentenced her to death, but she was rescued by Lancelot in the nick of time. After Arthur was killed, she entered a convent to spend the rest of her days as a penitent. See also: **Arthurian Legends**.

Guna (Sanskrit, 'rope, quality') The three qualities of **prakruti**, or matter, according to Indian philosophy. Guna is composed of *sattva*, 'clarity or goodness'; *rajas*, 'activity or passion'; and *tamas*, 'inertia or ignorance'. They produce pleasure, pain and indifference, in that order, and their continuing interaction accounts for the ever-changing nature of our existence. If guna is perfectly balanced, all is still, but also static. Only when guna becomes imbalanced is there change and therefore evolution in life.

Gurdjieff, George Ivanovitch (1872–1949) Mystic teacher and founder of the 'Gurdjieff system', a series of physical and psycho-spiritual exercises. Gurdjieff formed a theory that our reality is that we spend our lives asleep and believed these exercises (he called them 'the work') helped to jar people out of their somnambulist state.

Russian-born Gurdjieff was from his youth interested in the occult sciences and **spiritualism**, leaving home at an early age to seek out the truth of human existence. After extensive travel and initiation into secret cults and doctrines, he formulated his theory of the sleeping universe and attracted a large number of followers to his belief system.

Gurdjieff is also responsible for introducing to the West the use of the **enneagram**, which he claimed to have received from the Sufis of Afghanistan. He also wrote *Meetings With Remarkable Men*, an account of his early years and travels that continues to be popular today. See also: **P.D. Ouspensky, Sufism.**

Guru (Sanskrit *gu*, 'darkness', + *ru*, 'light') According to Hindu philosophy, a spiritual teacher who helps to dispel darkness and brings pupils, or **chelas**, into the light. A guru leads by example, in order to help devotees reach self-knowledge and **enlightenment**. Now used as a general term for a teacher or wise sage of spiritual disciplines.

Gypsy Magic, also **Romany Magic** Forms of magic and **fortune-telling** associated with the Romany people, more commonly known as gypsies. The word 'gypsy' is a corruption of 'Egyptian' where the Romany or 'Rom' were once thought to have originated. Recent findings suggest they may be descended from one of the races of Northern India.

As far back as the twelfth century AD, the Rom have been travellers, renowned for their dancing and musical skills, and for the divinatory arts of **palmistry**, **tarot** and **crystal-gazing**. These skills come from their religious beliefs, an intriguing blend of nature and goddess worship, folk magic and Christianity. In Rom society the witch or sorcerer (called a *chovinano*) held an honoured place in the tribe and was well trained in the arts of **herbalism** and other healing methods. To treat them disrespectfully was to bring down back luck on yourself, the origin of the 'gypsy curse'.

They strongly believe in the afterlife and the spirit world, reflected in their magical rites and cultural ceremonies. Today there are thought to be over three million Rom scattered across Europe, mostly in Russia, Eastern Europe, Greece and Turkey.

Hacking A classic movement in Swedish and holistic massage, where the sides of the hands are used in a light, springy, chopping movement. This is the 'typical' movement you see people mimic when they make a jokey attempt at massage. Hacking has a percussive effect on muscles and helps to tone the underlying tissue without stimulating the nerves. It is an invigorating, refreshing movement.

Hades, also **Ades, Aides, Aidoneus, Dis, Orcus, Pluto, Pluton** The Greek god of the underworld and dead, known as **Pluto** in Roman myth. He was one of the sons of Chronos (Time) and Rhea (Earth) and was one of the Olympiad, the 12 chief gods and goddesses of Greek legend who lived on Mt Olympus. Despite his high status, he preferred his kingdom, and abducted for his queen the goddess of springtime, Persephone. He tricked her into staying in Hades for six months of the year, which is how the Greeks explained the four seasons of the year (Persephone is in the underworld for autumn and winter).

Hahnemann, Dr Samuel (1755–1843) The founder of **homeopathy**. Hahnemann was a German physician who became disillusioned with the medical standards of his time, and resolved to find less barbaric and mortal ways of treating his patients. He first had the germ of the idea for homeopathy when translating *A Treatise on Materia Medica* by Dr William Cullen, in which that doctor claimed that cinchona bark (the raw material of quinine) was effective against malaria because of its bitter taste. Hahnemann felt this was wrong, and tested his idea by taking a dose of the bark although he was healthy. To his surprise, he immediately began to develop the same symptoms as those of malarial fever. As soon as he stopped taking the remedy, the symptoms lessened. They returned when he then again dosed himself with the potion.

Through many years of research and experiment, he began to assemble a stable of other naturally occurring substances that in large doses were toxic to people, but in extremely small doses (he called this the **minimum dose**) cured his patients. He went on to create an entire alternative medical system based on his theories, and in 1810 published his seminal work on the subject, *The Organon of the Rational Art of Healing*. It was the result of about 20 years' worth of research and experimentation, and it set out the principles of homeopathy which are still followed today. He continued to work and develop his theories up to his death, publishing five new editions of *The Organon* as well as many other works.

Hajj One of the **five pillars of Islam**, Hajj is the annual pilgrimage and an obligatory voyage expected from every Muslim who can afford it, for once in their lifetime. Pilgrims wear simple clothes that strip away distinctions of class and culture, so all stand equal before Allah.

Halloween, also **All Hallows' Eve, Hallowe'en** A holiday based on the **pagan** festival known as **Samhain** (31 October), that has evolved into a modern celebration of costumes, ghosts, jack o'lanterns and trick-or-treating.

Traditionally, Halloween was thought to be the one night of the year when the portals between our world and the afterlife were open, allowing spirits to roam free.

In Mexico it is celebrated as El Dia de los Muertos or 'The Day of the Dead' on 1 November, when families arrange altars of flowers, breads, fruits and sweets to 'feed' their deceased relatives who come back for a visit.

Trick-or-treating is thought to stem from the practice of 'souling' – children would go from door to door asking for money for the poor and a 'soul cake' for themselves. For every cake received, they would say a prayer on behalf of the dead loved ones of the donors. The beloved Jack o' Lantern pumpkin was originally a hollowed-out turnip with a candle in it, to use as a lantern when out walking on this auspicious nights of ghosts and ghoulies.

Halomancy, also **Alomancy** (Greek *halo*, 'salt', + *manteia*, 'divination') A form of **divination** or fortune-telling using salt. The diviner forecasts future events by throwing salt up into the air or into a fire. The way in which the grains of salt fall, or the patterns they make upon landing, are interpreted for good or bad omens. These practices are probably the basis for our salt-based superstitions, such as that spilling salt brings bad luck into the house, and that throwing a little salt over your left shoulder should ward off misfortune.

Handfasting A marriage ritual practised by **pagans** that magically (but not legally) binds a couple together. Magical energies are raised within a sacred space and the actions of a god or goddess are invoked by spells and chanting. The two people involved construct the vows of the ceremony, and will agree on the length of the union (so no life-sentences there, unless desired). Although a pagan priest or priestess will preside over the ceremony, the couple perform the actual ritual; thereby they 'marry' each other as opposed to 'being married' by the priest.

Handwriting Analysis see **Graphology**

Hare, The also **The Rabbit** In **Chinese astrology**, the fourth sign of the **zodiac**. You are a Hare if you were or will be born in the years 1939, 1951, 1963, 1975, 1987, 1999 or 2011. The Hare is the sign of virtue in Chinese mythology, symbolising longevity, virtue and prudence. Those born under this sign have refined tastes, and are self-assured and emotionally detached. They can appear to be snobbish, but overcome this by their intelligence and ability to command respect for their work. Their Western zodiac equivalent is **Pisces** and their ruling planet is **Neptune**.

Haruspicy, also **Aruspicy**, **Extispicium**, **Extispicy**, **Hieroscopy**, **Splanchomancy** (Latin *haru*, 'entrails', + *specere*, 'look at') A form of **divination** by means of the examination of the entrails of sacrificed animals. After the priest or diviner completed his observations, the entrails would be burned in a sacrificial fire. The method evolved from ancient Babylonian ritual and was handed down to the Greeks and Romans, who even set up a special official, the *haruspex*, to oversee the practice. The entrails of many different animals could be used (and also, rather horribly, those of people) but sheep, goat and ox were most common.

The underlying theory was that when an animal was sacrificed to a god or goddess, the deity absorbed the essence of the animal and created a direct link back to the priest or priestess. When they opened up the carcass, they were seeing into a god's mind and could interpret the future, or answer a question, based on the size and shape of the entrails. Haruspicy is still practised in remote parts of the world, and forms a part of some black magic rituals. See also: **Augury**.

Hatha Yoga see **Yoga, Hatha**

Hathor (Egyptian, 'House of Horus') The quintessential feminine goddess of ancient Egypt and the equivalent of the Greek goddess of love, **Aphrodite**. Hathor was the daughter of the sun king **Ra** and considered to be the consort of the sky-god **Horus**. She is often depicted as a cow with a sun disk between her horns, or as a fair maiden wearing a ceremonial headpiece with horns and disk. For that reason, the cow was a sacred animal. Like many of the female Egyptian deities, she had many faces – one of them being the cruel and vengeful goddess **Sakhmut**. In that role she was one of the 'Eyes of Ra', the deity who avenged herself against the enemies of Egypt.

Haunt, Haunting (Old French *hanter*, 'frequent a place') Places and events where ghosts and earth-bound spirits of the departed manifest themselves. These locations are often associated with places the dead visited in life (like gardens or pubs), or have some spiritual significance to the deceased, like churches, graveyards, castles or old buildings.

Hay Diet see **Food Combining**

Heart Meridian A channel or **meridian** of **chi** energy running through the body that affects the heart, according to **Traditional Chinese Medicine**. It is associated with the **fire element**, has **yin** energetic qualities and is partnered with the **small intestine meridian**, which is **yang**. Heart meridian energy controls the body and mind, and unites all other meridians to function efficiently. If heart energy is weak, it will affect energy throughout the body. Chi is strongest in this channel between 11 a.m. and 1 p.m. and conversely the weakest between 11 p.m. and 1 a.m. Both left and right sides of the body have this meridian, which begins under each arm and runs to the edge of the fifth finger.

Heather   A flower essence made from the heather blossom. This emotionally healing tincture is one of the **Bach Flower Remedies**. Dr Bach said that this is indicated for 'those who are in need of company and companionship. They are talkative and hold on to a person's attention for as long as possible while they go into detail about their problems or personal life'.

Heaven   The place where the spirits of the good go after death. Depending upon your belief system, heaven can be the cloud- and angel-packed domain of the Judaeo-Christian God, or a paradise garden for the righteous, as depicted in **Islam**. The ancient Greeks thought that heaven was Mt Olympus, where the gods resided. Although Buddhists do not believe in a supreme being, they do believe in **nirvana**, a state of unknowing bliss that is only possible after you reach **enlightenment**. Hence the phrase 'ignorance is bliss', which can be a heaven of sorts. See also: **Christianity**, **Hell**, **Judaism**, **Purgatory**.

Hecate, also **Hekate**, **Trivia**   One of the triple goddesses of Greek myth; she is known as Luna in her guise as moon goddess, Diana as earth goddess and as goddess of the underworld, Hecate or Persephone. She is a creature of black witchcraft and **necromancy**, and is sometimes referred to as the 'Diana of the Crossways' because she presides over places where three roads meet (considered bad luck). Hecate is a significant figure in the rites of the **Eleusinian mysteries**.

Hedge Witch   A woman who is a solitary practitioner of **Wiccan witchcraft**, so-called because of the old tradition of witches planting hedges of hawthorn around their house to mark a sacred boundary. A hedge witch keeps to all of the sacred principles of Wicca, celebrates the **sabbats** and **esbats** that mark the wheel of the witch's year, but does not belong to a group or **coven**.

Hell   A place where the wicked go, after death. Different religions have different ways of depicting this unsavoury afterlife – **Christian** and **Islamic**

tradition believe hell is a fiery pit of eternal torment, while the ancient Greeks and Mesopotamians thought it a sort of grey underworld (like **Hades**). Jewish traditions are caught between the eternal fire of **Gehenna** and the cave-like environs of **she'ol**. Hindis have their Naraka 'situated beneath the earth and beneath the water'. Memorably, Jean-Paul Sartre felt that hell was other people. Wherever hell is, it is an unpleasant dimension and you are better off not planning eternity there. See also: **Heaven**, **Purgatory**.

Hellerwork An offshoot of the bodywork therapy **rolfing**, which uses deep-tissue massage and 'movement reeducation' to relieve muscle pain and tension. Hellerwork was developed by Joseph Heller (no, not of *Catch-22* fame but a NASA aerospace engineer) in the 1980s and is based on his idea that tense, stressed muscles throw the body out of vertical alignment. Once this tension is banished through treatment, the body can return to its proper alignment, producing an improvement in health and spirit. Although not scientifically validated, proponents of Hellerwork testify that it helps ease back and neck pain, and improves impaired mobility and athletic performance.

Hera, also **Juno** The Greek goddess of marriage and childbirth, known as Juno in Roman myth. She was the jealous wife of **Zeus**, king of the gods, best known for creating the peacock, a bird sacred to her. She was one of the Olympiad, the 12 chief gods and goddesses of Greek legend who lived on Mt Olympus.

Herbalism, Herbal Medicine, also **Phytotherapy** The therapeutic use of plants known as herbs to promote healing, cure illness and enhance well-being. Herbal medicine uses all plant parts – leaf, seed, stem, flowers, root, bark – for the relief of certain complaints, conditions and ailments. Like **massage therapy**, herbalism has been known and used as long as there have been people, and even animals instinctively chew on plants they know have a beneficial effect (think of your cat eating grass and you have the theory). Herbs have been used in **witchcraft** and **paganism**, in **magic** rituals, in preserving and flavouring food, as integral parts of religious and spiritual ceremonies, in folk remedies, and in cleansing and purifying toxic environments. Most of our pharmaceutical drugs are based on or derived from healing plants, which are mentioned in scriptures from all the great religions of the world.

Herbs work to do all of these things because of their physiological effect on the body. They work biochemically, triggering neurochemical responses in the body. They contain certain alkaloids (from which more conventional drugs are synthesised) that have specific effects on the body; for example, willow bark is high in salicylic acid, the active ingredient in aspirin. Herbs also have nutrient values to the body that assist growth and stimulate self-healing mechanisms.

There are many systems for using herbs. External systems include **aromatherapy** (in which the essential plant oils are extracted and used on the body), ointments, salves, lotions, poultices, douches or enemas, herbal baths and inhalation. These methods rely on their healing alkaloids being absorbed through the skin (or nasal/intestinal membranes). Internal systems require consumption of herbs to be absorbed through the digestive process and include decoctions, tisanes, infusions, capsules, tablets, tinctures, syrups and mastication (chewing). Either method releases the healing chemicals into the bloodstream through which they eventually reach the brain, which explains the physical neurotransmitter response. What is not as easy to explain is the energetic properties of **life force** that herbs possess, which help to balance the body's essential energies and promote a return to physical and mental health. It is this concept of vibrational bioenergy that explains the healing properties of therapies like **Bach Flower Remedies** and **homeopathy**.

The Western approach to herbal medicine usually applies only one or two herbs to counteract a specific ailment, but Eastern systems like **ayurveda** and **Chinese herbal medicine** utilise a number of plant substances, to arrive at a formula mixed specifically for their patients.

The main thing to remember in herbalism is to consult a properly trained, qualified practitioner – unfortunately there are too often tales of accidental poisonings, organ damage and deaths that occur from the improper use of these plants. See also: **Flower Essences, Vibrational Medicine**.

Hermes, also **Mercury** The Greek messenger of the gods, himself the god of travel, business, wealth, communication and thieves. He is known as **Mercury** in Roman myth. He was the son of **Zeus** and the nymph Maia, and was a rogue of high order. He invented the musical instrument the lyre, which he traded with Apollo for the **caduceus**, a staff with two winged serpents. He is often depicted carrying the caduceus and wearing a hat with wings, to speed him on his messenger duties. He was a member of the Olympiad, the 12 chief gods and goddesses of Greek legend who lived on Mt Olympus.

Hermeticism A belief system based on various occult traditions, including **alchemy**, **astrology** and **theosophy**. Elements of Christian mysticism and the worship of the Graeco-Egyptian god Hermes/Thoth formed the basis of this doctrine. The patron saint of this movement is Hermes Trismegistos, a legendary ancient founder of alchemy who wrote down all of his occult secrets on an 'Emerald Tablet', which was supposedly discovered in the 300s BC and brought to Europe by Alexander the Great. These and other of his writings form a major part of the mystical tracts known as the 'Hermetica'.

Herne, Herne the Hunter In British mythology, the name of the **pagan** horned god of the hunt, animals, death and male fertility. In folklore he is referred to as Jack-in-the-Green, and in Celtic spirituality he is known as **Cernunnos**. Herne is one of the deities worshipped in **Wicca** (called the **horned god**), and is the archetypal nature god, depicted as a stag or bull and sacrificed each year in an endless cycle of life, death and rebirth.

His special festival in the yearly calendar is **Beltane** (also known as May Day), where he symbolically mates with **Aradia**, the earth goddess in her role as maiden, thus ensuring life continues for another year. He is also the leader of the wild hunt, to identify with his prey, and is often depicted careening recklessly over the hills, with the mad scent of the kill in his nostrils. See also: **Celtic Wheel, Green Man, Morris Dancers**.

Hero's Journey The idea that all myths and legends are essentially the same story, that of a 'hero's journey'. **Joseph Campbell**, a noted 'mythologist' and professor of comparative literature, formulated this theory after extensively studying the work of German anthropologist Adolph Bastian (1826–1905) and Swiss psychoanalyst **Carl Jung**. Bastian proposed the idea that myths from all over the world seem to be built from the same 'elementary ideas'. This fitted into Jung's theory of the **collective unconscious** where dwelled **archetypes**, images and figures which represented the entirety of human experience. Campbell took the concept of archetypes and grafted it onto the 'elementary ideas', arguing that all myths deal with the same issues of personal discovery through a quest or journey. He called this the 'monomyth', and it has three main elements to it: Departure, Initiation and Return.

In the first stage, Departure, the hero is untested, usually young and naive, living a pastoral life, or is fundamentally innocent. The father is usually absent from the hero's life in some way, and he has been raised exclusively by his mother, or is an orphan. This is interrupted by the 'call to adventure' – for example a message is delivered, or a mysterious stranger asks for a favour. After some delays, the hero sets out on the journey to complete a quest – finding a lost object, fulfilling a prophecy, etc. The first 'threshold of adventure' is crossed when something unpleasant happens, or a trial is faced (probably not successfully).

This sets the stage for Initiation. No longer completely innocent, the hero sets out to learn how to overcome his trials. He meets and learns from mentors and soldiers how to improve his survival skills, or how to solve the puzzle. Inevitably, there's a girl or goddess, and some sort of temptation that must be overcome. There is a symbolic reconciliation with the father figure and then the hero attains a mythic, godlike status that enables him to complete his quest.

The third stage is the Return, which is usually epitomised by the hero's reluctance either to stop fighting, or to not seek revenge. Eventually there is flight or rescue, and the hero returns, crossing the threshold to home, changed forever by his experiences, and master of both worlds.

Campbell wrote all of this down in *The Hero with a Thousand Faces*, first published in 1948, and still one of the most respected works available on mythology and legends. In it, he compared cultural myths from the Native Americans, ancient Greeks, Hindus, Buddhists and Mayans, as well as Norse and Arthurian legends and the Bible, which illustrated the hero's rite of passage.

The concept of the hero's journey is still echoed in our popular culture, from books like the Harry Potter series and *The Lord of the Rings* trilogy to movies like *Star Wars* and *The Matrix*.

Hexagram A pictorial symbol composed of six lines of varying pattern used in the Chinese oracle, **I Ching**. Each line of a hexagram is composed of either one long, unbroken line, called a 'firm' or **yang** line, or two short lines with a break in the middle, called a 'yielding' or **yin** line. The hexagram itself can be divided into two **trigrams**, which are the building blocks of the 64 possible hexagram symbols.

Ta Yu
wealth

Ch ien
modesty

Y
enthusiasm

Hexagrams

Hierarchy of Needs A theory of motivation formulated by psychologist **Abraham Maslow**, which states that we need to satisfy basic needs for such

Hierarchy of needs

necessities as food, shelter and safety before we can seek to assuage higher-level psychological needs like those for belonging and self-esteem.

He expressed his idea in the form of a pyramid of five motivational factors. At the base of the pyramid, the lowest level, the motivation is provided by Physiological Needs for food, water, shelter, oxygen and sleep. Next up come Safety Needs for security, then up from that come Belonging and Love Needs. At this level, we are motivated by our wish for love, acceptance and belonging. The fourth level up is Esteem Needs for achievement, education, competence and respect. At the apex of the pyramid is the Need for Self-Actualisation, where our motivating factor is the need to realise our fullest potential. Ironically, Maslow discovered that only one per cent of the overall population reach this level, and that typically they were middle-aged or over.

The hierarchy of needs has been applied to many professional fields outside of psychology including sociology, business, medicine and self-development strategies like **neurolinguistic programming**. See also: **Humanistic Psychotherapy**.

Hildegard von Bingen Twelfth-century Christian abbess who experienced ecstatic religious visions after years of dutiful contemplation in a Benedictine monastery. She spent ten years, from 1140 to 1150, recounting her interpretations of these mystic revelations of Christ. Hildegard penned nine books and many poems and songs which survive to this day, including a play set to music called the *Ordo Virtutum*.

This German nun's greatest gift is her wisdom about the healing properties of plants, animals, trees and stones. Hildegard regarded the world as part of God's creation, with every part and power of nature within it divine.

Hinayana Buddhism see **Theravada Buddhism**

Hinduism The third largest religion in the world after **Christianity** and **Islam**. Hinduism is a collection of thousands of different spiritual traditions and multiple deities that originated on the Indian subcontinent. Some believe Hinduism to have one central god, **Brahma**, but others believe in the triad of

Brahma, **Vishnu** (whose incarnation is **Krishna**) and **Shiva** (also known as Mahesh). There are some Hindus who believe in an even greater number of gods and goddesses, all with their place in the pantheon of heaven. All these different sects, however, base their beliefs on a central canon of ideas and hold certain texts sacred to their faith.

Hindus call their religion *Santana Dharma* (Eternal Religion) or *Vaidika Dharma* (Religion of the Vedas), but the term Hinduism is the most commonly used in Western culture. The name 'Hindu' is widely believed to be an ancient Persian corruption of the word Sindu (the river Indus), as the faith may have taken hold in the Indus Valley civilisation sometime between 4000 and 2200 BC.

There are four major texts in the Hindu canon: the **Vedas**, the **Mahabharata**, the **Upanishads** and the **Ramayana**. From these works come the major gods and goddesses, and the major beliefs. Central to all is the idea of the '**transmigration** of the soul'. Hindus believe in **samsara**, also known as the 'wheel of rebirth'. Everyone is caught up in a cycle of birth, life, disease, old age, death and reincarnation, caused by a bad **karma** of greed, hatred and ignorance. After you leave this earthly existence (i.e. you die) your soul is put back into another body – not necessarily human. Because it is possible that any living creature could be a reincarnated person, Hindus believe in non-violence towards any life form, which is why you often see cows with garlands in India.

The only way to escape samsara is to achieve **enlightenment** in this lifetime; you can do that by following the three aims of Hinduism. They are **karma** (action), **bhakti** (devotion), and **jnana** (contemplation). Then you will attain **moksha**, the ultimately blissful goal of liberation from endless death and rebirth.

One of the more controversial aspects of Hinduism has been the **caste system**. Although abolished by law in 1949, it is still influential in Indian culture.

There are two great festivals of Hinduism. The first is Holi, the Hindu new year held on the last full moon day at the beginning of spring. It is a fresh start, transcending barriers, and all grievances are forgotten. The second is **Diwali**, also known as the 'festival of lights'. Celebrated in late October/early November, it is a family-orientated holiday symbolising the victory of righteousness and the lifting of spiritual darkness. Relatives and friends gather together to offer prayers, celebrate and distribute sweets to the less fortunate.

Hippocrates (460–377 BC) Greek physician traditionally accepted as the father of Western medicine, and supposed author of the eponymous oath of all doctors: 'first do no harm'. Hippocrates felt that healing could not take place without considering the entire person, the *holos.* He also formed the theory of 'like cures like' that was later incorporated into the **Law of Similars** in **homeopathy**. He strongly believed in the healing powers of herbs and **massage**, so in effect you could say he was the world's first **holistic** practitioner.

Hippomancy (Greek *hippos*, 'horse', + *manteia*, 'divination') A form of **divination** using horses. Although known in other ancient cultures, it was especially popular among the Dark Age Celts of England and Ireland, who would keep white horses in a sacred grove of trees for this purpose. These horses were made to walk straight after being hitched to a sacred cart and auguries were drawn from their movements and neighing to predict the likely outcome of events. This is a form of **augury**, divining the future based on various signs and omens mostly related to animals.

Holism also **Holistic, Holistic Medicine, Holistic Therapy** (Greek *holos*, 'whole') A philosophy or therapeutic routine that aims to treat the whole person, mind, body and spirit, rather than just the symptoms of the diseases or imbalances they are showing. To holistic practitioners, the underlying cause of illness may not be physical in origin, so it is useless just to treat its physical manifestations. The intention of holistic therapy is less to intervene (in the form of surgery and drugs), thus only allowing the patient to take a passive role, than to encourage the patient to be active in their recovery, either through a change in lifestyle or in thinking patterns. The therapist assists in this return to health through the use of body treatments such as massage, reflexology or acupuncture, or through administering remedies from homeopathy or herbalism, all of which will have an effect on the essential energies of the patient in question.

Holistic therapies often have a higher rate of success than orthodox medicine in helping people manage non-critical, chronic illnesses. See also: **Alternative Therapy, Energy Medicine.**

Holly A flower essence made from the holly bush. This emotionally healing tincture is one of the **Bach Flower Remedies**. Dr Bach said that this is indicated for 'hatred, envy, suspicion, revenge, jealousy – all the feelings that eat away at the love within us'.

Holy Grail According to Christian tradition, the cup used by **Jesus Christ** at the Last Supper, and supposedly brought to Britain by Joseph of Arimathea. It was thought the Grail was a magic vessel with miraculous healing powers.

The origin of this part of the myth seems to lie in old Celtic tales about magic cauldrons like the goddess **Ceridwen's cauldron of inspiriation**. The Grail is also a symbol of purity and virtue, and for that reason it was sought after by **King Arthur** and his Knights of the Round Table. See also: **Arthurian Legends**.

Homeopathy (Greek *homolos*, 'same', + *pathos*, 'suffering') The alternative medical system based on the principles that 'like cures like'. The theory behind homeopathy is that substances that make you ill in large doses can also cure, in small enough doses. These diluted substances can be made from plants, minerals or animal products (like bee stings).

The founder of homeopathy, **Dr Samuel Hahnemann** (1755–1843), was an early nineteenth-century German physician who became disillusioned with the medical standards of his time. He formulated homeopathic principles based on a number of experiments on himself and other willing subjects. Through many years he assembled a basic stable of homeopathic remedies and practices. His work was carried on and developed by a number of other practitioners, most notably the American physician Dr Constantine Hering (1849–1916) who wrote the *Repertory to the Homeopathic Materia Medica*, which gives practitioners a framework for defining how to match remedies to personality types.

There are four basic principles to classic homeopathy. The first is the **law of similars** (like cures like). The second is the **minimum dose** (the right dilution of the right substance) and the third is the **single remedy** (the one substance that most closely models a disease's symptom is the right remedy). The idea of treating with just one remedy has been supplanted in recent practice by a more accurate mix of several remedies. The fourth and final idea is to treat the whole person, not just the symptoms. The reason for this **holistic** treatment is the **vital force** (life energy, similar to **chi**) present in every individual. Homeopaths believe their remedies work because the correct potions vibrate at the same energetic frequency as the individual being treated. This harmonious resonance stimulates the body's immune response, and allows healing to take place.

The idea of sympathetic energy vibrations is why homeopaths ask so many questions of their patients. In order to prescribe the right remedy, they need to determine which one of 15 **constitutional types** is predominant in your personality. If the wrong remedy is given, nothing happens with the body/remedy energies. If the right one is given, the mutual buzz sets off self-healing. As most people are a combination of constitutional types, it will often take a careful combination of different remedies to effectively treat a physical or mental ailment, particularly if it is of long duration.

There are 15 different premier remedies (called **polychrests**) that lend their name to the different constitutional types, although there are 72 standard remedies used by qualified homeopaths. See also: **Doctrine of Signatures, Potencies, Tincture, Vibrational Medicine**.

Honey A natural product with significant healing properties, produced by bees from flower nectar. Because of this curative power, honey was once thought of as the 'nectar of the gods' (so believed the medieval Christian saint, St Ambrose) and the **Bible** speaks of the Promised Land as 'flowing with milk and honey'. Babylonians worshipped a honey deity, and honey was used in their sacrificial offerings to the gods as protection against witchcraft.

Ancient cultures knew of honey's potency, particularly in healing wounds and skin inflammations, and it is mentioned in the **Vedas**, the **Koran** and the **Talmud**. In Egypt, honey was used on surgical dressings, the Chinese used it to treat smallpox scars, and **Hippocrates** thought it had the ability to heal ulcers. It was a common ingredient in medieval medicinal potions, and even used in World War I to treat burns, bedsores and wound-related skin ulcers.

Honey works both internally and externally. It is an easily digestible, nutritious source of energy, suitable for convalescents and other fragile people. In concentrated doses, honey has been shown to kill the *Helicobacter pylori*, the bacterium that causes many gastric ulcers. The small amount of pollen present in honey, ingested over time, has alleged benefits for asthma and allergy sufferers. On external wounds, honey works because of its high sugar content, which creates an atmosphere hostile to bacteria.

Honey completes its reputation as a miracle worker by being considered a potent aphrodisiac and fertility potion in many different world cultures; the ancient Greeks took it mixed with milk and with 'the meat of an ass' to raise their ardour. It was also a standard ingredient in the Sultan of Istanbul's harems, and in Hindu India it is still given to a groom on his wedding day.

Honeysuckle A flower essence made from the honeysuckle blossom. This emotionally healing tincture is one of the **Bach Flower Remedies**. Dr Bach said that this is indicated for 'those who thoughts linger in the past at the expense of their enjoyment of the present: when the mind dwells on happy memories, relives some unpleasant incident or yearns for how things used to be'.

Hornbeam A flower essence made from the blossom of the hornbeam bush. This emotionally healing tincture is one of the **Bach Flower Remedies**. Dr Bach said that this is indicated for 'those who feel they have insufficient strength to face the day ahead, or task at hand. Those who procrastinate and put things off until tomorrow'.

Horned God Generic term for a plethora of different male gods in **paganism**, mythology and **magic** traditions. Some version of a horned god appears in almost every culture in the world, where he is traditionally associated with the hunt, animals and male fertility. In **witchcraft** he is the symbol of male sexuality, and when **Morris dancers** go about with antlers on their head, they are depicting the Horned One. Jack-of-the-Green, Pan, **Cernunnos**, **Herne the Hunter**, Dionysus and Bacchus are but a few of his names.

In **Christianity**, this term is used to describe **Satan**, the fallen angel and chief architect of evil in the world. It is thought that 'Horned One' was ascribed to the Devil when the Christian Church was in the process of converting formerly pagan societies and wanted to discourage worship of the old gods.

Horoscope (Greek *hora*, 'time', + *skopos*, 'observer') In **astrology**, a map of the heavens at one specific point in time, which details the positioning of the planets in the **zodiac** signs and **houses**. Astrologers interpret the location of particular planets in this celestial diagram, and their relationship to a person's birth sign, to make a prediction for the future. The most important horoscope is your **birth chart**, which determines your **sun sign** and is the jumping-off point for other horoscope charts that may be drawn up for you thereafter. Horoscopes can be done to determine the most favourable conditions for any particular event or venture.

Where you were born is as significant as *when* you were born. The date and time of your birth determines your sun sign, but the place you were born will portray where the planets lie on the horizon and define your **ascendant** or rising sign. This in turn determines where the planets fall in the **houses** of your birth chart. Both signs and houses are significant in defining who you are, and what the future holds for you.

Horse, The In **Chinese astrology**, the seventh sign of the **zodiac**. You are a Horse if you were or will be born in the years 1930, 1942, 1954, 1966, 1978, 1990, 2002 or 2014. The Horse is the sign of ardour in Chinese mythology, symbolising prestige and a distinguished career. Those born under this sign are cheerful and independent, and possess immense charm. They are outgoing individuals who work with incredible stamina. Horses can be restless and impatient, however, but can usually salvage a situation with their own brand of charisma. Their Western zodiac equivalent is **Gemini** and their ruling planet is **Mercury**.

Horseshoes A general symbol of good luck, especially if the shoe is found by chance. Although mainly used now to decorate greetings cards and wedding cakes, they were originally believed to be a powerful form of protection against witchcraft. The horseshoe would be nailed above a door, so that evil would be unable to enter an abode. Their protective power came from being made out of iron, a substance fatal to witches, **fairies** and other malevolent spirits. Whether placed over a door or worn as an ornament, horseshoes must be placed with open ends uppermost or the luck will run out. See also: **Evil Eye**.

Horus, also **Harseisis, Hr, Hru** The sky god in Egyptian mythology, who in some traditions is the son of **Osiris** and **Isis** and in others Osiris' brother. The name Horus is a general catch-all for many different Egyptian warrior gods; he is most often depicted as a hawk or as a hawk-headed man, bearing a sword.

His eyes were the sun and the moon. On the nights of new moons, he would be blind, and considered dangerous as he might inadvertently hurt someone in his warrior's rage. His consort is **Hathor**, and he avenged the death of his father Osiris by overcoming **Seth**, his brother and murderer.

House In **astrology**, the heavens taken as a 360-degree circle divided into 12 sections. These sections (which correlate to two hours of time in our 24-hour day) are referred to by their numbers, such as 'the first house', 'the second house', etc., and speak to a particular component of one's life like home, career, money or relationships. They are each influenced or 'ruled' by a particular planet and sun sign. See also: **Ascendant, Horoscope**.

Human Design System A recent self-actualisation theory designed by Canadian teacher and poet Ra Uru Hu, which determines whether or not your inherent 'nature' is fixed by genetics or open to change. A complex chart is drawn up that involves your date, time and place of birth, and determines where you fall into one of five basic genetic types. Included also are elements of DNA amino acid groupings as well as **I Ching** astrology, all of which help you answer the question: Can I change?

Human Potential Movement A **holistic** self-development and spiritual movement based on **transpersonal** and **humanistic psychology**, and the ideas of **G.I. Gurdjieff**. In order to achieve your full potential as a person, you need to examine your past behaviours, thoughts and experiences, sometimes evoking unpleasant memories. The movement started in the early part of the twentieth century, but did not reach its apotheosis until the early 1960s in California, with centres (most notably the Esalen Institute) for therapies like primal scream therapy, EST and transactional analysis. There, participants eager to attain their potential would subject themselves to difficult physical and verbal sessions designed to break down the ego barriers of the past.

Since then, people have found less painful ways of developing the self, and the human potential movement has fallen out of fashion.

Humanistic Psychology An approach to psychology that emphasises personal growth and how to achieve your full potential. Its prime founder and philosopher is Abraham Maslow, who is best known for formulating the **hierarchy of needs**. He, along with George Kelly and Carl Rogers, developed humanistic psychology to deal with concerns they felt other schools of psychotherapy, like behaviourism and psychoanalysis, ignored. Theirs was a **holistic** approach, to consider a person's conscious and unconscious thoughts and behaviours, instead of just what may be at work beneath the surface in the unconscious mind. Humanistic psychotherapists also believe in the genuine good of the individual, and that, despite setbacks, we all strive to be better than ourselves. Humanists also pay attention to the spiritual dimension of someone's personality, using the concepts of **yin** and **yang** to explain character traits.

This positive view of human nature has deeply influenced **new age** thought and holistic healing therapies, including the **human potential movement**.

Huna The native religion of Hawaii, based on a belief system of healing magic and nature spirits. The philosophy of ancient Polynesian healers, which lay at the heart of this religion, can be summarised in the following seven principles: the world is what you think it is; there are no limits; energy flows where attention goes; now is the moment of power; to love is to be happy with; all power comes from within; and effectiveness is the measure of truth. Master healers are known as **kahunas**.

Hunch A feeling or guess based more on **intuition** than on hard facts. People with **psychic** abilities often report making decisions based on hunches rather than logic. See also: **Extra-sensory Perception, Precognition**.

Hundredth Monkey A phenomenon noticed among a group of monkeys, which prompted biologist Rupert Sheldrake to formulate the theory of **morphic resonance**. A study on the behaviour of macaques (rhesus monkeys) was conducted between 1952 and 1962 by a group of Japanese primatologists, on Koshina Islet off the coast of Japan. Monkeys on the island started to eat sweet potatoes left for them on a sandy beach. One young monkey discovered that rinsing them in the sea was an effective way to get rid of the sand sticking to them, and soon all the monkeys on the island copied him. When the hundredth monkey did this, something happened. On a neighbouring island that had no physical contact with the first island, observers suddenly noticed that all the monkeys on *that* island and the mainland were also starting to wash their sweet potatoes in the sea before eating them. This phenonenon was first documented by Lyall Watson in his 1979 work *Lifetide*, but was popularised by noted American author Ken Keyes Jr in his book *The Hundredth Monkey*.

This phenomenon is also used as a way to describe the mass power of a group of like-minded individuals, when suddenly there appears to be a mass-transfer of information without any communication; the likes of which were hitherto only known by a chosen few of the group.

Hydromancy, also **Hydrascopy**, **Ydromancy** (Greek *hudro*, 'water', + *manteia*, 'divination') An ancient way of predicting the future by means of water or rain. Water was considered a sacred element by most cultures and therefore incorruptible. Because of this quality, it would always show the truth of a person or situation.

This form of **divination** used several different methods to reach its conclusions. The colour, ripples and speed of water flowing in a river or artificial stream were studied and interpretations made based on the patterns formed. Another method would be to drop a stone in water and count the subsequent number of circles formed. A third method would use a ring suspended by a string and dipped into a vessel of water. The number of times the ring would strike the side of the container, and the number of ripples it created when it hit the water, would be considered of great portent.

Many other forms of hydromancy exist, some quite grisly. An ancient German custom was to throw newborn children of questionable parentage into a sacred spring or river. If the child was a bastard, he would drown. If he was legitimate, he would swim and be saved. Variations on this theme ultimately led to the seventeenth-century practice of throwing suspected witches into water to prove or disprove themselves guilty of witchcraft.

Hydrotherapy, also **Hydropathy** (Greek *hudro*, 'water', + *therapeia*, 'healing')
The use of water in the treatment of illness and disease. It is also deeply
relaxing, so is often used for stress-related conditions.

The healing powers of water have been known since prehistory and every
culture has stories of sacred springs and pools with miraculous cures attached
to them. Baths and bathing for therapeutic purposes formed a large part of
ancient Greek, Egyptian, Indian and Native American practice, and were
important to social life in Roman society.

There are two schools of hydrotherapy: the medical and the spiritual. The
medical approach uses mechanical and thermal aspects of water to stimulate
healing. It exploits the body's reaction to hot and cold, and to the effects of
pressure and sensation on the skin. Nerves stimulated by water at the surface
of the body help to kick-start the immune system, lessen the production of
stress hormones, invigorate the circulation and digestion and relieve pain.

In general, hot water quiets and soothes the body, and cold water
stimulates. Common techniques include baths and showers, steam inhalation,
hot and cold compresses, body wraps and douches.

The spiritual approach uses the same methods but the intention is
different. Water, like any natural element, has energetic qualities. It is one of,
if not the most important, substances to life and can be used to help balance
the flow of energy in a sick or ailing person. Water treatments can be external
(like those described above) or internal. 'Taking the waters' to aid health is a
very old tradition, and while this can be done to imbibe the minerals in the
liquid, it can also help flush toxins out of the body. Healing energies can also
be directed into water via **vibrational medicine**, or **magnet therapy**, which
enhances the already positive energy field water possesses.

Hypericum, also **St John's wort** (Greek *hyper*, 'over', + *eikon*, 'apparation')
The plant *Hypericum perforatum*, whose dried tops and flowers are used in **herbal
medicine** to treat a variety of ailments. The best-known use of hypericum, or
St John's wort as it is more commonly known, is to treat depression and
seasonal affective disorder, and in Germany it is prescribed more often than
any pharmaceutical antidepressant, with few side effects noted. This plant has
been known since the time of the ancient Greeks to be effective in treating a
troubled mind, and was used to vanquish evil spirits and ghosts thought to
cause mental illness.

Early Christians believed the herb first grew when St John the Baptist was
beheaded on the orders of King Herod, as its flower petals ooze crimson resin
when rubbed.

The active ingredient in hypericum is a substance called 'hypericin', which in clinical trials has been shown to stabilise the brain's level of the 'happy' chemical serotonin. It is also effective in treating premenstrual tension, anxiety and insomnia, and helps in reducing inflammation in wounded areas.

Hypericum is also the name of a homeopathic remedy used to treat wounds and is said to have anti-tetanus properties. This remedy can also relieve nerve pain, such as sciatica, and is the number one remedy for whiplash.

Hypnosis, Hypnotism The induction of a half-waking, half-sleeping state of awareness, where a person apparently loses voluntary control over their thoughts and actions, and is receptive to suggestions made to them during this state. Hypnosis bypasses the conscious mind, with all of its ego blocks and ingrained thoughts and habits, and allows the hypnotist to contact the unconscious directly. Hypnosis works by invoking a **trance** in the subject through various concentration and relaxation exercises.

Friedrich Anton Mesmer (1733–1815), an Austrian doctor, used magnets to practise a form of hypnotism he called 'animal magnetism'. Although he was later branded a stage charlatan, his ideas about the trance state intrigued a Scottish doctor, James Braid, who developed Mesmer's techniques into a more reputable science.

Hypnosis is currently used in three ways: the first, stage hypnosis, is meant mostly as entertainment, where the hypnotised subject often carries out silly pranks while in a trance. A second use of hypnosis is to help the subject recall details their waking mind may have forgotten. This is the sort of hypnosis sometimes carried out on witnesses by the police. The third, **hypnotherapy**, is a therapeutic tool used to bring about positive change in a person's habits or health. Self-hypnosis would fall under this category, because of the emphasis on self-improvement. See also: **Mesmerism.**

Hypnotherapy (Greek *hupnos*, 'sleep', + *therapia*, 'healing') A therapy that uses hypnosis to overcome physical, mental and emotional ailments. Hypnosis is the induction of a half-waking, half-sleeping state of awareness, where a person apparently loses voluntary control over their thoughts and actions, and is receptive to suggestions made to them during this state. Hypnosis bypasses the conscious mind, with all of its ego blocks and ingrained thoughts and habits, and allows the hypnotherapist to directly contact the unconscious. This communication allows the suggestion of healthy ideas to be implanted in a person's subconscious, and makes it easier to break bad habits. Hypnotherapy is particularly useful in treating the following conditions: post-traumatic stress disorder, phobias, bedwetting in children, smoking, eating disorders, irritable bowel syndrome, panic attacks, weight loss and low self-confidence.

In a typical session, a reputable therapist will discuss with you your reasons for wanting to undergo hypnosis as well as what you would like to accomplish, and take a full physical and mental health history. The first step to inducing a **trance** state is a series of relaxation exercises. The therapist will deepen this state by engaging you in visualising a particular place you find relaxing, safe and calm. How long it will take you to fall into a trance will depend upon your susceptibility to being hypnotised (everyone is different). Once in a trance, the hypnotherapist will address your subconscious mind with helpful suggestions, like, 'When you smoke you will find each cigarette less satisfying than the last one,' or 'When you see a spider, you will feel relaxed and not run out of the room shrieking for your husband to come and kill this teeny, tiny creature.' Before you are brought back to total awarenesses you may be given a post-hypnotic suggestion that enables you to self-induce the same state of relaxation and suggestion (called self-hypnosis).

Hypnotherapy has been proven to have a high rate of success in helping people make positive changes in their lives, but carries some bad press from work carried out by charlatans or 'stage hypnosis' pranks that backfire. The best way to guard against this is to only go to a reputable practitioner with documented success, ideally a psychologist who practises hypnotherapy.

I Ching (Chinese 'Book of Changes') Chinese book of advice and **divination** in use for over 3,000 years. Its origins are lost in myth but the inspiration for it is said to be cracks on the shell of a legendary Emperor's pet tortoise sometime in the twenty-fourth century BC. Certainly by 1000 BC it was in use and the philosopher sage **Confucius** wrote down interpretative meanings for each of the possible pictograms during the sixth century BC.

The connection to a tortoise's shell becomes apparent when you look at the I Ching, which consists of a set of 64 **hexagrams**, a symbol composed of six lines of varying pattern. Which hexagram applies to your situation is dependent upon you casting down coins, yarrow sticks or stones to create two sets of **trigrams**. Trigrams are three lines of **yin and yang** that represent the natural **elements**, and are the building blocks of all hexagrams. There are eight possible combinations of trigrams, each with particular attributes and qualities associated with them. Once all the sticks or coins have been thrown and the hexagram constructed, the I *Ching* is consulted to interpret the resulting pictorial diagram.

Prior to casting and consulting the I *Ching* as an oracle, it is recommended that you meditate or otherwise calm your mind. The Chinese believe that your conscious mind power and energy determine which hexagram is constructed and jangling, cluttered thoughts combined with a lack of focus tend to produce false results.

While time-consuming and difficult to understand, the I *Ching* is considered an infallible source of divination, respected by such figures as **Carl Jung** and the Dalai Lama for its accuracy and relevance. See also: **Taoism**.

IQ, also **Intelligence Quotient** A numeric rating of your intelligence, based on answers to a standardised test of different measures of brain function such as spatial and verbal ability, numeric reasoning and memory. This 'score' is based on the ratio between your mental age and chronological age. The average IQ is 100, with 95 per cent of the population testing between 70 and 130. Those above 130 are considered to be 'geniuses'.

The whole IQ testing system has come under recent scrutiny because of the way in which the test is administered, and the conditions of testing can influence the score, especially if the tester and test-taker do not come from the same cultural background. See also: **Emotional Intelligence**, **Psychometric Test**.

Icthyomancy (Greek *ikhthus*, 'fish', + *manteia*, 'divination') A form of **divination**, mostly outdated, examining the shape and/or entrails of a fish for significant omens. See also: **Augury**.

Id (Latin, 'it') According to **Sigmund Freud**, the unconscious part of the mind that represents the instincts, whose focus is on gratification of biological drives like sex, thirst and hunger. This dark, inaccessible area of the personality has only one reality – to satisfy its own selfish needs. When a child is born, the id is all that there is to his persona. As the child grows and develops, the **ego** and **superego** step in to control the id in socially acceptable ways. The id is also the seat of primitive emotions like anger and fear, and its desires are expressed through dreams, which is why Freud thought their interpretation was an important part of the psychoanalytical process.

Ignatia One of the 15 major **polychrests**, or major remedies in **homeopathy**. It is also a **constitutional type**, which is a way homeopaths have of classifying different patient profiles. The fitting constitutional remedy acts preventatively and curatively on its matching personality types – for example, a person with an Ignatia constitution will respond well to the Ignatia remedy almost regardless of the illness they are suffering from. Ignatia people are likely to be dark-haired women with a dreamy, artistic nature. They have a tendency to be clingy in relationships and often suffer from mood swings. They are prone to nervous and digestive upsets, as well as sore throats, and are very sensitive to pain. The biggest use of the Ignatia remedy is for acute emotional trauma, like grief, hysteria due to a relationship break-up, etc.

Illuminati A secret brotherhood of magical practitioners, called **adepts**, who have received this esoteric knowledge through 'illumination' from an outside, transcendent deity or entity. This brotherhood was rumoured to have started with the ancient Egyptians (although this cannot be verified) and became most popular in Europe in the mid-eighteenth to mid-nineteenth centuries. Although the concept of 'illuminati' has been known to mystic occult societies since the Middle Ages, it has been popularised in recent years by the writings of Robert Anton Wilson and Stuart Wilde.

Imbolc, also **Candlemas, St Brigid's Day** (Celtic 'in the belly of the womb') The **pagan** celebration that marks the halfway point between winter and spring (29 January–2 February). Imbolc celebrates the return of light to the world after dark winter. Christianised as 'Candlemas', it is traditionally when all the candles for the coming year would be made, to symbolise the light coming out of darkness. It is one of the four great **sabbats** (holy days) of a **witch**'s year; she marks it together with other magic practitioners with feasting, rites and bonfires.

Imbolc also celebrates the Celtic goddess **Brigid** (who later became St Brigid in Christian tradition). Brigid was the goddess of inspiration and the arts, and this was considered an auspicious time of year for planting seeds of thought, thus incubating creative and artistic ideas. One of the customs associated with Imbolc was making a 'Bridie doll', a female figure constructed from a sheaf of oats and dressed up in women's clothing. Later in the year, the

Bridie doll would be buried in the earth as part of fertility rites. See also: **Celtic Wheel**, **Paganism**.

Impatiens A flower essence made from the impatiens blossom. This emotionally healing tincture is one of the **Bach Flower Remedies**. Dr Bach said that this is indicated for 'those who are inclined to impatience and irritation with slowness. They want things done in a hurry and are therefore in a hurry themselves'.

Incantation (Latin *incantare*, 'chant, bewitch') A series of words used in **magic**, to infuse power into spells or charms. Incantations worked because they supposedly invoked sacred vibrations, which would reach a god or deity and connect you to their source of power. They can be used either for good (as in white magic) or for ill (as in sorcery and black magic).

Incubus A male **demon** or **spirit** who disturbs the sleep of a woman, often subjecting her to horrifying nightmares or unpleasant sexual intercourse. Think *Rosemary's Baby*. The female equivalent of the incubus is the **succubus**.

Indian Head Massage, also **Champissage** (Sanskrit *champi*, 'head') A **holistic** massage technique that involves working along specific points on the head, to stimulate the flow of **prana** (the body's energetic life force). This massage encourages the body to heal and to rebalance itself. It is based on principles found in **ayurvedic medicine**, the ancient healing system of India. Practised in that country for over a thousand years, champissage has a number of health and beauty benefits. It stimulates the circulation of the scalp, which nourishes the hair roots, and leads to fuller, thicker hair. It releases tension in the head, neck and shoulder muscles, and can help with the pain of migraines or jaw problems like Temporomandibular joint syndrome (TMJ), especially if any of these conditions are due to stress. It also helps the body to remove waste and toxins that are clogging up the system, by stimulating both blood and lymph circulation. Finally, it is incredibly relaxing, and people report feeling both calmed and energised after a treatment.

Inedia see Breatharism

Integral Yoga see Yoga

Intuition (Latin *intueri*, 'consider') The ability to understand something immediately through instinct rather than analytical thought or conscious reasoning. In its most extreme form, intuition can be considered **extra-sensory perception (ESP)**.

Iridology The study of the iris of the eye in order to diagnose health imbalances in the body. Iridologists believe that different areas of the iris represent different parts of the body and if you see discoloration, flecks, streaks or marks in one eye area, the corresponding body area will likely be ailing. Even if illness or disease is not present, it can show an area that is weak and where you should watch your health.

Iridology also classifies people as belonging to one of three constitutional

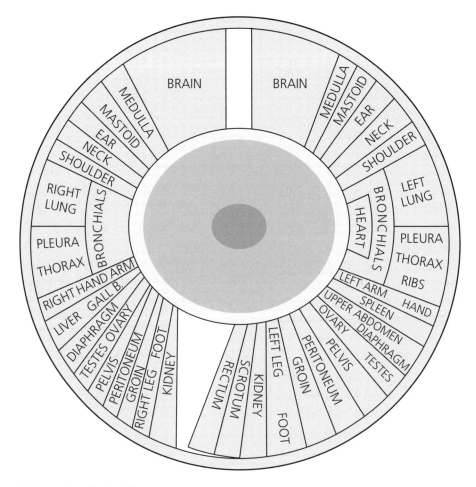

Iridology chart for the left eye

types. Blue and grey-eyed people are lymphatic constitutional types. They are prone to health problems like skin, throat and lung irritations, catarrh, diarrhoea, arthritis, eye irritations and fluid retention. Brown-eyed people are haematogenic constitutional types, and tend towards blood diseases like anaemia, hepatitis, jaundice, muscle spasms, digestive disorders, diabetes and circulatory disorders. Finally come hazel-eyed (part blue/brown or green/brown) people, called the biliary constitutional type. These poor chaps are prone to all of the woes of blue and brown-eyed types but have the added burden of a tendency to flatulence and constipation as well.

Iridology works best as a diagnostic tool and as a way to guard against future illness, and naturopaths combine it with other therapies to improve health. Despite the accuracy that iridology has shown in correlating iris marks with ill-health, it is not accepted in conventional medicine circles. See also: **Naturopathy**.

Isis (Egyptian, 'throne') One of the major goddesses of Egyptian mythology, who was the consort of the god **Osiris** and mother to **Horus**, the sky god. Isis had magical powers and was one of the nine gods of the **Ennead** council of deities. She was a fertility goddess, sometimes depicted as a woman with a ceremonial headpiece of horns and sun disk, and often associated with another goddess, **Hathor**.

Isis is best known for her part in the Osiris myths. After he was dismembered by his brother **Seth**, Isis searched for the missing pieces of her husband's body and magically reassembled it so he could travel to the afterlife, and so she could bear his son, Horus. She raised Horus in secret, and when Horus was grown he avenged his father's death by killing Seth.

Isis was one of the most popular of Egyptian goddesses, and she had many temples erected in her honour well into the Roman era. She is still revered in many **goddess** traditions, including witchcraft and **Wicca**, as a powerful figure of fertility and magic.

Islam (Arabic *salam*, 'submission or peace') The second largest religion in the world, based on the central belief that there is only one god, Allah, whose final prophet and true messenger was **Muhammad**. It is sometimes termed an 'Abramic religion' as it arose out of the covenant that the Jewish prophet Abraham made with the Lord.

Muhammad the Prophet (570–632) founded Islam around AD 622, in the city of **Mecca**. He received a revelation from the angel Gabriel to convert his countrymen from their pagan, polytheistic beliefs and deliver them from their moral oppression and decadence. Islam quickly grew and by AD 750 had spread as far east as China and as far west as Spain.

The fundamental beliefs in Islam are that there is a single, indivisible God (Allah is the Arabic word for God). Second, that Muhammad was the final messenger of God in a line that included Adam, Noah, Abraham, Moses, David and Jesus. Therefore all the writings of these prophets – the **Torah**, the **Bible** and the **Koran** – are sacred scriptures. Like those of Jewish and Christian faith, Muslims believe in a day of judgement after death, where unbelievers and sinners will be punished and the righteous will be rewarded with a place beside God in paradise. Muslims do not, however, believe that Jesus was the son of God and the only route to heaven. Instead, to return to God it is only necessary to sincerely repent of your sins and submit your will to Allah.

The five central practices of Muslim faith are called the **five pillars of Islam**. All Muslims must perform the sacred duties of the pillars, to be true to their religion. These form the framework of a Muslim's life, and are based on admonitions from the divine prophet Muhammad, in the holy book the Koran. They are: **Shahadah**, the declaration of faith; **Salah**, the routine of daily prayers; **Sawm**, fasting during the holy month of **Ramadan**; **Zakah**, tithing a percentage of assets to charity; and **Hajj**, the pilgrimage to Mecca, which every Muslim who can afford it must make once in a lifetime.

There are three main sects of Islam. Sunni Muslims constitute 90 per cent of all believers, and follow three main sources of Islamic law: the Koran, the Hadith (the Prophet's teachings and sayings), and consensus of Muslims. They are mainstream traditionalists, who are comfortable pursuing their faith within secular societies.

Shi'ite Muslins are followers of the Jafri school, and constitute less than 10 per cent of all Muslims. Their leaders promote a strict interpretation of the Koran and close adherence to its teachings. They also believe that there were 12 Imams (perfect teachers) who followed the Prophet with holy writings. The twelfth and final Imam has yet to appear, but when he does will guide all humans to justice and peace.

The third sect, with only a small percentage of followers, is the mystic tradition of **Sufism**. Sufis believe that it is possible to commune with Allah in this life, not the next, and strive for altered states of consciousness through mysticism and prayer.

There are no organised holidays in the Muslim calendar outside of the ninth month of the Islamic calendar, called Ramadan. During this holy month, fasting is required from just before dawn until sunset, as ordered by Allah in the Koran.

Muslims must also follow other precepts – they should avoid consuming alcohol and drugs and eating unclean foods (especially pork), and refrain from gambling.

Isolation Tank   see Flotation Therapy

Iyengar Yoga   see Yoga

Jade   A **crystal** gem that is said to have great powers of healing and protection. Jade remains the crystal most revered by the Chinese, where traditionalists still think it is of divine origin. Jade was also sacred to the ancient Egyptians, who believed it was associated with Maat, goddess of truth. When given as a gift, it was said to bring good fortune. Jade is reputed to help strengthen the heart, kidneys and immune system by cleansing the blood, also to enhance fertility and dispel negative emotions. In magic, jade is used to help you remember your dreams and use them to solve your problems.

Jainism   (Sanskrit *jina*, 'the conqueror') An Indian belief system that follows the philosophy of Mahavira, a contemporary of **Gautama Buddha**. Many Jainist beliefs are similar to those found in both **Buddhism** and **Hinduism**, with a few important differences. Jainists do not accept the authority of the **Vedas**, the ancient scriptures of India that show how you can reach enlightenment. Instead, they believe that only by achieving complete purity of the soul can one attain liberation. It is an austere sect, advocating fasting, meditation and living in solitude. Fundamental is the concept of *ahisma*, 'non-violence', so strict Jainists will not even step on an insect lest they kill it. That is why they famously are always seen carrying a broom – they sweep the path in front of them as they walk, to avoid stepping on anything, and wear a cloth over their mouths just in case they inhale a fly (never a pleasant thing).

The other four virtues they follow are truth-speaking, not stealing, chastity and non-attachment to worldly things. These, plus their other two requisites for salvation – right faith and right knowledge – are the Jain commandments. Jainism is mostly restricted to India, with approximately three million practising believers.

Jesus Christ (Greek *khristos*, 'anointed one' translating Hebrew *masiah* 'messiah'). A Jewish itinerant preacher, born in the Judean province of the Roman empire (modern-day Palestine) sometime between 4 and 7 BC, who Christians believe was the Son of God. Muslims believe that Jesus was one of Allah's prophets, succeeded by his last and great prophet, Muhammad. Although Jesus was proclaimed in his day as the long-awaited saviour of the Jewish people, most schools of Judaism do not accept that he is the Messiah prophesised in their scriptures.

There is no evidence to suggest that Jesus actually existed outside of the anecdotes told of his miraculous birth, life, death and ministry in the New Testament of the Christian Bible, most specifically the Gospels of Matthew, Mark, Luke and John. Matthew and John were the only two to have contact with Jesus during his lifetime; Mark was the nephew of the apostle Peter, and Luke was a Greek physician who converted to Christianity after Jesus' death and resurrection. Regardless of the lack of empirical documentation, Jesus has had a profound effect on the life and history of a large majority of the world's population, with Christianity the single largest religious tradition in existence. See also: **Christianity, Islam, Judaism, Virgin Mary.**

Jing, Jing Essence The word for the essential, ephemeral fluid of the body in Chinese medicine and philosophy. Along with **chi** (energy) and **shen** (spirit) it constitutes one of the main forces in the human body and is an essence inherited from our parents at birth that determines how robust our constitution will be, according to **Traditional Chinese Medicine.** The amount of jing at birth is the quantity we have for the rest of our life and can only be diminished, never replenished. A good example of a person with weak jing is one who develops dark circles under their eyes that do not go away despite treatment and rest. As jing is depleted, the body ages. When jing is gone, we die. It is also referred to as 'kidney energy' because it is circulated through the blood and the energy of blood is stored in the kidneys.

Jinx (US *jynx*, 'wryneck') Slang term for anything that brings bad luck, derived from the name of a Native American species of bird which was used in **witchcraft** rituals.

Jivi Mukti Yoga   see **Yoga, Hatha**

Jnana (Sanskrit, 'contemplation') One of the three aims of **Hinduism**, jnana is engaging in contemplative acts like study and **meditation** in order to increase your knowledge of higher consciousness. Seeking jnana, along with performing **bhakti** (devotion) and changing your **karma** (actions) will allow you to attain **moksha**, the ultimately blissful goal of liberation from endless death and rebirth. See also: **Yoga**.

Jnana Yoga see **Yoga**

Judaism The religion of the Jewish people, characterised by their belief in a monotheistic God, and that they are his chosen people. Judaism as both a religion and a culture emerged in the ancient Near East approximately 3,000 years ago. It is sometimes termed an 'Abramic religion' as it arose out of the covenant that the prophet Abraham made with the Lord.

Jews believe that God is the creator of the world and the universe, that he alone should be worshipped and that the first five books of holy scripture (called the Torah) were revealed to Moses by the creator. This divine being also monitors the activities of all people, rewarding individuals for good deeds and punishing them for evil ones. Although Jewish belief is the foundation of the Christian faith, Jews do not believe in the concept of original sin, nor do they think that a saviour is necessary to enter the kingdom of heaven. Instead, life in the afterlife is determined by your actions and behaviour in this world, and believers are able to sanctify their lives and draw closer to God by keeping his divine commandments.

The main holy books of Judaism are the Tanakh and the Talmud. The Tanakh is composed of three groups of books that Christians refer to as the Old Testament: the Torah (also known as the Pentateuch), the Nevi'im and the Ketuvim. The Talmud contains stories, laws, medical knowledge, debates about moral choices and mores, composed of material from two main sources: the Mishnah and the Gemara.

All Jewish practices and customs are based on these scriptures. The main ones are: observation of the Shabbat (Sabbath) as a day of rest, starting at sundown Friday evening; strict discipline in the areas of social conduct, personal behaviour and diet (some dietary restrictions are similar to those in **Islam**); regular attendance of Jewish males at synagogue; and observance of the annual festivals of the Jewish year. The main festivals are Pesach (Passover), held each spring; Rosh Hashanah, the Jewish new year (autumn), which culminates in Yom Kippur (day of atonement); Hanukkah, the eight-day feast of lights, held in November/December; Sukkoth, Purim and Shavuoth.

There are many different schools of thought followed within Judaism, including Hasidic, Orthodox and Reform traditions, but they differ only in their interpretation of the Jewish laws, not in the laws themselves.

One of the most significant events that can happen in a Jew's life is the moment they make the transition from childhood to adult status. This is cause for celebration in the Jewish religion, and marked by a special ceremony. At 13 boys reach the status of Bar Mitzvah and at 12 girls achieve Bat Mitzvah. After this, you are recognised as an adult and are personally responsible for following the Jewish commandments and laws.

Jung, Carl Gustav (1875–1961) Swiss psychologist who is one of the seminal philosophers in **new age** thinking, and the psychologist most referred to in the **holistic** world. Jung was the founder of the analytical school of psychology (also known as **Jungian psychology**) and, next to Freud, the most influential author of psychoanalytical theory. Jung coined phrases and mind–body concepts we take for granted like 'introvert–extrovert', complexes, projection and repression, and he is responsible for injecting the element of spirituality into psychology. Prior to that, people's thoughts and behaviours were only considered in scientific terms: what can be experienced and observed. Jung acknowledged that there were elements of our personalities which could not be explained in rational terms, and that only by considering mystic aspects could a person come to terms with their psychological problems and neuroses.

Early in his career, Jung worked closely with **Sigmund Freud**, whom he considered a friend and mentor, and gladly embraced Freud's theories about the unconscious mind. Freud's emphasis on sexuality as the root cause of all crises soon drove Jung to formulate his own theories about the way our identity is structured. He defined our 'self' as the **psyche** – our mind, soul or spirit. The psyche was divided into two aspects: the **ego**, which represents our conscious awareness, and our 'personal unconscious', which represents those unknown parts of us. Some parts of our unconscious (the **persona**) the ego will recognise but other parts, especially taboo or socially unacceptable beliefs, our ego will repress. That hidden element of the psyche is the **shadow**. Our persona and shadow are constantly in struggle with each other; they are opposing polarities but still interdependent like **yin** and **yang**.

Sometimes when the struggle becomes too great between the persona and shadow, a crisis erupts. It is at that time that the **collective unconscious** makes itself known. Jung believed that this was a psychic realm shared by everyone, where all the elements of human experience are stored. These elements express themselves in the form of mythical **archetypes**, which the collective unconscious uses to restore the individual psyche to health with its insights.

Later in his life, Jung became fascinated by the mystical elements of **astrology**, **I Ching** and **alchemy**, and by **mandalas**, which he felt pictorially represented the wholeness of the self. He was a great believer in the language of dreams, visions and fantasies, and he believed in **paranormal** concepts like **precognition** and **psychokinesis** (once scaring Freud with a display of his own psychokinetic abilities).

When he died in 1961 he left behind a voluminous body of written work and a respect for mysticism and spirituality in what hitherto had been the very mechanistic science of psychotherapy. See also: **Anima, Hero's Journey, Synchronicity, Zeitgeist.**

Jungian Psychology, also **Analytical Psychology** An approach to psychology founded by **Carl Jung** that interprets mental and emotional disturbances as an attempt to discover spiritual and personal wholeness. Jung believed that every person has a story to tell, some of it hidden away in their unconscious. In telling this story, images and symbolic figures called **archetypes** rise up from the **collective unconscious**, a **psychic** realm that we all share. These archetypes reveal wisdom and knowledge that will help a person heal their crises and become more familiar with the less positive aspect of their psyche, the **shadow**. This acceptance of your public face to the world (called the **persona**) as well as your shadow will lead you to a healthy psychological balance.

Other important aspects in Jungian psychology are the interpretation of dreams, fantasies and visions, and exploring the spiritual and creative impulses you feel. See also: **Anima, Peak Experience, Synchronicity.**

Jupiter The fifth and largest planet in our solar system, named for the Roman king of the gods. In **astrology**, Jupiter is the planet of expansiveness and prosperity, and is associated with compassion and good fortune. It also represents your outer personality and aspirations. Traditionally, Jupiter rules capitalism, celebration, higher education and courts of law, as well as luck, philosophy and religion. It is the ruling planet of the zodiac sign **Sagittarius** and co-ruler of **Pisces**.

Jyotisha Shastara see **Vedic Astrology**

Ka The ancient Egyptian definition of **life force**, the essential energy of all living beings. Ka was considered the spirit and life force of both humans and gods, and when a person was born, his ka was created with him, but lived in the eternal realm of the immortals. When a person died, he would be reunited with his ka, which would protect him against the dangers of the afterlife. See also: **Chi**, **Prana**.

Kabbalah, also **Cabala**, **Cabalah**, **Cabbala**, **Cabbalah**, **Kabala**, **Kabalah**, **Kabbala**, **Qabala**, **Qabalah**, **Qabbala**, and **Qabbalah** (Hebrew *QBL*, 'to receive, accept, oral tradition') The ancient Jewish mystical tradition that promises spiritual enlightenment to those who follow its precepts. Originally, Kabbalah was a study of methods for controlling spirits and **demons** through the magical use of their name and numbers associated with them. It hearkens back to primitive beliefs that to merely speak certain sounds was to allow you access to parts of the divine (see **Sound Healing**, **Mantra**).

Until the thirteenth century AD, Kabbalah was an oral tradition. The practice crystallised in medieval Spain and France when Moses de Leon, a Spanish Kabbalist, wrote the **Zohar** (the 'Book of Splendour'), a record of the rituals and practices that had previously been kept secret.

While Kabbalah is largely mathematical in nature, it concentrates on the configuration of magical words, anagrams, angel and demon names and the most holy, the secret name of **God**, **Tetragrammaton**.

Central to Kabbalistic belief is the **Tree of Life**. This is a diagrammatic representation of the ten different spheres of knowledge (known as 'sephiroth') that man must achieve to attain wisdom or the 'godhead'. Also key is the idea that the 22 letters of the Hebrew alphabet are sacred elemental symbols of the universe (known as the **arcana**), and to be able to decipher them is to understand life. A way to access the arcana's energy is to chant the sounds of each letter. The arcana are also linked to the ten sephiroth on the Tree of Life to form branches or 'pathways'. This means that there are 32 different ways to reach enlightenment, all of them by long and hard study only.

The Kabbalah is by nature hard to explain because of the emphasis on revealing its secrets only by initiation. Despite this hidden knowledge, it has heavily influenced many occult traditions, including **theosophy**, **numerology**, **Gnosticism**, **Golden Dawn**, alchemy and **tarot**, as well as rituals practised in **Wicca**, **paganism** and **witchcraft**. See also: **Pathworking**.

Kachina Spirits of the Native American Hopi tribe, who emerge from the earth at the winter solstice and remain until the summer solstice. They are protective ancestral spirits, represented either by dancers or dolls, painted in the colours of the six cardinal points of direction. These are: yellow for the north, red for the south, white for the east, turquoise for the west, black for sky and grey for the earth.

Kahuna (Hawaiian, literally 'keepers of the secret') Magician priests of the **Huna** religion in Hawaii, who use their powers to control **mana**, or the life force, for healing and clairvoyant purposes. Also used as a term of respect to indicate a master of an art, as indicated by its facetious application in 1960s surf and sand movies ('The Big Kahuna').

Kali Ray TriYoga see Yoga, Hatha

Kali/Kali Ma (Sanskrit, 'black') The bloodthirsty Hindu goddess of destruction, whose terrible aspect represents the shadow side of human nature. She is one of the incarnations of **Shakti**, the goddess of feminine energy and the wife of **Shiva**. Taunted by Shiva because of her dark skin, she transformed into **Kali**, the bloodthirsty goddess who in her violent dance of rage nearly trampled Shiva to death beneath her feet. Known as the demon killer and depicted wearing a necklace of skulls, for many years in India male human sacrifices were offered to her as encouragement to continue to decapitate demons threatening the world.

Many Hindus believe that Kali actually was the supreme creator of the universe and not **Brahma**, as portrayed in more conventional Hindu canons. According to them, it was from her and by her that Brahma, **Vishnu** (who calls her 'mother and grave') and Shiva came into being.

For all her violent ways, Kali is worshipped as the ultimate mother, source of life and death in this world. See also: **Hinduism**.

Kapha (Sanskrit, 'earth and water') One of the three body types, or **doshas**, in ayurvedic medicine, that determine who you are physically and mentally, and what you need to do to keep healthy. The kapha dosha is composed of earth and water energies, with the following results. Kapha types are inclined to be heavily built, gain weight easily and have difficulty taking it off. They also have slow digestions and metabolisms. They have soft, fleshy skin and are also emotionally 'soft' – caring individuals with great empathy for others. They have a tendency to dislike change and get stuck in a rut.

Kapha types have a sweet tooth and hate to exercise, which is bad because they need to eat less heavy and sweet food and exercise more to keep healthy. A kapha's great failing is laziness; their strength is their tolerant, loving disposition. Mostly, kaphas should: get plenty of exercise, avoid heavy foods and vary their routine.

Karma A central idea in **Buddhism** and **Hinduism** that actions of body, speech and mind in this life have consequences in our next life, due to **reincarnation**. This concept helps the believer to explain the reasons for misfortunes one might encounter in life. In other words, a cosmic 'cause and effect' from our past lives operates in our present existence. A bad karma in this life can be overcome for your next life by changing present behaviour. Consequently, if you wish to live happily in the world after death, or in your next incarnation, you need to sow the seeds of happiness now by 'right action'. See also: **Samsara**.

Karma Yoga see **Yoga**

Ke Cycle, also **Conquest Cycle, Control Cycle** In Chinese philosophy and medicine, the cycle of the five natural elements (water, wood, fire, earth, metal) that shows how one element controls another element. It appears in pattern as a five-point star, in a series of checks that, taken as a whole, balance out all the **chi** in the universe. Water will keep fire in check and fire makes metal usable. Metal cuts and tames wood and wood, through its roots, stabilises earth. Earth defines the boundaries of water. Taken to extremes, as in dysfunctional health, it could also be called the 'destruction' cycle because water unchecked will douse fire, fire will melt metal, metal will destroy wood, lack of wood will make earth crumble or too much wood will become parasitic to earth and, without earth, water has no boundaries. See also: **Five Element Cycle, Shen Cycle**.

Kelpie A Scottish mythological creature, a water-dwelling **fairy** or **demon** with **shape-shifting** abilities. Kelpies appear either as handsome youths with seaweed hair, or as water horses which drag unwary horseback riders to their deaths if they venture too close to their lairs.

Kephalonomancy (Greek *kephale*, 'head', + *manteia*, 'divination') An unusual form of **divination** that determined the guilt or innocence of those accused of crimes. The head of a goat or an ass would be baked and then molten carbon would be poured on the head while the names of the accused would be read out. If a crackling noise was heard during this reading, it would occur when the guilty party was named. Mostly practised among the ancient southern Germanic clan of Lombards.

Ki (Japanese, 'life force') see **Chi**

Ki Healing see **Reiki, Energy Medicine**

Kidney Meridian A channel or **meridian** of **chi** energy running through the body that penetrates the kidney, according to **Traditional Chinese Medicine**. It is associated with the **water element**, has **yin** energetic qualities and is partnered with the **bladder meridian**, which is **yang**. Kidney meridian energy is the main storehouse of chi for the body and rules birth, development and maturation. If someone lacks 'kidney energy' it means that their constitution is fundamentally weak and can only achieve health relative to the amount of kidney energy, or **jing essence**, they possess. Chi is strongest in this channel between 5 and 7 p.m. and conversely the weakest between 5 and 7 a.m. Both left and right sides of the body have this meridian, which begins on the sole of each foot and runs up the leg and torso to end below the clavicle.

Kinesiology A method of manual muscle-testing to diagnose imbalances in the body. This technique is based on Chinese medicine principles about health and illness, and connects them with the theory that muscles, organs and glands tap directly into the body's energetic pathways, called the **meridians**. If a particular muscle is weak, so will the energy in a particular meridian be. Kinesiology can then further be used to find out the source of the weakness – is it a disease? Is there some sort of food or substance that you are allergic to, and which weakens you by its mere presence? Are you emotionally stressed? This information is gathered and then another form of healing therapy like massage, osteopathy, nutritional medicine (and so on) is used to unblock body energy and help stimulate self-healing mechanisms. Properly applied, kinesiology can also assist in healing.

There are over 50 forms of kinesiology, including 'Touch for Health', but all use the same method of muscle-testing. In a typical session and after a full health history is taken, the kinesiologist will move your arms and legs into particular positions, and you will engage in a gentle strength-resistance exercise with the therapist. They are trained to judge whether the action of the muscle is energetically strong or weak. In the case of food and other allergies, a small amount will be placed on your hand or stomach, or under your tongue, and your muscles will be tested for their response to it.

Although using kinesiology for diagnosing illness and imbalances has a following in many healing therapies, conventional medicine does not accept this as a valid method of discovery. Alternative practitioners, however, find it an invaluable tool.

Kirlian Photography   A method of recording and photographing the **aura** of a living being, named after the Soviet professor Semyon Kirlian who discovered the technique in 1939. Kirlian photography records the high-frequency energy patterns given off by the aura, resulting in photos of differently coloured coronas of dazzling light and shadow. It may possibly one day be used to diagnose disease at the auric level.

Kneading   A classic movement in Swedish and holistic massage, where the therapist kneads muscles like bread dough. This lifts muscle away from the bone and quickly increases blood circulation, which helps to increase elasticity and tone as well as to remove toxins. It has a sedative effect on muscles if performed slowly, and a stimulating effect if performed briskly, making it an excellent part of therapy for improving sports performance.

Knights Templar   A company of medieval French knights, formed in 1118, that grew into a powerful secret organisation still believed to be in existence today. The Order of the Poor Knights of Christ and the Temple of Solomon – or Knights Templar for short – began with nine well-intentioned noblemen whose plan was 'as far as their strength permitted, they should keep the roads and highways safe…with a special regard for the protection of pilgrims' who were travelling to Jerusalem. The order took vows of chastity and poverty, and, in the fervour of the early Crusades, grew rapidly to a large company of warrior knights.

The Knights Templar established a chapter in Jerusalem itself, and were installed in the stables of what was considered the ruins of the 'Temple of Solomon', destroyed when the city fell to the Romans. This choice of residence was a deliberate one, because of persistent rumours that the Jewish high priests had managed to hide the treasures of the temple, including the Ark of the Covenant, before it was sacked and burned. There are accounts of the Knights excavating the stables' surrounds, and it is said that they discovered not only vast treasure including the Ark and the **Holy Grail**, but also a set of ornate gold thrones dedicated to Yahweh, the **God** of the Jews and (surprisingly) to Ashara, considered Yahweh's feminine counterpart by ancient Semitic Jews.

The Knighthood grew into a powerful brotherhood of wealth and commerce with influence stretching from the Holy Land back to Spain, France and even England. They were also great builders, and the magnificent Cathedral at Chartres, designed and financed by Templars, represents their crowning achievement.

Such success breeds envy and, unluckily for the Knights Templar, the jealous included Philip le Bel (1268–1314), the King of France. On a flimsy pretext, he had the main council of Templars arrested in Paris and accused them of heresy. On the King's orders, the Templar high command were tortured for several years, but Philip was never able to discover the Templars' fabled wealth and store of Holy Treasures, which vanished without a trace. The open arm of the organisation also disappeared, but it is rumoured that they still exist, perhaps in certain sects of **freemasonry**, and that somewhere lies the fortune of the Knights Templar, waiting to be discovered.

Koan, Koans A riddle without a logical answer, used by Zen Masters in **Zen Buddhism** to stimulate the mind of a disciple towards **enlightenment**. A classic koan is: 'Listen to the sound of one hand clapping'.

Koran, also **Qur'an** (Arabic, 'recitation') The holy book of **Islam**, believed by Muslims to be the words of their God Allah, as dictated to his Prophet **Muhammad**, by the archangel Gabriel. It was originally a collection of disparate oral teachings and written manuscripts, but was later assembled into one coherent text. Some Muslims maintain that the true Qur'an resides in heaven, and will be revealed to the faithful in the afterlife. (In the West, this holy work is spelled Koran but Muslims prefer the spelling Qur'an.)

Kripalu Yoga see Yoga, Hatha

Krishna One of the most popular incarnations or **avatars** of the Hindu god **Vishnu**, and best known for his starring role in the **Bhagavad Gita**. Krishna served as seer and guide to Prince Arjuna during the epic battle between warring factions, but was killed when the arrow of a hunter struck him in the heel. His death marked the start of the Kali **Yuga**, the present age of man, which began circa 3120 BC and will continue for 432,000 years. See also: **Hinduism**.

Krishnamurti, Jiddu (1895–1986) Noted **theosophy** spiritual leader who became Hollywood society's favourite guru between the two world wars of the twentieth century. He was discovered in Adyar, India, at the age of 15 by the well-known theosophist, C.W. Leadbeater, and transplanted to England, where he was proclaimed to be an incarnation of Buddha called Lord Maitreya.

He eventually decided to cast off theosophy and his celebrity status as guru, and concentrated instead on yogic philosophy. He travelled the world giving lectures and wrote many books of spiritual commentary before dying in 1986 at the age of 91.

Kriya Yoga see Yoga

Kriya, Kriyas (Sanskrit, 'purify') Cleansing rituals in **yoga**, which have profound results for both the physical and subtle body. These practices range from the simple, steam inhalation treatments and nostril-breathing exercises, to the complicated like *dhauti* – swallowing a sterilised muslin cloth and then regurgitating it to cleanse the stomach. In **kundalini** practices, kriya is also defined as a physical or mental response to the awakening of this serpent energy, as one must become 'pure' to accept kundalini energy and therefore attain higher consciousness. See also: **Tantra**.

Kundalini (Sanskrit, 'the coil in the hair of the beloved') In Hindu and Buddhist philosophy, the primal **psychic** force which sleeps like a coiled snake at the base of the spine. This dormant feminine energy is symbolised as a sleeping serpent coiled three and a half times round the base of the central **nadi** (energy channel) of the body, the *sushumna*. On either side of the sushumna are the *ida* (female) and *pingala* (male) energy nadis. They spiral like a double helix around the sushumna and exit at the nostrils. **Kundalini yoga** and **tantric** practices are designed to get energy flowing through these three nadis, which is why there is an emphasis on sexual ecstasy – male and female qualities must be invoked to awaken kundalini. Once awakened, kundalini energy is directed up the sushumna so that it may climb upwards and illuminate the brain, leading to heightened awareness and, ultimately, **enlightenment**.

Kundalini Yoga see Yoga, Kundalini

Labyrinth (Greek *labyrinthos*, 'double-headed axe') A complicated, maze-like structure or path with twists and turns, where the goal is to seek the centre without getting lost. The term came from the Greek myth of Theseus and his battle with the half-human, half-bull Minotaur of Knossos on the island of Crete. Legend has it that the Minotaur was so monstrous that the only way to imprison him safely was to place him at the centre of a convoluted maze.

Labyrinths are now recognised as a universal symbol of transformation, created to help us find our own spiritual meaning and destiny. It has become common practice for people to 'walk the labyrinth', following the single winding path to the centre and back out again. These labyrinths may be found at sacred sites like Chartres Cathedral, or in the English village of Saffron Walden. Labyrinths may also be specially constructed or drawn for the purpose of contemplation. This has been described as a meditative experience, where getting to the heart of the maze helps focus you on getting to the heart of your own concerns and questions.

In **paganism**, maze and labyrinth-walking were an important part of the fertility rites of the festivals **Beltane** and **Eoastre**. According to tradition, a young man would enter the maze to rescue the maiden imprisoned at the centre. The reward was obvious (it *was* a fertility rite). Labyrinths were also

Seven circuit labyrinth   Chartres-style labyrinth

Two variations on the labyrinth

thought to represent the map to the underworld, which the spirit of a dead person had to negotiate to reach the afterlife. If they got lost in the maze, they were doomed to float about in limbo.

In **Christianity**, the labyrinth symbolises the path we all must take to find salvation, which is why you find so many mazes and labyrinths located on sacred ground.

Lachesis One of the 15 major **polychrests**, or major remedies in **homeopathy**. It is also a **constitutional type**, which is a way homeopaths have of classifying different patient profiles. The fitting constitutional remedy acts preventatively and curatively on its matching personality type – for example, a person with a Lachesis constitution will respond well to the Lachesis remedy almost regardless of the illness they are suffering from. Lachesis people are stormy, creative types, who tend to be talkative and dogmatic. They have a tendency to burn the candle at both ends and find it difficult to control their emotions. They are susceptible to varicose veins, heart and circulation problems, and nervous upsets.

Lagnasad, also **Lammas**, **Lughnasadh** (Gaelic Lugh, 'the god Lugh', + ndsad, 'games') The **pagan** harvest festival, held on 31 July and one of the eight witches' **sabbats** of the year. Lagnasad is named for the Celtic god of fire and light, Lugh, and is a celebration of nature's abundance of the past year. Another name for this festival is Lammas, or 'loaf-mass', in keeping with the harvest theme. The rituals enacted on Lagnasad are associated with the traditional worship of the old god. Lugh is symbolically cut down and reborn in the bread made from harvest grains, the same way the sun is 'cut down' from the sky each autumn and 'resurrected' in the spring.

Lakshmi The consort of the Hindu god **Vishnu**, and the goddess of wealth and prosperity. Lakshmi was originally a sea goddess, worshipped as the deity of beauty and fortune.

Lama (Sanskrit, 'high mother') In **Tibetan Buddhism**, a teacher or monk of high rank and acknowledged wisdom, often the head of a monastery. These advanced meditators are often candidates to achieve **rinpoche** status, delaying their own ascension to **nirvana** by consciously choosing **reincarnation**, so they can continue to teach and lead others to **enlightenment**. The most famous recognised reincarnated lama is the **Dalai Lama**. He is fourteenth in a succession that began with Gendun Drup in 1391.

Lammas see Lagnasad

Lampadomancy, also **Lychnomancy** (Greek *lampad*, 'torch', + *manteia*, 'divination') A form of **divination**, first practised in ancient Greece, using the light from an oil lamp or torch flame. The diviner stares intently at the light and makes oracular interpretations based on the actions and movements of the flame. An alternate method is to examine the spots of carbon deposited on a piece of paper held over the flame. Lampadomancy is a form of **pyromancy**, divination by fire.

Lancelot du Lac, also **Launcelot** The greatest knight in the legendary British **King Arthur**'s court, and a key player in Arthurian legends. A mostly virtuous knight and good friend to Arthur, he nevertheless became embroiled in a tortuous affair with Queen **Guinevere** and, when the matter was discovered, left the court. He later returned to rescue the Queen from execution.

Lancelot had one son, **Galahad**, by Elaine of Corbenic, a knight's daughter. After the final battle in which Arthur was killed, Lancelot retired to a hermitage to do penance for his sins. See also: **Arthurian Legends**.

Lao Tzu, also **Lao Tse, Lao Tsu, Laotze, Laozi** (604–531 BC) Semi-legendary Chinese sage of the fifth century BC and the founder of **Taoism**. Lao Tzu is also credited with authorship of the text **Tao Te Ching**, which sets out the philosophy of 'The Way' – how to live in harmony with nature and the universe.

There is little else known about Lao Tzu. He may have been an older contemporary of **Confucius** (551–479 BC), and is rumoured to have been an archivist for one of the petty rulers of the age. His name can loosely be translated as 'old master' or 'old boy', which leads some to believe that he never existed at all. Whatever his story, there is no doubt that the literary work he purportedly left behind was the foundation for one of the great faiths of the world, and an endless source of enlightenment to countless generations of readers.

Larch A flower essence made from the blossom of the larch tree. This emotionally healing tincture is one of the **Bach Flower Remedies**. Dr Bach said that this is indicated for 'those who lack confidence in their ability: those who do not believe in themselves, are afraid of failure and do not try'.

Large Intestine Meridian A channel or **meridian** of **chi** energy running through the body that affects the large intestine, according to **Traditional**

Chinese Medicine. It is associated with the **metal element**, has **yang** energetic qualities and is partnered with the **lung meridian**, which is **yin.** Large intestine meridian energy is the great detoxifier of the body, transforming and eliminating surplus physical and mental matter. It also has to do with letting go of the past, especially negative emotions and experiences. Chi is strongest in this channel between 5 and 7 a.m. and conversely the weakest between 5 and 7 p.m. which is why healthy individuals often start the day with a bowel movement. Both left and right sides of the body have this meridian, which begins by each index finger and runs up the arm to the nose.

LaStone Therapy An **alternative therapy** treatment that combines full body massage with the placement of hot stones on strategically important energy points of the body (also known as the chakra centres). These stones are marble and basalt, and work to draw out negative energies from the body and help create a connection to the earth. Hot stones are also used in the massage part of the treatment, and a final rubdown is given with alternate hot and cold stones, to finish the treatment. See also: **Crystal Healing, Massage Therapy**.

Lavender (Latin *lavare*, 'to wash') Plants of the genus *Lavandulae*, which have a number of uses in **herbalism** and **aromatherapy**. This versatile plant is known for its healing, balancing properties and is used in many different **space clearing** and **magic** rituals. Lavender is also known for its calming properties, and its essential oil can safely be used neat on the skin to help heal burns and scar tissue. Properly applied, this oil is also excellent in helping to induce sleep in the young, and in the anxious. Because of its antibacterial properties, lavender is a traditional ingredient in household cleaning and has a long history of cosmetic use since Roman times, whence the plant's name, meaning 'to wash', derives.

Law of Cure The idea, in **homeopathy** and other alternative therapies, that the body heals in a very specific way given the right treatment or remedy. It states: 'All healing starts from the head down, from the inside out, and in reverse order as the symptoms have been acquired'. Dr Constantine Hering (1800–1880), the American 'Father of Homeopathy', formulated the law when he tried, ironically enough, to disprove homeopathy's effectiveness and ended up a convert.

Law of Similars In **homeopathy**, the concept that 'like cures like'. Substances that make you ill in large doses can also cure, in small enough doses. **Samuel Hahnemann**, the founder of homeopathy, formulated this theory, which states: 'To achieve a gentle and lasting cure, always choose a drug capable of provoking a disease similar to the one it is to cure'. Hahnemann based this law on work originating with the fourth-century-BC Greek physician **Hippocrates**.

Laya Yoga see Yoga

Lecanomancy A form of **divination** that interprets the ripples in a pool of water. See also: **Hydromancy**.

Left-handed Path Phrase used to describe the path of black magic and **sorcery**, where there is intention to harm a person, property or other living being, or use force against a person's free will. The left-handed path was given these negative connotations because the word 'sinister', Latin for 'left', has become associated with harm or evil.

Lemuria A mythical community of the Pacific Ocean from 25,000 years ago that Theosophists believe was covered over by the biblical flood. Unlike Atlantis, which was said to have had a flourishing, cosmopolitan society prior to its destruction, Lemuria was not as culturally advanced. Theoretically, all that is left of Lemuria's land mass are the peaks of Kauai, Hawaii to the north and Easter Island to the south. People living in this community were known as the 'Mu'. See also: **Theosophy**.

Leo The fifth sign of the **zodiac** in Western **astrology**, and the **sun sign** for those born between 23 July and 23 August. The symbol of Leo is the lion, and the ruling planet is the **sun**. Leo is a **fixed sign** influenced by the **fire element**, with 'power' the best single word to define those born under it. They know exactly what their role in life is: to be admired. They are the leaders of the zodiac and are courageous, noble, proud and loyal, but can be prone to arrogance and attention-seeking tactics. You cannot ignore a Leo: they have vivacious personalities and bottomless amounts of energy.

A meal with a Leo will be a bountiful royal banquet, with tables groaning with rich, dramatic foods and the finest wines. In health, Leos tend to have back and neck problems, as well as diseases of the heart. They benefit from herbs to alleviate aches and pains, as well as blood-purifying tonics.

Levitation The act of raising either a person or an object from the ground by supernatural means. This might be through **psychokinesis**, or through **magic**, or by visiting spirits from the other side. **Fakirs**, **yogis** and other

Eastern holy men often practise levitation as a demonstration of the mental control they have over themselves and other matter.

Ley Lines Naturally occurring bands of energy running through, along and beneath the earth that possess great spiritual, astrological and healing qualities. The phrase was first coined by Alfred Watkins in 1921 when he was out riding on horseback. Coming over a crest in the Bredwardine hills of Hereford, Watkins suddenly noticed that the ancient mounds, churches and burial sites in the area were all built along straight lines. He theorised that these places of spiritual significance must have been purposefully placed along a worldwide power network of such lines, criss-crossed and interconnected. The word itself comes from the Anglo-Saxon *lea* or *leigh*, meaning 'grassy track'.

Ley lines are the earth's equivalent of **chi**, the energy channels and **meridians** that run throughout the human body. Like chi, ley lines emit electromagnetic energy that can be located and measured, most notably through **dowsing**, and are known throughout every world culture. In Ireland they are known as' fairy lines', in China as 'dragon paths' and in Polynesia as 'lines of light'. Australian aboriginals follow ley lines (called dream paths) when they travel in **dreamtime** and it is no coincidence that many of Britain's most holy and ancient sites are located on these subterranean energy channels. **Feng shui** practitioners use 'dragon paths' to align buildings for the most positive energies available and many **pagan** religions perform ceremonial rites where these lines intersect; considered locations of particularly powerful resonance.

Libanomancy see Capnomancy

Libra The seventh sign of the **zodiac** in Western **astrology**, and the **sun sign** for those born between 23 September and 23 October. The symbol of Libra is the scales, and the ruling planet is **Venus**. Librans are a **cardinal sign** influenced by the **air element**, with 'harmony' the best single word to define them. Those born under Libra tend to be balanced, peace-loving individuals who make good diplomats. Librans are like chameleons, in that they fit in almost anywhere, but this can be interpreted as indecisiveness. They can also be vain at times, but are so agreeable about it that you easily forgive them.

An ideal meal for a Libran combines a discriminating array of delicacies, presented with exquisite sensibilities. They are also prone to a sweet tooth. In health, Librans can get very stressed if they are not living and working in harmonious conditions, and they can have weak kidneys. Herbs to tone that organ, as well as to aid nervous exhaustion, benefit Librans.

Life Coach (American) Late-twentieth-century term for a one-to-one trainer who evaluates and assesses a person's life with the intention to map out motivational life changes. These changes take into account the spiritual, physical, emotional and business factors of the individual using techniques gleaned from various psychological therapies. See also: **Cognitive Psychotherapy, Neurolinguiustic Programming**.

Life Force The generic term for universal life energy that animates all existence and permeates all things. It operates both within our physical bodies and in the world around us. Sceptics and hard scientists do not believe in it, although quantum physicists are getting close to acknowledging its existence. George Lucas did not get it that far wrong when his *Star Wars* film character Obi-Wan Kenobi described life force or 'The Force' as 'an energy field created by all living things. It surrounds us and penetrates us. It binds the galaxy together'.

Every culture on earth has a term for the concept of life force, some more recognisable that others: **chi** (China); ki (Japan); **prana** (India); rlun (Tibet); wakan (Native American Sioux); **mana** and huna(Polynesia); elima (African Congo); tondi (Sumatra); tinh (Vietnam); el (Israel); bioplasma (Russia). Medieval alchemists called it 'vital fluid', ancient Greeks 'pneuma' and the ancient Egyptians **ka**.

Our life force is what makes up our **aura**, and this bioelectric field can actually be detected and photographed through **Kirlian photography**. The closest the scientifically oriented West can come to life force, however, is the weak phrase the 'will to live', although there are growing traditions that acknowledge this energy, in alternative therapies like **homeopathy** and **vibrational medicine**. Christian tradition would term our life force 'the soul', but even that does not really describe the energetic properties of the united mind and body. 'It is as difficult to explain prana as it is to explain god,' yogic master B.K.S. Iyengar said, and he was right.

Light Healing A general term to describe any number of therapies that use light to promote healing. These range from the use of light boxes to combat seasonal affective disorder (SAD) to more esoteric treatments involving colour, crystals and nutrition. They all work on the same basic principles. Light, whether natural or artificial, affects the amount of hormones secreted by our pineal, hypothalamus and pituitary glands. The closer the light our bodies receive is to sunlight, the better. Sunlight also provides vitamin D, an essential body nutrient, which is absorbed through the skin.

Light, or rather refracted light in the shape of colour, is also significant when it comes to our personal energy field, the **aura**. Because colour is essentially light, it has its own energy vibration. These vibrations can be manipulated (using different shades and hues) to balance out low energies in our aura, or to calm down over-agitated areas of our personal energy.

Health conditions that have shown improvements after light therapy include skin conditions like acne and psoriasis, jet lag, sleep disorders, dyslexia, some forms of cancer, lupus, ME and even diabetes. It is especially good for convalescing patients.

Whatever the method used, light therapy has been shown to be effective in both conventional and alternative medicine treatments. See also: **Chakras, Colour Therapy, Crystal Healing**.

Lilith (Hebrew, 'night monster') The first wife of the biblical Adam, according to Hebrew tradition, who was a vengeful, dark creature. Lilith was reportedly a member of the **demon** race, the first group of entities to inhabit the earth, later superseded by mankind. Their pairing was an abortive attempt to unite the two races, and Lilith was soon deposed by Eve.

Lithomancy (Greek *lithos*, 'stone', + *manteia*, 'divination') A form of **divination** using precious gems and stones. The crystals (all different types) are cast (like dice) out onto a dark-coloured cloth while a question about the future or a particular situation is asked. The stones are then read according to the general pattern in which they fall, with the brightest stone the most significant of the lot. Another method is to sketch out the diagram of a compass marked with north, south, east and west. The crystals are placed into a bag and five stones (one for each compass point and one for the centre of the circle) are selected and placed clockwise from east, with the last stone in the middle. What meaning each stone or gem has depends entirely on the individual properties of each crystal, and where it is placed on the compass.

Liver Meridian A channel or **meridian** of **chi** energy running through the body that penetrates the liver, according to **Traditional Chinese Medicine**. It is associated with the **wood element**, has **yin** energetic qualities, and is partnered with the **gall bladder meridian**, which is **yang**. Liver energy controls the movement of blood throughout the body and affects both conscious and unconscious thinking. Chi is strongest in this channel between

1 and 3 a.m. and conversely the weakest between 1 and 3 p.m. Both left and right sides of the body have this meridian, which begins at the big toe then runs up the leg and torso to end below the ribs.

Loch Ness Monster A mythical dinosaur-like creature that supposedly inhabits Loch Ness in Scotland. Despite numerous alleged sightings and research projects, 'Nessie's' existence has yet to be incontrovertibly proven. See also: **Cryptozoology**.

Lodestone Rocks which are naturally magnetic like iron ore, that also have magical and healing properties. The ancient Greek physician Galen, in 200 BC, recorded using lodestones to relieve pain, and there are many folk remedies that use lodestones to draw out illnesses of all kinds, including fevers and infections.

Medieval Arabian magicians believed lodestones contained a living spirit. A single lodestone would be held over a wound or painful area on the body, and the illness would be attracted to the lodestone through sympathetic magic. Lodestones were also used in **spells** to attract love and money to the spellcaster. See also: **Magnetic Healing**.

Logos (Greek, 'word, study') 1. In **Christianity**, the Word of God, or the general principle of reason, judgement and creative order in the universe. 2. In magic and some religious traditions (particularly **Kabbalah** and **Gnosticism**), the term used to refer to a name or sound of a deity, and merely uttering the 'logos' of a god could endow you with the power he/she holds. See also: **Abracadabra, Tetragrammaton**.

Lomi Lomi Massage, also Hawaiian Temple Massage, Hawaiian Wave Four Hands Massage A full-body **massage** treatment given by two therapists, in a specific technique that originated in Hawaii. The two practitioners work in unison and perform almost a synchronised 'dance' over your body. Massage movements are long and flowing, in order to bring deep relaxation and, in doing so, balance the essential energies (see **chi**) in the body. Lomi Lomi stimulates circulation and the lymphatic system, encouraging the body to feel recharged. It is an especially good treatment for sensitive types for whom other forms of massage would be too vigorous.

Lotus Plant of the genus *Nymphaea*, this species of the Asian water lily is a sacred symbol in several different cultures, most notably Egyptian, **Hindu** and **Buddhist** beliefs. It features heavily in the **creation myths** of ancient Egypt, where the sun god **Ra** created himself from amidst chaos and first emerged from the petals of the lotus blossom. Ra's ability to be reborn each day made the lotus a symbol of resurrection, with lotus flower motifs found on the walls of tombs and in other Egyptian funeral art. Egyptians also used lotus flowers in aphrodisiacs and as a nutritive tonic, and today it remains the national flower of that country. **Lakshmi**, wife of the Hindu god **Vishnu** and goddess of fortune and prosperity, is portrayed as sitting on a lotus, her traditional symbol. Buddhists consider the lotus to be a sacred flower and a symbol of purity and **enlightenment**. The flower grows in mud but rises above the muddy water, which shows that from the imperfection and instability of all life it is possible to attain **nirvana**.

Lotus Position   Cross-legged seated posture used in **meditation**, **yoga** and various spiritual practices, mainly **Buddhism**. When you sit down, take your lower left leg and put it on top of your right thigh, and then take your lower right leg and put it on top of your left thigh. When a person is seated in this position they roughly resemble a **lotus** flower in full bloom, hence the name. This posture also helps to retain vital energy in the body, rather than letting it dissipate.

Lourdes   There in 1858, a fourteen-year-old shepherdess of poor health, Bernadette Soubirous, had a series of eighteen visions of the **Virgin Mary**. At the site of her visions, a spring of waters bubbled up that was later accredited with miraculous healing powers. Bernadette told everyone about her visions, a spring of waters bubbled up that was later accredited with miraculous healing powers. Bernadette told everyone about her visions and the healing reputation of Lourdes waters spread throughout Catholic Europe. After subsequent investigation of further miracles by the Roman Catholic Church, the spring was designated a holy place. After this edict, the surrounding community swelled to accommodate the flood of miracle-seekers. Now, over two million people each year make the pilgrimage to Lourdes to seek physical and spiritual healing, with many claiming to be healed by their faith and the water. Ironically, Bernadette herself was never cured of her many ailments and died at the early age of 35.

Lovelock, James   British atmospheric scientist and former consultant to NASA (b.1920) who formulated the **Gaia theory** that the earth is a living, evolving organism. In 1979 he published his ideas in *Gaia: A New Look at Life on Earth*. He continued to work and expand on his theory, publishing two further books, *The Ages of Gaia: A Biography of our Living Earth* and *Gaia: The Practical Science of Planetary Medicine*. He summed up his life and the great impact his work has had on our view of the world and environment in his 2000 autobiography *Homage to Gaia – The Life of an Independent Scientist*.

Lucid Dream, Lucid Dreaming Term used to describe a situation where the dreamer is aware they are dreaming. This conscious state of mind can be harnessed to change the course of a dream or nightmare through specific techniques, and is fast becoming a useful therapeutic tool. Celia Green, of the Institute of Psychophysical Research in Oxford, coined the phrase in her 1968 book *Lucid Dreams*.

Lugh, Lug (Gaelic, 'shining one') The Irish **pagan** sun god, who is patron of arts and crafts in Celtic spirituality, and leader of the *Tuatha de Danaan* (court of the **fairies**) after he deposed **Dagda**. Lugh is celebrated at the **sabbat** harvest festival of **Lagnasad**, in early August. At that time, Lugh is symbolically cut down and reborn in the bread made from harvest grains, the same way the sun is 'cut down' from the sky each autumn and is 'resurrected' in the spring. See also: **Celtic Wheel**.

Lung Meridian A channel or **meridian** of **chi** energy running through the body that affects the lungs, according to **Traditional Chinese Medicine**. It is associated with the **metal element**, has **yin** energetic qualities and is partnered with the **large intestine meridian**, which is **yang**. Lung energy is responsible for absorbing chi from outside the body and the lung is considered the organ most affected by grief (as an example, the use of the phrase 'it hurts to breathe'). Chi is strongest in this channel between 3 and 5 a.m. and conversely the weakest between 3 and 5 p.m. Both left and right sides of the body have this meridian, which begins just above the clavicle and runs down the arm, ending at the thumbnail.

Lycanthropy (Greek *lukos*, 'wolf', + *anthropos*, 'man') The magical belief that it is consciously possible, through witchcraft or sorcery, to transform into the form of an animal, most likely a wolf. Lycanthropy accounts for the many legends of **werewolves**, and is similar in practice to a **shaman**'s ability to **shape-shift** into a totemic animal.

Lycopodium One of the 15 major **polychrests**, or major remedies in **homeopathy**. It is also a **constitutional type**, which is a way homeopaths have of classifying different patient profiles. The fitting constitutional remedy acts preventatively and curatively on its matching personality type – for example, a person with a Lycopodium constitution will respond well to the

Lycopodium remedy almost regardless of the illness they are suffering from. Lycopodium people cannot stand illness, least of all their own. They can lack confidence and have a low self-esteem, yet present to the world a sarcastic and arrogant facade to hide these facts. They suffer from anxiety-related conditions, including digestive upsets and insomnia.

Mabinogion (Welsh *mabinogi*, 'a story for children') A collection of 11 medieval Welsh poems and stories, alleged to have been the work of the legendary bard **Taliesin**, but most likely composed by hundreds of anonymous storytellers over hundreds of years. The original stories were preserved in two Welsh collections, 'The White Book of Rhydderch' (c.1300–25) and 'The Red Book of Hergest' (1375–1425), although fragments of these tales appear otherwise, the earliest dated to AD 1225, with some scholarly debate that they could have been written as early as 1060.

In 1849 Lady Charlotte Guest first collected together this ensemble of myth and folklore and published it under the name *Mabinogion*. It consists of four branches, or tales: Pwyll Prince of Dyfed, Branwen the Daughter of Llyr, Manawyddan the Son of Llyr and Math the Son of Mathonwy; plus a collection of seven other songs, poems and legends featuring many exploits of Britain's King Arthur, the legend of Gwydion, and the birth of Taliesin.

Whatever its origin, the *Mabinogion* is a colourful and rich narrative featuring Arthurian legend, Celtic gods and goddesses, heroes, beasts, penance and vindication, kinship and kingship, battles and quests. See also: **Celtic Spirituality**.

Macrobiotics (Greek *macro*, 'large, long', + *bios*, 'life') A dietary therapy that follows a set of rules combining oriental medical principles with Western nutritional medicine. Macrobiotics looks at the interaction between our food choices, our lifestyles, and the environments in which we live. It is a course some seriously and terminally ill people take to help to completely **detoxify** their body, so that their entire energies can be focused on healing. There is some anecdotal evidence to suggest that individuals have been able to prolong their lives and recover from illnesses like cancer, heart disease and diabetes using macrobiotic diets, and it can be combined with more orthodox medical treatments for serious conditions. Most who follow this routine do it to maintain wellness.

Macrobiotics arose out of twentieth-century Japanese dietary therapies developed by Michio Kushi and Georges Ohsawa. This cultural trend is reflected in the choice of foods available in the macrobiotic diet, which is essentially vegan and heavily influenced by oriental cuisine. You are directed to a specific dietary regime based on whether or not you live in a temperate or tropical climate. For persons living in a temperate zone, the breakdown of daily foods is as follows: 50 per cent whole cereal grains, vegetables 20–30 per cent, beans and sea vegetables 5–10 per cent, soup (water and vegetable based) 5–10 per cent. The only beverages allowed are non-stimulating, non-aromatic tea, whole grain coffee and spring water. You may have fish one to three times a week, and fruits or fruit desserts made from fresh or dried fruits two to three times per week, and only fruits grown in a temperate climate. You can snack on pumpkin, sesame or sunflower seeds.

This is what you cannot have: sugar, salt, meat, animal fat, eggs, poultry, dairy products, chocolate, honey, any other coffees, teas, soft drinks or fruit juices, hot spices. In addition, special attention is paid to how foods are grown and prepared: no artificial colours, all organic grains and produce, no canned, frozen or irradiated foods, no microwaving, frying, electric ovens or stoves. There is also a number of environmental changes you need to make too numerous to go into – suffice to say that although macrobiotics is a very restrictive dietary regime with many complicated rules to follow, in extreme circumstances and illness many have found it healing and it has increased their quality of life. See also: **Nutritional Therapy**.

Magic (Greek *magike*, 'art of the magus', from Arabic *magus, magi*, 'wise man, men') The art of harnessing the psychic and natural powers of the universe to influence events, persons, objects and circumstances for one's own purpose. This is accomplished through the ritual use of appropriate incantations, spells and charms to focus the practitioner's intent upon conducting and manifesting the energies of the **elements** of nature and of spirit entities. If the magician's intention is benign (to harm no one) then it is considered white magic; if the intention is to harm a person, property or other living being, or use force against a person's free will, then it is black magic.

Magic can be performed by a solitary practitioner, called generically a 'magician', or conducted in large ceremonial groups. However with many participants, in order to harness magic, certain procedures must be followed. First is the use of the magic circle. This area provides a sacred space where energies of a spell or ritual can be concentrated, and protection from negative forces outside the circle can be assured while the channels between dimensions and consciousness are open. A magic circle is cast using special tools like an **athame** or a **wand**, which symbolise that the energies of the elements **air, fire, water** and **earth** are present in the circle. Together, these four elements make up a fifth called **ether** or **akasha** that is pure spirit and allows magical work to take place.

To perform magic, the ritual takes place in four stages: the Focus, which defines the purpose of the ritual; the Action, where the focus is endowed with elemental energies; Raising the Power, where these energies are charged and amplified; and the Release of Power, when the climax of the spell is reached.

There are many different types of magic: black, celestial, ceremonial, contagious (objects that have been in contact with each other still have a link), defensive, destructive, **Enochian**, high, image, imitative, low, mortuary, natural, protective, sexual, sympathetic (like affects like) and white. Each has its own traditions and forms an intrinsic part of religions and belief systems throughout every world culture. See also: **Divination, Gypsy Magic, Paganism, Theosophy, Wicca, Witchcraft, Zoroastrianism.**

Magnet Therapy, also **Biomagnetic Therapy, Magnetic Therapy, Magnetic Wave Therapy, Magnetotherapy.** The self-help use of magnets to improve health and ease pain. It is based on the theory that magnets can help to rebalance the electromagnetic energy field that surrounds the body. It is also claimed that magnets are capable of electrically charging iron atoms in red blood cells so they work more energetically. This circulatory speed-up means that toxins are removed more quickly, muscle and joint pain is relieved, and natural healing processes are stimulated. As magnets contain a positive/negative charge, they also aid the flow of **chi** (life energy) through the body.

Magnets need to be used in specific ways (size of magnet, alignment of its polarity, etc.) to work. Magnets can be inserted into mattress pads, jewellery like bracelets and necklaces, shoe insoles, fabric patches and wraps, back supports and seat cushions. Magnetic wands (similar in appearance to swizzle sticks) can be used to magnetise water both for ingestion and bathing.

Although there is plenty of anecdotal evidence supporting this therapy, it is not currently accepted in conventional medicine circles. Clinical trials are, however, being carried out so this situation could change.

Magnet therapy is particularly good for relieving pain associated with arthritis, back and neck problems, joint inflammations and sprains, repetitive strain injury, headaches and fibromyalgia.

Magus, Magi, Magician (Greek *magike*, 'art of the magus', from Arabic *magus, magi*, 'wise man, men') A general term for a person who practises **magic.** According to Christian legend, the Magi were three wise men, most likely Chaldean magicians and astrologers who visited **Jesus** and his mother, the **Virgin Mary.** The Magi – Kasper, Melchior and Balthasar – had seen in their portents and in the stars that Jesus was to be the 'King of the Jews' so they gifted him with gold, frankincense and myrrh.

Mahabharata (Sanskrit, 'The Great History of the Bharatas or Mankind') The great Hindu epic poem written during the sixth century BC by the mythic author Vyasa, which contains within it the work **Bhagavad Gita.** The *Mahabharata* is at heart a political work, which formed a manifesto of sorts for India's ruling and warrior castes, although on the surface it appears to be a mythic fable about the exploits of the Hindu god **Krishna,** and the great conflict between cousins that decided the future path of Hindu culture. With 18 books and 100,000 couplets, it is also thought to be the world's longest literary work; eight times longer than Homer's *Iliad* and *Odyssey* put together.

It opens with a war between two rival factions, the Pandavas and the Kauravas, symbolising the epic struggle between good and evil. The fifth book is the *Bhagavad Gita,* which is presented in the form of a dialogue between **Krishna** and Prince Arjuna, who is both his son and pupil. Arjuna questions the necessity of going to war, especially as he is pitted against former teachers, friends and relatives that he is likely to kill. Krisha answers by saying, 'When a man sees that the God in himself is the same God in all that is, he hurts not himself by hurting others: then he goes to the highest Path.' In other words, making the right efforts will lead you to enlightenment, or **nirvana,** because the battle is for the kingdom of the soul, not the kingdom of the land.

The three main themes covered in the *Bhagavad Gita* are jnana, 'the light of knowledge'; bhakti, 'love and devotion'; and '**karma**', the right action. These themes, incidentally, are three of the four paths to enlightenment through **yoga** (the fourth yogic path, raja, is mentioned but not in detail).

Many of the other books contained within the *Mahabharata* contain scraps of other songs, poems and philosophical treatises. By the end, the family struggle at the heart of this epic is resolved, leading to peace and reconciliation.

Mahatma (Sanskrit *maha*, 'great', + *atman*, 'soul') Title of respect on the Indian subcontinent for a great man or wise sage, like Mahatma Gandhi. In **theosophy,** mahatma also indicates someone with supernatural abilities or powers.

Mahayana Buddhism (Sanskrit, 'great way or vehicle') The oldest school of Buddhism, which uses Sanskrit as the primary language of reference. Mahayana is called Northern Buddhism because it took hold in China, Korea, Japan and Tibet. The Mahayana practitioner follows all the basic tenents of **Buddhism**, but believes that his path to enlightenment is more likely if he concentrates on serving and benefiting others. **Zen Buddhism** and **Tibetan Buddhism** both arose from this school of worship.

Maitreya Buddha see Buddha

Mana (Polynesia, 'life force') Term used by native Polynesian and Melanesian cultures to describe the energy of the universe, the life force inherent in all matter and living beings. It also forms part of their beliefs about the spirit world, that the 'mana' of a dead person, or the powers of a sacred object, can be transmitted to someone alive for their magical use. See also: **Huna, Kahuna**.

Manayana see Mahayana Buddhism

Mandala (Sanskrit, 'magic circle or disc') A circular visual representation of the universe that focuses on **Buddha** and Buddhist themes. Diagrammatic in nature, these detailed and colourful drawings are said to be the formal geometrical expression of sacred vibrations and are used as a focus point for the practice of **meditation**. When a person concentrates on a mandala, they are able to establish a connection with the infinite, and therefore travel further on the path towards **enlightenment**.

Mandala

Mandalas are also used in Western mystic traditions to represent the relationships between symbols in Kabbalism. In **Jungian psychology**, a mandala is considered an important dream/**archetype** symbol that represents the universe or wholeness of the self. See also: **Jung, Tibetan Buddhism**.

Mandrake The plant *Mandragora officinarum*, whose roots are used in magic and other supernatural traditions. Despite its use in love potions, in medieval European cultures it was considered a herb of unsavoury and rather sinister reputation, because its roots resembled the form of a human being. To this day, it retains this negative status in folkloric traditions throughout Europe. It was also commonly found under the bodies of hanged men at crossroads, since it was said to thrive on the last emissions of their death throes.

According to superstition, when the mandrake was harvested, it would shriek, driving the hearer insane. All of these attributes are probably due to the high level of psychotropic compounds in the plant, which can give rise to delirious, fantastic visions.

Mantra (Sanskrit, 'uniting and holding') A set of words made up of sacred syllables and sounds used for developing the mind and transcending consciousness. In **Buddhism** a mantra expresses the path to **enlightenment**, and is chanted while meditating to self-induce a trance state. The more a mantra is chanted, the more effective and powerful it becomes. When chanted to music, a mantra is called a raga.

Mantras are also used in Hindu rites to enhance a guru's power and are often passed down to initiates.

In recent years it has also come to mean one's personal life philosophy and/or goal which, if repeated long enough, might be realised.

Mantra, also Nada Yoga see **Yoga**

Mars The fourth planet in our solar system, with a reddish tinge to it. This hue explains why it is named for the Roman god of war. In **astrology**, Mars is the planet that rules your desires and determination. It stands for initiative, your will to succeed and how you deal with your temper. Mars also symbolises the archetypal male in the cosmos. Traditionally, Mars rules armies, blood, cars, engineering, passion, sport, stamina and aggression. It is the ruling planet of the **zodiac** sign **Aries**, and the co-ruler of **Scorpio**.

Maslow, Abraham (1908–70) One of the founders of **humanistic psychology**, and the author of the seminal theories the **hierarchy of needs** and **peak experience**. Maslow believed in the intrinsic goodness of human nature, and felt that psychotherapists should work with a patient to achieve their highest potential. He also felt that the whole of a person's psyche should be examined to discover the root causes of neuroses and psychoses, and not just the workings of the unconscious mind (the favoured idea in psychological circles up to the 1950s and '60s). He was one of the first psychologists to bridge the gap between mental, physical and spiritual experience, and influenced movements like the **human potential movement** and **neurolinguistic programming**.

Massage, Massage Therapy (Arabic *mas'h*, 'press softly') The kneading, stroking or pressing of the muscles and soft tissues of the body for therapeutic purposes. Massage therapy is an ancient healing art, known throughout the centuries in all cultures as producing physical, psychological and spiritual benefits. Not surprisingly, there are different schools of massage based on these differing effects.

One of the earliest remedial practices, massage was first documented in Chinese writings c. 3000 BC. Massage treatments and their healing properties were also discussed in the holy Hindu texts, the **Vedas**. Knowledge of this bodywork travelled the Silk Route from the Orient and was documented in Arabic writings, which were translated into Greek and incorporated into Western medicine and therapy. **Hippocrates**, the Greek physician and author of the eponymous oath, applied diagnostic principles to the theory of massage and infused it with a degree of respectability as a healing art.

'Swedish massage', so called because it was developed by Swede Per Henrik Ling in the early nineteenth century, best exemplifies the physical school of massage. His six classical massage movements are: **effleurage**, **petrissage**, **kneading**, **hacking**, **cupping** and **tapotement**. Ling defined an objective for each movement and classified them either as 'active' or 'passive', depending on their physiological effect. Most masseurs today are taught these six movements as the foundation for any serious touch therapy. This school of massage concentrates on producing physical benefits, which include: relief and relaxation for tense, painful muscles; increased blood circulation and flow of nutrients to muscles and bone (which can speed healing, the reason massage is used so often in recovery from sports injury); improved blood circulation to skin; stimulation of lymphatic drainage, which promotes rapid removal of toxins and waste products from the body; decreased heart rate and lowered blood pressure due to muscle relaxation.

Physical massage methods are also utilised for their psychological effects on the body, but these mind benefits are the primary focus for **holistic** massage. As the name suggests, this school works on the whole person, and often incorporates theories of **energy medicine** into its practice. Psychological benefits of massage include reduction of stress and promotion of a feeling of well-being, often because of the release of endorphins in the body after a treatment. The goal for a holistic masseur is to promote these effects as well as to work to balance the flow of life energy (known in various traditions as **chi, prana, vitalism, life force** and **ki**) throughout the body, while still providing the physical benefits of massage. **Shiatsu, rolfing, champissage, reflexology,** and **aromatherapy** are examples of this form of massage.

Finally there is the 'spiritual' school of massage, which sometimes includes little or no touch at all, and whose aims are all in aligning energies in the body. Examples of this massage school are **therapeutic touch, reiki, zero balancing** and **polarity therapy**.

Massage continues to be one of the most popular of all alternative therapies, as it is non-invasive and, with a few exceptions, safe for anyone from children to Chelsea Pensioners. As with any alternative therapy, however, it is best to find a fully trained and qualified practitioner to administer massage, as there *are* circumstances under which massage therapy is not appropriate.

Mayan Calendar, Mayans An ancient Meso-American tribe (AD 200–900) who invented a calendar of remarkable accuracy and complexity. It was based on astronomical observations and advanced mathematics that made it capable of projecting dates far into the future. It used three different dating systems in parallel with each other: the long count, the *Tzolkin*, or divine calendar, and the *Haab*, or civil calendar. It had a year of roughly 260 days of 20 months, and was used in some unknown way in Mayan religious ritual.

The Mayan calendar is of particular interest because it theoretically predicts the date that the world will come to an end: 21 December AD 2012. Until that date passes, there will be many wondering about the worth of their long-term investments, and whether or not 'carpe diem' (seize the day) is a better philosophy of life.

Mecca A holy city in **Islam**, where the Prophet **Muhammad** was born and where the Ka'bah, the grand mosque and first house of Islamic worship, is located. When Muslims make their daily prayers, they face towards Mecca, and the goal of every devout Muslim is to make pilgrimage (or **Hajj**) to Mecca once in their lifetime.

Medical Intuitive A person with a specific set of **spiritual healing** abilities. A medical intuitive can instantly and accurately visualise the anatomy of the human body and its energy field, the aura, and correctly diagnose the root causes of disease and illness. They then can direct their own healing energies to the afflicted area to facilitate a return to health.

Medicine Man A medical, magical practitioner who uses his spells and potions to cure the sick, protect his community from evil and contact **spirit guides** for wisdom and divination purposes. The medicine man is mostly found in Native American cultures, but is also known as a **witch doctor** among indigenous tribes of Africa and South America, and in parts of Australasia and Polynesia. See also: **Shaman, Shamanism**.

Medicine Wheel A ritualistic stone circle or hoop used by Native North Americans to tell time, follow the seasons and conduct spiritual ceremonies.

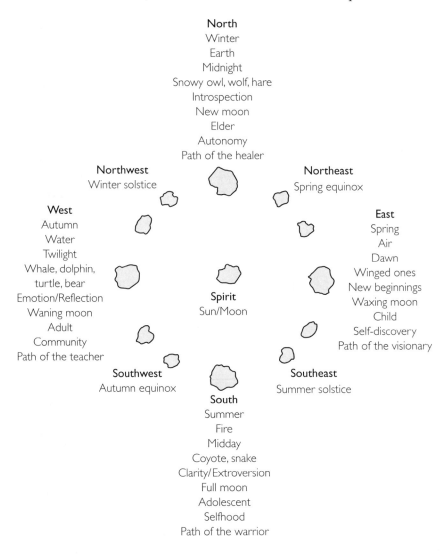

North
Winter
Earth
Midnight
Snowy owl, wolf, hare
Introspection
New moon
Elder
Autonomy
Path of the healer

Northwest
Winter solstice

Northeast
Spring equinox

West
Autumn
Water
Twilight
Whale, dolphin,
turtle, bear
Emotion/Reflection
Waning moon
Adult
Community
Path of the teacher

East
Spring
Air
Dawn
Winged ones
New beginnings
Waxing moon
Child
Self-discovery
Path of the visionary

Spirit
Sun/Moon

Southwest
Autumn equinox

Southeast
Summer solstice

South
Summer
Fire
Midday
Coyote, snake
Clarity/Extroversion
Full moon
Adolescent
Selfhood
Path of the warrior

The Native North American medicine wheel

It is similar in nature to the **Celtic wheel of the year**, and also to the **ba-gua** diagram used in **feng shui**, as it has both time and direction noted on it. Although the assignment of colours, elements and spirit beings to parts of the wheel differed from tribe to tribe, the four compass points (north, south, east, west) and the same four colours (red, white, black and yellow) were always present on the wheel. It is also similar to the magic circle of the four natural elements used in **Wiccan** and witchcraft magical ceremonies.

Meditation (Latin *meditari*, 'contemplate or measure') A contemplative technique of focusing your mind on a specific object or thought, for religious, spiritual or relaxation purposes. This often leads to feelings of great calm or peace in body and soul. There are many different ways to meditate – in silence or with the aid of chanting, or listening to music. Sometimes the focus of concentration can be on a picture like a **mandala** (as in Tibetan Buddhism) or on the rhythm of your breath and posture. Whichever approach is used, you will need a quiet environment and a fixed period of time when you will not be interrupted. Next, you choose the thing you wish to focus on, like your breath or a particular word or phrase, or a physical object, and get into a comfortable position (lying down is not recommended as you might go to sleep). The goal is to achieve a state of 'mindfulness' – where you are aware of what is going on around you, but are detached from your immediate surroundings, almost in a light **trance** state.

Meditation is an important spiritual practice among many religions, including **Sufism**, and Jewish and Christian mystical tradition, but is most closely associated with **Buddhism** and with **yoga**. Meditation is used in the context of Buddhist teachings to indicate the controlling and directing of one's mind inward in the quest for **enlightenment**. Although meditation can be done while walking, standing, sitting or lying down, usually emphasis is placed on sitting meditation (called **zazen**).

There is a number of documented physical and psychological benefits to meditation, many of them arising out of a research project from Harvard Medical School Professor Herbert Benson. He discovered the **relaxation response** in transcendental meditation practitioners in the 1970s. Even 20 minutes of meditation reduced blood pressure, heart and breathing rates, reduced muscle tension and slowed the metabolism.

Follow-on studies have shown meditation can help relieve stress and anxiety, headaches, migraine, fatigue, depression, insomnia and chronic pain. Mental benefits include increased feelings of energy and confidence, as well as the calming of overactive minds and imaginations.

Medium People who serve as a conduit between our physical world, and that of the spirit realm. These 'go-betweens' are often people who already possess other **psychic** abilities, and know the precise means of invoking a mediumistic trance. This trance allows a medium's 'control' entity to possess them – this entity is one that regularly works with the medium, and can be thought of as a spiritual doorman for the other ghosts and powers invoked. When the control or other entities are in possession of the medium's body (called **channelling**), this may manifest itself in physical ways, like a change of voice, gestures and mannerisms specific to the deceased spirit. A medium will usually have no memory of what has taken place during their trance state.

There is a special type of medium who practises what they call 'soul rescue' – they contact a ghost or spirit to persuade them to move on to the afterlife. These ghosts are those with trapped souls, who either do not know they have died, or cannot bear to leave their own home. See also: **Séance, Spiritualism**.

Megaliths (Greek *mega*, 'large', + *lithos*, 'stone') Large prehistoric monuments of stone consisting of rows of single standing rocks or circular arrangements in a table-like format. Megaliths are often deliberately placed on **ley lines** (the earth's energy network) and appear to have astronomical and healing associations. They also seem to have spiritual meanings in **paganism**, although their original builders and creators are unknown.

Megalithic monuments have been found all over the world, from Carnac in Egypt to **Stonehenge** in England and Easter Island in the Pacific Ocean. When they are arranged in post and lintel style, they are known as 'dolmens'; when aligned in rows of sole standing stones, they are known as 'menhirs'. See also: **Cailleach, Geomancy, Sacred Geometry**.

Mehndi The decorative art of applying temporary henna tattoos on the skin, dating back over 5,000 years. Mehndi originated in ancient Egypt, where the remains of bottles filled with henna paste have been found in burial tombs in the Valley of the Kings.

Mehndi has been a part of cultural traditions in North Africa, the Middle East and India for many years, used for special occasions and celebrations like weddings (where the hands and feet of the bride are painted), births, deaths and even first menstruations. Although men sometimes have henna tattoos applied, it is more usually a female custom because in earlier times women were thought to be vulnerable to evil spirits at times of significant life events. Mehndis were considered a form of painted-on **amulets**, a protective tattoo against the evil eye and other misfortunes. In our day, mehndis are considered body art. These delicate henna patterns of flowers, leaves and other geometric designs are applied to the hands, wrists, arms, feet and ankles, but they can also be used to decorate other parts of the body.

Menhir (Breton men, 'stone', + hir, 'high') A tall standing stone erected in prehistoric Europe, particularly Britain and Ireland, where they are associated with the Celtic pagan goddess, **Cailleach**. See also: **Megaliths**.

Merc. Sol. One of the 15 major **polychrests**, or major remedies in **homeopathy**. It is also a **constitutional type**, which is a way homeopaths have of classifying different patient profiles. The fitting constitutional remedy acts preventatively and curatively on its matching personality type – for example, a person with a Merc. Sol. constitution will respond well to the Merc. Sol. remedy almost regardless of the illness they are suffering from. Merc. Sol. people are very introverted, and tend to be easily offended. They require a stable existence to function effectively, and in particular to control their temper. They are susceptible to respiratory ailments, and to problems with the mouth and throat. Women of this type often suffer from chronic thrush.

Mercury The first planet in our solar system and the closest to the **sun**. Mercury is named for the Roman winged messenger of the gods. In **astrology**, Mercury is associated with the mind, with communications, information and sharp money practices. It represents the way you think and the way you process information. Because Mercury has the shortest transit (only 88 days to circle the sun), every four months or so it appears to go **retrograde** (backwards) from the earth's point of view. When this happens, anything under the influence of Mercury becomes garbled and confused – goes 'backwards' just as the planet apparently does.

Traditionally, Mercury rules the written word in all its forms, logic, computers, telephones. It is the ruling planet of the **zodiac** signs **Gemini** and **Virgo**.

Meridians Rivers of bioelectric energy (also known as **chi**) that circulate in the body along specific channels, according to **Traditional Chinese Medicine**. These rivers of energy bring life to every cell in the body. When a person is healthy, chi flows freely through their meridian channels. When disease or injury occurs, chi becomes blocked and unequally distributed throughout the body. A variety of therapies, including **acupuncture**, **acupressure**, **shiatsu**, **reflexology** and **Chinese herbal medicine**, work to redistribute chi evenly

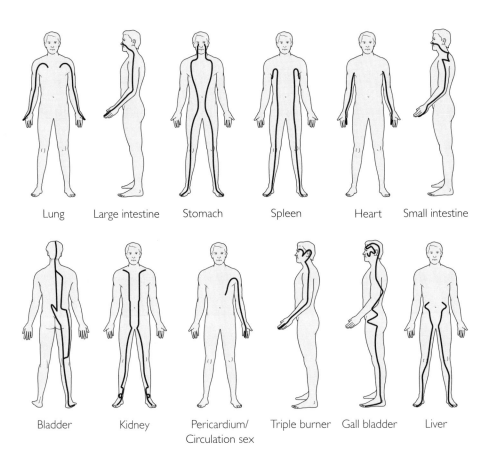

Lung   Large intestine   Stomach   Spleen   Heart   Small intestine

Bladder   Kidney   Pericardium/   Triple burner   Gall bladder   Liver
                    Circulation sex

The principal meridians

along meridian lines. Although skilled Chinese physicians and acupuncturists work with a much more complex meridian map, there are 12 main meridians, six that start or finish in the hands (**heart, small intestine, pericardium/circulation-sex, triple warmer, lung** and **large intestine**) and six that start or finish in the feet (**stomach, spleen, bladder, kidney, gall bladder** and **liver**). Two vessels (central and governing) start and end on the head and torso, and function as a prime energy source and as a junction and clearing house for the other meridians.

Chakras are also aligned on the paths of the central and governing vessels. The direction of energy flow is determined by whether or not a meridian is **yang** or **yin**. Yang energy flows downwards from the sun and so those meridians run from the fingers to the face (as if a person has their arms raised) or from the face to the feet. Yin energy, from the earth, flows upwards from the feet to the torso and from the torso along the insides of the arms to the fingertips.

Meridians are bilateral, meaning that there are two sets of identical meridians, one on each side of the body, and they are named according to the organ energy they affect. Each meridian has a corresponding partner of opposite polarity, meaning one of the pair will be yin and the other yang. A meridian also has particular affinities with one of the Chinese **five elements**, with a whole host of corresponding qualities associated with each. See also: **Acupuncture**, **Five Element Cycle**.

Merlin Wizard, enchanter and prophet to the legendary ruler of Britain, **King Arthur**. He is best known for his role in overseeing Arthur's conception, and in ensuring that Arthur took the throne through magical means. His name is Latin for the Welsh *Myrddin*, a sixth-century bard who reportedly had the 'gift of sight', otherwise known as **precognition**. At the end of his long life, he fell into the clutches of the sorcerous witch, Nimue (also known as Viviane) who stole his magic and imprisoned him with an enchantment.

In some traditions, Merlin is a Celtic Druid, who used his magical abilities to enable Arthur to gain and retain his power. In all traditions, he is pictured as scholar and adviser to the King, and his genius guides Arthur's reign. See also: **Arthurian Legends**.

Mermaids, Mermen, Merpeople (from Latin *mare*, 'sea') Mythological half-fish, half-human creatures, which had the upper torso, head and arms of a person and the bottom half of a fish. Mermaids in particular were considered bewitching temptresses, bare-chested, who liked to sit on rocks in the ocean, singing and combing their long tresses. Or so the lonely sailors, at sea for years without women, thought. These sightings were considered to be unlucky, no doubt hearkening back to the tale of Ulysses and the **Sirens**, who lured the unwary to their deaths.

Merpeople are **elementals**, nature spirits of the water, who have the ability to change their fish-like tail into human legs and venture onto dry land. According to legend, a merman or mermaid occasionally fell in love with a human. If the loved one hid the merperson's tailskin, or a precious object like a shell necklace or other jewellery, the water spirit would be doomed to stay on dry land until the object was recovered. If you could trick a merperson into being baptised, they would gain a soul and never be able to return to life in the sea.

Tales of mermaids and mermen are known throughout many cultures – the ancient Greeks called them nereids and thought them divine; Irish folk called them merrows; and Germans, the Lorelei. It is now believed that all the sightings of these legendary creatures were actually of manatees or dugongs, marine mammals of the large and lumpy sort. So much for myth, then.

Mesmerism An early form of **hypnosis** used by Friedrich Anton Mesmer (1733–1815) during the late eighteenth and early nineteenth centuries. Mesmer himself called it 'animal magnetism', because he believed that magnetic force shot through his fingertips or eyes and induced a **trance** state. He used magnets and iron shavings in his work, which became an act for the society circles he travelled in. Eventually Mesmer was branded a charlatan, but his early work in hypnotism prompted more reputable folk to research and develop the phenomenon into a valid therapeutic technique.

Metal Element One of the **five elements** in Chinese philosophy and medicine that make up the 'building blocks' of the universe. In **Traditional Chinese Medicine**, metal is associated with the **lung** and **large intestine meridians**, and with the season of autumn. Metal represents grief and sadness and protects the body from outside physical influences as well as emotional assault. The colour white, dryness, pungent or aromatic tastes, the skin, body hair, nose and smell, the sound of weeping and elimination of body wastes are also associated with this element.

In the five element cycle, metal generates or gives birth to **water** and controls **wood** and in turn metal is given life by earth and controlled by **fire**. This interdependent relationship to other elements has implications in health. If someone has weak metal energy they will be prone to colds, allergies, asthma, dry skin and constipation. Mentally, they may appear cold and judgemental. Left unchecked, this could then go on to weaken other elemental energies and lead to other health problems in the way that poor toxic waste elimination (weak metal energies) could lead to gallstones or even cirrhosis in extreme cases (weak wood energies). See also: **Taoism**, **Yang Yin**.

Metamorphic Technique An esoteric physical therapy roughly based on the same principles as **reflexology**. Metamorphic technique works more on changing patterns of our personality and behaviour, and maximising our potential, than directly on balancing body energies in health. In the 1960s Robert St John, a British naturopath and reflexologist, developed this technique based on his belief that life begins at conception, not birth. He thought his specific method of manipulating foot reflexes provided a transforming trigger for change or 'metamorphosis'.

St John and his followers have had some therapeutic success in working with mentally handicapped children and those with learning disabilities, although his theories are not accepted by the main bulk of reflexologists and other alternative therapists.

Meteoromancy see Astromancy

Michael see Archangel

Michaelmas The **pagan** celebration that surround the autumn **equinox** (21 September) and the last of the eight great **sabbats** of the **Celtic wheel of the year**. It is the second and last 'harvest festival' of the year, representing a drawing in of bounty to survive the following winter. In the Celtic story of the year, this is the date when the god of darkness wins control of the day from his brother, the god of light.

Michaelmas is named after the Christian St Michael (his actual day is 29 September), patron saint of high places, replacing earlier pagan sun deities. **Druids** mark this day by climbing up to the top of high hills and ceremonially saying goodbye to the sun for another year.

Midsummer, Midsummer's Eve The pagan festival that surrounds the summer **solstice** (21 June), which marks the high spot of the year and the zenith of solar magical energies. It is also associated with fertility rites that celebrate the sexual joining of the archetypal mature earth goddess with the archetypal sun god, making June the optimum time for marriage and conception.

Druids mark this date by keeping watch through Solstice Eve, and continue their celebrations until noon of the Solstice Day; this too is one of the eight **sabbats**, holy days of a **witch**'s year. Midsummer's Eve is also the one night of the year when you can see **fairies** and **elementals**, nature spirits and powers that otherwise keep themselves hidden from man.

Pagans see the solstice as a time for love, marriage, friendship, magical energy and strength. Fires are lit on this evening to keep away evil spirits and light the way for revellers.

Midsummer is also associated with the Christian feast of St John the Baptist, celebrated on 24 June. The flower **St John's wort** is at full bloom in this season, making it the sacred flower of midsummer. See also: **Celtic Wheel**.

Mimulus A flower essence made from the mimulus blossom. This emotionally healing tincture is one of the **Bach Flower Remedies**. Dr Bach said that this is indicated for 'those who are afraid and lack courage. For everyday, known fears, and for those who are shy, or timid'.

Mindfulness see Vipassana

Mind-Maps, also **Mind-mapping** A learning technique developed in the late 1960s by English psychology lecturer Tony Buzan, following his research into note taking. Mind maps aid memory recall and help generate ideas by association using graphics. They utilise different cortical skills – word, image, number, logic, rhythm, colour and spatial awareness – to produce a single visual representation of an idea or concept. To make a mind map, one starts in the centre of the page with the main idea, and draws lines outwards in all directions to produce a growing and organised structure composed of key words and key images. Unlike a flow chart, which can only express visual ideas in a linear fashion, a mind map resembles a spider web, with the main idea the centre of the web and related concepts and associations branching out and connecting to each other independently of the centre.

Minimum Dose In **homeopathy**, the term for the right dilution (also known as 'potentation') of the homeopathic remedy appropriate for treating a particular illness or condition. The more it is diluted, the deeper-acting the remedy becomes.

Moksha, also **Moksa** (Sanskrit, 'liberation') In **Hinduism,** the ultimate goal of liberation from the process of **samsara**, the continuous cycle of birth, death and rebirth. Much like **nirvana**, you can only achieve moksha by carefully following the precepts of Hindu belief, and by changing your **karma** (actions) in this life.

Molescopy The art of reading moles, for the purposes of **divination** or to define a person's character. Molescopy was practised throughout many different cultures (like ancient Egypt, Greece and Rome), but reached its height (some say its frenzy) during Europe's medieval period. Then it was often taken to be a way of foretelling a person's future, or more ominously, as a sign of witchcraft (called a witch's mark).

Where the mole was located on the body was significant – for example, moles located over the heart meant a person was wicked; on the right armpit they signified wealth or honour (on the left armpit, the opposite). Astrologists believed the colour of moles was influenced by different planets. This practice is now considered somewhat out-of-date, mostly because of the random nature of mole scatters, and the means to apply artificial moles (like beauty marks and tattoos) that create false predictions.

Mondo, Mondos Questions and answers that defy logic, used by Zen

Masters in **Zen Buddhism** to stimulate the mind of a disciple towards **enlightenment**. See also: **Koan**.

Mongolian Overtone Chanting, also **Overtone Singing**, **Overtoning**, **Throat Singing** A unique method of chanting on one note found only in Central Asia – Mongolia, Tuva (native Siberia) and Tibet. Listeners often describe the sound as unearthly, angelic and bell-like. It all has to do with the way the mouth, larynx and throat are manipulated by the singer: it is possible for the note to take on different harmonic qualities, even if the pitch of the note stays the same. When more than one chanter is involved, the harmonies can become quite hair-raising, but spiritually very moving. In Tibet, in a few **Tantric Buddhism** monasteries, it is done by the monks as part of ceremonial practice. Mongolian overtone chanting is becoming increasingly popular in the West, and there are workshops run in the UK and US, with practitioners claiming it has a powerful therapeutic effect.

Monkey, The In **Chinese astrology**, the ninth sign of the **zodiac**. You are a Monkey if you were or will be born in the years 1932, 1944, 1956, 1968, 1980, 1992, 2004 or 2016. The Monkey is the sign of fantasy in Chinese mythology, symbolising intelligence and resourcefulness. Those born under this sign are lively, fast-thinking and witty. They are intuitive and yearn for constant variety. They can become irritated and impatient, however, with slower-thinking individuals. Their Western zodiac equivalent is **Leo** and their ruling planet is the **Sun**.

Moon Signs In **astrology**, the sign of the **zodiac** the moon occupied at the time of your birth. To many astrologers, your moon sign tells more about you than your **sun sign**, because the location of the moon at the particular hour of the particular day of the particular year you were born is so precise. **Horoscopes** used to refer to a person's moon sign, not sun sign, but that changed in the early part of the twentieth century, when newspapers started to list daily horoscopes. Putting in the long tables necessary to determine your moon sign was too bulky, so instead astrologers used a person's sun sign, of which there are only 12. Your sun sign deals with the outer you and is therefore more general than your moon sign, which deals with the inner you.

Moon, The The earth's only natural satellite and, in **astrology**, the most important body in the heavens outside of the **sun**. Known as the 'Queen of the Night', the moon represents the emotional and unconscious aspects of our personality and the **moon sign** was once considered more important in casting a **horoscope** than the **sun sign**. She represents the divine mother goddess, and traditionally rules water and the oceans, nursing, reproduction, silver, the stomach and tears. She is the ruling planet of the **zodiac** sign **Cancer**.

It has been known for thousands of years that if you time your activities to different phases of the moon, you are likely to have greater success in achieving a particular aim. Indian culture has a school of **astrology** called **Panchang**, organised around that very idea. This concept of lunar timing drives sceptics crazy because it cannot be explained through scientific means. Certain research has shown, however, that the phases of the moon have an effect on human and animal life. At the full moon there are more births, and doctors do not schedule elective surgery, as haemorrhage is more common in the operating theatre. Farmers have known for years that seeds sown with a waxing moon have better rates of growth. In general, a waxing moon helps to make things grow (plants, money, relationships). A full moon marks a time where matters are clarified and confidence increases and it can also cause (as seen above) intense physiological changes and increase emotional tension. A waning moon is a good time to try and resolve old problems, and a new moon is the best time to start anything new.

Moonstone, also **Fish-eye**, **Water Opal**, and **Wolf's-eye** A **crystal** gem long associated with the moon by ancient cultures up to the present. In magic, moonstones were used during the waxing moon in love spells and during the waning moon to foretell the future. The moonstone protects travellers and brings success and good fortune, especially in love. It is the quintessentially feminine stone, and in **crystal-healing** bring ease to period pains and similar disorders. Moonstones are said to enhance a person's innate **psychic** abilities, and are a great balancer of emotions.

Morphic Resonance A term created by biologist Rupert Sheldrake in his 1981 publication *A New Science of Life* to explain how groups of living organisms can suddenly learn behaviours previously exhibited only by a small membership of the group. He thought there was 'the basis of memory in nature ... the idea of mysterious telepathy-type interconnections between organisms and of collective memories within species'. In simpler terms, if you have an animal like a rat that learns a trick in one place, another rat in another place will learn the trick more easily. The more rats that learn the trick, the more others will learn it. Sheldrake felt that there was some sort of 'morphogenetic' field surrounding each specific organism, and when something new occurred to one of them, every other organism of the same species would feel the ripple effect, even if they were not physically present, as this new information 'resonated' within the first organism's morphogenetic field.

He coined this phrase as a creative response to the challenges set by nineteenth-century scientific debates over the development of organisms. Sheldrake also thought it best explained the phenomenon of the **hundredth monkey**.

There is much scientific scepticism about morphic resonance, but advanced studies in physics are beginning to discover the interconnectedness of all living things, as well as unexplained electromagnetic fields surrounding all matter.

Morrigan, The In Irish mythology, a triple **goddess** (maid, mother, crone) of renewal, death and fate, and the fierce goddess of battle. She appears in the guise of a fighting warrior maiden, urging on soldiers to glorious deeds and afterwards as carrion, scavenging the bodies of the dead. The Morrigan is one of the incarnations of **Cailleach**, the Irish goddess of death. See also: **Celtic Wheel, Paganism**.

Morris Dance, Morris Dancers The most widely known ceremonial dance form in England; originally derived from ancient **pagan** and **Druid** fertility rituals. The name comes from the 'Moorish' dancers of Spain, and is first mentioned in English documents of the fifteenth century.

The dancers are usually male and wear a special costume of tights and tunics with wooden clogs on their feet or wooden taps on their shoes. They have ankle bands with many small bells, wear holly wreaths on their heads, and carry tall straight canes with flowing scarves. One of the dancers will portray antlers on his head, symbolising **Herne** the Hunter, the pagan god of male fertility, and traditional consort to the Mother Earth **goddess**. The dance is slow and rhythmic, with much foot-pounding and shaking of bells. The insistent tapping steps, hanky-waving and bell-ringings were once thought to awaken slumbering spirits of the fields after their winter hibernation. Leaping is a reminder to them to allow grain to grow high, flocks to multiply, and people to prosper. The final gathering circle dance mimics the path of the sun as it blesses the earth.

In recent years, growing numbers of women have become Morris dancers, although the intent of the dancing remains the same. See also: **Beltane, Horned God, Paganism**.

Mount Olympus The home of the Greek gods of mythology, in particular the 12 gods and goddesses who made up the ruling council, the Olympiad. They were: **Zeus, Hera, Poseidon, Demeter, Apollo, Artemis, Mars, Aphrodite, Athena**, Hephaestus, Hestia and **Hermes. Hades**, the god of the underworld, was also a member, but preferred the gloomy depths of his dark realm.

Moxibustion (Japanese *moe,* + *kusai*, burning herb) A therapeutic technique used in **acupuncture** to enhance needling or to energetically warm up specific acupuncture points. A small core of moxa (the dried leaves of a Chinese mugwort-like herb *Artemisia vulgaris latiflora*) is placed on a point and ignited. Alternatively, a small plug of moxa is placed on the end of an inserted needle and ignited. A moxa stick may also be lit and waved around the affected area for a gentle warming.

Mu see **Lemuria**

Muhammad, also **Mohammad, Mahomet** (Arabic, 'praised one') The founder of Islam, also known as the Prophet. Muhammad (570–632) was born in **Mecca** and lived a fairly ordinary life for his time, until he was 42. Spiritually troubled, he retreated to a cave in the hills above Mecca where he received a vision from the archangel Gabriel (Jibril) who revealed to him the first revelation of many that were collected into a single text, the **Koran**. Gabriel also said that Muhammad had been ordained a prophet of the one true God, **Allah**, and that he therefore should lead the people from their present immorality to righteousness and salvation.

Despite considerable opposition to his teachings, Muhammad continued over the next 23 years to receive messages from Allah, and constructed the tenets of Islam we know today. He eventually moved north to the city of Medina, where he became a powerful leader and was firmly able to establish the Islamic faith before his death in AD 632.

Beside the Koran, Muhammad is responsible for the other main text consulted by Muslims, the *Hadith*, a collection of his teachings and sayings.

Mummies, Mummification A funerary practice of ancient Egypt, employed at least since 2400 BC, where the body of a dead person (or in some cases those of animals like cats and dogs) would be carefully embalmed using a method not dissimilar to the modern one. First, the intestines and other organs were removed and the body cavities filled with preserving substances like bitumen, salt, incense and spices. The organs that had been removed were placed in 'canopic jars', and buried with the owner. The body would then be sealed in layers of linen wrappings, often with sacred objects such as **scarabs** and other symbolic **amulets** wrapped among the bandages. Finally, the deceased would be laid to rest in a series of airtight coffins, which preserved the body.

This elaborate ritual was all carried out because of the Egyptian belief that the body would still be required in the afterlife. If the mummies lay undisturbed, the natural process of decay would be eliminated – and those found in excavations over the last 100 years or so remained preserved.

Contrary to Hollywood myth, no empirical evidence has so far been found to support the existence of 'the mummy's curse', nor has anyone yet been attacked by a flailing, bandage-ridden monster. See also: **Egyptian Book of the Dead**.

Music of the Spheres A theory of the Greek mystical mathematician **Pythagoras**, who related the orbits of the sun, moon and planets to a musical scale. Not regarding it as a mere metaphor, he described it as 'a divine symphony beyond the perception of most humans, played by the planets as they spun along in their orbits'.

Mustard A flower essence made from the mustard blossom. This emotionally healing tincture is one of the **Bach Flower Remedies**. Dr Bach said that this is indicated for 'depression for no apparent reason. An unhappiness that descends and then lifts like a passing cloud but without an identifiable cause'.

Mutable Signs In Western **astrology**, the four signs of the **zodiac** (**Sagittarius**, **Gemini**, **Virgo** and **Pisces**) that share a certain versatility and willingness to compromise. They thrive on constant change, and are called 'mutable' because when the sun enters their sign the season is about to change.

Myotherapy, also **Trigger Point Therapy** (Greek *myo*, 'muscle') A technique developed by American fitness expert Bonnie Prudden in the 1970s for defusing trigger points (tender, irritable and painful spots) in muscles. These points are known in other health systems, like Traditional Chinese Medicine, and in Swedish massage, but Prudden combined her skills as a masseuse with a specific combination of pain-relieving injections, heating and cooling, and exercise to bring relief to stressed muscles. Myotherapy relieves any soft-tissue pain, but is particularly good for pain associated with repetitive strain injury, accidents and sport injuries as well as fibromyalgia and related conditions.

Mysticism (Greek *mustes*, 'initiated person') A belief that union or absorption into an ecstatic religious experience will allow you to become one with the god or deity you are worshipping. You will then be given secret knowledge inaccessible by the intellect or any other means. The experience of surrender must be total, and can be obtained through contemplation, invocation of trance states through music, chanting or dance, or focused meditation.

Nadis (Sanskrit) Channels of **prana** (energy) that run through the body, similar to **meridians** in Chinese medicine and philosophy. There are over 72,000 nadis but the three principles are pingala, which carries male or solar energy (known as 'ha' energy) through the body; ida, which carries female or lunar energy (known as *tha*) and the central channel called sushumna, which lies along the axis of the spine. **Yoga** aims to channel prana into the sushumna, as all the **chakras**, or focused energy centres of the body, lie along this nadi. Activation of these three main channels is necessary to arouse **kundalini** energy, vital in **kundalini yoga** and any **tantric** practices.

Nag Hammadi Library A collection of religious and philosophic texts discovered in 1945 buried in a large stone jar in the desert outside Nag Hammadi, Egypt. Among these manuscripts were the lost 'gospels' of **Gnosticism**, long believed to be apocryphal scriptures lost in antiquity. The library itself is a diverse collection of texts that the Gnostics considered to be related to their heretical philosophy in some way. There are 45 separate titles in the library, including a copy of *The Gospel of Thomas*, attributed to Jesus' brother James, *The Gospel of Mary*, *The Apocryphon of James*, and *The Dialogue of the Saviour*.

Other texts that explore the mystic traditions at the heart of early Christianity were subsequently banned by more conservative Church leaders.

Natrum Mur One of the 15 major **polychrests**, or major remedies in **homeopathy**. It is also a **constitutional type**, which is a way homeopaths have of classifying different patient profiles. The fitting constitutional remedy acts preventatively and curatively on its matching personality type – for example, a person with a Natrum Mur constitution will respond well to the Natrum Mur remedy almost regardless of the illness they are suffering from. Natrum Mur people are introspective and sensitive and are prone to suppressing their emotions. They appear to be totally self-reliant but can be somewhat inhibited in personal and business situations. They are susceptible to colds and flu, but do not acknowledge their illness no matter how sick they feel. The remedy Natrum Mur is often used to treat grief, especially amongst those people who hide or refuse to deal with this feeling.

Naturopathy, also **Naturopathic Medicine** A combination of natural therapies, modern science and folk wisdom used to treat illness and restore health. This approach is based on the belief that the body will heal itself, given the right circumstances. Producing these right circumstances is the goal of naturopaths, who seek to find out the underlying reason for the imbalance, rather than merely alleviating symptoms. They do this through different methods including: physical examination, **iridology**, **kinesiology**, X-rays, blood and urine tests, and hair analysis.

Once the underlying cause of illness is found, a naturopath will use any number of different therapeutics to stimulate the body's self-healing processes. They may prescribe homeopathic or herbal formulas, or changes in nutrition and exercise. Naturopaths also believe in helping to cleanse the system through a number of means: fasting, massage, hydrotherapy, **colonics** and other **detox** routines. In all of their therapies, a naturopath will insist on the patient being a willing participant in the healing process, and taking responsibility in making lifestyle changes to improve and maintain health.

Near-death Experience A phenomenon reported by people who have been declared clinically dead, but are later revived. They report an altered state of consciousness where they feel they are travelling through a tunnel towards a loving, bright light, or that they are floating above their body watching medical efforts to revive them. This sort of experience is classified as a type of **out-of-body experience**, where the **astral** and physical body separate.

Necromancy, also **Nagomancy** (Greek *nekros*, 'corpse', + *manteia*, 'divination') Methods of **divination** via communication with the dead, either through contacting the spirits of the departed, or through the grisly practice of using a dead person's corpse. Necromancy differs from other contacts with the spirit world, like mediumship, in that occult magical rituals are used to compel the ghost, or corpse, to submit to the summoner's will. This black magic often required not only a burnt sacrifice but also a blood-drenched altar to perform the ritual (the more 'precious' the blood, the stronger the magic).

It was extensively practised throughout the classical world but the best-known example of it was described in the **Bible** (1 Samuel 28). This passage describes the visit of the Israeli King Saul to the Witch of Endor, for the purposes of summoning the spirit of Samuel, the departed prophet. The episode was thought to provide irrefutable biblical evidence for the existence of witchcraft.

Nei Jing see Yellow Emperor's Inner Classic

Nephelomancy see Aeromancy, Austromancy

Nephthys, also **Neb-hut**, **Nebthet** (Egyptian, 'mistress of the house') One of the major goddesses of Egyptian mythology, considered to be the 'friend of the dead' because she accompanied souls into the afterlife, and comforted the deceased's loved ones. Nepthys was also the goddess of childbirth, in consort with her sister **Isis**. She is nearly always depicted as a woman with the hieroglyphic symbols of her name (a basket and a house) above her head. In most traditions, Nephthys is the youngest daughter of **Nut**, and sister to **Osiris** and Isis, and sister-consort to **Seth**, or sometimes **Ra**. She is also considered to be the mother of **Anubis**, the dog-headed god of death.

Neptune The eighth and second most-distant planet in our solar system; discovered in 1846 and named for the Roman god of the oceans. In **astrology**, Neptune rules the collective unconscious, and is associated with all emotions and intuition, hidden potential and with unknown dreams, fantasies and wishes. It is also the planet of creativeness and artists, poets and playwrights. The transit of Neptune is 165 years, spending 14 years in each sign of the **zodiac**. Because of this great length of time, it is hard to see daily or even yearly how Neptune influences our lives. Its effects are best seen in the establishment of new cults and religions. It is the co-ruling planet of the zodiac sign **Pisces**.

Neurolinguistic Programming (NLP) A self-help technique developed by linguist John Grinder and psychologist Richard Bandler in the early 1970s. Neurolinguistic programming (also known as NLP) helps to bring about personal change by teaching you how to reprogramme your brain using language, thought and behaviour. Influenced by the psychotherapeutic work of Gregory Bateson and Milton Erickson, Bandler and Grinder put together a theory that combines elements of behavioural cognitive therapy with sophisticated linguistic techniques. The emphasis is on teaching a variety of communication skills, and using self-hypnosis to motivate yourself. It is sometimes termed 'study of the structure of subjective experience', because what you perceive your reality to be, is what it is.

The theory of NLP is not precisely new. Shakespeare's Hamlet said, 'There is nothing either good or bad but thinking makes it so' and that idea would resonate with an NLP trainer. What is unique about NLP is the specific technique that can be taught, so people can make effective changes in their lives. It has applications in business, health management, and education.

First NLP trainers call themselves 'modellers' because they model what thoughts a person should think and what behaviours they should adopt based on successes in related fields. An example would be using NLP to improve athletic prowess. An NLP trainer would find out exactly what a world-class athlete thought, said and did during a winning performance. He would then create a 'model' of behaviour and thought based on this winning athlete, and modify it for his client, the aspiring sports star.

The great benefit of NLP is that it states: 'No one is wrong or broken.' If the first modelling technique does not work, then the right communication model was not put together by the trainer, and it is back to the drawing board. Despite scientific scorn, many have found NLP a useful technique to rewire their negative thought patterns, and attain desired self-improvement.

New Age General term to describe a movement that combines different aspects of Western and Eastern thought into new societal thinking, especially in the areas of spirituality, health and self-development. The school of 'new age' teaching became popular in the 1960s and 1970s in the Western world partly as a reaction against the failure of Christianity and secular humanism to provide spiritual and ethical guidance for the future, and because influential Eastern texts like the teachings of Buddha, the **Vedas** and **I Ching** became widely available in English.

After the Chinese invasion of Tibet, Tibetan Buddhists were scattered in a diaspora all over the world; the Dalai Lama escaped to the West, and their gentle teachings appealed to capitalist cultures weary of materialism. This same fatigue led to the re-emergence and revitalisation of older **pagan** beliefs and holistic health practices already present in the Western world, as well as growing concern over the effects of pollution and waste on the earth's eco-system.

The final explanation must belong to a prevalent concept in new age thinking – it was bound to happen. According to **astrology**, our world will shortly be moving from the Age of Pisces, which has dominated thought and culture for the past 2,000 years, into the **Age of Aquarius**, characterised by an interest in spirituality and intuition, and an increasing belief in the **collective unconscious**. Ultimately, this 'new age' will transform our thinking and bring us together into one united global community.

Nine Star Ki, Nine Ki Astrology Specific type of Japanese/Chinese **astrology** that uses principles of **feng shui** to determine the qualities of your own personal energy field of **chi**. This energetic quality can be defined using your birth date to arrive at your 'ki number' between one and nine. The method of arriving at your ki number is similar to practices used in **numerology**. To work it out, write down the year you were born, using the Chinese calendar (so if you were born before February, you use the preceding year). Next add the last two digits together. This will give you your number, unless it is over nine, when you add it together again to arrive at a single digit. If you were born in 1978, you would first add 7+8=15, then 1+5=6. Six would be your ki number and you could then read an interpretive guide as to your general character and temperament.

Nine star ki is often used in determining the compatibility of couples, arriving at one of three possible answers: positive, neutral or negative.

Ninth House In **astrology**, the **house** or part of the heavens in your birth chart that describes your spiritual and philosophical outlook on life. It also concerns matters about travel, higher education and publishing ventures. It is ruled by the sign **Sagittarius** and the planet **Jupiter**. See also: **Ascendant**, **Horoscope**.

Nirvana, also **Nibbana** (Sanskrit, 'blowing out') State of ultimate bliss and enlightenment in **Hinduism** (sometimes called 'moksha') and **Buddhism**, which means the end of all suffering and liberation from endless existence. As this term also denotes the extinguishing of a fire, it carries the connotations of stilling, cooling and rest. When a soul has attained nirvana, it achieves total peace.

Niyama (Sanskrit, 'individual conduct') Moral code in **yoga** concerning personal behaviour that includes striving for the following: purity or cleanliness; contentment; austerity; the study of texts; and awareness of and devotion to the divine. Niyama is one of the 'eight limbs' or **ashtangas** that are mentioned in the **Yoga Sutras** of Patanjali, whose practice will lead to enlightenment.

Noosphere see **Chardin, Pierre Teilhard de**

Northern Paganism Pagan traditions and beliefs based on the mythology of Ancient Norse and Anglo-Saxon gods and goddesses. Followers usually call themselves heathens instead of pagans, although in every other respect they are the same: they honour the same cycles of nature, perform the same magical rites, and worship the same **goddess** archetype of the Earth Mother. The English terms for the days of the week all come from this mythological culture.

Norse deities are divided between spirits that epitomise natural elements called the Vanir, and the more familiar panoply of deities called the Aesir. The faith itself is called Asatru, or Odintru, as the god **Odin** is its principal inspiration.

According to Odintru, the universe consists of nine worlds, each a branch on the Yggdrasil, an ancient ash tree similar in appearance to the **Kabbalistic tree of life**, which makes some speculate that at one time, long ago, the two faiths were connected. The nine worlds of Yggdrasil are: Midgard, the land of ordinary mortals; Asgard, land of the Aesir; Hel, the land of the dead; Vanaheim, home of the Vanir and Freya's hall; the land of fire; the land of Light Elves; the land of Dark Elves; the land of Ice Giants; and the land of fog. Many of the deities and spirits that inhabit these lands are still found today in the symbols of the **runes**.

There are three magical traditions in Northern Paganism: *Seidr*, which is **shamanistic** in nature; *Galdr*, the written and spoken side (dealing with runes); and *Taufr*, which deals with protective **amulets** and **talismans**. These are practised and celebrated in the eight great **sabbats** (pagan festivals), the **wheel of the year**, as well as the **esbats**, the monthly gatherings on the night of the full moon. See also: **Paganism**.

Nostradamus (1503–66) Famous French seer whose prophecies are still causing controversy. Among his many predictions that are said to have come true are: the French Revolution, the great Fire of London, the rise of Hitler, and the moon landing. He was erroneously credited with predicting the attack on the World Trade Center in 2001; the verses upon which that judgement was based were manipulated to fit the context of 11 September.

Born Michel de Nostredame, his upbringing and early adult life were unremarkable. He trained as a doctor but soon after the death of his wife and two children from plague, he started to develop his visionary reputation. In 1555 he published *The Centuries*, the book of prophecy for which he is known. The title refers not to future ages, but to the groupings of verse in which his visions were written out, in groups of 100. He deliberately made the references in his prophecy obscure, using metaphoric and highly imaginative symbols in his efforts to remain ambiguous.

There are 942 separate predictions and only a handful mention a specific date. Nostradamus claimed that he could have put dates to all of them, but feared to do so lest he be accused of witchcraft and heresy. Interestingly, he predicted that the 'King of Terror' was scheduled to appear in July 1999, heralding the end of the world. As we are still here, it is safe to say that not every prediction he made has come true.

Numerology, also **Numeromancy** (Latin *numerus*, 'number', + Greek *logos*, 'word, study') The use of numbers in magic and **divination**. Numerology is based on the idea that the universe is mathematically constructed and the vibrational energies of all things can be expressed through numbers.

The Classical Greek mathematician and philosopher **Pythagoras** first set down the basic principles of numerology in the fifth century BC. He thought there were connections between gods, men and numbers that could be codified and used to foretell the fate of a person, or future events, when certain number patterns appeared. In his time, these principles were applied to **arithmancy**, an early form of numerology.

In numerology's present form, each number from nought to nine has a specific meaning and numerical values are given to each letter of the alphabet. Any number larger than nine can be reduced to a single number by adding all the digits together. This reductionism is the main tool when numerology is used for making predictions. Consider the number 732. $7+3+2=12$; then $1+2=3$. The qualities of 732 are equivalent to the symbolic number 3. Using these as a guide, the patterns of different dates and a person's name can be analysed to define character and temperament, and to predict likely outcomes in the future.

Nut The sky goddess in Egyptian mythology, and member of the **Ennead**, the council of gods and goddesses which ruled over the country. Nut personified the skies and the heavens and represented the barrier between the forces of chaos and the order of our world. Nut was daughter of **Shu** and **Tefnet** and consort to the god **Seb,** the earth god. She was depicted as a nude woman covered in star constellations, and her fingers and toes touch the four cardinal directions of north, south, east and west.

Nutraceuticals A manufactured term for foods (often also referred to as functional foods) engineered and marketed as having specific medical or physiological health effects. Examples include margarines with plant compounds added to help reduce cholesterol levels in the blood, yoghurts and yoghurt drinks containing friendly or probiotic bacteria claimed to promote gut health, or calcium-fortified breakfast cereals. There is currently no legislative body responsible for overseeing the production of nutraceuticals, although the Food Standards Agency does monitor research claims made by food companies on supposed health benefits.

Nutritional Therapy The use of diet, vitamins, minerals and supplements to improve health and increase vitality. Conventional medicine already recognises diet as a major factor in causing and preventing disease, but nutritional therapy actively seeks to use 'food as medicine'. Nutritionists also look at the way the environment around an ailing person may affect them, as well as lifestyle factors that may be affecting their uptake of vitamins and other nutrients.

In a typical session, a nutritionist will spend a long time talking to a client, seeking to discover unhealthy diet and lifestyle patterns. They often use **iridology** (using the iris of the eye to diagnose imbalances in the body), muscle-testing (called **kinesiology**), or testing of hair, urine or stools, to see which areas of the body are affected by poor nutrition. Once test results have been analysed, the nutritionist can suggest dietary changes, or food, vitamin or mineral supplements, to aid a return to health.

Nutritional research has found that many long-term health problems with vague symptoms – things like bloating, thrush, fatigue, aches and pains – are often due to food intolerances. For whatever reason, the body sometimes interprets certain foods as being 'toxic' to the system. When a certain tolerance level is exceeded, ill-health can result. Eliminating these toxic substances can allow the body to flush the system clean and, in the process, stimulate self-healing mechanisms.

Nutritional therapy has helped many sufferers from the following ailments: irritable bowel syndrome, headaches, migraine, chronic fatigue syndrome, arthritis, circulatory disorders, menstrual problems, asthma, eczema and allergies, lending truth to the statement 'An apple a day bugs the BMA'. See also: **Naturopathy**, **Optimum Nutrition**.

Nux Vomica One of the 15 major **polychrests**, or major remedies in **homeopathy**. It is also a **constitutional type**, which is a way homeopaths have of classifying different patient profiles. The fitting constitutional remedy acts preventatively and curatively on its matching personality type – for example, a person with a Nux Vomica constitution will respond well to the Nux Vomica remedy almost regardless of the illness they are suffering from.

Nux Vomica types are best described as 'workaholics'. They are highly strung, impatient and prone to anger, but tend to be dynamic entrepreneurs. They work hard and play hard, and most of the ailments they are susceptible to are attributable to that fact. They are also prone to insomnia, headaches, tension, irritable bowel syndrome and ulcers. The remedy Nux Vomica is the number one homeopathic treatment for a hangover.

Oak A flower essence made from the blossom of the oak tree. This emotionally healing tincture is one of the **Bach Flower Remedies**. Dr Bach said that this is indicated for 'those who have an inner strength – the plodders who soldier on through life despite its pitfalls'.

Occult, Occultism (Latin *occulere*, 'to hide') General term for practices involving secret or hidden knowledge, usually of an esoteric or magical nature. It is also applied to mystical societies like those of the **Rosicrucians** and **Freemasonry**. See also: **Mysticism**.

Odin The head god of Scandinavian mythology, known for his all-seeing eye of knowledge. See also: **Northern Paganism**.

Ogham A Celtic tree alphabet developed by **Druids**, and used as a **magic** and divinatory tool. During the Roman conquest of Britain, the ogham was also used to transmit secret wisdom and knowledge through times of pagan persecution. There were 20 original symbols, each representing a different tree, later increased to 25. These symbols were etched on staves (sticks) of wood, named 'ogham staves' after Ogma, the Druidic warrior god. Ogham staves were also associated with colours, birds, animals and kings, and served to transit various elements of Celtic lore. The tree alphabet was also used as a tally system in accounting, and was inscribed on stones for a more 'permanent' record of information. Ogham was usually written vertically from top to bottom in inscriptions and horizontally from left to right in manuscripts.

In **divination**, a Druid would gather together the ogham staves in his hand and, after asking a question, cast them down onto the ground, as in **runes** and

I Ching sticks. He would then make an interpretation based on the patterns formed from the staves, and the symbols that were uppermost in the casting.

Although use of the ogham died out after Britain's conversion to Christianity, a quintessential ogham stave is in use to this day. The maypole, used in May Day celebrations throughout Europe, was originally a phallic symbol of the Sky Father in **Beltane** fertility rituals, designed to celebrate the union of heaven and earth. See also: **Paganism**.

Alder: Fearn　　Ash: Nuin　　Birch: Beith　　Elder: Ruis

Examples of the Ogham alphabet

Olive A flower essence made from the blossom of the olive tree. This emotionally healing tincture is one of the **Bach Flower Remedies**. Dr Bach said that this is indicated for 'tiredness, fatigue, exhaustion. When one has been working hard, studying or concentrating and feels drained as a result'.

Om One of the most well-known **mantras** in **Hinduism** and **Tibetan Buddhism**. Om is considered a sacred and powerful syllable because it is

believed to be the origin of all other sounds in the universe. It symbolises the absolute. People chanting it can channel some of this universal energy and power to themselves, so the more you repeat it, the more potent it becomes.

Om

Om Mani Padme Hum (Tibetan, 'the jewel is in the lotus') The **Tibetan Buddhist mantra** of unconditional love and compassion. This mantra is chanted by the devout Buddhist or spun about in **prayer wheels** in order to invoke the powerful benevolent attention and blessings of Chenrezig, the embodiment of compassion. Each syllable of Om Mani Padme Hum (pronounced Om Mani Pémé Hung) has the purpose of transforming the six base emotions of vanity, jealousy, desire, ignorance, avarice and anger into wisdom and enlightenment. It purifies you and protects you from harm and illness, as well as from negative emotions that are seen as the cause of endless rebirths.

Omen A foretelling of some future event through some sort of portent, which can be interpreted as either a positive or negative sign. Omens often arise from performing different forms of **divination**, and **oracles** often made prophecies based on seemingly insignificant signs or objects. See also: **Augury**.

Oneiromancy, also **Oniromancy** (Greek *oneiros*, 'dream', + *manteia*, 'divination') The study of dream interpretation for the purposes of divining the future, outlining prophecy and analysing the subconscious of an individual. Dream interpretation has a long, documented history, starting with the biblical prophet Joseph. He not only dreamt that his brothers would one day bow down to him in homage (as they did) but also successfully interpreted the portents of the Pharaoh's dream of harvest plenty followed by horrendous famine.

The ancient Chaldeans, Chinese, Egyptians, Hindus, Native Americans, Greeks and Romans all believed in dreams as a means of foretelling the future, although then they were regarded as messages from the gods as opposed to workings of the subconscious mind. It was also thought that a person's soul was freed in dreams to travel about in the spirit realm, thus establishing a direct connection to the gods and their wisdom, and sometimes to past lives.

In Egypt and Mesopotamia, dream interpretation was the job of an expert class of priests and priestesses, and the Roman seer Artemidorus wrote down a guide to interpreting dreams that is still consulted today. Oneiromancy is still practised today, with many **precognitive** and prophetic dreams recorded that have later come true.

Dream interpretation has also been legitimised by the psychoanalytical work of **Sigmund Freud** and **Carl Jung**. Jung in particular believed that dreams brought back archetypal memories from the **collective unconscious**, expressed in symbolic language. These dream symbols could then be interpreted and help the dreamer to gain insight into their past and future. See also: **Astral Projection, Lucid Dreaming**.

Opal A precious gem and crystal with profound magical, spiritual and healing properties. The common misconception that an opal is unlucky only came into being in Victorian times due to the influence of Sir Walter Scott's fictional tale *Anne of Geirstein*. Prior to that, Indo-European cultures from ancient Greeks onwards believed that the stone shielded the wearer from any contagion and warned of poison. Opals enhance intuition and positive/negative beliefs, and balance the emotions as well as bringing good luck and money to business leaders.

Optimum Nutrition A phrase coined by leading nutritional authority Patrick Holford to describe 'giving yourself the best possible intake of nutrients to allow your body to be as healthy as possible and to work as well as it can'. It is also a system of analysing your nutritional requirements and taking account of your lifestyle to come up with an individual eating programme. In 1984 Holford founded the Institute for Optimum Nutrition (ION), a charitable and independent educational trust for the furtherance of education and research in nutrition. The ION has served as a nutrition and environmental consultancy to public and health officials throughout the world. See also: **Nutritional Therapy**.

Oracle (Latin *orare*, 'speak') An intermediary between the gods and those seeking divine counsel or prophetic visions. The high priest or priestess who served as the mouthpiece of the deity would usually induce or fall into a trance state (similar to a **medium**) and channel the wisdom of the gods who would temporarily possess them. Oracles delivered cryptic answers, probably for protection against those who would not want to hear what they had to say. The best-known oracle of the ancient world was the one at Delphi dedicated to the Greek god Apollo, which was also known as the Pythian Oracle. See also: **Sibyl**.

Orc see **Goblin**.

Orgone Energy A 'primordial cosmic energy' that is present everywhere throughout the universe, according to controversial psychoanalyst **Wilhelm Reich**. Orgone energy is a motivator for such things as gravity, galaxies, failed political revolutions and even sexual orgasms (no word as to whether it is responsible for failed sexual orgasms). In the body, orgone energy is known as 'bio-energy'. Reich thought that unlike other concepts of life force like **chi** or **prana**, orgone energy was measurable and could be collected in specially constructed accumulators made of wood or metal (which he made available for a small fee from select outfits). These devices, or 'shooters', as they were known, could distribute this energy where needed to cure just about any medical disorder.

Ornithomancy, also **Oionoscopia**, **Oionoscopy** (Greek *ornith-*, 'bird', + *manteia*, 'divination') A form of divination using birds to interpret events and foretell the future. Omens were inferred from their behaviour, appearance and even their song. Ornithomancy was very popular in ancient Greece and in ancient Rome it was part of the national religion. In all cultures, certain birds had certain meanings. An eagle was believed to foretell triumph after a struggle; a dove was a favourable omen for lovers (hence the appearance of doves at grandiose weddings); an owl was considered a bird of ill-omen in Rome although it was heralded in Greece as a wise companion to the goddess Athena.

In English folklore, magpies, crows and rooks were thought to be unlucky, although you could reverse the luck either by saluting or spitting at the auspicious bird (leading to the famous saying 'one for sorrow, two for joy', etc.).

Sailors still believe sighting an albatross foretells storms and that harming an albatross brings bad luck. Modern-day ornithomancy is more concerned with the predictive behaviour of birds, particularly prior to natural catastrophes like earthquakes and volcanic eruptions, when they act out of character. Bird appearance and behaviour also still play a role in weather prediction, especially in determining how hard a winter might be. See also: **Augury**.

Osiris The great god of Egyptian mythology, who was considered the lord of the afterlife. Along with his consort, **Isis**, Osiris was revered as a fertility god and was father to **Horus**, the sky god. Osiris was a member of the **Ennead**, the ruling council of Egyptian gods and goddesses. One of his major duties was to judge souls in the afterlife to determine their final reward. For this reason, he was greatly feared in Egyptian society.

Osiris was one of the four children of the gods **Seb** and **Nut**. His sisters were Isis and **Nepthys** and his brother was **Seth**, who killed and dismembered him, scattering his body throughout Egypt. Osiris' sister-consort Isis gathered all the pieces together and, through her magic arts, reassembled his body. This was not enough to return life to Osiris, but Atum-Ra the father god took pity on Isis and allowed him to live in the afterlife as king of the dead.

Osteopathy (Greek *osteon*, 'bone', + *pathos*, 'suffering') A method of diagnosing and treating musculoskeletal disorders through the manual manipulation of muscles, bones, joints, ligaments and connective tissue. Osteopaths use a variety of bodywork techniques, like massage, stretching and forceful realignment of vertebrae and other joints, to ease muscle tension and restore the body's natural self-healing abilities.

Osteopathic treatment is often recommended for pain in the back, neck, shoulders, arms and legs, especially pain caused by accidents, injuries and poor posture.

Osteopathy is often confused with **chiropractic** and there are some similarities. The main difference is that chiropractics use X-rays more in treatment and focus only on joint and vertebrae movement, while osteopaths are less likely to use X-rays, instead focusing on muscle and joint movement.

At a typical session, the osteopath takes a detailed medical history and asks about your symptoms and how they affect your lifestyle. They look for the causes of a problem as much as for ways of treating it – for example, does your back hurt after a day's work because of the way you sit at the computer? Is it your chair? Is it because of recent injury to the neck? The osteopath will then ask you to carry out a series of movements so they can assess your mobility, either by simple observation or by palpating (feeling) the affected areas.

Treatment may be merely massage, or it may involve 'adjusting' or 'realigning' your spine or other joints. If this is done, the osteopath places your body in a particular posture (it could be standing, sitting or lying on a couch) and, using pressure, takes the vertebrae or joint to the end of their normal range of movement. Then the joint is given a sharp tap, which allows it to spring back into position. The force for this motion is not painful, but is often accompanied by a loud popping noise or 'click'. This scary sound is actually harmless, as the click is the gas bubble between joints popping when there is a change of pressure between the two bones.

Dr Andrew Taylor Still, an American army doctor, developed osteopathy in the mid-1870s after concluding that the body was similar to an engine. If it was well-tuned and structurally sound, it would function at an optimum level. If any part of the structure came out of alignment, it would adversely affect other systems. At first there was strong opposition to Still's idea, but from shaky beginnings it has grown to become a respected and accepted part of medical practice.

UK osteopaths must be registered with the General Osteopathic Council (which has rigorous standards of education and training in place) in order to practise in this country.

Ouija Board   A device used to seek out messages from ghosts, spirit beings and other entities in **spiritualism**. The word 'Ouija' is made up of the two words for yes in French and German (*oui* and *ja*) and it is one of the most controversial methods of spirit communication, because it appears to attract malevolent spirits to it. A noted psychic, Craig Hamilton-Parker, says that 'playing with the Ouija is the spiritual equivalent of opening up your house and asking in anyone who's passing. So you shouldn't be surprised if your guests then go ahead and try and wreck the house.' Because of this aspect, it is not considered a very reliable form of **divination**.

The board is made of wood or plastic, with a smooth surface. Printed on the board are the letters of the alphabet, the numbers one to ten, and the words yes and no. During a **séance** or other contact session, each participating person places a finger on the pointer (called a **planchette**) and asks for a message to be delivered. The planchette, under the control of the contacted spirit, whizzes around the board spelling out the answer.

No one knows who invented the Ouija board but the first one was sold in the US in 1891. Many people make their own boards, using an upturned glass or coin as a planchette.

Ouroboros, also **Oroborus, Uroboros, Oureboros** (Greek, 'devouring its tail') A mystical symbol of a serpent swallowing its own tail. This symbolises the cyclical nature of life and death, that one feeds the other in a never-ending process. In **alchemy**, it also represented the ability to transcend the dual good/evil nature of man and become a pure individual.

Ouspensky, Peter Demianovich (1878–1947) Russian follower of mystic **G.I. Gurdjieff**, who was better able to explain Gurdjieff's cosmological theories than the man himself. Ouspensky is better known as a mathematician who attempted to link that scholarly science with the more ephemeral arts of **magic, occultism** and religion. He is the author of several notable works of **new age** thought, including *Tertium Organum, In Search of the Miraculous* and *A New Model of the Universe*.

Out-of-body-experience (OBE or OOBE) The feeling that your spirit or consciousness is separate from your physical body, floating either just above it or at some distance from it. During this experience, details are recorded and can be recalled once back in the body, with many case histories of unconscious patients being able to recount events that happened when they were supposedly knocked out. Out-of-body experiences can be deliberately invoked, as in **astral projection**, or they can be spontaneous, as in **near-death experiences**. See also: **Astral Travel**.

Ox, The In **Chinese astrology**, the second sign of the **zodiac**. You are an Ox if you were or will be born in the years 1937, 1949, 1961,1973, 1985, 1997 or 2009. The Ox is the sign of tenacity in Chinese mythology, symbolising enduring prosperity through continuing effort. Those born under this sign are open-minded, practical people who are seldom ruffled by the unexpected. Oxen are home-loving and usually devoted to their families. They can become miserly, however, and need to guard against materialism. Their Western zodiac equivalent is **Capricorn** and their ruling planet is **Saturn**.

Pagan, Paganism (Latin *paganus*, 'villager or rustic dweller') General term used to describe a number of belief systems that hold nature, magical ritual and particularly **goddess** traditions in reverence. Pagans do not believe in an actual figurehead of a god, but instead are pantheistic, which means that for them the divine is in everything, and the universe itself is divine. If anything, they are nature worshippers, who closely tie their practices to the seasonal cycle of the year, and believe spiritual aspects and **life force** reside in everything, be it animal, vegetable or mineral. As such, pagans are earthly sensualists, celebrating sexuality and fertility in a series of rituals and lifestyle choices. Invoking the powers of nature and particularly of the divine feminine through goddess worship and magical practices is also a key element of paganism.

There are many traditions in pagan practice, but the five most common are: **witchcraft** and **Wicca**; **Druidry**; **shamanism**; **Celtic spirituality**; and **Northern paganism**. Growing schools of thought include eco-paganism and cyber-paganism, also known as 'green spirituality', and some traditions in the men's movement and in feminism. Each of these approaches emphasises one or more of the above elements over others, but holds in common the reverence for nature and the two major tenets of paganism: 'As above, so below' and 'An' it harm none, do what you will.'

Pagan is also a derogatory term used to describe someone who does not hold Christian beliefs, a distancing technique first implemented by early Church fathers to discourage the old teachings and nature gods and goddesses that were worshipped prior to their flock's conversion to Christianity. See also: **Celtic Wheel, Esbats, Paganism, Pantheism, Sabbats**.

Pali Language dialect of India, closely related to Sanskrit, in which the sacred texts of **Theravada Buddhism** are written. Although Sanskrit Buddhist terms are better known, every concept and tenet of Buddhism has a Pali equivalent term. See also: **Buddhism, Theravada**.

Palmistry Predicting the future or telling a person's fortune by interpreting the lines, shapes and markings on their hand. It is also known as *chiromancy*

(Greek for 'hand divination') and has been practised since ancient times in cultures ranging from China and India to Egypt and the classical world. Palmistry was immensely popular during the Middle Ages and reached its height in nineteenth-century society with 'Cheiro', an Irish palm-reader and seer born in 1866 (from whom we get the names chiromancy and **chirognomy**, the study of personality traits). Cheiro read the palms of the rich and famous, including Oscar Wilde, Rasputin and Edward VII when he was Prince of Wales.

Palmistry differs from other forms of **divination** because it focuses both on predicting the future and on interpreting personality and character traits. This is done by looking at all aspects of a hand's appearance, including size, shape, texture, colour, size and shape of nails and fingers, and temperature. Primary focus is on the markings, or lines and mounts of the hand. Traditionally, your left hand is passive, and indicates inherited traits of personality, abilities and weaknesses (the past), and your right hand is active, and indicates your individuality and how you have fulfilled your own potential, the person you have made yourself (the future). These meanings are reversed if you are left-handed. As you age, lines will appear on the hands, which will indicate how you have fulfilled your potential, and what experiences you have had. These additional lines can be read like a road map of your life journey.

There are three major interpretive lines on your hand: the heart line, head line and life line (all horizontal). The heart line is the top line running from side to side, and deals with love and relationships, emotions and the spirit world. Next, running from side to side, is your head line, which deals with the intellectual part of your nature. Below that runs the life line, which indicates how strong your intrinsic life force is, and your chances for a short or long life. There are many other secondary lines used in interpretation as well.

The mounts on your hands are the other great indicators of who you are and where you are going. They are the seven fleshy contours located at the base of each finger and lower palm, named after the seven traditional astrological planets, each symbolising a particular trait or quality.

The Mount of Jupiter is located under your index finger and is used to assess your strength of character. The Mount of Saturn is found under the second (middle) finger and signifies how you cope with difficulties in life. The Mount of Apollo or the Sun is under your ring finger and refers to your artistic and creative abilities, and the Mount of Mercury is located under your little finger, signifying your inventiveness and communication skills. The Mount of Mars is located down the palm, below the Mount of Mercury, and indicates your courage and physical strength, and below that, next to the

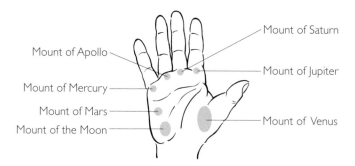

The mounts, in palmistry

junction of wrist and palm, is the Mount of the Moon. This is connected with your imagination, dreams and intuition. Finally there is the Mount of Venus, located below the thumb, and it signifies love, passion and affection in your life. It is also considered the 'fount' of your personality.

If the lines and mounts on both hands appear identical at first, it means you have not changed the destiny given to you. If the hands vary greatly, you have exercised your free will to change your destiny. However your hands appear, age and experience will be recorded on them, as the memory of life is written on the body.

Panchang A system of Indian **astrology** based on the cycles of the moon. Panchang relies heavily on working with the heavens to discover the times that are best for different actions. As with regular astrology, there are times when it is not auspicious to try and clarify problems with a loved one, or to make major purchases. Panchang uses a daily planner to help a person chart out, months at a time, the best times for different types of activity in love, career or health. Days are classified according to certain qualities – swift, fixed, light, tender, fierce, dreadful and challenging are but a few of them.

Panchang horoscopes can be cast for you, or you can work one out with the help of an **ephemeris** that shows the movements of the moon for your particular geographic location for months and years ahead.

Pantheism (Greek *pan*, 'all', + *theos*, 'god') Both a belief system that tolerates and accepts all gods as divine, as well as the idea that god is in everything, i.e. that the universe is god and god is the universe. Pantheism is a key element in **paganism**.

Paracelsus, Phillipus Aureolus (1493–1541) Medieval alchemist and owner of the best middle names anywhere (Theophrastus Bombastus von

Hohenheim). He was a Swiss doctor who later became fascinated with the then-new practice of **alchemy**, and studied a number of esoteric and occult texts from ancient Egypt and Greece. He was also one of the first **holistic** medical practitioners, regarding disease as a form of imbalance in the body, and was instrumental in developing the **Doctrine of Signatures**, one of the founding principles of **homeopathy**.

In his alchemical studies, Paracelsus concentrated more on the transmutation of the soul than on that of base metal into gold. He supposedly was the recipient of the secret of the **Philosopher's Stone**, although there is no record he was ever successful in producing the elixir of immortal life, as he died in 1541.

Parakinesis see Psychokinesis

Paramita (Sanskrit, 'reaching the other shore'; also, 'attaining the state of emancipation') A central tenet of **Buddhism**, that each and every person has the potential within to become a Buddha because infinite wisdom exists within the human mind. Through the discipline of the six paramitas, a person's innermost wisdom will well up. The six paramitas are: dana-paramita – loving acts, the practice of love that gives; sila-paramita – seeking simplicity by observing the five precepts, similar in nature to the Ten Commandments in Judaeo-Christian religion; ksanti-paramita – perseverance, waiting patiently until the time is ripe; virya-paramita – making a diligent effort and the achievement of goals; dhyana-paramita – daily practice of the **eightfold path** and **meditation**; and prajna-paramita – receiving deep, transcendental wisdom that allows an individual to communicate with their own guardian and guiding spirits.

Paranormal (Greek *para*, 'irregular', + *norma*, 'precept, rule') Events or phenomena that cannot be explained by normal scientific methods, or by the laws of nature. See also: **Parapsychology, Supernatural**.

Parapraxis Technical term for a 'Freudian slip', coined by **Freud** himself, who seemed to think that it demonstrated the unconscious at work. He defined the following behaviours as parapraxis: forgetting people's names; forgetting something you intended to do; a slip of the tongue or pen; misreading or mishearing something; losing or temporarily mislaying things; bungled actions and accidents; and remembering things incorrectly. Freud thought that all of these things were the **subconscious**'s way of dealing with painful or socially unacceptable thoughts, and the mistakes were made because a person had conflicting intentions in their head. In other words, the Freudian slip reveals what a person is *really* thinking.

Parapsychology (Greek *para*, 'irregular', + Greek *psukhe*, 'breath, soul, mind' + *logos*, 'word, reason') The study of unusual mental phenomena that cannot be explained by normal scientific methods, like **telepathy**, **out-of-body experiences** and **ESP**.

Paroptic Vision (Greek *para*, 'irregular', + *optikos*, 'seen') The **paranormal** ability to see using other organs than the eyes. The most common form of paroptic vision is visual perception through the skin.

Patanjali see **Yoga Sutras**

Pathworking A way of expanding your consciousness for personal development, that originated in the Jewish mystical religion **Kabbalah**. Since the 1960s, pathworking has grown in popularity from its Kabbalistic roots and is used in Western culture as a means to gain greater spiritual awareness. The technique used in pathworking is a type of **visualisation** that is very similar to **guided imagery** or a **vision quest**, but has specific magical connotations. Through the use of a guide or mediator, you are led into a semi-trance state during which you are asked to paint pictures in your mind using occult and archetypal symbols. Often, these symbols are the same as those on **tarot** cards, or from the Kabbalistic **Tree of Life**. Once the visualisation is complete and you come back to full awareness, the things you experienced can be used to reject destructive habits and improve yourself.

Peak Experience An ecstatic moment of intense feeling, where the entire body and mind of a person are lost in bliss. The phrase was coined by psychologist **Abraham Maslow** to describe getting totally absorbed in an experience where you have 'total fascination with the matter in hand, getting lost in the present, detachment from time and place'. Often it can be your response to events like perfect sexual experiences, a religious ritual, parental love or childbirth, or aesthetic appreciation in communing with nature, listening to music or viewing great art.

Peak experiences can sometimes arise from such practices as physical exercise, **meditation** and altruistic behaviour. Maslow felt that it was fulfilled people who could have peak experiences of enjoyment, and then go on to the plateau experience, where they achieved an ongoing sense of connection, confidence and happiness with the universe.

Pegasus The mythical winged horse of Greek legend. He sprang from the blood of the monster Medusa, when the hero Perseus cut off her head. He became a favourite of the Greek goddesses, the Nine Muses, and is a symbol of poetic inspiration.

Pendulum (Latin *pendulus*, 'hanging down') A device used in **dowsing** and

divination to answer questions and locate lost items or people. It consists of a weighted object or crystal suspended from a fixed point. The weight is able to swing freely to and fro and acts like a pointer (in dowsing) or in answering yes or no questions (in divination). A pendulum is also used in **radiesthesia** to locate the source of illness in the body.

Pendulum

Pentagram, Pentacle (Greek *penta-*, 'five') The five-pointed star, and an

important symbol in **magic**. In white magic, it represents the five natural **elements** of **earth, air, fire, water** and **ether** (**akasha**). The pentagram is a symbol of power and protection, and when it is placed on a disc, or a circle is drawn around the outside, it is called a pentacle. If a pentagram is inverted, then it means the practitioner is involved in black magic, or Satanism. See also: **Witchcraft**.

Pentagram

Pericardium Meridian, also Circulation-Sex Meridian. A channel or **meridian** of **chi** energy running through the body that affects the pericardium, or lining of the heart, according to **Traditional Chinese Medicine**. It is associated with the **fire element,** has **yin** energetic properties and is partnered with the **triple warmer meridian**, which is **yang**. Pericardium energy regulates and controls emotions and protects the heart, physically and energetically. Chi is strongest in this channel between 7 and 9 p.m. and conversely weakest between 7 and 9 a.m. It begins on the chest then runs down the arm to end by the nail of the middle finger.

Persephone, also **Proserpine**, **Kore** In Greek mythology, the daughter of **Demeter** and **Zeus**, and unwilling bride to **Hades**, the god of the underworld. She is known as Proserpine in Roman myth. Persephone, who personified springtime, was abducted by Hades and taken to his dark realm to be his queen. She pined away for the surface of the earth and particularly for her mother, the goddess **Demeter**. In rage at Hades' tricks, Demeter, the goddess of the harvest, cursed the land and humankind started to die. She persuaded **Zeus** to allow Persephone to come back, but as the unfortunate girl had eaten six pomegranate seeds, she was doomed to be Hades' queen for six months of the year.

This myth reflects the origin of the four seasons of the year – autumn is when Demeter says goodbye to Persephone, who takes her place at Hades' side throughout winter. When spring arrives, Persephone is reunited with her mother and summer comes. See also: **Eleusinian Mysteries**, **Goddess**.

Petrissage A classic movement in Swedish and holistic massage, where the therapist compresses the muscles against underlying bone. It is a deep movement, which stimulates circulation in the muscle and bone. Petrissage is also a very warming movement, and is good for strengthening weakened muscles.

Peyotism The use of psylocebic plants like peyote cactus, jimson weed and mushrooms to attain an altered state of consciousness, contact **spirit guides**, or gain higher spiritual knowledge through psychedelic visions. It is a technique mainly used in **shamanism**, where a specific set ritual of preparation and ingestion is followed to keep the shaman from accidentally poisoning himself. Peyotism was a prominent feature of **Carlos Castaneda**'s spiritual/anthropological adventures. See also: **Vision Quest**.

Philosopher's Stone In **alchemy**, a magical catalyst that reputedly had the ability, among other things, to change base metals into gold. It was also believed that the Philosopher's Stone was the original substance from which all metals derived, held together all the elements of the universe, had extraordinary healing powers and was the key to immortality and all the knowledge in the world. The Philosopher's Stone was not believed actually to be a stone, but a powder or elixir, and attempting to discover its formula was one of the three main goals of alchemy.

Phoenix (Greek *phonios*, 'blood-red') Mythical bird associated with the sun in the legends of many different cultures. It is a beautiful, graceful bird, with colourful red and gold plumage and a long, decorative tail. In Egyptian and Arabic tales, the phoenix is consumed by the flame of the sun but arises reborn from the ashes; in China, it was considered an envoy of the gods. The firebird of Russian tales could grant magical wishes to those pure of heart.

The tears of a phoenix were considered to have unique healing abilities, and it had a singing voice of unearthly purity and heartrending beauty.

The phoenix figures heavily in Christian tradition as a symbol of resurrection and the triumph of life over death, and in alchemical belief as a symbol for the **Philosopher's Stone**.

Phosphorus One of the 15 major **polychrests**, or major remedies in **homeopathy**. It is also a **constitutional type**, which is a way homeopaths have of classifying different patient profiles. The fitting constitutional remedy acts preventatively and curatively on its matching personality type – for example, a person with a Phosphorus constitution will respond well to the Phosphorus remedy almost regardless of the illness they are suffering from. Phosphorus people are kind and affectionate, and great fun to be with. They do not deal very well with emergencies, however, and are prone to stress-related ailments. They also are susceptible to respiratory trouble, stomach ailments and neuralgia.

Phrenology, also **Cranioscopy**, **Bumpology** (Greek *phren-*, 'mind', + *logos*, 'word, study') Study of the bumps of the head that give a guide to general character and mental capacity. This system, which was very popular in the late nineteenth/early twentieth centuries, has now been largely discredited, leaving only the intriguing sight of white porcelain heads with strange black diagrams littering junk shops worldwide.

Theoretically, the sizes of the bumps indicate which instincts are well developed in you and which are only slight. No bumps in a particular area indicates an imbalance in the quality associated with that area.

The head is divided into 22 different areas with different characteristics assigned to each area. Each bump has a specific name: self; invention; judgement; music; argument; humour; beauty; generosity; kindliness; enthusiasm; practicality; ambition; energy; determination; cautiousness; dignity; constancy; reason; love of children; courage; love; colour.

Phrenology is closely related to **physiognomy**, which is considered a more legitimate divinatory method. See also: **Chinese Facial Analysis**.

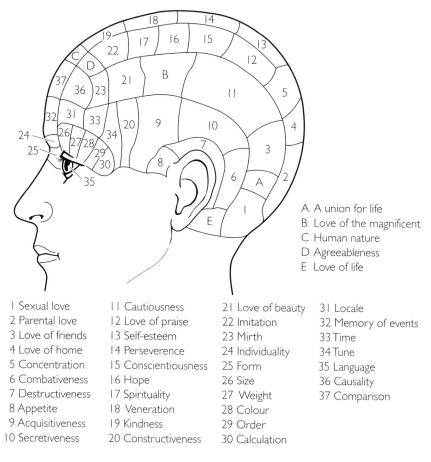

A A union for life
B Love of the magnificent
C Human nature
D Agreeableness
E Love of life

1 Sexual love	11 Cautiousness	21 Love of beauty	31 Locale
2 Parental love	12 Love of praise	22 Imitation	32 Memory of events
3 Love of friends	13 Self-esteem	23 Mirth	33 Time
4 Love of home	14 Perseverence	24 Individuality	34 Tune
5 Concentration	15 Conscientiousness	25 Form	35 Language
6 Combativeness	16 Hope	26 Size	36 Causality
7 Destructiveness	17 Spirituality	27 Weight	37 Comparison
8 Appetite	18 Veneration	28 Colour	
9 Acquisitiveness	19 Kindness	29 Order	
10 Secretiveness	20 Constructiveness	30 Calculation	

A phrenology map

Physiognomy (Greek *phusiognomonia*, 'judging of a man's nature by his features') A method of reading fortunes and characters in people's faces based on their physical features. The eighteenth-century mystic Johann Kaspar used astrology to classify facial characteristics, devising seven different types of face based on the astrological charts of that time. Since then, the term has expanded to cover any methods that use facial features to interpret people's inner nature and ultimate fate, many of them based on scientific theories of evolution. It is closely related to the more structured practice of **Chinese facial analysis**, although the spiritual underpinnings of each theory are quite different.

Phytotherapy, see Herbalism, Herbal Medicine

Pig, The In **Chinese astrology**, the twelfth sign of the **zodiac**. You are a Pig if you were or will be born in the years 1935, 1947, 1959, 1971, 1983, 1995, 2007 or 2019. The Pig is the sign of honesty in Chinese mythology, symbolising wealth, prosperity and comfort. Those born under this sign appear placid, sincere and trusting. They are intelligent and dutiful, and prefer the status quo. At times they can be gullible and over-indulgent, but they are intensely loyal to their friends and families. Their Western zodiac equivalent is **Scorpio** and their ruling planet is **Mars**.

Pilates A disciplined and focused physical fitness programme, designed to strengthen the soft tissues of the body (muscles, ligaments, joints). Pilates involves a series of very controlled, slow, concentrated movements performed with the help of a spring resistance machine. The aim of this resistance exercise is to lengthen and strengthen the muscles group by group. Pilates also utilises mind-body techniques like **visualisation** to enhance the physical methods, leading many to term this system as 'yoga with machines'.

Josef Pilates, a German who emigrated to England shortly before World War I, first developed the technique. Sickly as a child, Pilates became obsessed with physical fitness and took up a plethora of sports in adulthood to improve his body image. Interned during hostilities, he first devised his eponymous exercise methods, and after the war set up a studio in New York where his earliest disciples were ballet dancers like Martha Graham. Pilates has long been known in dance and acting circles as 'the' method to sculpt your body, but has only become more widely popular in recent years as a result of our celebrity-obsessed culture. Although many come to Pilates on the back of media endorsement, most stay because of its effectiveness as a fitness regime and as a positive body–mind system.

Pine A flower essence made from the blossom of the pine tree. This emotionally healing tincture is one of the **Bach Flower Remedies**. Dr Bach said that this is indicated for 'those who feel guilty and blame themselves, even for something that was not their fault, harbour a guilt complex or have a guilty conscience from which they are unable to set themselves free'.

Pisces The twelfth sign of the **zodiac** in Western **astrology**, and the **sun sign** for those born between 20 February and 20 March. The symbol of Pisces is two fish, and the ruling planets are **Jupiter** and **Neptune**. Pisceans are under a **mutable sign** influenced by the **water element**, with 'intuition' the best single word to define them. Those born under Pisces are sensitive, sympathetic and imaginative, but can be somewhat dreamy and impressionable. They are spiritual and deeply interested in mysticism, but do not always concentrate on the mundane business of life as much as they should.

The ideal Piscean meal is a buffet full of exotic, subtle dishes to be savoured, accompanied by an exquisite wine. In health, Pisceans are prone to overextend themselves and suffer from low energy. They may also suffer from foot problems. Drying foods and stimulating herbs benefit the zodiac's dreamer.

Pitta (Sanskrit, from *tapa*, 'to heat') One of the three body types, or **doshas**, in ayurvedic medicine, that determine who you are physically and mentally, and what you need to do to keep healthy. The pitta dosha is composed of fire and water energies, with the following results. Pitta types tend to be evenly proportioned, of average height, and are confident, ambitious individuals. They have keen intellects and love to solve problems, but can be controlling and dominating if they are not careful. They seldom gain or lose much weight. They have a tendency to perspire quite a bit, and are warm when everyone else is cold. Accordingly, they do not like hot weather much. Pittas have a tendency to fevers, acid indigestion and ulcers and should take care not to overdo time in the sunshine, as they are also prone to sunburn. To keep healthy, pitta types should avoid red meat and sour, salty foods, eating instead sweet and astringent food like salads, chicken and fish. Mostly, pittas should avoid excessive heat and excessive steam, and eat cooling, non-spicy foods.

Placebo Effect (Latin *placere*, 'to please') A beneficial improvement in health not attributable to any drug or medical treatment, but instead based on the patient's belief in a false (or placebo) drug or treatment administered in its place. It is the one thing most sceptics of any alternative therapies cite as the reason these treatments work. One theory as to why the placebo effect works is as follows: the patient's faith in their therapy actually alters the brain chemistry, causing them to produce more beneficial substances like endorphins, which soothe and relax the body. Another theory states that the actual attention the patient receives from the practitioner is more healing than the treatment itself.

There is no doubt that the placebo effect exists, and there have been a number of reputable medical studies to back this up. What is less clear is how this can explain the effectiveness of such therapies as **homeopathy**, **herbalism** and **acupuncture**, which have been proven to work despite their use in double-blind research projects. See also: **Allopathic**, **Complementary Medicine**.

Placket A small pocket or pouch used in **witchcraft** to gather together ingredients for spells and rituals. It is mostly used to hold pictures or letters of the person for whom the spell is intended, and is commonly put onto an altar or other consecrated place. See also: **Charms**, **Wicca**.

Planchette (French, 'little board') A triangular piece of wood on two wheels, with a writing instrument or point attached to one corner. It is used in séances to perform **automatic writing**, or with an **Ouija board**. You rest your fingertips lightly on the top of the planchette, and the **spirit** summoned actually moves the pen or point around to spell out messages.

Playback Theory The theory used to explain **hauntings**, especially those where a particular scene or sequence of events is played over and over. If the emotions of a scene were strong enough or if someone died in a violent or disturbing way, the intense amount of energy involved in this incident could make an 'imprint' on the environment, the same way that a voice is 'imprinted' onto a tape recorder. The clearest example of this is the spirit of Catherine Howard, doomed wife of King Henry VIII, who haunts the long gallery at Hampton Court Palace. Reliable accounts from palace cleaners and tourists report seeing her ghost screaming and running down the hall, in a 'playback' of her final desperate attempt to plead with Henry for mercy. In 2000, a team of scientists from Hertfordshire University, using high-tech detection devices, were able to record empirical data that seemed to confirm an unusual amount of psychic activity in the long gallery.

Pluto The ninth and most distant planet in our solar system, named for the dark and mysterious Roman god of the underworld. As it was not discovered until 1930, there is some dispute as to how much influence Pluto has in **astrology**. Most astrologers, however, believe it represents the search for ultimate truth and perfection. It also stands for hidden and unconscious powers, in particular **psychic** abilities. It is the co-ruling planet of the **zodiac** sign **Scorpio**.

Polarity Therapy A bodywork touch therapy based on energy medicine principles found in several disciplines, most notably ayurveda. Dr Randolph Stone, a naturopath, osteopath and chiropractic, developed this healing art after 50 years of worldwide study of alternative therapies. He felt that the key to health was in balancing the body's subtle energies, also known as 'life force'. Stone mapped out what he called 'The Energy Anatomy of Man', which showed the electromagnetic fields around the body and how our life force should appear in balance, or health.

Like any magnetic field, energy can be either positive or negative. Polarity seeks to balance the flow of this energy/life force between positive and negative poles, through an exchange between the giver and receiver of a session. Like **prana** or **chi**, our energy flow can become blocked, and a polarity therapist will work on releasing blockages to gain the positive/negative balance necessary for health.

There are four ways to balance body energy: triggering polarity or chakra points on the body with light touch therapy; stretching exercises, called polarity yoga or polarity energetics; an approach to nutrition based on the philosophy's principles; and mental–emotional balancing exercises.

Although polarity therapy on its own is not appropriate to treat primary health conditions, it provides a useful adjunct to traditional medical and psychological therapy, especially in resolving emotional trauma.

Poltergeist (German *polter*, 'a noise', + *geist*, 'spirit') Term for a ghost or other **discarnate entity** which specialises in making sounds and moving things about a house or building, often resulting in breakages. These spirits can sometimes be malevolent but on the whole are considered merely nuisances. Some believe that poltergeists are actually manifestations of **telekinesis**, due to a reported frequency of occurrences in households of disturbed adolescents, which can become hotbeds of seething frustration and emotional tension. See also: **Ghost**, **Spiritualism**.

Polychrest The 15 major remedies used in **homeopathy**. Polychrests also lend their name to the 15 **constitutional types** of people, the system homeopaths use to classify the personality types of their patients. In general, the fitting polychrest acts preventatively and curatively on its matching personality type – for example, a person with a Calc. Carb. constitution will respond well to the Calc. Carb. remedy almost regardless of the illness they are suffering from. There are 15 polychrests, each with different characteristics: **Argent. Nit.**; **Arsen. Alb.**; **Calc. Carb.**; **Graphites**; **Ignatia**; **Lachesis**; **Lycopodium**; **Merc. Sol.**; **Natrum Mur.**; **Nux Vomica**; **Phosphorus**; **Pulsatilla**; **Sepia**; **Silica** and **Sulphur**.

Polytheism (Greek *polus*, 'many', + *theos*, 'gods') A belief or a belief system or religion that holds there is more than one god, supreme being or deity that is worthy of worship. Polytheism is a key element in many of the world's great religious movements, including **Taoism**, **Hinduism** and **paganism**.

Poseidon, also **Neptune**   The Greek god of the oceans, known as **Neptune** in Roman myth. He was one of the sons of Chronos (Time) and Rhea (Earth) and was a member of the Olympiad, the 12 chief gods and goddesses of Greek legend who lived on Mt Olympus.

Possession   A mental and spiritual condition where a person feels that they have been taken over, or 'possessed', by an outside spirit entity. This entity controls all aspects of their actions and personality. Possession can be benign, as when a **medium** is possessed during a séance, but more often it is an unwelcome phenomenon where a malevolent demon or spirit takes up residence in an unwilling subject. See also: **Exorcism**, **Spiritualism**.

Potencies   In **homeopathy**, the number of times the mother **tincture** of a substance is diluted. If one drop of tincture is added to 99 drops of water or alcohol and successed (shaken), this is known as a '1c (centesimal) potency'. If a drop of this is diluted again in the same way, it is known as a '2c potency'. Most homeopathic remedies operate at a 30c for acute health conditions, but 6c potency for emergencies and chronic conditions.

Potions   (Latin *potare*, 'to drink') A liquid or drink with healing, magical or poisonous properties, used in **witchcraft**, **alchemy** and **sorcery**.

Prakruti, also **Prakriti** (Sanskrit, 'matter') The Indian philosophical equivalent of **yin**, prakruti is the primitive matter from which the cosmos is made, representing the female principle in **prana**, or universal life energy. **Purusha** is in an interdependent relationship with prakruti, the pure consciousness or spirit of the universe.

Prakruti itself is made up from a balance between three **gunas**, or qualities of matter. These are *sattva*, 'clarity'; *rajas*, 'activity'; and *tamas*, 'inertia'. They produce pleasure, pain and indifference, in that order. Prakruti and purusha and they way they interact are vital in **tantric** practice and belief. In **ayurvedic** medicine, prakruti also describes the unique combination of the elemental energies, the **doshas**, that govern our physical constitution, intellect and personality.

Prana   (Sanskrit, 'life force') The intangible life force of the universe that operates both within our physical bodies and in the world around us, according to Indian religion, philosophy and medicine. It is known in many other cultures by different names, such as **chi** (Chinese), ki (Japanese) or **ka** (ancient Egypt).

Prana has many different layers of meaning and describes how we can be mind, body and spirit. According to yogic theory, we exist in both a physical and subtle body (also called an etheric or **astral body**). The subtle body has four distinct but connecting layers, or 'sheaths'. The first layer, or 'pranic sheath', contains **nadis**, pathways through which our personal prana flows. It is along the central nadi channel, called the sushumna, that our personal energy centres, the **chakras**, are located. The second inner layer is the 'mental sheath', or subconscious mind, followed by our 'intellectual sheath', which holds our consciousness and ego. Finally there is the 'bliss sheath', which contains our true self and soul, akin to the Freudian **id**.

The physical body also has a complex system of prana distribution, important in maintaining health. Body prana can be divided into five sub-types; each with control over specific areas of the physical body. The first is also called prana and it circulates in the area of the heart; it flows upwards and controls breathing. The second is apana, which circulates at the abdomen; it flows downwards and controls elimination. Samana circulates at the middle of the body and controls digestion and metabolism, and udana circulates at the throat and controls speech and sleep. Finally, vyana circulates throughout the whole body and controls the nervous system, endocrine system and blood circulation.

It is important for both the physical body and subtle body to have a balanced, unrestricted flow of energy. Many things, including illness, unhealthy lifestyle or stress can cause this flow to stagnate or become trapped. When prana becomes blocked or depleted, we get sick. When prana is completely gone, we die. Fortunately, practices like **ayurveda** and **yoga** work to rebalance energy in the body, to enhance healing and promote well-being. See also: **Hinduism**.

Pranayama (Sanskrit, 'breath control') Control of the breath in **yoga** so that it may tune the body, calm the mind and ultimately be used as a route to deeper levels of consciousness. Pranayama is one of the 'eight limbs' or **ashtangas** that are mentioned in the **Yoga Sutras** of Patanjali, and both stimulate the flow of **prana** (life energy) throughout the body, as well as raise the level of oxygen distribution around the system. These breathing exercises help to bring more blood and nutrients to the muscles, aiding in physical performance of **asanas** (postures). Pranayamas also help the body to relax, lowering the heart rate and blood pressure.

Pratyahara (Sanskrit, 'sense withdrawal') Turning the senses away from the external world to the internal, spiritual world, according to **yoga**. Pratyahara is one of the 'eight limbs' or **ashtangas** that are mentioned in the **Yoga Sutras** of Patanjali, whose practice will lead to enlightenment. Pratyahara is considered necessary to allow a yoga practitioner to more fully concentrate and meditate on his quest for mental, physical and spiritual union that is the ultimate goal of yoga.

Prayer Wheel A metal drum (called *mani* wheels by the Tibetans) filled with written prayers, used during Tibetan Buddhist religious ceremonies for spreading spiritual blessings and well-being. Rolls of thin paper inscribed with the **mantra** of unconditional love and compassion, **Om Mani Padme Hum**, are wound around the drum's axle and spun round and round. Buddhists believe that viewing a written copy of this mantra has the same effect as chanting it: it invokes the powerful benevolence of Chrnrezig, the embodiment of compassion. Mani wheels are always spun clockwise, as viewed from above, because doing so rotates the syllables of the mantra in the order they are read and follows the direction of the sun.

Precognition (Latin *prae*, 'before', + *cognoscere*, 'know') The ability to know impending events before they happen through **extra-sensory perception**. Precognitive visions may or may not be unpleasant, but a form of precognition, **premonition**, usually predicts a disaster of some sort.

Predestination (Latin *prae*, 'before', + *destinare*, 'establish') The belief that our fate has been established prior to life; that we have no choice or free will but can only follow our destiny.

Premonition (Latin *prae*, 'before', + *monere*, 'warn') The ability to know impending events before they happen through **extra-sensory perception**. These events are mostly ones you would wish to avoid, like accidents, terrorist attacks or natural disasters. They usually come to the **psychic** individual in the form of dreams (if asleep) or visions (if awake).

Prophecy (Greek *prophetes*, 'one who speaks before') A prediction of the future based on divinatory methods, mystical visions or the guidance of a supernatural deity or supreme being. There are many famous prophecies and their spokesmen, prophets, throughout history. The Christian **Bible** has a large number of prophecies mentioned throughout its text, most famously the New Testament Book of Revelations, in which St John writes down his vision of the apocalyptic end of the world. **Nostradamus** (1503–66) also discusses future history in his cryptic verse, and Joan of Arc (1412–31) was said to have visions of the future of France, which inspired her military campaign. Proving the truth of prophetic writings is more problematic, as many visions given to prophets are vague and are not verified until after the supposed event has taken place. See also: **Divination**.

Pseudopods (Greek, 'would-be limbs') A phenomenon noticed in mediumship, where extra limbs seem to protrude from a **medium** or at some distance from the medium, during a **séance** or other spiritualist meeting. It is thought that these pseudopods are actually part of the medium's **astral body**, and are similar to **ectoplasm**.

Psi An acronym derived from 'paranormal sensory information' and used to describe **ESP**, **psychokinesis** and other related powers. Psi is also a letter of the Greek alphabet, and was traditionally associated with **psychic** phenomena, because it was the first letter of the word *psukhikos*, meaning 'breath, soul, mind'.

Psionics An alternative medicine system that combines medical **dowsing** techniques (known as **radiesthesia**) with homeopathy and a diagnostic triangle called a 'W.O.Wood chart' (named after the man who invented the device). On the bottom right-hand corner of the triangle goes a blood sample from the patient, on the bottom left-hand corner a 'diagnostic witness' (homeopathic substance) and at the apex of the triangle sits a homeopathic remedy. A **pendulum** is then dowsed over the chart, and when the correct remedy has been found it will remain in perfect balance.

Psyche (Greek *psukhe*, 'breath, life, soul') 1. According to **Carl Jung**, the psyche is the mind or spirit of a person, consisting of the conscious part of the brain, the **ego**, and the unconscious, the **shadow**. When the ego and shadow are in harmonious balance, a person is mentally healthy and mature. When either ego or shadow dominates the personality, psychological crises and neuroses can occur. See also: **Anima, Jungian Psychology**.

2. A beautiful mortal maiden in Greek mythology, with whom the god **Cupid** (or **Eros**) fell in love. She responded to him but lost him through indulging her curiosity about his appearance (he only came to her at night). Eventually Cupid and Psyche were reconciled and she was made immortal. Psyche is the personification of the human soul, and a symbol of the union between the mortal and the divine.

Psychic (Greek *psukhikos*, 'breath, soul, mind') A person with **extra-sensory perception (ESP)**, who can possess a host of different **paranormal** powers ranging from **clairvoyance**, **telepathy** and **precognition** to an ability to read a person's aura or tune into that person's aspirations and feelings. Psychic is also used as an umbrella term to describe the essence of these paranormal powers.

Psychic Protection A phrase use to define routines and rituals designed to protect your own personal energy from attack or attrition. These routines can be quite detailed, such as conjuring up specific **spells** and charms to defend against concerted psychic attacks like **voodoo** or a **curse**. Psychic protection rituals can also be employed by healers prior to treating someone (so they avoid picking up the ill energy of a patient) or merely as a guard against everyday energy drains, like pollution, a bad commute, or angry or depressed people.

Methods vary. Most involve the use of **visualisations**, where you imagine yourself surrounded by some sort of shield or bathed in healing light, to form a 'duk rak' (a Romany Gypsy term for a psychic shield). One can also wear crystal shields or **amulets** for protection. The theory behind all these routines is to activate and strengthen the energies of your **aura**, the measurable, bioelectric field that surrounds everyone. This aura fortification not only protects you against psychic attack, but also helps to revitalise a person's psyche. See also: **Psychic Vampire**.

Psychic Surgery A healing technique where the psychic apparently operates on the physical body, removing tumours and diseased organs, and repairing damaged tissues. They claim the power to cure comes from a higher being or god, and that they merely channel this energy. Although it sounds similar to **spiritual healing**, it does not have the same rate of success or body of evidence to support it. This controversial method is mainly practised in Brazil and the Philippines, where several high-profile successes were proved to be false. Psychic surgeons have had some limited success in triggering self-healing mechanisms in their patients, but the jury is still out on the authenticity of this healing system. See also: **Placebo Effect**.

Psychic Vampire A term used for someone who sucks mental energy from a person. This 'drain' can be either through a concerted spiritual attack, like **curses** or **voodoo**, or through the mere presence of a fatigued, gloomy person. Although the phrase is slangy and somewhat facetious, everyone will recognise a person who lowers your energy rather than raises it. This sort of person never feels satisfied with anything or anybody, they need constant reassurance, they have consistent low self-esteem and they always want you to make it feel better. They are not, however, interested in getting better but merely in feeding off the optimism and caring of others, which is why they seek out nurturing individuals.

How you fend off psychic vampires depends upon the type of attack it is. If there is serious bad mojo involved, certain **spells** and rituals can help. Otherwise, it is best to indulge in some **psychic protection** routines to safeguard yourself.

Psychoanalysis see **Freud, Sigmund**

Psychokinesis, also **Parakinesis** (Greek *psukhikos*, 'breath, soul, mind', + *kinesis*, 'motion') The wilfully intentional movement of objects and people through the air without any apparent physical means. How these objects are moved is either through **paranormal** means like a **poltergeist**, or by thought or will power alone – a 'mind over matter' act. If the movement is spontaneous, it is known as **telekinesis**.

Psychometric Tests (Greek *psyche*, 'mind', + *metrios*, 'measure') Tests used to assess a wide variety of abilities and attributes such as intelligence and personality. They are often used by employers as part of their selection process, and increasingly used by institutes of higher learning to weed out less promising (in their opinion) candidates. There are two basic types of psychometric test: aptitude tests, which assess your abilities; and personality questionnaires, which help to build up a profile of your character and temperament.

Aptitude tests (also known as cognitive, ability or intelligence tests) are designed to assess your critical reasoning skills under strictly timed conditions. A typical test would have three separate sections each testing a different ability – verbal reasoning, numerical reasoning and spatial reasoning. Typically, 30 minutes would be allowed for 30-plus questions, and how you 'score' is based on a comparison with a 'norm group's' scores.

A personality questionnaire focuses on aspects like: how you relate to other people; your work style; your ability to deal with your own or others' emotions; your motivation, determination and general outlook; and your ability to handle stress. Unlike aptitude tests, there is no average score, but instead a character profile is produced of the person best suited to the job (or course of study) at hand. The closer you fit that profile, the better chance you have of doing the job successfully, which of course influences candidate selection by potential employers.

Psychometry (Greek *psukhe*, 'breath, soul, mind', + *metria*, 'measurer') The **psychic** ability to receive impressions of a person or an event merely by holding objects belonging to or related to the subject. A person with this talent will be able to describe in great detail characteristics, personality traits and emotional states of the owner, and 'play back' an event in their head akin to viewing a video. A personal item, like a watch, piece of clothing or jewellery works the best, because the owner's **life force** energies have had time to become infused into the material. When a psychometrist holds this item, they are picking up on the vibrational energies stored therein.

Psychometry has been around as long as there have been people, but the phrase was not coined until 1842, when American scientist and professor of medicine Dr Joseph Buchanan discovered that 80 per cent of his students could register the effects of pharmaceutical drugs simply by holding them. When an emetic was handed to several of these students, they could only escape vomiting by stopping the experiment.

Psychoplasm see Ectoplasm

Psychosynthesis see Transpersonal Psychology

Pulsatilla One of the 15 major **polychrests**, or major remedies in **homeopathy**. It is also a **constitutional type**, which is a way homeopaths have of classifying different patient profiles. The fitting constitutional remedy acts preventatively and curatively on its matching personality type – for example a person with a Pulsatilla constitution will respond well to the Pulsatilla remedy almost regardless of the illness they are suffering from. Pulsatilla people (often women) are affectionate, gentle but also easily influenced and can be needy/dependent. They enjoy being out of doors, and love children and animals. They are prone to women's ailments, coughs and colds, and tend to get weepy when feeling off colour.

Pulse Diagnosis One of the four diagnostic techniques used in **Traditional Chinese Medicine** to determine ill-health. The pulse is traditionally taken at the radial artery on the wrist as a way of coming directly into contact with the patient's chi, which is stored in the lungs. The pulse is checked on each wrist, along the **lung meridian** in three separate areas, with attention paid to its depth, speed and strength each time. An experienced

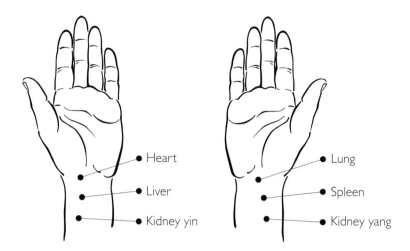

Pulse diagnosis

practitioner will be able to locate nine different pulses on each wrist, and each pulse corresponds to a particular internal organ. If the quality of a pulse shows up as weak, it indicates a corresponding weakness or imbalance in the energy of that organ. See also: **Tongue Diagnosis**.

Pure Land Buddhism The Pure Land, or Dharma, school emphasises chanting the many names of the Buddha and pure intent as a path to enlightenment and is most popular on the Indian subcontinent. Little emphasis is placed on strictly following all the teachings and tenets of Buddhism, and one is not even required to read the Buddha's teachings to attain **nirvana**. It is also known as amidism.

Purgatory (Latin *purgare*, 'to make clean, to purify') According to the Catholic Church, a place or condition of temporal punishment for those who are not entirely free from sin or fault, or have not fully paid for their transgressions. Purgatory is the region in the afterlife where you can (and need to) rectify mistakes you made in your life, before the final decision is made by **God** on whether you are **heaven**- or **hell**-bound for eternity. See also: **Christianity**.

Purusha (Sanskrit, 'spirit') The Indian philosophical equivalent of **yang**, purusha is pure consciousness or spirit, representing the male principle in **prana**, or universal life energy. Purusha is in an interdependent relationship with **prakruti**, the matter from which the cosmos is made. Prakruti and purusha and they way they interact are vital in **tantra** practice and belief.

Pyramid Power The belief that pyramids, or sitting beneath a pyramid shape, can endow a person with unique healing and psychic powers. It is thought by some that pyramids act as repositories or transformers of the electromagnetic energies of the earth and atmosphere. The unique geometric shape of a pyramid funnels vibrational energy from the ground up to the point of a pyramid. In the meantime, cosmic or solar radiation is attracted to the point at the top of the pyramid, in a 'lightning rod' effect. The resulting collection of energy 'supercharges' the atmosphere within the pyramid.

A number of experiments with pyramid power have been carried out, with some unusual results. In one, a cardboard model pyramid would sharpen a blunt razor blade and keep it sharp provided it was placed in a certain orientation to the earth's north/south pole axis. In another, plants grown in a pyramid-shaped greenhouse increased in growth by over 150 per cent in comparison to plants raised in exactly the same growing conditions, including soil and location, but in a greenhouse that was not of a pyramid shape.

Pyramid power is best known for focusing and endowing psychic abilities (the ancient Egyptians thought pyramids awakened the god who sleeps in the soul); and for demonstrating specific healing properties. By placing a pyramid beneath a bed or chair on which the subject is sitting, or directly pointing a pyramid towards the source of pain, relief is experienced within a short time. Many people also report increased energy and tranquillity after a meditative session under a pyramid.

Pyromancy (Greek *pyros*, 'fire', + *manteia*, 'divination') A number of **divination** methods using fire, for predicting the future and uncovering hidden knowledge. These ranged from throwing objects into the fire and observing their behaviour to interpreting the movement and sound of flames.

Fire, one of the primary **elements** of the universe, was considered inherently pure. Anything sacrificed to the fire (precious possessions, plants and herbs, animals and sometimes people) was considered purified and thus an acceptable gift for the gods. In the temples of ancient Greece and Rome, fires burned continuously, tended only by chaste vestal virgins.

Pyromancy can be subdivided into a number of specific methods including **capnomancy** (interpreting smoke patterns), **halomancy** (throwing salt into fire), **lampadomancy** (staring at a single flame) and **spodomancy** (interpreting the patterns of ashes and cinders).

Pythagoras (580–500 BC) Greek mathematician, known for his eponymous theorem, who was also the father of many mystical and divinatory practices, including **numerology**. He thought that there were connections between gods, men and numbers that could be codified and used to foretell the fate of a person, or future events, when certain number patterns appeared.

Pythagoras believed the entire universe could be interpreted using numbers and, centuries before telescopes were invented, attempted to analyse the orbits of the sun, moon and stars. He also formulated the theory of 'the **music of the spheres**', describing it as 'a divine symphony beyond the perception of most humans, played by the planets as they spin along in their orbits'.

Quartz (Slavic *twardy*, 'hard') The most versatile type of **crystal**, used for **divination**, healing and magic rituals. Quartz is a general term for a number of different crystals including amethyst, citrine and topaz, but clear quartz has the most use in **crystallomancy**, where it is the substance used to make crystal balls and **scrying** mirrors. Quartz is also used to rid the environment of unhealthy vibrations, and is excellent for cleansing an area too full of electromagnetic toxins, like computer-laden offices.

In magic, quartz is used as a protective **amulet** against evil, and for enchantments and charms. Rose quartz, a pink form of the stone, has special powers to attract affection so it is heavily featured in love spells and potions. Quartz also enhances a person's ability to foretell the future, and has been employed for this purpose, in many different cultures, for thousands of years.

Ra, also **Re** The great sun god of Egyptian mythology. Ra was the most important of all the gods as he personified the source of all life, the sun. One of his aspects was **Atum**, and in his role as Atum-Ra he created the world, starting with **Shu** (Air) and **Tefnet** (Moisture). They in turn created **Seb** (Earth) and **Nut** (Sky), who bore **Osiris, Isis, Seth** and **Nepthys**. Together these nine gods formed the **Ennead**, the ruling pantheon of deities holding sway over all of Egyptian thought.

Ra was said to have created mankind from his tears, but humans were ungrateful and plotted against him. In furious betrayal, Ra convened the Ennead and they agreed to an agent of destruction – the Eye of Ra, personified by the lion goddess **Sakhmet**. In her guise as avenging fury, the fierce lioness hunted humans down and revelled in their slaughter. The terrible fate he inflicted on mankind moved Ra to pity, and he called Sakhmet off. Still deeply saddened by human deceit, Ra withdrew into the heavens and appointed the god **Thoth** to be humanity's guardian and teacher.

Radiesthesia A method of medical **dowsing** that uses a **pendulum** to determine whether or not someone is sick. The pendulum is held over the body and the direction (clockwise, counterclockwise, left to right across the body, towards the body at right angles) in which it rotates or swings provides an indication of illness. Measures can then be taken to rebalance the flow of energies (called **life force**) throughout the body and restore health. See also: **Psionics**.

Radionics An alternative medicine system based on medical **dowsing** (called **radiesthesia**). This method, developed by Dr Albert Abrams in the early twentieth century, uses a 'black box' instead of a pendulum to detect and manipulate vital energy patterns in the body. All bodies radiate an electromagnetic field and Abrams claimed his device could tell healthy from diseased tissue, based on changes in the vibrations of a person's electric field as the body was scanned. Radionic instruments could then be retuned to emit 'healing vibrations' that would cure illness. After a brief heyday, Abrams' theories were discredited and have yet to regain scientific respect.

Radionics is still practised in the UK, US and Australia, although not widely, and the equipment and treatments can be very expensive.

Raja Yoga   see Yoga

Ramadan   The ninth month of the Islamic calendar, and a holy time because it was the month in which the **Koran** was revealed to the Prophet **Muhammad**. During this holy month, all Muslims over the age of 12 are required to fast from just before dawn until sunset, as ordered by Allah. See also: **Five Pillars of Islam**.

Ramayana   (Sanskrit, 'song of rama') One of the two great epic poems of ancient India that helped to form its culture, written some time prior to the sixth century BC (mostly by the poet Valmiki) and composed of over 24,000 couplets. It tells the story of Prince Rama, an incarnation of the god **Vishnu**, and his quest to save his beautiful princess wife Sita from the evil designs of Ravana, the demon-king. The *Ramayana* is a fantastical tale, full of monkey gods and evil stepmothers. After Rama saves Sita, he rather unfairly asks her to take a series of horrendous tests to prove she has been faithful to him, which she does – fair play and purity win the day. At the end, Rama is crowned king.

What may appear to be just a fairy tale actually deals in mythic form with the prehistorical conflict of the Aryans with the natives of India, the land they have plundered and conquered, and the battle to integrate these two cultures together.

Raphael   see Archangel

Rapture, The   The fundamentalist Christian belief that true believers will be spared the apocalypse at the end of the world, as described in the **Bible**. The Rapture is based on several verses in the Book of Revelations, in particular 3:10, where the faithful are promised they will be spared the trials and tribulations to come. This will be accomplished 'in the twinkling of an eye', by being snatched up by the Lord alive, without any clues left in the earthly realm as to your whereabouts. See also: **Christianity, Jesus Christ**.

Rastafarianism   (Amharic *ras*, 'head', + *tafari*, 'god') A religious faith specific to the African-Caribbean black community, founded in 1930 and based mostly in Jamaica. Rastafarians believe in the divinity of His Imperial Majesty Emperor Haile Selassie of Ethiopia, who they say was the god promised years earlier by prophetic writings.

Rastas mainly follow codes of conduct spelled out in the **Bible**, in particular Leviticus and Numbers, which specify diet, lifestyle and morality. Hair in both men and women is left uncut, as this symbolises breaking away from the 'Babylonian' system of Western society. In particular, dreadlocks are the result of the Nazarene Oath set out in Numbers 6:1-6, where they are considered a sign of devotion to God.

Rastas are proscribed by biblical edicts from many different foods (think Orthodox Judaism). Many also reject Western medical care, in particular blood transfusions, instead relying on unique combinations of herbs and other plant medicines (source of the infamous 'ganja' reputation). Rastas believe that their children are of paramount significance and they are accorded when young the status of princes and princesses. The transition to adulthood is marked by a change of designation to kingman and empress, as they are considered to be of the same lineage as their holy Emperor Jah Rastafari, the living God of Creation.

As Rasta status is determined by bloodline, you many not be converted or 'become' a Rasta. You just are, and no amount of reggae and dreadlocks will convince a true believer otherwise.

Rat, The In **Chinese astrology**, the first sign of the **zodiac**. You are a Rat if you were or will be born in the years 1936, 1948, 1960, 1972, 1985, 1996, 2008 or 2020. The Rat is an admirable character in Chinese mythology, symbolising shrewdness, enterprise and prosperity. Those born under this sign are assertive, intelligent and ambitious. They possess innate charm and have a quirky sense of humour. Rats can at times appear impatient and even insensitive, but are born leaders and succeed even against impossible odds. Their Western zodiac equivalent is **Sagittarius** and their ruling planet is **Jupiter**.

Rebirthing A technique of breath control and exercise that, when performed in a controlled manner, leads to a feeling that you are re-experiencing the trauma of your birth. Leonard Orr, the founder of rebirthing, discovered the technique in 1975 while practising a form of maha **yoga** exercise. He felt that it helped to resolve repressed attitudes, negative emotions and low self-esteem that supposedly originated with your experiences before and during your birth.

Rebirthing practitioners instruct their clients in specific breath exercises that trigger hyperventilation and, during the ensuing physiological response, encourage their patients to reenact their birth. According to theory, this leads to a cathartic rush of emotions and leaves you with an increased amount of physical and psychic energy.

Rebirthing is a controversial process, as there is no formalised system of training or accreditation for rebirthers, just a voluntary code of practice. It was erroneously connected to the death of a young American girl in the 1990s, when two therapists allegedly used rebirthing techniques in an ill-fated bonding ritual with her foster parents.

Red Chestnut A flower essence made from the blossom of the red chestnut tree. This emotionally healing tincture is one of the **Bach Flower Remedies**. Dr Bach said that this is indicated for 'those who are afraid for the safety and well-being of those they care about: over-anxious and fearful'.

Reflexology, Reflex Zone Therapy A **bodywork** therapy where pressure and massage applied to one area or 'zone' of the body (usually the feet, sometimes the hands) activates healing effects in another part of the body. The 'zones' are actually ten bands of energy (called **chi**) that run vertically throughout the body. Each foot or hand, then, can be divided into five separate zones, with 'reflex' areas in each corresponding to all the major organs, glands and body parts.

Foot reflexology is considered more powerful than hand reflexology,

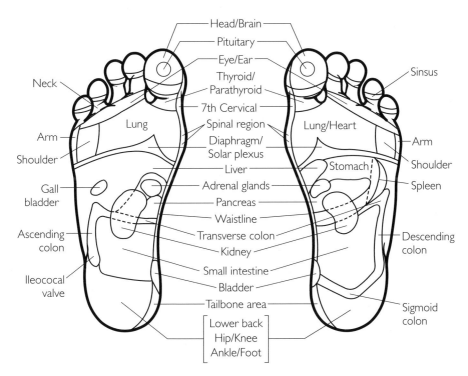

Reflexology chart

mostly because the foot is larger and it is easier to locate precisely the reflex points that need working.

Forms of reflexology have been known for millennia, with references found in ancient Chinese, Indian and Egyptian texts. Modern reflexology began, however, with American Dr William H. Fitzgerald, in 1915. He noticed that applying pressure on one part of the body produced a numbing effect in another, and he mapped out the ten body zones of energy, similar to **meridians** in Chinese medicine. Physiotherapist Eunice Ingham, who took the idea of 'zone therapy' further in the 1930s, maintained that all parts of the body could be treated by pressing certain areas of the foot. She coined the phrase 'reflexology' and mapped out the foot reflex points we know today.

When the foot reflexes are 'worked' by a practitioner, several things happen. First, crystalline deposits of waste products (composed usually of calcium and uric acid) that accumulate around nerve endings on the foot are broken up, 'crunched' and taken away by the lymphatic system. This helps to detoxify the body. Second, most of the body's nerves end in a 'reflex' on the feet; when these reflexes are pressed, they stimulate the nerve in a pleasant way. This relaxes the nerve and increases the flow of positive neurotransmitters like endorphins in the brain. Third, like any therapy that seeks to balance chi, reflexology helps break up blockages and regulate the flow of energy, so the body's self-healing mechanism is stimulated. It is similar to **acupuncture** in theory, but less invasive.

Reflexology can help many ailments, but is particularly good for stress-related conditions like insomnia and migraine, also asthma, sinusitis, wound healing, back pain and general pain relief, gynaecological problems, constipation and healing emotional crises.

Regression, Past-life Regression, Past-life Therapy The journey into past lives and incarnations while under hypnosis. This form of **hypnotherapy** is designed to carefully regress you back in age until you cross the threshold of your present birth and consciousness. Then a window can be opened to your unconscious mind, where buried memories of your previous life are stored. The purpose of the therapy is to help you heal any unresolved traumas hanging around from past existences, in order to improve your life in the present. When these memories are discovered, the therapist helps you to visualise more positive endings to your past lives, as most do have unhappiness attached to them.

There is some debate as to the merits of past-life therapy due to its attachment to the theory of **reincarnation**. Respected psychotherapist Dr Brian Weiss, of Columbia and Yale Universities and currently Chairman

Emeritus of Psychiatry at Mount Sinai Medical Center in Miami, firmly believes in its worth. His own scepticism was eroded when a troubled patient he was treating suddenly began spouting memories of a past life, which included remarkable revelations about Dr Weiss' own dead son. The patient then started to resolve her own present trauma by dealing with memories of her past.

The other side of the argument states that the therapy only works on people predisposed to believe in reincarnation and past lives in the first place, a point proved in a controlled study where 85 per cent of subjects told they would be able to recall a past life, did, and of another group told they would not, only 10 per cent produced a past-life memory. As it is not yet possible to scientifically prove the existence of reincarnation the debate continues, but a growing body of psychotherapists considers it a useful tool to help patients diagnose the root cause of their psychological problems, and to find a way to achieve better mental health. Through the process of remembering, symptoms diminish, and a strong sense of relaxation and well-being often emerges.

Reich, Wilhelm (1897–1957) Controversial psychoanalyst who is best known for his use of various bodywork methods in psychotherapy. He thought that there was a physical 'bioelectric flow' of energy through the body. When emotions and sexual instincts are repressed, bioelectric flow is blocked. The body holds these repressions as 'body armour' but this shield can be dissolved using a series of approaches, including deep breathing, massage and physical movement called **bioenergetics**.

Reich is also responsible for the concept of **orgone energy**, which makes bioenergetics seem positively staid in comparison. He courted controversy throughout his life for his theories, faced many charges of medical quackery and was jailed for criminal contempt in 1957, dying the same year before his release.

Despite the dubious nature of the man, his psychoanalytic theories have many reputable advocates, with glowing testimonials from those undergoing Reichian therapy. His bodywork concepts have heavily influenced other schools of thinking, most notably **rolfing** and **feldenkrais**.

Reiki (Japanese *rei*, 'universal', + *ki*, 'life energy') A system of healing through the manipulation of body energies. Reiki masters, called 'initiates', are specially trained to act as channels for 'universal life energy', using their hands in particular patterns to funnel healing power down into an ailing patient. Similar to **therapeutic touch**, the therapist's hands are either moved above the body, with minimal physical contact between the practitioner and the client, or are placed directly on the body, using specific healing movements and massage to direct the healing energy. Dr Mikao Usui (1865–1926), a Japanese doctor, founded reiki healing following 14 years' research into Christian and Buddhist scriptures for an alternative to orthodox medicine. After a 21-day meditation on a mountaintop, Usui was knocked over by a beam of light from the heavens, and he saw bubbles of light containing symbols he had previously seen in his studies. He took this vision to mean the symbols themselves had healing power and started to use them in his practice, with amazing results.

Usui kept these symbols secret and passed them along only to a chosen few he trusted to carry on his work. Reiki made its way west to the US via Kawaio Takata, a Japanese woman who learned it from one of Usui's pupils.

Training to be a reiki master is an exhausting, expensive process. There are three levels of training and only the highest level of pupil attains the rank of 'master' and is shown Usui's healing symbols. The theory behind reiki is simple, and familiar to anyone who has been exposed to the concept of body energy, whether in **Traditional Chinese Medicine**, **ayurveda**, or **spiritual healing**. Everyone has a personal energy field that, in health, runs around and through our bodies in an even harmonious flow or vibration. When we get ill, energies become imbalanced. Reiki seeks to rebalance these energies to help stimulate the body's self-healing mechanisms.

In a typical session, you are asked to participate by focusing on your own 'healing intention'. You lie or sit down in a comfortable position (no clothes need to be removed) and the initiate goes into his ritual to channel beneficial vibrations into your body's energy centres, the **chakras**. You may feel warmth or tingling in these areas, and most report feeling very relaxed after treatment.

Reiki is said to be effective in healing emotional and spiritual crises as well as physical health problems. Reiki practitioners, like spiritual healers, can also perform absent healing on a patient not physically present. The one caveat to add, however, is that the healing energies being manipulated are not merely those of the reiki practitioner, or those of the patient. It comes from an outside source: a channel that cannot be identified, and some reiki masters claim they receive their energy from **spirit guides** during healing sessions. Anyone questioning of spiritualist practices should be aware of this fact. See also: **Absent Healing, Vibrational Healing**.

Reincarnation The doctrine that maintains that after death one is reborn in another physical body, a new existence in 'carnate flesh'. Reincarnation is a central tenet of many spiritual traditions, in particular ancient Egyptian mythology, **Hinduism** and **Buddhism**. According to these beliefs, you take a body and an existence that is commensurate with your **karma**. You can then be born in different realms of existence, including animal bodies as well as various hellish and heavenly states. Reincarnation into a higher life form next time around guarantees you a reward for the efforts you make now. If you are able to finally achieve **enlightenment**, then you can escape the endless cycle of birth, death and rebirth by attaining **nirvana**.

Belief in reincarnation is not limited to practising Buddhists or Hindus. For many people the idea that we come back is substantiated by tales from **past-life regression therapy**, or from cases of spontaneous memory recall of past existence that can be backed up with corroborating facts and figures.

Traditional reincarnation involves going from one human body to another. Belief that you could return in an animal or non-human form is called **transmogrification**.

Relaxation Response A phrase coined by Harvard professor and cardiologist Dr Herbert Benson in his 1970s studies on **autogenic therapy**. Triggering the relaxation response in the body turns off the chronic release of stress chemicals in the brain, so the body can engage its self-healing mechanisms.

Remote Viewing The ability of some individuals to experience and describe locations, events and objects beyond the range of the physical eye, usually because of distance. The phrase was coined in 1972 by a team of investigators at Stanford University in California after they carried out a series of experiments on the phenomenon. After ten years of research, they concluded that remote viewing is a **psychic** power that occurs spontaneously, and that there is no way to determine why one person would be better at it than another. The only exception to this was the fact that if a person later visited the site they previously 'remote viewed', that person probably did better in the original test. This seems to point to **precognition**, where people have visions of future events or places. See also: **Extra-sensory Perception (ESP)**.

Rescue Remedy A **Bach Flower Remedy** recommended for emotional emergencies or traumas. This essence is comprised of five separate flower remedies: **impatiens, clematis, rock rose, cherry plum** and **star of bethlehem**. A small amount (one to five drops) of the tincture is taken either neat or in a glass of water, and repeated at half-hour intervals as needed. Available as a cream, Rescue Remedy can also be applied to the skin to remove the shock and subsequent pain from a bruise or minor burn.

Retrograde In **astrology**, a planet that appears to be moving backwards in the skies of the **zodiac** from our earthly perspective. All planets other than the sun and moon turn retrograde and, when they do, the expression of their unique energy is changed. Mercury, for example, is the planet of communication, transport and perception. When it goes retrograde (as it often does), appointments are missed, people quarrel over misunderstood messages, and cars, trains and phones break down. Things improve in the area of planetary influence when a planet goes 'direct', that is, appears to be going forwards again.

Rhabdomancy (Greek *rhabdos*, 'rod', + *manteia*, 'divination') A form of **divination** performed by using sticks, better known as **dowsing**. Twigs of wood (preferably **hazel**) are used as a rod to seek out hidden things, particularly underground water or silver. The term also applies to interpreting the flight of an arrow for oracular purposes.

Rhapsodomancy (Greek *rhapsoidia*, 'song, ode', + *manteia*, 'divination') A form of divining the future which involves throwing open a poetry book and selecting a passage at random to answer a specific question. Rhapsodomancy is a form of **stichomancy**, divining the future using books in general. See also: **Bibliomancy**.

Right-handed Path Phrase used to describe the path of white magic, where the magician's intention is benign, causing harm to no one, or for purposes of healing. In other words, a path of light and spiritual illumination. See also: **Wicca**.

Rinpoche (Sanskrit, 'precious one') Also known as a tulku, this is the title given to recognised reincarnated spiritual practitioners in **Tibetan Buddhism**. Tibet instigated a lengthy search and testing system to find the **reincarnations** of advanced meditators or **lamas**, on the understanding that such people had promised to return to earth in order to bring all living beings to enlightenment. Once a rinpoche is recognised in a new incarnation, he is then reinstated in his former position, usually at a very young age, to carry on the spiritual work he had been engaged in during his previous life. The most famous recognised reincarnated lama is the **Dalai Lama**. He is fourteenth in a succession which began with Gendun Drup in 1391.

Rising Sign see Ascendant

Ritual A stylised ceremony or form of practice designed to invoke a religious or magical deity. There are often specific routines and formalised behaviour that need to be followed in order to successfully gain access to the power or blessing of the god. Sometimes, rituals are performed to placate angry deities, as in ritual sacrifice. See also: **Magic, Spells**.

Rlun see **Chi**

Roc, also **Rukh** In Arabian myth and legends, a huge bird capable of carrying off elephants and other large animals, which it fed to its young. Its egg was as large as 148 hen's eggs and looked like the dome of a mosque. It is best known from the tale of 'Sindbad the Voyager' from 1001 *Arabian Nights*, where Sindbad hitched a ride back to civilisation on the roc's leg after being marooned on an island. Some think it is possible that the roc was actually one of the last remaining pterodactyls (flying dinosaurs) that somehow escaped extinction and lived in medieval Arabia.

Rock Rose A flower essence made from the rock rose blossom. This emotionally healing tincture is one of the **Bach Flower Remedies**. Dr Bach said that this is indicated for 'terror, panic, nightmares and other fears of a horrifying nature'.

Rock Water A flower essence made from the rock water blossom. This emotionally healing tincture is one of the **Bach Flower Remedies**. Dr Bach said that this is indicated for 'those who are strict with themselves, set themselves high standards and targets and demand perfection of their efforts'.

Rodomancy see **Astromancy**

Rolfing A bodywork therapy which uses deep-tissue massage and 'movement reeducation' to relieve muscle pain and tension. Rolfing was developed by Ida P. Rolf (1896–1979), a biochemist and therapist who discerned a correlation between muscular tension and repressed emotions. Once this tension is banished through treatment, the body can return to its proper alignment, producing an improvement in health and spirit.

Rolfing is often compared to **chiropractic** in that realigning the spine is of prime importance, but goes further to say that *every* part of your body must be aligned or ill-health will result. Unlike **chiropractic**, rolfing is not as rigorously regulated nor does it command much respect from the medical establishment. Rolfers claim that the technique has been scientifically validated and proponents testify that it helps ease back and neck pain, and improves impaired mobility and athletic performance. It is, however, only available from qualified rolfers from the Rolf Institute in Boulder, Colorado.

Rooster, The In **Chinese astrology**, the tenth sign of the **zodiac**. You are a Rooster if you were or will be born in the years 1933, 1945, 1957, 1969, 1981, 1993, 2005 or 2017. The Rooster is the sign of candour in Chinese mythology, symbolising protection and keeping misfortune at bay. Those born under this sign are flamboyant types with lively minds. They love to study, make friends easily and are glamorous. They can be conceited and opinionated, but are not prone to grudges or sulking. Their Western zodiac equivalent is **Virgo** and their ruling planet is **Mercury**.

Rose Quartz see Quartz

Rosicrucians Blanket term for a number of **esoteric** and **occult** sects which based their teachings on those of Christian Rosenkreuz (1378–1484). Rosenkreuz (literally 'rosy cross' in German) was a monk who travelled extensively throughout the Middle East, studying mystic traditions from these lands. On his return to his native land he founded with fellow monks the Order of the Rosy Cross, where they applied the lore of magic and healing Rosenkreuz had learned on his travels.

Rosenkreuz's teaching might have remained consigned to obscurity but for the publication sometime between 1614 and 1616 of three books he supposedly wrote. (They were probably actually written by Johann Valentin Andreae, a Wittenberg theologian of that time.) These writings inspired the formation of a 'secret brotherhood of Rosicrucians', with roots in occult and mystic science and philosophy.

There are several organisations today claiming links or lineage to this original secret society, which purport to have the esoteric answers to all of life's questions.

Rumi-Jelaluddin Mevlana Rumi (1207–73) was a mystic poet of **Islam**, who founded the order of **whirling dervishes**, a subsect of **Sufism**. He believed 'whosoever knoweth the power of the dance, dwelleth in God', so he and his followers would whirl themselves about in a rhythmic dance, provoking a **trance** state that Rumi thought led to direct communication with the Almighty Allah.

He also produced a prodigious output of literature and verse, writing poems of rare beauty and passion, many about love and wine. Rumi felt that the way to God was through experiencing ecstasy, and his best-known work, *Mathnawi*, captures the essence of the joyful, transcendent experience that is at the heart of Sufi philosophy.

Runes (Old Norse, 'whispered secret mystery') A form of **divination** using a set of 24 small tablets or stones with Norse symbols inscribed on them. It is a type of fortune-telling called **sortilege** (casting lots) as chance decides what runes will be chosen. After a question is asked, up to three runes are selected at random, and the symbols interpreted to fit the situation. They may first be cast down on the ground and if a character appears upside down, it reverses the meaning of the rune.

Kaunaz
torch;
inner light

Gebo
gift;
sacred mark

Wunjo
bliss;
perfection

Runes

Rune characters are made up of combinations of vertical and diagonal lines, each with elemental and symbolic meaning. For example, the rune 'kenaz' means 'torch'. It represents guidance, inner strength, inner light or intuition. Reversed, it means a loss of material possessions.

Runes were created by the Germanic peoples, the English, Germans and Scandinavians, sometime between 1300 and 1200 BC (based on archaeological finds). They were made of wood, metal or stone, and the act of inscribing the name of a natural element endowed the rune with its sacred power. This made runes popular not only in fortune-telling, but also when used as a protective **amulet** against evil. Each rune was also associated with a different Norse deity, who served as a guiding spirit to the person using them.

Runes fell out of favour when the Christian Church began to persecute rune-casters and other Northern pagans, who were burnt at the stake up until the seventeenth century. As pagan traditions have been rediscovered by a technology- and science-weary society, the use of runes in divination and guidance has started to rise again. See also: **Northern Paganism**.

Sabbat (Hebrew *shappath*, 'sacred or holy time') The eight days of the year when **pagans** and witches, particularly white and **Wiccan** practitioners, meet together. These festivals coincide with the **Celtic wheel** of the year, with the four main sabbats **Samhain/Halloween, Imbolc/Candlemas, Beltane/May Day** and **Lagnasad/Lammas** aligned with the four most important seasonal changes in the year. These are times for cleansing the old and welcoming the new, by lighting great 'bane' or 'bone' fires (made from rubbish and old bones). The four minor sabbats, **Yule, Midsummer, Eoastre** and **Michaelmas** coincide with the winter and summer **solstices** and the spring and autumn **equinoxes**. See also: **Paganism**.

Sacred Geometry (Greek *ge-*, 'earth', + *metres*, 'measurer') The idea that joins the concept of mathematical harmony and ratio to revered natural formations and buildings. Sacred geometry combines the theories of the 'golden mean' and pi (the numeric expression of the golden mean) with repeating patterns in nature and architecture, which represent the spiritual connection between the human and the divine. In other words, we respond with awe and reverence to certain structures, either man-made or natural, because they conform to the mathematical rules of the 'transcendent' golden mean, which adds order and proportion to the landmark. Some think that sacred geometry is the universal language of the subconscious, causing the five human senses and the psychic **sixth sense** to respond instinctively to the proportions.

Examples of sacred geometry at work are the Taj Mahal, Externsteine (Dragon Stones) in Northern Germany, Machu Picchu in Peru, Da Vinci's great artwork 'The Last Supper', Glastonbury Tor, **Stonehenge**, the pyramids of ancient Egypt and Mexico, Mt Fuji and Mt Everest. See also: **Geomancy, Labyrinths, Megaliths**.

Sadhana General term in **Hinduism** to describe spiritual or physical exercises, which lead to self-realisation and ultimately **enlightenment**.

Sagittarius The ninth sign of the **zodiac** in Western **astrology**, and the **sun sign** for those born between 23 November and 21 December. The symbol of

Sagittarius is the archer, and the ruling planet is **Jupiter**. Sagittarians are a **mutable sign** influenced by the **fire element**, with 'expansive' the best single word to define them. Those born under Sagittarius are visionaries, always on the quest for spiritual enlightenment. They are flexible, open-minded and extroverted, but can be rash and reckless. They are unconventional and if something does not serve their immediate aim, it is ignored.

The ideal meal for a Sagittarian is – food! And lots of it. Sagittarians love to cook (many chefs are born under this sign) and they are great entertainers. In health, their inability to say 'no' to anything leads them to suffer from their excesses, especially in food and drink. They tend to have accidents and undergo particular problems with their muscles and joints. Detoxifying herbs benefit this sign, as well as general tonics: Sagittarians tend to heal fast but can always use that extra push to support their unflagging energies.

Sakhmet, also **Sekmeth** The vengeful, bloodthirsty lion goddess of Egyptian mythology. Sakhmet represented the destroyer aspect of the feminine goddess archetype, and she was **Ra** the sun god's terrible instrument of revenge against deceitful, unrepentant man. In this guise as avenger goddess she was called the 'Eye of Ra', and accompanied pharaohs into battle as a warrior goddess just because she liked the blood. Sakhmet was also considered the 'Lady of Pestilence' as she sent down plagues and disease, but paradoxically was also considered the goddess of healing.

Salah One of the **five pillars of Islam**, which is the name for the obligatory prayers which are performed five times a day, and are a direct link between the devout Muslim and Allah. Prayers are said at dawn, noon, mid-afternoon, sunset and nightfall, and therefore determine the entire rhythm of the day. The devotee must kneel on a special prayer rug, facing east towards **Mecca**.

Salamander (Greek *salambe*, 'fireplace') A mythical lizard believed to live in the flames of a fire, that could burn you if you touched it. In the language of **alchemy** and **magic**, the salamander is the symbol of the element **fire**.

Samadhi (Sanskrit, 'illumination') The ultimate goal in **yoga**, samadhi is the highest of the 'eight limbs', or **ashtangas**, mentioned in the **Yoga Sutras** of Patanjali that will lead to enlightenment, and the final stage of the 'inner path'. To reach samadhi is to be so clearly focused on a single point that you reach absolute unity between mind, body and spirit. This unity leads to a blissful state of transcendence.

Samhain (Celtic origin, 'summer's end') The festival of 31 October, also known as **Halloween**, and the traditional start of the **pagan** calendar (also known as the **Celtic wheel of the year**). Samhain is the main witches' **sabbat**, and a time for cleansing the old year and welcoming the new seasonal cycle by lighting great 'bane' or 'bone' fires (made from rubbish and old bones), but also to honour the forces of death, as rebirth and life can only occur in nature if the previous cycle ends. Samhain was also thought to be the one night of the year when the portals between our world and the afterlife were open, allowing spirits to roam free. The bonfires lit that night served to light the path of departed souls to the other side, and chase away malevolent spirits. Samhain rituals are potent for protection, overcoming old fears and for preparing for the dark winter ahead.

Samsara The endless round of existence as defined in **Hinduism** and **Buddhism**, also known as the 'wheel of rebirth'. Everyone is caught up in a cycle of birth, life, disease, old age, death and reincarnation, caused by a bad **karma** of greed, hatred and ignorance. Samsara can be transcended by following the path to **enlightenment**. A soul is condemned to an eternal cycle of birth and death until enlightenment is achieved and **nirvana** (Buddhist) or **moksha** (Hindu) is attained.

Sangha (Sanskrit) In **Buddhism**, a term commonly used to denote monks, nuns, or the spiritual community that offers support for one's own spiritual endeavours. Named after the first disciples of Shakyamuni **Buddha**.

Satan (Hebrew, 'an enemy') The embodiment of evil according to Jewish, Christian and Islamic religion, and in many schools of thought throughout the world. He is the great enemy of God and has temporary status as king of our mortal world, because he was able to (and still does) tempt mankind into sinning.

The **Bible** relates that he was once one of the highest of **angels** in the celestial realm, until he rebelled against God and was kicked out of heaven with his followers (called **demons**).

He is known by a host of other names (appropriately Legion is one of them) including the Prince of Darkness, the Devil, Mephistopheles, Beelzebub, Diablo, Old Coots, Eblis, Old Harry, Old Nick, Old Scratch, the Serpent, Son of the Morning Star and Son of Perdition. There are over 33 names for Satan in the Bible alone, and hundreds of titles and nicknames in other cultures for this entity. It is common not to refer to him directly by name, lest you call his unwelcome attention to you. This tradition originated with Kabbalistic practices, where to utter the sound or name of a deity or entity was to access their power for you.

There are some who revere him as a god, as a source of black magic and great power, and perform rituals extracted and perverted from standard Christian practice. This worship of the devil is known as 'satanism'.

Satori In **Zen Buddhism**, a flash of insight into the true nature of reality. This insight is attained through meditation, question and answers, and through the contemplation of illogical riddles.

Saturn The sixth planet in our solar system and the furthest that can be seen with the naked eye. Named for the Roman god of old age and time, Saturn proceeds through the heavens at a stately pace. In **astrology**, Saturn represents your inner personality and how you cope with the restrictions, fears and barriers in your life. It is associated with limitation and difficulties. Despite this, it can also symbolise meeting challenges with fortitude and perseverance. Traditionally, Saturn rules agriculture, architecture, old age, time and mortality. The transit of Saturn is 28 to 30 years, the longest planetary cycle that will occur in a person's life. It is the ruling planet for the **zodiac** sign **Capricorn** and the co-ruler for **Aquarius**.

Sawm, also **Sawn** One of the **five pillars of Islam**, which is the rite of obligatory fasting from sunrise to sunset during the holy month of **Ramadan**. Abstinence is required from all food and drink (except water), as well as smoking and conjugal relations.

Scarab An ancient Egyptian symbol of rebirth and immortality. The dead were often buried with carvings and jewellery in the form of a scarab, usually inserted in between the linen wrappings that bound their body, to ensure their passage to the underworld. One purpose of the scarab **amulet** placed over the heart during mummification was to ensure that the spirit of the dead spoke the truth before **Osiris**, the lord of the afterlife.

Psychoanalyst **Carl Jung** considered the scarab to be an important **archetype** of rebirth and, in his writings, cited its appearance in a case study as a prime example of **synchronicity**.

Scientology A movement that bills itself a religion, started by American science-fiction writer L. Ron Hubbard in the mid-twentieth century. It blends elements of psychology, **occultism** and the best of Hubbard's story-telling techniques into a self-help belief system. The main text used in Scientology is

Dianetics, purportedly one of the best-selling books of all time. Scientology enjoys the patronage and testimonials of a number of high-profile celebrities, who aim to spread its goal of spiritual evolution through esoteric psychological testings and manic proselytising efforts.

Scleranthus A flower essence made from the scleranthus blossom. This emotionally healing tincture is one of the **Bach Flower Remedies**. Dr Bach said that this is indicated for 'those who are indecisive, debating the pros and cons of every situation – hesitating "shall I, shan't I?"'.

Scorpio The eighth sign of the **zodiac** in Western **astrology**, and the **sun sign** for those born between 24 October and 22 November. The symbol of Scorpio is the scorpion, and the ruling planets are **Mars** and **Pluto**. Scorpios are a **fixed sign** influenced by the **water element**, with 'intensity' the best single word to define them. Those born under Scorpio are passionate individuals: they are the sensualists of the zodiac. They tend to be psychic, purposeful and very focused, but can be vengeful and secretive.

To match this 'all-or-nothing' persona, a Scorpio's ideal meal is cooked from exotic and adventurous ingredients. They are the ones chomping down strange cuts of offal and semi-poisonous puffer fish. It comes as no surprise that in health they suffer from excess – they are often prone to bladder or bowel complaints and can be tense individuals. They would benefit from herbal tonics to detox impurities from the body, and to lighten up the infamous Scorpio intensity.

Scrying, also **Skrying** (Latin *describere*, 'write down, perceive') A form of **divination** using reflective objects or crystals. If you stare long enough at the surface of the reflection, you become receptive to messages from the spirit world, which either reveal the truth of a matter or predict the future. Crystals are particularly effective in focusing the mind and providing a gateway to the altered consciousness required to correctly divine the truth.

Scrying was practised in ancient Egypt and Chaldea, and was a favourite fortune-telling method of Dr **John Dee**, official astrologer to Queen Elizabeth I. The crystal ball used by gypsies is the best-known tool used in scrying, although you can also use shiny stones, a mirror or bowls/pools of water. See also: **Catoptromancy**.

Séance (French, 'sitting') A meeting of a group of people who wish to communicate with the **spirits** of loved ones, or other supernatural entities. It is led by a **medium**, who acts as a go-between for the group and the spirit world. Contrary to popular belief, it is not necessary to sit around a table and join hands in order to conduct a successful séance, unless all you want the contacted entity to do is lift or rap the table. See also: **Spiritualism**.

Seb, also **Geb**, **Keb** The earth god in Egyptian mythology. Seb was the son of **Shu**, the air god, and **Tefnet**, the moisture goddess. His sister-consort was **Nut**, the sky goddess, and their children were **Osiris**, **Isis**, **Seth** and **Nepthys**. He was depicted as a man with either green or black skin – the green representing all living things, and the black the fertile mud of the Nile river. He sometimes took on the image of a goose, his sacred animal, and was known as 'the Great Cackler' for that reason.

Second House In **astrology**, the **house** or part of the heavens in your birth chart that describes your attitudes to money, possessions, wealth and security. It is ruled by the sign **Taurus** and the planet **Venus**. See also: **Ascendant, Horoscope**.

Second Sight A term used to describe **clairvoyance**, the ability to look beyond the normal world and obtain information about a person, event or situation through **ESP** or other paranormal means. See also: **Precognition**.

Secret Doctrine see Blatvatsky, Madame

Self-hypnosis see Hypnotherapy

Sema, Sama see Whirling Dervishes

Sephiroth, Sethiroth see Tree of Life

Sepia One of the 15 major **polychrests**, or major remedies in **homeopathy**. It is also a **constitutional type**, which is a way homeopaths have of classifying different patient profiles. The fitting constitutional remedy acts preventatively and curatively on its matching personality type – for example, a person with a Sepia constitution will respond well to the Sepia remedy almost regardless of the illness they are suffering from. Sepia people are elegant, seemingly extroverted and self-possessed. This facade, however, disappears at home with their loved ones, where they can appear peevish and irritable. They are prone to extreme fatigue, weep easily, but conceal their vulnerability. Mostly women, Sepia types are susceptible to a host of gynaecological ailments, and lack of libido.

Seraph (plural **Seraphim**)   A winged **angel** that represents light, ardour and purity in mythology and Christian thought. Seraphs are tall, mysterious beings of light, the highest of the ninefold celestial angel order. They guard the throne of **God** and are depicted as having three wings. See also: **Cherubim.**

Serendipity   (Latin *serenus*, 'clear, fine, calm') An occurrence or sequence of events that by chance turn out to be happy or beneficial. The phrase was actually coined by Horace Walpole in 1754 after reading a fairy tale called *The Three Princes of Serendip,* in which the heroes 'were always making discoveries, by accidents and sagacity, of things they were not in quest of'.

Seth, also **Set, Setekh, Seti, Setish**   The god of chaos and evil in Egyptian mythology, best known for murdering and dismembering his brother **Osiris**, the god of the afterlife. Seth was also considered the deity of war, deserts and storms. Seth was one of the sons of **Seb**, the earth god, and **Nut**, the sky goddess, and his sister-consort was the goddess **Nepthys**. He was also a member of the **Ennead**, the ruling council of Egyptian gods and goddesses.

Despite his unsavoury reputation, Seth was the protector of the barge of the sun god **Ra**, during its nightly journey through the perilous underworld. He was often depicted as half-man, half-beast, and sometimes considered the patron god of animals.

Seventh House   In **astrology**, the **house** or part of the heavens in your birth chart that describes the relationships in your life – in partnerships and love and with enemies. It is ruled by the sign **Libra** and the planet **Venus**. See also: **Ascendant, Horoscope.**

Shadow, The   According to **Carl Jung**, the hidden or unconscious aspects of our selves, both good and bad, that our conscious self (also known as the **ego**) has either repressed or never acknowledged. Jung thought that the shadow was one of two aspects to our **psyche** (mind), the other one being our ego, which presents itself to the world in our 'persona', or public mask. The shadow is mostly composed of those elements we find distasteful, like taboo desires, childish fantasies and resentments, and uncivilised impulses. These unacknowledged elements still find a way to be heard, by our 'projecting' those qualities onto others. This projection is a convenient way of being able to blame others for our own faults.

Despite the negative connotations of the shadow, acknowledging and 'assimilating' it into your ego is a sign of a healthy psyche. The presence of our own shadow serves us as a moral barometer, to allow us to distinguish between good and evil, and to learn compassion in our dealings with others. See also: **Jungian Psychology**.

Shahadah One of the **five pillars of Islam**, the Shahadah is the declaration of faith that all Muslims must make in order to be righteous believers. 'There is no god except Allah, Muhammad is the Messenger of Allah.'

Shakti The consort of the Hindu god **Shiva**, and the embodiment of the feminine in the mystic life force, **prana**. Together with her male counterpart Shiva, Shakti energy is utilised to awaken the dormant power of **kundalini** in **tantric** practices and beliefs. In **Hinduism**, Shakti is a goddess with a dual nature, representing the loving, nurturing aspects of women as well as their destructive powers. As Parvati, the wife of Shiva, she is a gentle mother to the two gods **Ganesha** and Skanda. Taunted by Shiva because of her dark skin, she transforms into **Kali**, the bloodthirsty goddess who in her violent dance of rage nearly trampled Shiva to death beneath her feet.

Shakti is also known as Durga, the warrior goddess.

Shaman (Native Siberian *sha'man*, 'to heat up, to burn, to work with fire') A healer-magician-priest figure who usually serves as wise man to tribal peoples of the Americas, India, Australia, Japan, Siberia and Mongolia, as well as in some northern European pagan traditions. In different traditions, shamans are also known as **medicine men** or **witch doctors**. They can access altered states of consciousness and tap into the elemental powers of nature and spirit, for the health and well-being of their people. They are often well-versed in practices including **herbalism** and **spiritual healing**.

Shamans are also able to enter into communication with the gods and spiritual beings, and often consult **spirit guides** in the form of animal guardians called **totems**. Shamans also guide their people to maturity by helping them to contact their own totem guides, or through the use of psychogenic or psychedelic substances.

Shamanism, Shamanic Drumming, Shamanic Healing The spiritual practices of a **shaman**, a person who is able to access altered states of consciousness through the use of **spirit guides** and psychedelic substances, and through invoking a trance state using rhythmic drumming, chanting or dance. Once in a trance, a shaman is able to access his guardian spirit, also known as a **totem**, for healing, guidance and advice.

Shambhala In **Tibetan Buddhism**, a mysterious lost land located somewhere beyond the peaks of the Himalayan mountains. This mystical kingdom is a hidden paradise of green valleys and lush vegetation, and those who find it attain spiritual wisdom and all the esoteric knowledge of the universe. For many Buddhists, Shambhala does not exist on this earthly plane, but instead will return to our existence one day so that its inhabitants can usher in a new Golden Age. The legend of Shambhala was the inspiration for James Hilton's Shangri-la, the fictional paradise of his novel *Lost Horizons*.

Shape-shifting A deliberate act of transforming from human to animal form, through magical or spiritual means. Witches, **shamans**, and sorcerers practise this supernatural ability to increase their understanding and knowledge about a particular situation, or to gain the power the chosen animal, bird or mythic creature possesses. Types of shape-shifting include a witch taking on the role of her **familiar**, or a shaman transforming into a tribe's **totem** animal to seek out advice and wisdom for his tribe. One particular form of shape-shifting is called **lycanthropy**, where a man turns into a werewolf.

Sheep, The In **Chinese astrology**, the eighth sign of the **zodiac**. In some Chinese cultural traditions this sign is referred to as 'the Goat' or 'the Ram', although all the characteristics remain the same. You are a Sheep if you were or will be born in the years 1931, 1943, 1955, 1967, 1979, 1991, 2003 or 2015. The Sheep is the sign of art in Chinese mythology, symbolising creativity, social status and career success. Those born under this sign are reserved, creative types, with strong spiritual values. They are often dreamy and sensitive, but have a tendency to take on too much work and hate confrontation. Their Western zodiac equivalent is **Cancer** and their ruling planet is the **moon**.

Shen (Chinese, 'mind-spirit') In Chinese philosophy and medicine, the individual consciousness of a person, also known as the soul. They believe that it is housed in the blood and stored in the liver. Along with **chi** (energy) and **jing** (blood) it constitutes one of the main forces in the human body. See also: **Taoism**.

Shen Cycle, also **Creation Cycle**, **Production Cycle** In Chinese philosophy and medicine, the cycle of the five natural elements (water, wood, fire, earth, metal) that shows how one element generates, or 'creates', the next element. Water causes new plants to grow in spring to create wood, which in turn is destroyed by fire and returns to ashes and earth. Earth is the source of metal, which, being cold, causes condensation to appear as water. The Chinese also call this the 'mother–son' cycle, as one element 'gives birth' to the next, in a continuous and interdependent circle. See also: **Five Element Cycle, Ke Cycle**.

Sheol (Hebrew *she'ol*, 'cave') The Jewish version of the afterlife, where the spirits of the departed dwell in underground caves. Most people think it is one of the two Jewish versions of **hell**, the other being **Gehenna**. See also: **Heaven, Judaism**.

Shiatsu (Japanese, 'finger pressure') A **holistic** massage technique that uses fingertip pressure to stimulate energy pathways on the body. These pathways, called **meridians**, circulate bioelectric energy (**chi** or the Japanese term **ki**) throughout the body along specific channels. When the flow of ki becomes imbalanced through blockage, pain or illness can result. The practitioner presses down on meridians to free up this bioelectric flow.

The meridians are pressed on specific points on the body called **tsubos**, which allows the shiatsu practitioner directly to affect your personal energy flow. There are over 600 of these points on the body, and many find them surprisingly sensitive to the touch. You can tell if your energy is becoming more balanced, because these tsubos cease to hurt when pressed.

Shiatsu practitioners work with their fingers, thumbs, elbows, knees and feet to press these points. They may also stretch, squeeze and rub sore areas to help relieve pain and to stimulate the circulation.

The therapy can be used for a wide range of different health conditions, but is most often recommended for any stress-related conditions like headaches, depression and anxiety, as well as digestive disorders, back and neck pain, sports injuries, circulatory problems, painful menstruation and cold-type conditions like catarrh, sinusitis and bronchitis.

Shiatsu is a form of **acupressure**, which is related in theory to **acupuncture**.

Shinto, also **Shintoism** Japanese state religion of ancient origin (seventh century BC) that combines elements of ancient nature worship with the later philosophical tenets of **Buddhism** and **Confucianism**. It is also known as *Kami-no-Michi*, 'The way of the gods', because believers thought that their emperor was a 'divine leader', in lineage actually descended from the sun goddess Amaterasu Omikami. In 1946 Emperor Hirohito formally renounced his divinity.

The most sacred places of Shinto are the temples of the sun goddess, where people still go and worship today.

Shiva (Sanskrit, 'kindly') One of the **trimurti**, or three main gods in **Hinduism**, primarily known as 'the destroyer of evil'. Shiva has many different aspects, some compassionate, some destructive and some erotic (he is worshipped in the form of a phallic symbol called *linga*). Shiva is also the male embodiment of **prana**, or life energy. Together with the energy of his female counterpart, **Shakti**, Shiva's energy is utilised to awaken the dormant power of **kundalini** in **tantric** practices and beliefs.

Many devotees of Shiva believe that he is the ultimate deity despite his dual nature. As Rudra, Shiva is the god of destruction and storms. As Pashupati, he is the lord of animals, and a gentle soul. These two aspects of his persona are shown in his well-known 'dance', which can express either love or hostility.

Shiva's consort is **Shakti**, who appears in many different guises. Gentle Parvati is the mother of his children, **Ganesha** and Skanda. Horrific and bloodthirsty **Kali** rips her enemies into pieces and tramples them underneath her feet. Like Shiva, Shakti has a dual nature.

Shu Ancient Egyptian god of the sky and one of the **Ennead**, the leading council of ruling gods and goddesses. He was created from the sole efforts of **Atum**, the supreme creator of the universe, along with his sister-consort, the goddess **Tefnet**. With her, he became the father of **Nut**, the sky goddess, and **Seb**, the earth god.

Sibyl (Greek *sibilla*) A woman who is able to foretell the future. The term came from ancient Greece, where sybils were prophetesses whose special function was to intercede with the gods on behalf of others. They usually lived in isolated places like caves or rocky precipices. The best-known sibyl in the ancient world lived at Cumae, near modern-day Naples. She guarded the temple to Apollo, which was supposedly the entrance gate to the underworld. Mythical Roman hero Aeneas consulted here before descending to Avernus (the underworld). See also: **Oracle**.

Sick Building Syndrome see Geopathic Stress

Sidda Yoga see Yoga

Sidhe see Fairies

Sigil (Latin *sigillum*, 'sign') A symbol, seal or **glyph** used in magic rituals of **witchcraft** and **occultism**. The symbol is constructed out of a set of written

words transformed into a picture. Ones you create yourself are the most potent, and can be used to enhance magical working by placing the symbol on pertinent letters, packages or clothing. They can also be used as focal points for meditation and contemplation, or to summon spirits and **angels**.

Sigils

Sikhism (Punjabi *shishya*, 'learner or pupil') An Eastern religion that originated on the Indian subcontinent in the fifthteenth century. Sikhism is thought to result from a combination of beliefs from the Bhakti movement within **Hinduism** and Sufi mysticism, although Sikhs would say it was a direct revelation from God. The founder of Sikhism, Shri Guru Nanak Dev Ji (known as Guru Nanak), infamously began his treatise with the statement: 'There is no Hindu, there is no Muslim.'

Guru Nanak (1469–1538) was born in the Punjab area of what is now Pakistan. His revelation that led to the new faith was followed by the teachings of a further nine gurus (regarded as reincarnations of Guru Nanak), up to the year 1708. The guru of that period, Guru Gobind Singh, decreed that there would be no further living gurus and, instead, divine relevation and authority would be centred in the 'Panth' (the believers) and the holy text, the Gurn Granth Sahib, more commonly known as the **Adi Granath**. Because of its divine nature, the Adi Granath is taken out and paraded on Sikh festivals as a visible sign of godhead.

Guru Nanak's vision of the path to enlightenment was revolutionary for its time, as it advocated sexual equality and tolerance of other religions – as long as those faiths sought enlightenment. Sikhs believe in one God who created the universe, and that all humanity is one. God does not care what religion you follow, as long as you conduct yourself in certain moral ways.

The core beliefs of Sikhs are as follows: the goal in life is to build a close, loving relationship with the single, formless God of 99 names. Sikhs believe in **samsara**, the endless round of death and rebirth, **karma** (how your actions in this life determine your path in the next) and **reincarnation**. The only way to transcend samsara is to reach enlightenment through leading a holy life in three dimensions: worshipping only the almighty (known as nam japna);

earning your own way in life (kirat karna); and sharing your time, talents and earnings with the less fortunate (vand chakna).

Strict Sikhs and those of advanced status aspire to Khalsa, the community of the pure. They undergo the Amrit Panth ceremony, a sacred ritual of initiation. After that, Khalsa Sikhs display the symbols of the five K's: the kesh, long uncut hair that is a symbol of spirituality; the khanga, a comb which is a symbol of cleanliness and orderliness; the kara, a steel bracelet worn on the right wrist as a reminder of the need for restraint; the kirpan, a double-edged ceremonial sword as a symbol of dignity; and the kachera, knee-length undershorts worn as a symbol of self-control and chastity.

Silica   One of the 15 major **polychrests**, or major remedies in **homeopathy**. It is also a **constitutional type**, which is a way homeopaths have of classifying different patient profiles. The fitting constitutional remedy acts preventatively and curatively on its matching personality type – for example, a person with a Silica constitution will respond well to the Silica remedy almost regardless of the illness they are suffering from. Silica types tend to be weakly, thin and pale, and are often susceptible to colds and flu. They can be indecisive and lack confidence, but despite all this, are hard workers. They suffer from a number of minor ailments of skin, teeth and hair, and are prone to frequent respiratory infections.

Single Remedy   In classic **homeopathy**, the one substance that most closely models a disease's symptom. Because of this, it is also the most effective remedy, properly diluted, to counterbalance the illness or condition.

Sirens   (Greek *seiren*, 'to bind or attach') In Greek mythology, sea nymphs who possessed alluring voices that could tempt a sailor to his doom on the rocks surrounding them. They are best known from the episode in Homer's *The Odyssey* where the hero Odysseus must navigate his ship past their habitat. In order to keep his sailors from falling prey to their seductive singing, he makes them stop up their ears with wax, and then commands them to lash him to the main mast so he can hear the sirens' songs. Odysseus told his sailors that no matter how hard he begged, they were not to untie him until the danger was past.

Another hero to thwart these temptresses was Jason, he of the Golden Fleece. When his ship of adventure passed the sirens, he had the legendary musician Orpheus on board. Orpheus outplayed the sirens, and the ship went on without incident.

Sivananda Yoga see **Yoga**

Sixth House In **astrology**, the **house** or part of the heavens in your birth chart that describes your health and your feelings towards the obligations in your life: duties, employment and service. It is ruled by the sign **Virgo** and the planet **Mercury**. See also: **Ascendant, Horoscope.**

Sixth Sense A slang term for **extra-sensory perception (ESP)**, because people who possess this ability can often perceive things beyond those with which their other five senses (sight, sound, touch, smell, taste) can provide them.

Sky-clad A Wiccan witch's preferred way of working a spell to better channel natural energies and to feel better connected to the earth and sky without the distraction of clothes. It also represents a return to purity and innocence. In other words, naked.

Small Intestine Meridian A channel or **meridian** of **chi** energy running through the body that affects the small intestine, according to **Traditional Chinese Medicine.** It is associated with the **fire element**, has **yang** energetic properties, and is partnered with the **heart meridian,** which is **yin.** Small intestine energy controls the assimilation of food and also of new experiences and feelings. Chi is strongest in this channel between 1 and 3 p.m. and conversely the weakest between 1 and 3 a.m. Both left and right sides of the body have this meridian, which runs from the little fingernail up the arm and neck to the ear.

Smudging The Native North American practice of energetically cleansing an environment through an ancient smoke ritual. It involves burning small bundles of herbs and sweet-smelling grasses to physically and spiritually cleanse anything from homes to people, and to replace negative thoughts and feelings with positive ones. Theoretically, as the smoke drifts upwards, it carries your desires and messages to **God,** or the 'Great Spirit' in Native American religion, who will grant them if your thoughts and intentions are pure.

During the ritual, you focus on something you want to change, or ask for blessings to come down to you. The choice of herb should be determined by your desired objectives. Lavender helps to restore a peaceful balance to an environment, and attracts loving energy and spirits. Rosemary is healing and stimulating, and helps to clarify problems. Sage, the herb most often used, is calming and healing, and usually combined with cedar and sweetgrass for an overall cleansing effect. Smudging is a form of **geomancy**, a practice that works with the natural magnetic and **life force** energies of the earth. See also: **Feng Shui, Space Clearing.**

Snake, The In **Chinese astrology**, the sixth sign of the **zodiac**. You are a Snake if you were or will be born in the years 1941, 1953, 1965, 1977, 1989, 2001 or 2013. The Snake is the sign of wisdom in Chinese mythology, symbolising wisdom, glamour and cunning. Those born under this sign are attractive, graceful and clever, with great powers of concentration. Snakes can be secretive and cunning, and are considered lucky with money. Their Western zodiac equivalent is **Taurus** and their ruling planet is **Venus.**

So Mote It Be Phrase use by magic practitioners, particularly white witches, to end a spell. It is, in effect, the equivalent of saying 'amen' or 'blessed be'. See also: **Wicca.**

Solstice (Latin *solstitium*, 'sun stands still') The twice-yearly time when the sun reaches its highest or lowest point in the sky at noon, which is marked by either the longest or the shortest day (hours of sunlight) of the year. In the northern hemisphere (reversed in the southern hemisphere), the summer solstice date is 21 June, and the winter solstice 21 December, but on the day before and the day after each of these dates the sun appears to rise and set at more or less the same point on the horizon, seeming to stand still in the sky. This illusion is caused by the tilt of the earth's axis in relation to the sun. In many religious traditions around the globe, the solstices are significant dates, and were especially so in ancient times when the sun's yearly patterns were not fully understood, and people always feared that when the sun disappeared in the winter, it would not return. These two great dates of midsummer and midwinter were also perceived as gateways for the soul on its journey into and out of life.

The solstices marked important dates in the **pagan** calendar of the year and were celebrated as festival days, **sabbats**. The summer solstice was known as **Midsummer's Eve** and the winter solstice as **Yule**, and special rites to mark their passing are still performed today. See also: **Celtic Spirituality, Celtic Wheel, Wicca, Witchcraft.**

Songlines Invisible lines of psychic energy that run across the Australian continent, according to aboriginal spirituality. They are called 'psi-tracks', a phrase coined by Swede Gote Andersson in 1987. He believed that the force of these energy lines was created by visualisation that extends between a person and the object on which they are focusing. This is why it is necessary for Aboriginals to walk songlines, to keep the psychic energy alive through visually reconnecting a person to the land. See also: **Dreamtime**.

Sophia (Greek, 'wisdom') The female embodiment of **God**, according to **Gnosticism** and some Eastern Orthodox sects of **Christianity**, who call her St Sophia. Sophia is the essence of feminine divinity, and is called by many **goddess** names in different cultures. For some she is the Christian **Virgin Mary**; in ancient Egypt she was **Hathor**; for ancient Greeks she was **Athena**; in the **Kabbalah** she is Shekinah; and for medieval alchemists and scholars she was Lady Sapientia, whose virgin daughters represented the seven liberal arts of academia. In whatever cultural tradition you consult, Sophia is the **archetype** of wisdom, and the great mother to all the world.

Sorcery, Sorcerer, Sorceress (Latin *sors*, 'lot') A form of **magic** that uses **spells** and **incantations** to summon up supernatural powers or spirits, mostly for evil purposes or to gain advantage. It is usually associated with black magic. Someone who practises sorcery is called either a sorcerer (if male) or a sorceress (if female). See also: **Left-handed Path**, **Witchcraft**.

Sortilege (Latin *sors*, sort-, 'lot, chance', + *legere*, 'choose') Divination by the casting or drawing of lots popular in ancient Rome (whose citizens considered the practice sacred to the god **Mercury**). It was usually done by casting dice, although drawing straws from a cluster provided an alternative method. Although it was most popular at the time of the Roman Empire, it is still practised today in Western culture, using dice or short straws, or taking a card at random from a pack of playing cards. See also: **Cleromancy**.

Soul The immortal **spirit** that resides within a person or (in some traditions) animals, plants and other organic material. The soul is the animating presence within our physical form, and represents the essence of who we are. It lives on after our death on this plane of existence and, depending upon your beliefs, gets reincarnated, lives in **heaven**, paradise, **hell** or **purgatory**, or is transmogrified into the animus of other living being. It is also the part of us that goes walkabout in **astral travel**. See also: **Astral Body**, **Chi**, **Ether**, **Life Force**, **Prana**, **Reincarnation**.

Sound Therapy, Sound Healing A healing method that uses the vibrational energy of sound, either the voice or a musical instrument. Sound therapists believe that every part of the body vibrates on a particular energy frequency. Dissonance in these vibrations equals imbalance and therefore stress or illness. Therapists use their own vibrational energy, either from instrumental music or vocal work, to counteract or correct this dissonance. Therapies using sound such as bells, drums and musical recordings appear to stimulate and regulate the body's endocrine system, providing many physical and emotional benefits. Sound therapy is said to aid deep relaxation as well as managing illnesses like seasonal affective disorder (SAD) and assisting pain management. It can also help to release painful memories and emotions trapped in the cellular structure of the body.

Space Clearing The practice of clearing clutter from your home or business, in order to improve the flow of natural energies through your environment. The goal of space clearing is to create greater harmony and balance in your life, by first creating it in your personal living spaces. It is very similar to other methods of **geomancy**, practices that work with the natural magnetic and **life force** energies of the earth. Many consider space clearing to be the first step in successfully applying **feng shui** principles to your living and working domains.

There are three kinds of clutter: physical, vibrational and internal.

Physical clutter relates to the mess and jumble of accumulated items in our house or office and needs merely to be reduced to have a positive effect.

Vibrational clutter relates to the unresolved and negative issues in our life, whether they be financial debt, unanswered phone calls and letters, or disrupted relationships. Dealing with these matters relieves pressure on the unconscious mind, resulting in more personal, positive energy.

Internal clutter is associated with our personal health, and is usually related to lifestyle choices or habits (good or bad). Balancing your internal environment, either through a change in habit or through energy-enhancing treatments like **acupuncture, reflexology** or **ayurveda**, will result in better health and an improved sense of well-being. See also: **Smudging**.

Spell (Anglo-Saxon *spellian*, 'to recount') A procedure performed by a witch, wizard or magician that is believed to make a tangible change to a situation. Spells are activated either by incantation (chanting) of ritual words or by invocation of powerful spirits, with the aid of magical tools and ingredients. They can be positive, as in wishing to improve a person's health, or negative, to coerce a person against their will. Whether or not a spell is good or evil depends on the intentions of the spellcaster. See also: **Left-handed Path, Wicca**.

Sphinx A mythical creature, usually female, with the head and breast of a person, the lower body and tail of a lion, and the wings of a bird. The best-known example is the statue of the Great Sphinx of Giza, Egypt. The Sphinx featured in both ancient Egyptian and Greek mythology, where she would

hide by well-travelled paths and pounce on unsuspecting travellers. She threatened to devour them unless they could answer her riddle: 'What creature goes on four legs in the morning, on two at noonday, and on three in the evening?' No one got the answer right until the Greek hero Oedipus, who said that the answer was man: who crawls on all fours as a baby, strides on two as a vital adult, and requires a stick (or third leg) when old. The Sphinx was so chagrined that she threw herself off a cliff and was killed.

Egyptian Sphinx

Spirit (Latin *spiritus*, 'breath, spirit') The animating essence within our physical forms; sometimes referred to as the **soul**. In many belief systems, the spirit lives on after death and can be contacted by a **medium** on our plane of existence. Spirit is the divine spark that defines who we are, and is an indivisible part of the three aspects of human existence: mind, body and spirit. See also: **Chi, Life Force, Prana, Spiritualism**.

Spirit Guide, also **Spirit Helper** A spirit entity that serves as a communications bridge, guardian or a guide in: **shamanism**, where they are often known as 'totem animals'; **spiritualism**, known as the medium's 'control' in a **séance**; or **witchcraft**, where they are known as a **familiar**.

Spiritual Healing Umbrella term to describe a number of methods in which a healer serves as a conduit or 'channel' for healing energies to be funnelled into a patient. This healing energy helps to stimulate the body's self-healing mechanisms, whether the problem is physical, spiritual or emotional. Depending upon your personal beliefs, this healing energy comes from God, a cosmic consciousness, **spirit guides**, or other entities of power.

Although the source of power comes from outside the spiritual healer, that person needs to possess an innate healing ability as well as the discipline to control the power for maximum benefit to the patient. They may not actually need to touch the patient, but keep their hands just above the body (as in therapeutic touch and reiki), or there may be a 'laying-on' of hands to concentrate and focus healing energy, called 'contact' healing. Sometimes healing can take place even when the patient and healer are in separate locations (see **Absent Healing**). Because it deals with the whole person and not just physical symptoms, spiritual healing is considered a **holistic** therapy.

People who attend a spiritual healing session report feelings of warmth or tingling where energy is directed, and often feel very relaxed and sometimes sleepy after treatment. Healers do not guarantee a 'cure' but this non-invasive form of healing has been found to be beneficial for the following conditions: chemotherapy side-effects, stress-related conditions such as anxiety and depression, migraines, tension headaches and recovery from major surgery. See also: **Vibrational Medicine**.

Spiritualism (Latin *spiritus*, 'breath, spirit) A practice based on the belief that we can communicate with the spirits of the dead. This is accomplished through purposeful contact with the departed, called a **séance**, via a **medium**. The medium goes into a trance and through their psychic ability is able to establish a link between our world and the afterlife. The spirits then 'speak' through the body of the medium, who is temporarily possessed by this incorporeal entity. This contact is taken as proof by believers that there is, indeed, life after death.

Spleen Meridian A channel or **meridian** of **chi** energy running through the body that penetrates the spleen, according to **Traditional Chinese Medicine**. It is associated with the **earth element**, has **yin** energetic properties and is partnered with the **stomach meridian**, which is **yang**. Spleen energy transforms food into chi and blood and can be affected when people become stressed or run down. Chi is strongest in this channel between 9 and 11 a.m. and conversely the weakest between 9 and 11 p.m. Both left and right sides of the body have this meridian, which begins by the big toe and runs up the body to end at the armpit.

Spodomancy, also **Tephramancy**, **Tuphramancy** (Greek *spodos*, 'ashes, embers', + *manteia*, 'divination') A form of **divination** that interprets the patterns of ashes, soot or cinders from a sacrificial fire. Popular among ancient cultures but not much in practice today.

Spontaneous Human Combustion, also **SHC** The odd phenomenon where a person appears to have spontaneously burst into flame, resulting in a complete immolation of nearly all body parts (sometimes an arm or leg is left), including bones – but where the clothes and surroundings are left completely intact. The burning is rarely witnessed and invariably fatal, but the few eyewitness accounts that exist state that a blueish flame shot out from the abdominal area, quickly engulfing the rest of the body. Despite extensive research into the phenomenon, no conclusive explanation as to why it happens has ever been reached. Fortunately, it is extremely rare.

St John's Wort see Hypericum

Star of Bethlehem A flower essence made from the star of Bethlehem blossom. This emotionally healing tincture is one of the **Bach Flower Remedies**. Dr Bach said that this is indicated for 'shock, the effects of serious news, bereavement, sorrow and grief'.

Steiner, Rudolf (1861–1925) Austrian-born mystic and educator who founded the Anthroposophical Society in 1909. Originally a member of the **Theosophical Society**, Steiner founded the Anthroposophical Society after he disagreed with the theosophists, although the basic tenets and beliefs of both schools of thought are virtually identical. Steiner believed that reality is essentially spiritual, and that you can train yourself to overcome the material world by accessing different planes of knowledge and existence through occult means. He also believed that colour would play an important part in medicine in the twentieth and twenty-first centuries.

Steiner is known too for his controversial education theories that include esoteric spiritual practices and colour healing as part of the standard curriculum. He established a 'school of spiritual science' in Stuttgart, Germany in 1919 for the children of workers at the Waldorf-Astoria cigarette factory. His methods of education were so well received that he went on to found 'Waldorf' schools in the USA. There are now over 600 Waldorf schools in over 32 countries. Steiner designed the curriculum of his schools around the theory that children pass through three seven-year stages and that education methods that take into consideration the 'body, spirit and soul' should be appropriate to those stages. See also: **Anthroposophy, Theosophy**.

Stichomancy (Greek *stikhos*, 'row, line of verse', + *manteia*, 'divination') A form of **divination** using books. A book is opened at random and a passage of text is selected. This passage can then be applied as an oracular answer to a question being asked. Several forms of stichomancy exist. **Bibliomancy** seeks spiritual insight by selecting a random passage from a holy book like the **Bible** or **Koran**. Rhapsodomancy uses poetry books. Stichomancy works best with 'yes or no' answers and is still in popular use today.

Stigmata (Greek *stigma*, 'a mark made by a pointed instrument') Wounds that appear spontaneously on the hands and feet, sometimes bleeding, in the same pattern as those left on Christ's body by the Crucifixion. They usually appear on Christian saints in a state of religious ecstasy, or can be a symptom of hysteria. St Francis of Assisi, in 1224, was the most famous person to exhibit stigmata, although there have been many cases documented since then. See also: **Christianity**.

Stomach Meridian A channel or **meridian** of **chi** energy running through the body that affects the stomach, according to **Traditional Chinese Medicine**. It is associated with the **earth element**, has **yang** energetic properties and is partnered with the **spleen meridian**, which is **yin**. Stomach energy is called the 'sea of nourishment' as it supplies food to all other organs. Stomach chi is strongest in this channel between 7 and 9 a.m. and conversely the weakest between 7 and 9 p.m. Both left and right sides of the body have this meridian, which begins under each eye and runs down to end next to the second toenail.

Stonehenge One of the most famous prehistoric monuments in the world, located on the Salisbury Plain in Wiltshire, England. Built in stages between 2800 and 1800 BC, it is oriented to mark the sunrise and moonrise at the summer and winter **solstices**. The original architects of and reasons for building this megalithic stone circle are unknown, but since the Roman conquest of England it is known to have been an important part of **Druid** practice and worship. Because of the precise solstice orientation of the stones, it is thought to have some astronomical significance.

The rock from which it is quarried is blue stone from the Preseli mountains of South Wales, over 217 km (135 miles) distant. This particular type of blue stone amplifies sound and when modern Druids and other **pagan** celebrants of the solstice stand in the centre of the circle, even the merest whisper can be heard from one side to another. As Stonehenge is also constructed along **ley lines**, it is thought this resonant quality of the stone might also be connected to the theory of **sacred geometry**, where the earth's energy can be tapped for magic ritual and healing.

Subliminal, Subliminal Self (Latin *sub*, 'below', + *limine*, 'threshold') An unconscious aspect of ourselves that perceives sensations, emotions and thoughts below the threshold of conscious thought. This perception could be of spirit beings and other entities beyond our plane of existence, or of taboo impulses not acceptable in society, especially those related to sex. Our unconscious reactions to these taboo ideas are what are harnessed in subliminal advertising. Advertisers use images and sounds to influence our consumer responses without us being aware of it.

Subtle Body see **Astral Body**.

Succubus A female **demon** or **spirit** who disturbs the sleep of a man, and has sexual intercourse with him. Unlike the male equivalent, **incubus**, whose attentions to a woman are horrifying, the succubus' attentions are not always unwelcome.

Sufism (Arabic, 'wearer of wool') The mystical branch of **Islam**, whose adherents believe they are on a spiritual journey towards God. This journey is referred to as *tariqah*, or 'the path'. Sufis dedicate themselves to the *tariqah*, live a simple life with few possessions, and follow all the precepts of more conventional Islamic belief, with the hope of achieving direct communion with Allah. Unlike traditional Islam, which teaches that you cannot become close to God until after death and judgement, Sufis believe it is possible to experience closeness to God while alive. The only barrier to this closeness is your own self, or **ego**, which Sufis call *nafs*. Fighting to overcome the dominance of *nafs*, therefore, is the Sufis' primary goal in life.

There are many esoteric traditions within Sufism, and many orders, which vary in their approach to overcoming *nafs*. One of the more unusual is the Mevlevi order, also known as **whirling dervishes**, for the sacred dance they perform to bring themselves into an ecstatic state of communion with the Almighty. See also: **Rumi**.

Sulphur 1. One of the 15 major **polychrests**, or major remedies in **homeopathy**. It is also a **constitutional type**, which is a way homeopaths have of classifying different patient profiles. The fitting constitutional remedy acts preventatively and curatively on its matching personality type – for example, a person with a Sulphur constitution will respond well to the Sulphur remedy almost regardless of the illness they are suffering from. Sulphur people are intellectual and highly imaginative, and tend to be disorganised and untidy.

They can be self-centred but are generous and good-humoured. They are susceptible to digestive and skin complaints, and suffer from male/female ailments in later life. 2. In **alchemy**, the symbol of **fire** and the male spirit. According to alchemists, Sulphur is one of the three 'vital ingredients' of life.

Sun Signs In Western **astrology**, the sign of the **zodiac** the sun occupies at the time of your birth. This defines your basic temperament, the outer you – when people ask, 'What sign are you?' they are asking what your sun, or birth, sign is. Each sun sign is associated with a particular planet, and they each have associations with one of the four natural **elements** (**air**, **earth**, **fire** and **water**). Sun signs can also be classified as one of three types (**cardinal**, **fixed** and **mutable**) depending upon where in the seasons of the year (winter, spring, summer, autumn) the sign falls.

Sun, The The centre star of our solar system and source of all light, warmth and energy. In **astrology** the most important planet, symbolising our essential self and personality. It describes the inner child and how you respond to life. It is the most significant planet when it comes to casting a **horoscope** for predictive purposes. Traditionally, the sun rules children, gold, fatherhood, health, laughter, pomp, royalty and stardom. It is the ruling planet of the **zodiac** sign **Leo**.

Superego According to **Sigmund Freud**, the part of the personality that represents the conscience. The superego gives us our sense of right and wrong, of pride and guilt, and what is or is not taboo behaviour. It is the opposite of the **id**, the unconscious part of us whose only desire is gratification of its own needs. The superego often gets us to act in ways that are acceptable to society, by denying the needs of the id.

An example might be extramarital sex. The id would be all for it, to gratify the sexual urge. The superego would produce guilt at the thought of breaking one of society's rules. The piggy in the middle of this contretemps is the **ego**, which seeks to balance out conflicting desires; its job is made no easier by the fact that the superego and id often operate on an unconscious level. If an adult is a reasonably mature individual, then the id, ego and superego will be acting in a balanced way. If not, then the result will be either childish, immature behaviour, or an overdeveloped set of guilt neuroses.

Supernatural (Latin *super*, 'above, beyond') Any occurrence, manifestation or object that is beyond the laws of nature and scientific reality. The phrase is often connected to different aspects of **spiritualism** or **magic**. See also: **Paranormal**.

Superstition (Latin *super*, 'over', 'above', + *stare*, 'to stand') Excessive belief in the power of supernatural events or phenomena to control our lives. Prime examples of this are believing that a broken mirror causes you seven years of bad luck, or saying 'Bless you' after someone sneezes. These customs are holdovers from a time when it was hard to explain how the universe worked and the borders between daily living and magic, religion and nature were much less defined than they are today.

Sutra (Sanskrit, 'thread') 1. In Indian philosophy and religion, sutras are texts comprised of aphorisms, treatises and fables, all with a common thread. These sutras provide guidance, advice and religious philosophy. 2. also **Sutta** (Sanskrit, 'thread') In **Buddhism**, the text of the oral teachings of **Buddha** or his contemporary disciples that lays out the path to **enlightenment**. See also: **Hinduism, Yoga Sutras**.

Svaroopa Yoga see Yoga, Hatha

Swami (Sanskrit *svamin*, 'master, prince') A spiritual teacher, holy man or magical practitioner, in Indian philosophy and culture. See also: **Hinduism**.

Sweat Lodge A Native North American group ritual of cleansing and purification for spiritual and physical purposes, using a specially constructed sweat bath. There is no one ceremony as each tribe has its own customs, but in general the same routine is followed. First, the lodge is built (or renewed if the structure already exists). People working on the lodge fast to help keep their intentions pure. Prayer is offered as the saplings (usually willow) are cut and tightly woven into a round or oval dome, with only a low, small opening to enter and exit. A pit is dug in the middle of the lodge to hold hot rocks, and tobacco is burnt as an offering to the Great Spirit.

The rocks are heated outside the lodge and placed in the pit, and water is poured over them to create steam.

The sweat lodge is kept in darkness, and the naked participant either meditates quietly or joins the group in talking, praying and singing sacred songs.

As with any **hydrotherapy**, there are many physical benefits to the sweat lodge. More significant is the spiritual benefit people report after this ritual.

Some receive visions, or experience a catharic emotional release. All emerge refreshed, and cleansed in body and spirit. See also: **Shamanism, Vision Quest**.

Sweet Chestnut   A flower essence made from the blossom of the sweet chestnut tree. This emotionally healing tincture is one of the **Bach Flower Remedies**. Dr Bach said that this is indicated for 'utter despair – heartbreaking anguish as though there is no end in sight'.

Synastry   In **astrology**, comparing two people's horoscopes to predict the likely outcome in a romantic relationship. Synastry is also used to determine the relationships between other types of 'pairings' – political parties, ideological camps, work mates and businesses, even countries. See also: **Aspects**.

Syncronicity   (Greek *sun-*, 'together', + *khronos*, 'time') The phenomenon of simultaneous events occurring that are related but have no discernible connection to each other. Psychoanalyst **Carl Jung**, who coined the phrase, felt these meaningful coincidences happened for a reason. Synchronicity occurs to provide access to the **archetypes**, which are located in the **collective unconscious**. These archetypes symbolise universal images and behaviours, and can help a troubled person to solve psychological crises.

Jung cited an example of synchronicity when working with a patient of his. He was listening to a young woman describing a dream she had had about a golden **scarab** (a common symbol in ancient Egyptian artefacts and hieroglyphics). As she spoke, he heard a tapping at the window and opened it. There he found a scarabaeid beetle, a beetle regarded as sacred by the ancient Egyptians. His patient was so surprised by this that she stopped being defensive and started to consider what it might mean. Jung pointed out that the scarab was an archetypal symbol of rebirth (the reason it is found in so many Egyptian tombs) and this realisation eventually led to greater maturity in his patient.

Jung was fascinated as to why synchronicity occurs, and spent much of the latter part of his life examining concepts of quantum physics to explain these coincidences. Eventually, he came to accept that the mysterious connection between the two seemingly unrelated aspects of mind and material world was that ultimately they were two different forms of the same thing, vibrational energy.

Synchronicity is an important concept in the mind/body/spirit canon, and in recent years has become popularised in other disciplines including the arts and literature. The clearest example of this is the book *The Celestine Prophecy*, by James Redfield.

T'ai Chi, also **T'ai Chi Yuan** (Chinese *tai*, 'grand', + *chi*, 'ultimate') A Chinese martial art consisting of a series of postures linked by slow, graceful movements and accompanied by meditative breathing techniques. It is an active form of **chi kung**, designed to restore and enhance a person's **chi** (vital energy) to promote health and well-being. It is also an effective system of self-defence, as it evolved out of kung fu practice.

T'ai chi originated with a thirteenth-century Taoist priest, Chang San Feng. He originally trained in the martial arts with the Buddhist monks of Shaolin. He adapted their hard techniques into the smoother, softer movements of t'ai chi after a visionary dream of a snake and a crane engaged in a dance-like fight. His teachings evolved into five main styles still in practice today: yang, wu, chen, woo and sun. Yang is the most commonly practised in the West and is characterised by large, open gestures.

T'ai chi movements are said to balance out fluctuating **yin** and **yang** energies in the body, ensuring a smooth flow of chi (energy) through a person's **meridians**. Studies have shown the regular practice of t'ai chi has certain health benefits. It is commonly recommended for stress-related health conditions and can reduce the incidence of falls in the elderly or those with balance disorders. It also helps to lower blood pressure and to improve the quality of health in people with multiple sclerosis, arthritis and other age-related ailments.

Taiji Symbol Yin/yang symbol, also known as **The Great Polarity**. See also: **Yang, Yin**.

Taliesin (Welsh, 'radiant brow') Legendary bard of Wales who is associated with stories of King Arthur and the goddess **Ceridwen**. He is also a historical figure who lived in Wales during the latter half of the sixth century, where he is said to have been a **shaman** and **shape-shifter** in the Druidic tradition, and direct forebear to the wizard **Merlin**.

In another Welsh tradition, Taliesin was once named Gwion Bach, servant to **Ceridwen**, the goddess of inspiration and wisdom. She had two children: Crearwy, a daughter, whose name means 'light' or 'beautiful'; and a son, Afagddu, meaning 'dark' or 'ugly'. To compensate the boy for his unfortunate appearance, Ceridwen brewed a magical potion called greal that would make him wise. The potion required boiling for a year and a day for the magic to develop and she foolishly left Gwion, her kitchen boy, in charge of the brew.

Towards the end of the year, Gwion (either by accident or on purpose) licked off three drops of liquid that had fallen onto his hand – and assimilated all the wisdom intended for Afagddu. Furious, Ceridwen chased Gwion across Wales in a wild, shape-shifting hunt: first he became a hare and she a greyhound, then he a fish and she an otter, then he a rabbit and she a hawk. Finally he became a grain of corn and she a hen, and she ate him. This did not end the magic, as Ceridwen became pregnant and nine months later gave birth to Taliesin.

After his birth, she put him in a coracle and sent him sailing off down the River Dee, where he was found and rescued by King Elphin the Unfortunate. Elphin was struck by the brightness of the baby's forehead and called him Taliesin, meaning 'radiant brow'. Taliesin grew up in Elphin's court and was tutor to Elphin's son, but misfortune befell him and Taliesin was sent packing. Thus he became a roaming bard and eventually ended up at Camelot, the home of King Arthur.

His musical talent was said to be unearthly, with the power to charm even **fairies** and wild animals. He supposedly penned the collection of Welsh myths, the **Mabinogion**, while on his travels, and when he died all other bards took on the name of 'sons of Ceridwen' in his honour.

Talisman A **charm** either carried on the body or displayed in a house; it attracts good luck to the owner. As opposed to the passive power of **amulets**, talismans are active in seeking out fortunate circumstances and can even bestow magical powers on the person carrying one. Horseshoes, four-leaf clovers, lucky coins or stones inscribed with the name of a personal god or saint are all examples of talismans. The Maoris of New Zealand still wear fish-hook pendants carved from greenstone called *hei matau*, which ensure that a person will never go hungry if he has his 'fish hook'.

Tantra, Tantric (Sanskrit, 'technique') A school of Hindu and Buddhist philosophy, which seeks **enlightenment** through ecstatic religious and sexual practices. The main goal of tantra is to awaken **kundalini** energy, the primal **psychic** force that sleeps like a coiled snake at the base of the spine. This can only be done by invoking the male and female energies of the universe, embodied by the Hindu gods **Shakti** and **Shiva** who created our existence through their divine play.

Tantrics believe that enlightenment comes only through attaining physical and sexual ecstasy, which is why there is an emphasis on carnal pleasures and intercourse in tantra. In tantric sex, orgasm must be delayed as long as possible, to allow the proper stimulation of kundalini energy. See also: **Kundalini Yoga**, **Tantric Buddhism**, **Tantric Yoga**.

Tantric Buddhism, also **Vajrayana Buddhism** A subsect of Buddhism also known as the school of the Mysteries because it combines esoteric magical and sensual practices with more traditional Buddhist belief. Most schools of Buddhism focus on overcoming self and denying body impulses to concentrate on the higher self. Followers of tantric Buddhism believe that their body is a temple and to indulge in its most sensual impulses, especially sexual, is to perform an act of worship. It is closely related to similar practices in **Hinduism**. Where tantric Buddhism does agree with more conventional Buddhist beliefs is in the importance of transcending the self in order to reach **enlightenment**, and in the idea that the physical world is illusory, and that we are all caught up in the endless cycle of our existence (**samsara**) until we can reach **nirvana**.

Tantric Yoga   see Yoga

Tao, also **Dao** (Chinese, 'the way') Fundamental principle in the Chinese religion **Taoism**. The Tao is a mystical concept, which can only be inadequately described in words. Tao is a state of being, of *wei wu wei*, 'doing-not-doing', that accepts we are all part of the flow of **chi** – the energetic life force that powers all nature and matter in the universe. The Tao is everything and everywhere and flows unchallenged and is unchallenging. It is ever changing but never changes. It can be experienced but obviously not defined. It just is.

Tao of Physics   see Fritjof Capra

Tao Te Ching, also **Daodejing** (Chinese, 'The Book of the Way') Mystical religious text of **Taoism**, supposedly written by the great Chinese sage **Lao Tzu** in the sixth century BC. It describes, in a series of 5,000 different Chinese characters (called pictograms), the necessary interaction and harmony of the three things that make up life: *tao*, the way, *te*, the power and *chi'ng*, the energetic **life force** that runs through all of us and the universe. If we are able to balance all three of these elements, then life will flow smoothly. This can be done through various mental and physical processes like breath control, dietary requirements, **meditation**, sexual techniques and alchemical processes, all of which are described in the book. Its main emphasis, however, is on 'the way', which is all about going with the flow, the action of non-action that characterises Taoist philosophy.

Taoism, also **Daoism**   (Chinese *tao*, 'the way') Chinese religion based on the philosophy of the concept of **Tao**. (Tao is a state of being, of *wei wu wei*, 'doing-not-doing', that accepts we are all part of the flow of **chi** – the energetic life force that powers all nature and matter in the universe.) Taoism is not something that can be quantified with words; instead it must be experienced. A Taoist might have coined the phrase 'Go with the flow', as you must acknowledge that there is no action to take to be fulfilled, but instead you must let nature take its course. This choosing to do nothing is, in itself, a choice, and one that balances out the natural energies of life, **yin** and **yang**. The secret to a happy life is harmonising the yin and yang aspects of every situation, to achieve the perfect balance of all elements in life. This requires continuous adjustment as life is change.

Taoism as a religious movement can be traced back to the appearance of its seminal text, the **Tao Te Ching**. Supposedly written by legendary sage **Lao Tzu** in the sixth century BC, the concepts of Tao expressed in it were in direct contrast to the conflicts and feudal warfare afflicting China at that time. The philosophy appealed to those weary of constant strife, and it quickly grew from a minority opinion to a major faith. By 440 BC, Lao Tzu was venerated as a deity, and Taoism was adopted as the official state religion.

Taoism does have some similarities with **Buddhism**, in focusing on 'living in the moment'. It also complements **Confucianism** as it focuses on inner thought and behaviour and Confucianism focuses on outer moral conduct. The three faiths coexisted peacefully in China until the communist takeover of 1949, when all three were officially banned. Since 1982 that blanket restriction has been eased somewhat and Taoism currently has about 20 million followers, mostly in Taiwan.

The influence of Taoism has spread far beyond China's shores, however, serving as a conceptual base for many practices like **Traditional Chinese Medicine**, **acupuncture** and **meditation**, and martial arts like **chi kung** and t'ai chi. Taoism, with its emphasis on stillness and 'just being, not doing' also appeals to many people frazzled and exhausted by the frantic pace of Western society.

Tapotement   A classic movement in Swedish and holistic massage, where the therapist uses their fingers to tap on the body. It is also referred to as 'vibrations', as the point of the movement is to create a humming sensation in the area being treated. It both sedates and stimulates the muscle nerves, depending upon the intensity and duration of the digital tapping.

Tarot A form of **divination** that uses a special pack of 78 cards to predict the future. There are many theories as to their origin, but they most likely came from Northern Italy, in the valley of the Taro River, sometime in the late fourteenth/early fifthteenth century AD. The oldest known set, dated around 1440 (known as the Visconti-Sforza deck), was created for the Duke of Milan's family.

The cards were used to play a bridge-like game called *tarocchi*. The fanciful pictures inscribed on the cards were inspired by costumed figures of the yearly pre-Lent Carnivale festival, although the actual images and symbolic language are much older, probably derived from the worship of the ancient Egyptian god, **Thoth**. This tradition of dramatic image and symbolic language has carried through to the modern deck.

When the game of *tarocchi* spread to France it was renamed 'tarot', and the deck was used merely for playing until the advent of the eighteenth-century vogue for the occult, when the cards acquired the mystical meanings ascribed today.

The 78 cards in a tarot pack are divided between the 22 cards of the major **arcana**, and the 66 cards of the minor **arcana**. The cards of the major arcana are considered to have greater divinatory significance because of the **archetypes** of fortune they portray. These cards are also similar to the meditative pathways on the **Tree of Life** in **Kabbalistic** tradition, so occultists believe that they have magical powers of their own.

Tarot is one aspect of **cartomancy**, which is fortune-telling using playing cards. Some of the 'rules' on how to lay out and interpret either tarot or playing cards are the same, but some fundamental differences apply. One is the symbolic nature of the major arcana cards (also called 'trump' cards). Each card has a dual meaning and where the card falls in the layout (called a 'spread') determines which meaning is applied.

For example, the trump card of Death can mean exactly that – death or misfortune to befall the person whose fortune is being read. However that would only be the applicable meaning if the Death card appeared in a particular place in the spread, and with a particular combination of other cards surrounding it. In other circumstances, the Death card could actually symbolise the 'death' of an old tradition and the 'birth' of a new one like divorce, a new job, first-time parenthood, etc. These dual meanings do not apply to interpreting a regular deck of playing cards when they are used in divination.

You should always use your own tarot deck, and the deck should be new, unused by anyone else. It is better to be given a deck than to purchase it yourself, but it is a myth that you should not *pay* for a deck, although some prefer to receive their deck as a gift. The reason for these beliefs is that your own personal energies will become invested or 'imprinted' in the cards. When you first get your tarot deck, the cards will feel stiff, almost unfriendly to you. That is because they are a 'tabula rasa', a blank slate waiting to take on your personality. After a deck has been used for some time, it becomes familiar; your readings become more accurate and more fluid because you are working directly with the mystical energies inherent in the cards, and you know intuitively what interpretations to apply when a card comes up in a particular combination and spread.

How you lay out your cards is also of importance. There is no right way or wrong way but, as with many divinatory arts, intuition is your best guide. There are nine general spread types, each with its own advantages.

Finally, a successful card reading depends upon the inherent **psychic** abilities of the tarot reader. This, although something that cannot be taught, makes the difference between a successful reading session and an uncertain prediction.

Tasseography, also **Tasseomancy** (French *tasse*, 'cup', + Greek *graphe*, 'writing', or *manteia*, 'divination'). The art of reading tea leaves for the purposes of **divination**. As tea originated in China, it makes sense that tasseography was an ancient Chinese practice. It spread to the Western world via nomadic gypsies in the mid-1800s and is still practised today. The leaves of the tea plant (like those of many other plants) are sensitive to recording energy vibrations in the environment around them. When a person drinks a cup of tea (or fresh ground coffee) the leaves or grounds pick up sympathetic vibrations from that person's **aura**. When the cup is subsequently turned over, the tea leaves form patterns that correspond to that energy.

Tea-leaf reading is carried out in three distinct phases. First, a cup of tea is made, using fresh leaves and a clean cup per person. Then you either drink or pour most of the liquid away, leaving just enough to swirl the leaves. Hold the cup in your left hand and ask the question you want answered, about a specific matter or the future in general. Swirl the cup clockwise three times, then invert the cup on the saucer and let the remaining liquid drain away. Quickly turn the cup upright and the leaves will have formed patterns on the inside of the cup.

The cup is divided into several different sections and symbols must be read according to where the tea leaves land (which indicates future timelines) as well as what pictures they form. Each symbol has a different meaning and there are hundreds of symbols that have been interpreted. Some are quite common, like a box or a fish, but there are also such odd symbols as a pair of scissors, rose, rattle, kite, duck, earrings, anchor, giraffe and the ever-popular camel.

Tasseomancy see **Tasseography**

Taurus The second sign of the **zodiac** in Western **astrology**, and the **sun sign** for those born between 21 April and 21 May. The symbol of Taurus is the bull, and the ruling planet is **Venus**. Taureans are a **fixed sign** influenced by the **earth element**, with 'persistence' the best single word to define them. Those born under Taurus are patient, reliable and concerned with material comfort for themselves and loved ones. They can, at times, be overpossessive and somewhat grumpy and lazy, but make up for these shortcomings with their loyalty, diligence and discriminating taste.

The Taurean is the gourmet and bon viveur of the zodiac, and suffers from a terrible sweet tooth, especially for chocolate. In health, Taureans are prone to throat and stomach ailments (must be all that rich food) and benefit from herbs to cool the throat and clean out the digestive system.

Tefnet Ancient Egyptian goddess of moisture and one of the **Ennead**, the leading council of ruling gods and goddesses. She was created from the sole efforts of **Atum**, the Supreme Creator of the universe, along with her brother-consort, the god **Shu**. With him, she became the mother of **Nut**, the sky goddess, and **Seb**, the earth god.

Telekinesis (Greek *tele*, 'at a distance', + *kinesis*, 'motion') The spontaneous movement of objects and people through the air without any apparent physical means. These objects are moved either through **paranormal** means like a **poltergeist**, or by thought or will power alone – a demonstration of 'mind over matter'. If the movement is intentional, it is known as **psychokinesis**.

Telepathy (Greek *tele*, 'at a distance', + *patheia*, 'suffering, feeling') The communication of thoughts, feelings and ideas through **psychic** means, especially **extra-sensory perception** (ESP).

Teleportation, also **Translocation** (Greek *tele*, 'at a distance', + Latin *portare*, 'carry') The transportation of an object or person across a distance, as if by magic. Teleportation is a common occurrence in **spiritualism**, where it is sometimes interpreted as communication from the 'other side'. See also: **Apport**, **Bilocation**, **Séances**.

Tenth House In **astrology**, the **house** or part of the heavens in your birth chart that describes your social status, your achievements and how important you want to be. It is ruled by the sign **Capricorn** and planet **Saturn**. See also: **Ascendant**, **Horoscope**.

Tetragrammaton In **Kabbalah** (Jewish mysticism) the sacred name of God, expressed as a series of four-letter groups: IHVH, JHVH or YHVH. This is the source of Yaweh, or Jehovah, which traditionally was too holy to write down and only used in the highest mystic rituals.

Thai Bodywork, also **Thai Massage** A school of massage and soft-tissue manipulation that originated in Thailand. This energetic bodywork combines elements of **ayurveda**, **yoga**, **Traditional Chinese Medicine** and **shiatsu** in the treatment. The main focus of Thai bodywork is helping to restore the even flow of energy (**chi** or **prana**) in the body. The therapist uses rhythmic compression movements on specific energy points, along with deep stretching movements and gentle rocking of muscles. This is all performed in a slow, almost meditative manner. It is deeply relaxing and, like all massage therapies, is excellent for helping to relieve aches and pains, especially those related to the back and neck.

Thalassotherapy (Greek *thalassos*, 'sea', + *therapeia*, 'healing') The many uses and curative effects of seawater and substances derived from the sea, like seaweed, mud and sand. It is the mineral and salt content of seawater and its relatively low ionisation that makes it such a beneficial substance. Thalassotherapy is a form of **hydrotherapy** that out of necessity is located in coastal centres. Several different methods are used. Sea-spray baths and showers, mud-pack facials, directed streams of water on problem areas of the body, steam rooms and salt scrubs are but a few of the ways to get the benefit of this therapy.

Conditions that are said to be helped by thalassotherapy include back problems, stress-related ailments, rheumatoid arthritis, heavy legs, menopause complaints and other gynaecological problems. It is also a useful aid in giving up smoking and weight loss.

It is a popular spa treatment all over the world, but particularly in France, where it is taken very seriously and where doctors often prescribe different courses and treatments for specific ailments.

Thanatology (Greek *thanatos*, 'death', + *logos*, 'word, study') The scientific study of death and **near-death experiences**. This blanket term covers a number of issues on the topic ranging from considering the needs of terminally ill patients and bereaved families to documenting **out-of-body experiences** in near-death situations.

Thanatology first acquired legitimacy from the pioneering work of Dr Elizabeth Kübler-Ross, who defined the five-stage grieving process (denial, anger, bargaining, depression, acceptance) now widely accepted in medicine. In recent years thanatology has grown to encompass beliefs about life after death, based on the growing number of documented near-death experiences. See also: **Astral Travel**.

Thaumaturgy, Thaumaturge (Greek *thaumatourgos*, 'one who works wonders') The practice of working miraculous things, especially by magic or supernatural powers. A thaumaturge is a term often applied to a magician. See also: **Magic, Theurgy**.

The Camino The famous pilgrimage trail of Santiago de Compostela, across Northern Spain, is also known as 'the Camino', which loosely translates as 'the road' or 'the way'. In medieval times it was one of three main treks that devout Christians yearned to take (the other two being to Jerusalem or Rome) although the Camino has been walked since Roman times. It is still one of the most important pilgrimages a Christian can make, but it is now also undertaken by non-Christians with the intent to find deep spiritual meaning and resolutions regarding conflicts in self.

The Camino is said to have special power as it follows **ley lines**, and the route lies directly under the constellations of the Milky Way. Many feel the combination of the earth power below their feet and energy from those star systems above it makes this a significant spiritual journey.

Theosophy, Theosophical Society (Greek *theos*, 'a god', + *Sophia*, 'wisdom') A school of mystical thought and belief with roots in occult and esoteric religions that arose out of the formation of the Theosophical Society. Founded in 1875 by **Madame Helena Blatvatsky** and Henry Olcott, the Society had three stated aims: to form a universal human brotherhood without distinction of race, creed, sex, caste or colour; to encourage studies in comparative religion, philosophy and science; and to investigate the unexplained laws of nature, power and magic. It attracted many prominent intellectuals of the time including Aldous Huxley, Frank Lloyd Wright and W.B. Yeats, who were involved in one of the Society's main activities, translating holy works from Eastern cultures. Much of the credit for the introduction to the West of Indian and Chinese religious and philosophical ideas must be given to the theosophists, who first translated into English many of the texts used today in **yoga**, **Buddhism**, and other **new age** movements.

One of the religion's later gurus was **Jiddu Krishnamurti**, who became the darling spiritual leader of the Hollywood set between the two world wars. **Rudolf Steiner** was also a theosophist before he quarrelled with the Society's leaders and formed his own sect, **anthroposophy**.

Theosophy is at heart a secret doctrine, which only reveals its true beliefs and practices to the initiated, and to what are termed 'Masters'. See also: **Gnosticism**.

Therapeutic Touch A type of healing system where the therapist moves his or her hands above the patient's body, 'massaging' the ill-balanced energy fields back into harmony. It also helps to regulate the flow of **chi** or life force throughout the body, which helps the patient to heal. Therapeutic touch is growing in popularity amongst the nursing community in the United States, where there are many training programmes in this technique. It is a form of **spiritual healing**, where the intention of the therapist and the receptivity of the patient must work together to stimulate the body's self-healing mechanisms. It can be performed by more than one nurse or therapist, but is most effective when the patient also engages in practices like meditation, visualisation or relaxation techniques.

Theravada, Theravadin Buddhism, also Hinayana Buddhism, Sthaviravada (Sanskrit *thera*, 'old', + *vada*, 'school', translated as the 'tradition of the elders') Early school of **Buddhism** as practised in the 'southern countries' of Sri Lanka, Thailand, Laos, Cambodia and Burma. Pali was the primary language of reference in this early school of Buddhism. The Theravadan practitioner strictly follows the tenets of **Buddhism**, and believes that keeping to the letter of the law will better lead to enlightenment.

Thermoauricular Therapy Alternative therapy involving the use of wax candles inserted into the outer ear to promote peripheral lymphatic circulations, and to relieve earache and glue ear. Also known as 'ear candling' or 'coning'. The technique was first practised in healing rituals by the Native North American Hopi Indians, which is why the candles are often referred to as Hopi Ear Candles. Benefits of the treatment include increased lymphatic drainage, enhanced energy flow and clean ears.

Theurgy (Greek *theos*, 'god', + *urgy*, 'work') The practice of working miracles either through divine intervention, or by calling upon supernatural powers. This is usually a beneficial form of **magic**, in which the miracle-worker seeks only to heal or to foretell the future. See also: **Thaumaturgy**.

Third Eye An invisible point in the centre of the forehead that corresponds to the brow **chakra**. It is known as the third eye for two reasons. First, because psychic visions and prophetic dreams seem connected to the energy that emanates from this chakra. Second, the eye-shaped pineal gland is situated in the brain behind this point on the skin. This may be why the French philosopher Descartes decided that the pineal gland was the seat of the human soul, the location of what we call the mind. The pineal gland does contain a complete map of the visual field of the eyes, and it plays several significant roles in human functioning. This 'all-seeing' ability is reputedly linked to psychic visions or **clairvoyance**.

Third House In **astrology**, the **house** or part of the heavens in your birth chart that describes the way your mind works, your ability to think and communicate, and your early education. It is ruled by the sign **Gemini** and the planet **Mercury**. See also: **Ascendant, Horoscope**.

Thoth, also **Djeheuty, Tahuti, Tehuti, Zehuti** The Greek name for the Egyptian god Djeheuty, who was deity of wisdom, inventor of writing and mediator between the upper gods and mankind. Thoth was appointed the 'scribe of the **Ennead**' and guardian of man after **Ra**, the sun god, nearly destroyed the ungrateful mortals. He is most often depicted as a man with the head of an ibis, holding a palette and pen.

Thoth also served as peacemaker between the quarrelsome gods, and was always present at the judgement of the dead. He questioned the souls of the deceased before recording the weights of their hearts against a feather. If the dead spoke the truth about their conduct in life, then the heart and the feather would balance, and they would be judged worthy of a blessed afterlife. If the soul lied, however, the heart and feather would not balance, and the unfortunate liar would be instantly thrown to a monster called Ammut ('devourer') who waited behind the scales.

Thoth was also considered the god of magic and the moon and, according to Egyptian tradition, he invented numbers. Because of this, he holds great symbolic significance in many **occult** and **esoteric** systems like **theosophy**, **numerology** and the **tarot**.

Threefold Law The belief in **Wicca** and other white magic practices that whatever you wish in a spell or magic actions you carry out against a person will come back to you threefold if you intend to create chaos, hurt the victim or force them to do things against their will. Much like doctors, white witches believe 'first do no harm', mostly because any harm would rebound on the practitioner.

Tibetan Book of the Dead Also known as Bardo Thodol, this is the **Tibetan Buddhism** guide to the soul's journey in the afterlife, prior to reincarnation into a new body. The soul or 'bardo body' goes through three stages. The first stage is the separation of the soul from its physical body and the earthly domain; the second is a recap of good and bad deeds from life, where past **karma** has shown whether or not **nirvana** has been attained, a process similar to that described in the **Egyptian Book of the Dead**, as well as the Last Judgement in **Christianity**; the third is a stage of the bardo body's carnal lust for the physical world – this curiosity draws a soul towards an earthbound couple engaged in intercourse at the moment of conception; the soul is then drawn into the newly created human life and is thus set for rebirth.

Tibetan Buddhism A school of Buddhist philosophy that combines **mahayana**, hinayana and vajrayana (**tantric**) traditions into a unique practice, which has become one of the most popular forms of **Buddhism** in the West. It emphasises service to others and living a virtuous life as a vehicle to **enlightenment** combined with meditation, tantric ritual and the teachings of the **Buddha**. His Holiness the **Dalai Lama** is the titular head and spiritual leader of Tibetan Buddhism.

Tibetan Medicine The traditional **holistic** healing system of Tibet, which draws on principles of **ayurveda**, **Traditional Chinese Medicine**, **herbal medicine**, **massage**, **yoga** and **meditation**. All of these traditions are combined with an understanding of Buddhist spirituality that seeks to transform you psychologically as well as heal your illness. It is a form of **energy medicine**, which states that disease and ill-health are a result of blockages in the flow of 'vital energy' through the body. This **life force** energy (known as rlun in Tibetan tradition) needs to be evenly balanced throughout the body and medical treatments are based on doing just that. Emphasis is also placed on treating the underlying causes of disease, as opposed to merely the symptoms.

In a typical session, the practitioner will use a variety of diagnostic methods similar to those used in Chinese medicine (**tongue diagnosis, pulse diagnosis**, extensive questioning about lifestyle and state of mind) as well as urine analysis. Treatments take four approaches: lifestyle adaptations; body therapies like massage or yogic exercises; changes in diet and the use of herbs and mineral supplements; and energy balancing treatments like **acupuncture** and **moxibustion**. Like many oriental healing systems, Tibetan medicine is most effective in treating illness and disease cause by an unhealthy lifestyle, or in alleviating chronic ailments like irritable bowel syndrome, ME, arthritis and fibromyalgia, which more orthodox medicine finds difficult or even impossible to cure.

Tiger, The   In **Chinese astrology**, the third sign of the **zodiac**. You are a Tiger if you were or will be born in the years 1938, 1950, 1962, 1974, 1986, 1998 or 2010. The Tiger is the sign of courage in Chinese mythology, symbolising optimism, humanitarianism and valour. Those born under this sign are fascinating, sociable characters. They strive to reach the top and have a strong rebellious streak. Tigers can be hedonistic and prone to burnout because of limitless enthusiasm, but have an amazing capacity for hard work. Their Western zodiac equivalent is **Aquarius** and their ruling planet is **Uranus**.

Tiki   An **amulet** or good-luck charm, worn in Polynesian cultures like those of Hawaii or the Maoris of New Zealand. A tiki is considered to be a powerful symbol of protection and is carved in the shape of Kane, the Polynesian sky god. Tikis are carved from mother-of-pearl, greenstone (a form of jade) or wood, and have large, oversized heads on top of squat little bodies.

Tincture   (Latin *tinctura*, 'dyeing', from *tingere*, 'to dye or colour') Medicines made by dissolving drugs or other healing substances (like herbs) into alcohol. This preserves their vital healing properties. Tinctures can be taken neat or used in diluted form in herbal and homeopathic remedies (where they are known as 'mother tinctures'). See also: **Herbalism, Homeopathy**.

Tongue Diagnosis   One of the four diagnostic techniques used in **Traditional Chinese Medicine** to determine ill-health. The tongue is considered to be the only internal organ that can be seen from the outside, so it functions as a mirror or X-ray for the health (or lack of it) in other parts of the body. The tongue is divided into areas representing various internal organs. If signs of disease or dysfunction occur in one part of the body, it will show up in the corresponding area on the tongue, similar to patterns on the feet in **reflexology**. Before each therapy session, a practitioner looks at a

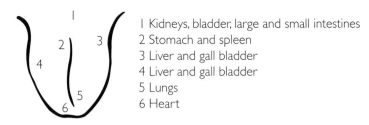

1 Kidneys, bladder, large and small intestines
2 Stomach and spleen
3 Liver and gall bladder
4 Liver and gall bladder
5 Lungs
6 Heart

Tongue diagnosis

patient's tongue colour, shape, coating and cracks or spots; changes in these factors during the course of treatment indicate whether or not a person is getting better or worse. See also: **Pulse Diagnosis**.

Totems Spirit guides that appear in the shapes of animals, each with a different symbolic meaning. Totems were also known as 'power animals' and the indigenous tribes of North America's Pacific Northwest associated themselves with a specific totem they felt represented the spirit of their personalities – for example, the deer is associated with fleetness of foot and thought, the eagle with noble vision, the bear with strong-willed protection. When a **shaman** or other member of the tribe sought wisdom from the spirit world, their guiding spirit would appear in the form of their selected totem.

The custom of the totem pole came from North America, where the native peoples of Northwest Canada and the US carved their selected totems into logs as protective **amulets** for their villages, and to channel the qualities of their tribal animals into the hearts of their tribes.

Touch for Health   see Kinesiology

Traditional Chinese Medicine, also **TCM** The holistic Chinese philosophy of medicine that puts a greater emphasis on prevention than on treatment of illness. A traditional Chinese saying states: 'Treating a disease once symptoms have occurred is like digging a well when thirsty' and in ancient China, physicians were only paid when their patients stayed well, not when they fell ill. TCM dates back almost 5,000 years and is based on Taoist principles surrounding the concept of **chi** (life energy). There is some evidence to suggest that this health system had its roots in ayurvedic practices imported from India and was combined with Taoist thought sometime in the fourth century BC. Originally a philosophy of nature encompassing **yin** and **yang** and the five natural elements of the universe, TCM evolved into a complex system of external examination and diagnosis of health and disease.

Four methods of treatment and prevention are used: herbal medicine, **acupuncture**, regulation of diet and nutrition, and building up the body through appropriate exercises, either active (martial arts, **chi kung**) or passive (**ta'i chi**, **tui na** massage). All of these practices are mentioned in two historical texts still used today: **Divine Farmer's Classis of Herbal Medicine** (*Shen Nong Ben Cao Jing*) written in the first century BC, and **Yellow Emperor's Inner Classic**, written in the third century BC. TCM practices were brought to the West in the seventeenth century by French Jesuit priests, and were standardised by Mao Tse-tung during the Cultural Revolution of the twentieth century.

TCM is based on the ancient Chinese belief that we are born with a finite amount of chi. This amount is determined by heredity and by the way we live our lives. We add to our chi by healthy living; we diminish it by inappropriate living habits. When our chi is depleted, we die. The body is composed of chi, **jing** (vital fluid) and **shen** (spirit), which together are referred to as the 'Three Treasures'. To maintain health, chi needs to be evenly balanced, flowing in harmony throughout the body. This will therefore balance out jing and shen.

The Chinese believe several factors lead to imbalance or disease: 1. the six excesses – wind, cold, heat, dampness, dryness and phlegm (these all relate to the **five element cycle**, as well as its diagnostic language). 2. the five emotions – joy, anger, sympathy, fear, and grief. 3. poor or intemperate eating and drinking. 4. too little or too much sexual activity. 5. too little or too much work or exercise.

Any of these can block the flow of chi through the body's **meridians**, and can lead to either excessive or deficient energies in the different elements/ organs of the body.

TCM practitioners use the philosophy of 'to see, to hear, to feel' to diagnose their patients and determine the energetic levels of the body. Their four main diagnostic methods are: 1. **tongue diagnosis** 2. wrist **pulse diagnosis** 3. palpation of sore areas and specific acupuncture points on the body, and 4. intensive, specific questioning on the patient's moods, symptoms, and lifestyle, past and present.

By putting all this information together, a unique picture of your health is produced, where any disease or illness is revealed as a pattern of disharmony in your chi. This diagnosis points to the type of treatment required to address the problem and set you on the path to recovery. The length of treatment will depend upon the root causes of your illness, which the practitioner will seek to eradicate along with any presenting symptoms. If a problem is of a chronic nature, or the illness is of long duration, it may well take a long time to get better.

Although TCM is primarily viewed in the West as an alternative medical procedure, it is the main healthcare option in China, which favours the use of herbs over acupuncture. This is the opposite of how TCM is used in the West, where acupuncture is better known. Reputable practitioners go through rigorous medical training and there exist a number of TCM professional organisations that issue licences only to qualified members, many of whom work through the NHS and other governmental health bodies. TCM methods work best with illnesses and diseases of a chronic nature (for example eczema, arthritis, autoimmune disorders) or accidents and environmental disorders (stress, obesity, unexplained gynaecological problems, back injury), where permanent changes are required to maintain health. See also: **Ayurveda, Chinese Herbal Medicine, Taoism**.

Trance (Latin *transere*, 'go across') A half-conscious state between sleeping and waking, where a person focuses entirely upon their internal thoughts and visions, and is unaware of their external environment. This altered state of consciousness can be induced in several ways: by hypnosis, by a medium during a **séance**, or by **shamans** via sensory deprivation, hallucinogenic substances, or rhythmic music and movement. A trance can be self-induced via the same methods or, in the case of **whirling dervishes**, by whirling around and around in a circle. See also: **Hypnotherapy**.

Transcendental Meditation A type of **meditation** advocated by 1970s guru Maharishi Mahesh Yogi, where the meditator concentrates on a particular **mantra** known only to them. This was the type of meditation the music group The Beatles engaged in. The object of transcendental meditation is to seek inner tranquillity and to increase spiritual awareness, and it is very popular in the United States, Britain and Australia.

Translocation see Teleportation

Transmigration A belief similar to **reincarnation**, that after death the **soul** can be born into another physical body. It differs from reincarnation in that this body can be either human or animal. Buddhists are comfortable with this idea, but Hindus do not like it at all. See also: **Buddhism, Hinduism**.

Transpersonal Psychology A school of psychology that seeks to understand what part mysticism, transcendent states and **peak experiences** play in forming personality and character. Roberto Assagioli (1888–1974), an Italian psychiatrist, developed this approach in the early twentieth century. He called it 'psychosynthesis': where the focus is to achieve a coming together of the various parts of an individual's personality. That person can then respond to the world in a way that is more life-affirming and authentic than before. Because their 'lower self' has been psychosynthesised together, they can focus on the 'higher' or 'transpersonal self'. This gives life purpose and meaning, which all people must feel to be psychologically healthy.

Psychosynthesis, along with **humanistic psychology**, is an integral part of thought in the **human potential movement**.

Tree of Life The complex, many-limbed symbol central to the practice of **Kabbalah**, the Jewish mystical religion. In Hebrew it is known as the *Otz Chiim*. This is a diagrammatic representation of the ten different spheres of knowledge (known as 'sephiroth') that man must achieve to attain wisdom or the 'godhead'. Connecting each of these spheres to one another are 22 'pathways', comprised of the letters of the Hebrew alphabet. Followers of Kabbalah must work their way up from the foundation of the tree by study and initiation into the secret knowledge of each level, before ascending to the next tier of wisdom.

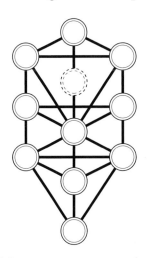

Tree of Life

The arrangement of the ten sephiroth is as follows: at the base is the foundation and tenth level, Malkuth, followed up by two rows of three (in ascending order and level: Yesod, Hod, Netzach, Tiphareth, Geburah, Chesed). Then a tier of two (Chokmah, Binah) followed by the highest level, the pinnacle of the tree and the mystical residence of the godhead, Kether. There are 32 ways to reach Kether (22 pathways plus 10 spheres), and the self-development work you do on the way is known as **pathworking**.

Tridosha see Dosha

Trigger Point Therapy see Myotherapy

Trigrams The building blocks for the pictorial symbols used in the Chinese oracle, **I Ching**. They consist of three lines each composed of either one long, unbroken line called a 'firm' or **yang** line or two short lines with a break in the middle, called a 'yielding' or **yin** line. These three lines of **yin** and **yang** represent the natural **elements**, with a total of eight possible combinations of trigrams.

Shake, Zhen
It manifests in quake and thunder

Subtle penetration, Sun
It works in those who lay out offerings

Trigrams

Each has a specific name, with particular attributes and qualities associated with it. Two trigrams are put together to form a **hexagram**, whose pattern is interpreted using the I Ching manual. See also: **Divination**.

Trimurti The three major gods of the Hindu canon: **Brahma**, **Vishnu** and **Shiva**. See also: **Hinduism**.

Tripitaka In **Buddhism**, the three pieces of canonical literature, assembled in the century following Shakyamuni **Buddha's** death. They are: the Buddha's original teachings; the historic philosophical dissertations of other 'buddhas'; and the rules regulating Buddhist priest and nun's lives. They are commonly referred to as 'the Buddha, the Dharma and the Sangha'. Buddhists also refer to their canon as 'Three Treasures', 'Three Jewels', 'Triple Gems' or 'Three Baskets'.

Triple Burner Meridian, also **Triple Warmer, Three Heater Meridian** A channel or **meridian** of **chi** energy running through the body that affects the metabolism, muscles and skin, according to **Traditional Chinese Medicine.** It is associated with the **fire element,** has **yang** energetic properties and is partnered with the **pericardium meridian,** which is **yin.** Triple burner energy, as the name suggests, is divided into three different body regions, each regulating and connecting all the organs together to ensure a steady flow of energy and heat. Chi is strongest in this channel between 9 and 11 p.m. and conversely the weakest between 9 and 11 a.m. Both left and right sides of the body have this meridian, which begins by the fourth fingernail and runs up the arm and neck to end at the eyebrow.

Trump Cards see Arcana

Tsubos (Japanese, 'vital energy points') In **shiatsu**, pressure points where **ki**, our innate body energy, can be accessed to stimulate our self-healing mechanisms.

Tui Na (Chinese *tui*, 'push', + *na*, 'grab'). A therapeutic massage technique used in China for over 2,000 years. Tui na is considered an integral part of **Traditional Chinese Medicine,** as it seeks to establish a harmonious flow of energy or **chi** throughout the body. Tui na focuses on specific problems and uses a combination of soft-tissue massage, acupressure techniques to directly affect chi, and manipulation techniques to realign the muscles, bones and ligaments. Herbal poultices, compresses, liniments and salves are often used to enhance the treatment.

This is in contrast to **Swedish massage**, which emphasises a full-body treatment and a lesser focus on localised weaknesses. For this reason, tui na is often used as an alternative or extension to other types of massage. Tui na is excellent in treating specific musculoskeletal disorders and chronic stress-related disorders of the digestive, respiratory and reproductive systems, but not as beneficial for general relaxation and stress-reduction.

Tulku see **Rinpoche**

Tumo (Tibetan, 'fierce woman') A specific **meditation** technique utilised by **Tibetan Buddhists** to keep warm despite snow, ice and freezing winds. The monks practise yogic methods of visualisation designed to rouse **kundalini** energy along with the chanting of sacred **mantras**, focusing on their navel region and imagining heat rising outwards from that spot to the rest of their body. These adepts are able to keep from freezing even in the lightest of clothing, using this technique. In 1924, the French author and explorer Alexandra David-Neel disguised herself as a young male acolyte and studied with a Tibetan master, exploring the mystical practices of Tibetan Buddhism. Her disguise was eventually penetrated when her habit of regular bathing (a practice unfamiliar to the Tibetans of that time) was discovered. Upon her return to the West, she wrote extensively about her travels and studies including tumo, which she had learned how to perform herself.

Theoretically anyone with a high mastery of Tantric yoga and Tibetan spirituality could learn to perform tumo, although the only successful practitioners documented have all been from Tibet.

Twelfth House In **astrology**, the **house** or part of the heavens in your birth chart that describes your subconscious wishes and desires, and defines how to move forwards in your life. It is ruled by the sign **Pisces** and the planets **Jupiter** and **Neptune**. See also: **Ascendant, Horoscope**.

UFO Short for Unidentified Flying Object, the term is most often applied to craft purported to be the transportation of alien visitors from outer space. These are objects that cannot be explained as any other phenomena, natural or manmade. The existence of **extraterrestrials** continues to be hotly debated, despite the fact that UFO incidents are subject to official investigation by every major government on earth.

The two best-known cases are the 1947 Roswell, New Mexico incident and the 1980 Rendlesham, Suffolk affair. In the first, an alien spaceship supposedly crashed and despite evidence to the contrary that this mysterious craft was a failed US Army experiment, many people still believe that there was a cover-up of the truth. The second one is more problematic. In December 1980, a UFO was radar-tracked falling to earth by several different systems, witnessed by a large number of people, and was investigated by three soldiers from the US Air Force base located nearby. These soldiers later reported a chase through wooded undergrowth involving mysterious beams of light. News of the incident was suppressed but leaked out to the press in 1984, and has yet to be fully explained away.

Reports of UFO incidents, while on the decline, do continue, with many credible witnesses and videotape evidence adding to the general population's belief that 'we are not alone.'

Unicorn (Latin *unus*, 'one', + *cornu*, 'horn') A mythical creature in folktale and heraldry, which appears as a horse (usually white) with a single, opalescent horn protruding from the forehead. Unicorns are powerful symbols of purity and it was thought no one could tame this fierce beast except the most virginal of young women. The horn of a unicorn was believed to have magical properties. It had the power to neutralise poison and could purify dirty, muddy water merely by being dipped into it. Powdered unicorn horn or its ashes were regarded as an antidote for snakebites, scorpion stings and rabid dogs.

Although the existence of a unicorn has never been documented, many popes and medieval royalty claimed to have articles made from unicorn horn. Most likely these were the tusks of the narwhal or walrus.

In many religions, the unicorn is a potent symbol. The unicorn is a divine creature belonging to the moon goddess, according to many pagan religions. In Christianity, medieval religious scholars and monks thought that it represented Jesus' purity, and his willingness to offer himself as a blameless sacrifice to save the world.

Upanishads, The (Sanskrit, 'to sit down next to') Esoteric texts of Hindu philosophy, which reflect on the mystery of death and emphasise the oneness of the universe. They are thought to have been written sometime between the eighth and seventh century BC, and form the basis of ideas later developed into the central tenets of **Hinduism, yoga** and **Buddhism**. There are over 108 treatises collected in *The Upanishads*, covering the four states of consciousness (waking, sleeping, dreaming and 'higher consciousness'). To obtain the last, higher consciousness, is the desired goal of all religious practice, for only there will you gain transcendence over the self.

Uranus The seventh planet in our solar system, discovered in 1781 and named for the Greek mythological god who personified the heavens. In **astrology**, Uranus represents liberation from the past and the breakdown of structures, and is associated with sudden change and inventions. It is also linked with sudden impulses, especially sexual ones. Uranus is also the planet of technology, telecommunications and inventions. Because the transit of Uranus is 84 years through the **zodiac**, its effects are best felt in generations, as opposed to individual years of our lives. It is the co-ruling planet of the zodiac sign **Aquarius**.

Uriel see Archangel

Urine Therapy, also **Amoroli, Urotherapy** The use of urine as a therapeutic substance, either by drinking your own urine (known as amoroli), or bathing skin and wounds in it. It is an ancient therapy, with mention of it in papyrus documents dating back to 1500 BC. Egyptians used it to cleanse burns. Ayurvedic scriptures dating from 1000 BC advocated the use of urine in poultices and enemas.

Despite the squeamish feelings this therapy may raise, there are some medical studies that show why urine has such beneficial effects. Urea, the solid constituent of urine, is very salty. When applied to a wound or troubled skin, it creates very high osmotic pressure, literally sucking all the water out of the area. This has a debriding, antiseptic effect on open wounds.

Amoroli has specific antifungal and antiviral effects, as well as sedative effects, because of the high level of melatonin in urine. It is particularly effective in fighting gout and oral infections, and many people swear by it as a cosmetic tonic for the skin.

Vajrayana Buddhism see Tantric Buddhism

Vampire (Hungarian *vampir* from Turkish *uber*, 'witch') A bloodthirsty creature of legend, based on the historical figure of Vlad Tepes, King of Wallachia, Transylvania. Vlad was known as 'the Impaler' for his habit of killing his enemies by impaling them on stakes. A vampire is a half-human, half-demon who must drink the blood of humans in order to survive. Vampires are the living dead, corpses who sleep by day and hunt by night, as sunlight is fatal to them. Any blessed object such as holy water or a cross may also harm them, but the only sure way to kill vampires is to behead them, burn them or stab them through the heart with a wooden stake. The tradition of the sun being fatal to vampires may have its roots in a rare blood condition, porphyria, which causes extreme photosensitivity, pale skin and enlarged incisor teeth.

The most famous vampire was Dracula, the fictional creation of Irish writer Bram Stoker. In his 1897 novel, many of the traditions we associate with vampires – sleeping in coffins, dislike of garlic, sunlight bad, night time good – were his creation. Central was the belief that, by his bite, a vampire could 'sire' another vampire.

The cult of vampires and vampirism has grown in recent years, due to the popularity of the Anne Rice novels of the Vampire Lestat, and the television series *Buffy the Vampire Slayer*.

Vastu Shastra, Vastu Vidyavaastu (Hindi, 'dwelling science') The ancient Indian art of placement in homes and buildings. It combines principles of **ayurveda** and **Vedic astrology** in the construction and design of buildings so that people will interact with their environment in energetically harmonious ways. It is the Indian equivalent of **feng shui**.

As in feng shui, the flow of energy, or **prana**, is of prime importance. Positive and negative energies must be balanced in order for prana to flow freely through a building, and bad design can block this energetic river. Vastu looks at how to rebalance these energies through the five elements: **ether** (known as **akasha**), **air** (vayu), **fire** (tejas), **water** (Jala) and **earth** (prithvi). A compass or **mandala** is used to diagram where the placement of doors and windows should be, and to determine whether or not architectural features encourage positive or negative energies.

Although vastu is best utilised when a building is in the design and construction phase, there are also solutions to be found for existing structures. The use of mirrors and artefacts, strategic treatments of light and colour, or even the simple re-arrangement of furniture can rebalance the energy of your rooms.

Vata (Sanskrit, 'to move') One of the three body types, or **doshas**, in ayurvedic medicine, that determine who you are physically and mentally, and what you need to do to keep healthy. The vata dosha is composed of ether and air energies, with the following results: vata types are light, flexible, fast-talking, fast-moving people. They are not afraid of change (in fact often seek it out) and easily grow restless. They tend to be slim, with little body fat. Vatas often have dry skin and poor circulation, which means they do not usually like cold weather. They should try to avoid bitter, pungent foods and instead eat sweet, sour and warming foods to balance their body humours. Mostly, vatas should: keep calm, keep warm, follow a regular routine.

Vedanta A collection of texts sacred to Hinduism that includes the **Vedas**, the **Yoga Sutras**, the **Upanishads** and the **Bhagavad Gita**. These writings and others form the basis of Hindu philosophy and yogic literature.

Vedas (Sanskrit, 'wisdom') The collection of four texts written sometime around 2500 BC, which constitute the beginnings of Indian philosophy and are the basis of the Hindu canon. These four 'hymns' are called *Rg Veda*, *Yajur Veda*, *Atharva Veda* and *Sama Veda*. Each section covers a different subject; together they tell the story of the creation of the universe and all of its parts. The *Rg Veda*, a collection of 1028, covers religious consciousness; the *Atharva Veda*, with its spells and sacrifices, forms the basis of Indian medicine or **ayurveda**; the *Sama Veda* is a collection of chants and **mantras**; and the *Yajur Veda* contains rituals and prayers. See also: **Hinduism**.

Vedic Astrology, also **Jyotisha Shastara** The form of **astrology** practised in Indian cultures. Vedic astrology is a **sidereal** system of prediction (as opposed to Western astrology, which is a tropical system), which means it uses fixed star constellations in conjunction with planets, to determine your **horoscope**. It is based on the true celestial position of the constellations, taking into account the precession of the equinoxes. Because of this, everyone's birth sign moves back a month (Arians become Pisceans, etc.). Sidereal astrologers believe that the standard sun signs and aspects give a person's general tendencies, but fixed constellations supply the particular, peculiar details and qualities of a person's character.

The other great characteristic is that Vedic astrology is steeped in the philosophy of the **Vedas**, one of the holy texts of Hindu religion and medicine. This means that the Vedic astrologer must have assimilated the philosophy of the Vedas and applied this moral religious aspect to his predictions. Vedic horoscopes indicate what a person's spiritual destiny should be in this lifetime (remember, the Hindu culture believes in **reincarnation**). If you choose to follow your destiny as predicted, you will be closer to escaping **samsara** (the endless cycle of death and rebirth). If you choose not to improve your **karma** in your present life, then you get the chance to do so in your next incarnation.

Venus The second planet in our solar system and the closest one to earth. Venus is named for the Roman goddess of love and symbolises the archetypal female in the cosmos. In **astrology**, Venus is associated with love, beauty and desire. It represents that which you most want, but also what you might want too much. As might be expected with the goddess of love, these excesses usually involve passions of some sort. Traditionally, Venus rules art, entertainment, music and beauty, love, marriage, sexual intercourse and fashion style. It is the ruling planet of the **zodiac** signs **Taurus** and **Libra**.

Vervain A flower essence made from the vervain blossom. This emotionally healing tincture is one of the **Bach Flower Remedies**. Dr Bach said that this is indicated for 'those who are incensed by injustice. They speak out to make their point known, and try to persuade others to believe in what they have to say. They work hard, are enthusiastic in all they embark upon, and are prone to become tense and highly stressed'.

Vibrational Healing, Vibrational Medicine Alternative healing method based on the idea that everyone has a personal field, composed of both electromagnetic and subtle energy, that vibrates at certain frequencies. According to quantum physics, biochemical molecules that make up the physical body are actually a form of vibrating energy. Illness affects how efficiently our personal energy vibrates and flows, and the aim of vibrational medicine is to restore these energies to a healthy balance. By doing so, the body will start to heal itself.

In order to treat this ailing energy field, you need to do more than alleviate symptoms. The root causes of illness must be identified and dealt with. Most vibrational healing is therefore considered to be **holistic**, as it often must deal with emotional and spiritual problems to solve a physical illness.

There are many types of healing practice that can be classified as vibrational medicine, including **reiki**, **flower essences**, **spiritual healing**, **therapeutic touch**, **colour therapy**, and certain aspects of **homeopathy** and **acupuncture**. The key to defining a therapy as 'vibrational' is to determine if it seeks to restore an imbalance of energy in the body. If this is the case, then the label fits.

Vinaya Buddhism A monastic form of **Buddhism** that focuses on studying Buddhist precepts (rules and regulations) as the path to enlightenment. Pure Vinaya followers are expected to be literate and to live a cloistered life, although lay people may practise some of the precepts.

Vine A flower essence made from the blossom of the grape vine. This emotionally healing tincture is one of the **Bach Flower Remedies**. Dr Bach said that this is indicated for 'those who are of a strong and dominant nature. The leaders who are tempted to use their position and strength to control others, taking no notice of their feeling or preferences, demanding obedience and acceptance of their orders'.

Viniyoga Yoga see **Yoga, Hatha**

Vipassana, also **Mindfulness** The state all Buddhists wish to achieve. Mindfulness is moment-to-moment non-judgemental awareness, or paying attention to whatever feelings or actions one is experiencing at the time. See also: **Meditation, Buddhism**.

Virgin Mary The mother of **Jesus Christ**, the 'Son of **God**', according to **Christianity**. Catholic Christians believe that she is actually the Mother of God and Queen of Heaven, immaculately conceived. Non-Christians view her as the personification of the ancient Mother **goddess**, representing the essence of the feminine power of the earth and the universe.

The Virgin Mary is usually depicted in one of two poses: as the gentle nurturing mother with the infant Jesus on her knees, or as the sorrowful mother, 'Mater Dolorosa', cradling her dead son.

Of her actual life, we know little but what the **Bible** tells us. Mary was a young Jewish woman of Nazareth, in Roman Palestine, who lived sometime between 20 BC and c. AD 45. She was probably in her early teens, and betrothed to a local carpenter, Joseph, when an **angel** of God appeared to her and said that, despite her virgin status, she was to be filled with the Holy Spirit and give birth to the long-awaited saviour of the Jewish people, the Messiah.

Despite the somewhat unbelievable circumstances of her divine pregnancy, Joseph married her and then follows the familiar Christmas story of Bethlehem, the Nativity, the Three Wise Men, the Flight into Egypt and a return to Nazareth when it was safe to do so.

She is mentioned in the course of Jesus' ministry but does not feature until his crucifixion, when Mary keeps vigil with him during his ordeal and death. After that, we know little.

Fortunately, there are plenty of folk legends and a disputed early Christian writing 'The Nativity of Mary', to fill in the blanks. As the **Black Madonna**, she represents the timeless power of the Earth Mother. She is also depicted as **Sophia**, the goddess of wisdom and the female counterpart of God. The result of all of these stories is a goddess myth of incredible sweetness that transcends national borders and allows anyone of any race or religion to access the divine feminine energy of the universe.

Virgo   The sixth sign of the **zodiac** in Western **astrology**, and the **sun sign** for those born between 24 August and 22 September. The symbol of Virgo is the virgin, and the ruling planet is **Mercury**. Virgos are a **mutable sign** influenced by the **earth element**, with 'perfection' the best single word to define them. Those born under Virgo tend to be methodical, meticulous and at times perfectionist. Virgos like to make sense of their world, and are excellent organisers of systems and structures. They are analytical and can appear cool and reserved, but bear in mind the old adage about 'still waters run deep'.

The ideal meal for a Virgo is a carefully planned affair, featuring plenty of fruits, nuts, vegetables and grains (they are the harvest goddesses of the zodiac, after all). They have discriminating palates and often end up as nutritionists and restaurant critics. In health, Virgos are prone to intestinal disorders and stress-related ailments. Herbs which act as a tonic to the digestive system, as well as relaxation techniques, will soothe the agitated earth goddess.

Virgula Furcata   (Latin, 'forked rod') A specific type of **dowsing** rod named by the German sixteenth-century father of geology Georgius Agricola

(1494–1555). It was usually constructed of hazel wood, which was thought to enhance the natural divining powers of a dowser. Modern-day dowsers use rods of other woods, or even of stainless steel.

Vishnu One of the **trimurti** or three main gods in **Hinduism**, who is the only one to take on different incarnations or **avatars** in his contacts with mankind. Vishnu is depicted as the preserver of the worlds created by **Brahma**, the Supreme Being. Whenever **dharma** (eternal order, righteousness, duty) is threatened, Vishnu travels to earth from his heavenly realm in one of his ten different incarnations. His two best-known forms have been Rama (of the **Ramayana)** and **Krishna** (of the **Bhagavad Gita**). Many Hindus believe that **Gautama Buddha** was one of Vishnu's avatars. He is married to **Lakshmi**, the goddess of wealth and prosperity. The one incarnation of Vishnu that has yet to be seen is **Kali**, who will appear when the world ends.

Vision Quest A Native North American ritual where one seeks to provoke a visionary trance, in order to commune with **spirit guides** for wisdom and power. It is usually undertaken by young men, especially those on the brink of adulthood. Prior to beginning the quest, the seeker spends a number of days purifying himself through fasting, or time in a **sweat lodge**. Usually, a tribe elder assists him in his preparations, and serves as a guide to provoke the start of the vision quest. The seeker then isolates himself out in the wilderness, in a small rectangular tent he has constructed, and will neither eat nor sleep until his quest is concluded. He prays for a message from Wakan Tanka (the Great Spirit) and a physical representation of the message or vision (such as a feather, rock, or piece of fur) will be given to the seeker from his spirit guide, who will appear in the guise of an animal. See also: **Pathworking**.

Visualisation(s) A technique utilising mental imagery and affirmation to produce positive change. This ability to make pictures in the mind can lead to better health and improved self-image, and help someone to attain a host of other personal goals. Although visualisation has formed part of religious practices for centuries (for example **Buddhism**) it first came to greater attention in the West through the 1977 publication of the book *Creative Visualisation* by Shakti Gawain. Her theory that people can use their imaginations to manifest their deepest desires quickly spread beyond esoteric spiritual circles into mainstream culture.

The technique is simple. First you find a quiet place and relax into a deep, meditative state of mind. Then you construct a detailed mental picture of whatever situation you wish to change. The third step is to imagine your desired outcome, to think out in great detail how change is possible; experience it as if it were already happening. Often this visualisation is combined with repeating a positive phrase of affirmation that you will attain your goal. The technique is repeated for days, weeks, months – until the desired change is attained.

Reputable research has shown that visualisation works; why is another matter. The growing field of psychoneuroimmunology, the study of the mind's effect on health and illness, has found it to be a particularly effective technique in fighting disease. A particular form of visualisation called **guided imagery** is used more and more in psychotherapy and medicine, especially for treating individuals with compromised immunity, life-threatening illnesses and/or chronic degenerative conditions.

Vital Force The phrase used by **Samuel Hahnemann**, the founder of **homeopathy**, to describe the life force or energy that exists within every human body. It is also known as **chi** in Chinese philosophy and **prana** in Indian thought. Hahnemann believed his homeopathic remedies worked because they stimulated the vital force, and encouraged the energies within the body to return to a healthy balance and, therefore, health.

Voluntary Simplicity, also **Downshifting** A phrase coined by author Duane Elgin in 1981 to describe a new ethos spreading through materialistic Western society. This new moral code is a conscious effort to simplify our lives through reduction of possessions, a shift or 'downshifting' of lifestyle including location, career and consumer goods, or acting in ways that conserve natural resources.

Voodoo, also **Vaudoux**, **Voudou**, **Vondoun** (West African *vodun*, 'god or spirit') A magical religion practised in Haitian and African communities in the Caribbean and Southern US, which combines Roman Catholic religious customs with African magical rituals. Animal blood sacrifices, spirit possessions, black sorcery, sexual routines and **shamanistic** trances are common features of this religion, although there are some sects which practise white magic. Voodoo probably came over from Africa to the New World via the slave trade, which some say is the reason for the ferocious anger at the heart of this religion.

One of the more unpleasant magic spells is for the voodoo practitioner to make a small doll or puppet in the shape of a person they wish to curse. They then 'torture' the doll, with the intention of causing the cursed one pain and harm. This 'voodoo doll' is probably something slaves got from their white masters, rather than the other way around, as 'puppet magic' has been practised in European cultures for a very long time.

It is said that voodoo priests also have the power to raise **zombies** (reanimated dead people) to do their bidding. Although voodoo is specific to Haiti and the Southern US, offshoots and related cults in different parts of the world include santeria, candomble (or macumba), obeah and hoodoo.

Walnut A flower essence made from the blossom of the walnut tree. This emotionally healing tincture is one of the **Bach Flower Remedies**. Dr Bach said that this is 'the remedy for change and any period of adjustment when one feels unsettled, and for those who are influence or distracted by the influence of others.'

Walpurgis, Walpurgis Night German name for **Beltane**, the spring pagan festival of fertility, held on 30 April, or May Day's eve.

Wand (Germanic *windan*, 'wind, bind') A wizard or witch's traditional implement that helps to control the energies of a **spell**, sending it in whichever direction the wand is pointed. In **magic**, the wand represents the **air element**, and is made from the wood of living trees. The best types of wood to use are hazel or elder, but willow wands are good for enhancing your wish and for working with the energies of the moon, rowan for healing and protection spells, ash for prosperity, oak for strength and endurance, and apple for binding love. Sometimes a crystal will be put on top of the wand, which has the effect of intensifying and focusing its directional power. See also: **Witchcraft**.

Water Element 1. One of the four natural elements harnessed in **pagan** rituals of **magic** and religious worship. In **Wicca**, a water **elemental** is one of the four spirits that energise a spell and bring its wishes into being. Water symbolises relationships, intuition and the natural cycles of birth, death and rebirth. It represents the female principle of **yin**, in the aspect of the moon **goddess**, and is especially potent in love matters. The magical tool associated with the water element is the chalice or **cauldron**. Water's colour is blue, and water is associated with the **zodiac** signs of **Cancer, Scorpio** and **Pisces**.

2. One of the **five elements** in Chinese philosophy and medicine that make up the 'building blocks' of the universe. In **Traditional Chinese Medicine**, water is associated with the **kidney** and **bladder meridians**, and with the season of winter.

Water represents the deep, hidden depths of a person, and the storage or 'inheritance' of genetic characteristics. The colour black, cold and cold weather, salty tastes, the bones, teeth and head hair; the sound of groaning and the ears and hearing in general are also associated with this element. Water flows deep and water people tend to be thinkers. In the five element cycle, water generates or gives birth to **wood** and controls **fire** and in turn water is given life by **metal** and controlled by **earth**. This interdependent relationship to other elements has implications in health. If someone has weak water energy they will often have dark circles under their eyes, have a weak back or bladder, weak bones or teeth, or hormonal problems. Left unchecked, this could then go on to weaken other elemental energies and lead to other health problems in the way that kidney disease (weak water energies) can lead to heart problems (weak fire energies). See also: **Taoism, Yang, Yin.**

3. One of the **five elements** in East Indian philosophy and medicine that defines the universe based on the spiritual concept of **prana**, or life energy. In **ayurveda**, the water element, also known as jala, is associated with the tongue, tastebuds and salty tastes, and has the elemental qualities of being liquid, cold and soft. In combination with the **earth element**, water forms the **dosha** (mind/body type) **kapha**, and, combined with the **fire element**, forms the dosha pitta. See also: **Hinduism, Tridosha.**

Water Violet A flower essence made from the water violet blossom. This emotionally healing tincture is one of the **Bach Flower Remedies**. Dr Bach said that this is indicated for 'those who are reserved, self-contained, dignified people who enjoy peace and quiet. May become cut off due to their need for privacy and may therefore appear aloof or unapproachable'.

Werewolf A person who turns into a hideous wolf on the full moon, feeding on human flesh. The legend of the werewolf probably came from the magical tradition of **lycanthropy**, the belief that it is consciously possible, through witchcraft or sorcery, to transform into the form of an animal.

Wheel of Rebirth see **Samsara**

Wheel of the Year see **Celtic Wheel**

Whirling Dervishes (Persian *darvesh*, 'religious mendicant') A subsect of **Sufism** (mystic **Islam**) whose adherents dance in circles, rhythmically chant or repeat **mantras** from the **Koran** in order to whirl themselves into religious states of ecstasy. Dervishes belief that, while in this **trance** state, they are better able to directly communicate with Allah.

The whirling dervishes trace their origins to the thirteenth-century mystic poet Jelaluddin Mevlana **Rumi**. The Mevlevli Order, as they are called in his honour, perform their sacred dance, the *sema*, in a set, ritualised way. During this ceremony, the dancer becomes a conduit for divine energy, with the power of heaven entering the upwards extended right palm and leaving through the lower, turned-down left palm. The dervish does not retain or direct the power; instead he accepts he is the true instrument of God so does not question this spiritual energy.

White Chestnut A flower essence made from the blossom of the white chestnut tree. This emotionally healing tincture is one of the **Bach Flower Remedies**. Dr Bach said that this is indicated for 'worrying thoughts and mental arguments that interfere with rest and peace of mind'.

White Goddess, The A work on the mythological and psychological inspirations for poetry and literature, published in 1948 by British poet and writer Robert Graves. Subtitling his book *A Historical Grammar of Poetic Myth*, Graves argued that the language of Northern European poetic myth was actually derived from magical rites conducted to invoke the power of the 'White Goddess – the Moon'. Some of these rituals for poets to 'invoke the power of the Muse' dated from Palaeolithic times.

Graves felt that the rituals used in the Western world corresponded to those used in Eastern cultures. There currently are doubts about Graves' scholarship, as *The White Goddess* was written in the period when Graves' first marriage was shattered by his involvement with Laura Riding, an American adventuress and witch. She was later to claim that the substantive content of *The White Goddess* was hers. Graves regarded Riding as his own personal muse, but was no longer with her when the book was published, so her contributions to the project went unacknowledged. Graves claimed the inspiration for the book to be his alone; it was partially based on an earlier work, **The Golden Bough** by James Frazer, published in 1922.

Wicca, Wiccan (Celtic origin *wicce*, 'wise') A major witchcraft movement of white **magic**, and an organised **pagan** religion of nature and goddess worship. Wicca is based on traditions dating back thousands of years to ancient Egypt and Greece, but in its present form only goes back to the mid 1950s and 60s, when two practising warlocks, Alex Sanders (1926–1988) and Gerald Gardner (1884–1964), standardised magical rituals, initiations and goddess beliefs into one codified, organised system. Their major influences were Charles G. Leland's book *Aradia* (published in 1899), Margaret Murray's two works *The Witch Cult in Western Europe* (1921) and *The God of the Witches* (1933), and Sir James Frazer's book **The Golden Bough** (1922). While Sanders and Gardner worked together, they still had some differences of opinion about Wiccan practice, which is why there are two strands of Wicca – 'Alexandrian' and 'Gardnerian'.

Wicca has many characteristics, but the most distinctive is that of the Wiccan Rede, which is akin to an oath of benign magical intent. It is long and quite complex but the final line sums up Wiccan philosophy: 'An it harm none, do what ye will'. See also: **Celtic Wheel of the Year, Paganism, Witchcraft**.

Wiccan Rede   The central tenet of the pagan religion Wicca : 'An it harm none, do what ye will'. This white witchcraft belief of using magic only for positive, non-coercive ends arose out of their other central belief of the **Threefold Law**. This form of karmic law states that any energies or magic used to create chaos, and/or force a person to actions against their will, would rebound threefold on the original magician.

Wild Oat   A flower essence made from the wild oat blossom.   This emotionally healing tincture is one of the **Bach Flower Remedies**. Dr Bach said that this is indicated for 'those who are at a crossroads in life and do not know in which direction they should proceed. They tend to feel unfulfilled and dissatisfied with what they have achieved, and have ambitions to do something of value'.

Wild Rose   A flower essence made from the wild rose blossom. This emotionally healing tincture is one of the **Bach Flower Remedies**. Dr Bach said that this is indicated for 'those who are unmotivated and resigned to all that happens. Not interested in change: happy with life the way it is. For apathy and resignation or feelings of staleness'.

Willow   A flower essence made from the blossom of the willow tree. This emotionally healing tincture is one of the **Bach Flower Remedies**. Dr Bach said that this is indicated for 'resentment or bitterness. For those who find it hard to forgive and forget, but dwell on negativity and their own misfortunes'.

Witch Ball Large, heavy glass balls coated with glossy reflective paint or patterns, designed to be hung in the windows of houses to deflect away black magic and the **evil eye**. These protective **amulets** were first made in the seventeenth-century English countryside and were widely popular up to the end of the nineteenth century. See also: **Witch Bottle**.

Witch Bottle (English) A counterspell against illness caused by witchcraft, in which a bottle filled with nails, pins and threads was buried in the hearthstones or foundations of medieval houses. The sick person's urine, several hairs and fingernail clippings were also placed in the bottle before it was tightly corked. This would break the magical link the witch had created with her victim and reverse the spell back onto the perpetrator, who would need to sever the ties to save herself. Still in common use in some parts of England into the twentieth century.

Witch Doctor A medical, magical practitioner who uses his spells and potions to cure the sick, protect his community from evil, and contact **spirit guides** for wisdom and divination purposes. The witch doctor can be found in tribal cultures of Africa, South America, and the Native North American Indians (where he is known as a **medicine man**), and in parts of Australasia and Polynesia. In some Caribbean cultures, he may be a **voodoo** priest. See also: **Shaman, Shamanism**.

Witchcraft, Witches (Celtic origin *wicce*, 'wise') A belief system of nature and **goddess** worship, magical practice and folk religion that incorporates a host of other traditions like **divination, herbalism** and **paganism**. A female practitioner of witchcraft is called a witch, and a male practitioner a warlock. Unlike **Wicca**, a decidedly white magical movement, witchcraft utilises both white and black magic, depending upon the choices made by the witch or warlock.

Its origins are shrouded in prehistory, but certainly there is mention of witches and witchcraft as far back as the time of Moses. Magic and sorcery were practised in ancient Babylonia, Egypt and Chaldea, and also throughout the classical world of Greece and Rome. Witchcraft did not acquire its negative connotations until the rise of the Christian Church, which taught: 'Thou shalt not suffer a witch to live'. There are infamous and horrendous tales of persecution, ranging from the witch-hunts of medieval England and Scotland to the Salem witch trials in colonial America.

The rhythm of a witch's year is organised around the schedule of **sabbats** and **esbats**, better known as the **wheel of the year**. These seasonal festivals and meetings provide a framework of worship and celebration, and a chance to gather together and concentrate their powers of magic.

The practice of witchcraft is ritualistic, involving precise use of a number of different tools (**athame**, **wand**, **cauldron**, **besom**, **grimoire**) and magic rituals like **spells**, **charms**, **incantations** and **potions**. Witches gain their magical power through harnessing the energies of the four natural elements of the universe: **earth**, **air**, **fire** and **water**. If witches decide to follow the Wiccan Rede of white magic: 'An it harm none, do what ye will', then it is said that they have taken the **right-handed path** of light and inspiration. If instead they use magic for their own means or for malevolent purpose, they have taken the **left-handed path**, of darkness and black magic.

Witches' Cradle A device used in **witchcraft** to induce sensory deprivation and movement, in the hope of enhancing fantasies and alteration in consciousness. Only advanced practitioners should attempt using it, and there are some who believe it is a harmful practice because the witch does not retain control, leaving her open to influences from malevolent spirits and powers. See also: **Left-handed Path**.

Wizard (Middle English wis, 'wise philosopher, sage') A magician with a high level of skill in summoning spirits and supernatural powers. See also: **Adept**, **Witchcraft**.

Wood Element One of the **five elements** in Chinese philosophy and medicine that make up the 'building blocks' of the universe. In **Traditional Chinese Medicine**, wood is associated with the **liver** and **gall bladder meridians**, and with the season of spring. Wood signifies dynamic movement and new beginnings. The colour green, the wind, sour tastes, the eyes, tendons and nails; the sound of shouting and the emotion of anger (the phrase 'gung-ho' means 'liver-fire' in Chinese) are also associated with this element. Wood-type people need to beware of overactivity, anger and overexuberance.

In the five element cycle, wood generates or gives birth to **fire** and controls **earth** and in turn wood is given life by **water** and controlled by **metal**. This interdependent relationship to other elements has implications in health. If someone has weak wood energy they will be prone to mood swings, depression, period problems, eye problems, gallstones, violent behaviour and alcohol and substance abuse. Left unchecked, this could then go on to weaken other elemental energies and lead to other health problems in the way that alcoholism (weak wood energies) can lead to stomach problems (weak earth energies). See also: **Taoism**, **Yang**, **Yin**.

Wraith The spectral double, similar to a ghost, of someone who has just died, is about to die or is in mighty big trouble. Relatives and friends often see the wraith of a loved one, almost always as a sign that someone has passed over. To see your own wraith (also called a **fetch**) is a sure sign of your imminent death.

Wyvern, also **Wivern** (Old French *wivre*, from Latin *vipera*, 'viper') A mythical creature depicted in folk tales and heraldry, a wyvern is a winged serpent similar to a dragon, but it has eagle's legs and a barbed tail.

Xenoglossisia, also **Xenoglossis**, **Xenoglossy** (Greek *xenos*, 'strange', + *glossa*, 'language, tongue', + *lalia*, 'speech') The phenomenon of 'speaking in tongues' either in Pentecostal Christian worship or in **spiritualism** when a person is under the control of an spirit entity from another realm. The language spoken can sometimes be identified as one not native to the speaker, coming out as a great torrent of words that at first hearing sound like gibberish. Sometimes it cannot be identified as any known language, although the speech patterns seem to indicate that it could be some sort of organised tongue. This has led some more credulous folk to believe that the person may be talking in angelic or otherwordly languages. Theories on the origins of xenoglossisia range from the Christian viewpoint of a gift from the Holy Spirit to the psychologist's view that it comes from our subconscious memory, which stores foreign languages possibly heard in childhood and subsequently forgotten.

Yama (Sanskrit, 'social conduct') Moral rules for interaction with others, according to **yoga**. Yama is one of the 'eight limbs' or **ashtangas** that are mentioned in the **Yoga Sutras** of Patanjali, whose practice will lead to enlightenment; this ethical code includes practising non-violence, truthfulness, non-stealing, moderation in sex and in all things, and non-greed.

Yang (Chinese *yang*, 'sunny') The masculine embodiment of **chi** (universal life energy). See **Yin/Yang**.

Yantra (Sanskrit, 'instrument) A visual counterpart to a **mantra** used in Buddhist meditation ritual. They are very similar to **mandalas** but tend to concentrate more on geometric patterns than on a pictorial representation of the Buddhist universe. They function the same way by providing a focal point in meditation. When a person concentrates on a yantra, they are able to establish a connection with the infinite, and therefore travel further on the path towards **enlightenment**. A yantra is also used in the worship of the Hindu goddess Shakti. See also: **Tibetan Buddhism**.

Yellow Emperor's Inner Classic, also **Inner Classic of the Yellow Emperor** Classic text in **Traditional Chinese Medicine**, written by Huang Di, the Yellow Emperor (2696–2598 BC) and still in use today despite its age. It was written in the form of a dialogue between the legendary ruler and his minister, Qi Bo, on the subject of medicine. The first part of the book, 'Simple Questions', talks about the 12 organs and their relationships, which correspond to the 12 **meridians** used in **acupuncture** and other energy therapies. Qi Bo described them as 12 government bureaucrats, who must work in harmony to achieve good health. The second part of the text, 'Spiritual Axis', focuses more closely upon the practice of acupuncture itself.

Yeti, also **Abominable Snowman** A white-furred, hairy man-beast of great strength that supposedly lives in the snow heights of the Himalayan Mountains of Tibet, known to the natives as *Metohkangmi*. The yeti's existence has yet to be proved despite countless sightings and research done by cryptozoologists. Whatever he is, he has relatives all over the world – in the mountains of the Northwest US and Canada, Native Americans have many tales of the Sasquatch, or 'Bigfoot', a brown-haired variation of the yeti, and Australian aboriginal legends mention the Yowie, characterised by its foul stench and dark, matted hair. See also: **Cryptozoology**.

Yin (Chinese yin, 'shadow') The feminine embodiment of **chi** (universal life energy). See **Yin/Yang**.

Yin/Yang, also **Taiji** (Chinese Taiji, 'great polarity') The Chinese Taoist idea that the energy of the universe (known as **chi**) and everything in it is based on a pair of opposing forces, yin and yang. The four main characteristics of Yin and Yang are: they are in opposition to each other; they are interdependent; they consume each other; they transform each other. One cannot exist without the other.

The **I Ching**, although best known in the West as a work on Chinese fortune-telling, is a classic Taoist text that introduced the concept of yin and yang for the first time during the later third/early second century BC. Chi, or all life energy, lies at the top of the existential pyramid of the universe. Below that, chi is divided into yin and yang, which can then be further divided into the **five elements** of the natural world.

Chinese philosophy often presents chi as a mountain with two sides, one in full sunshine and one in shadow. Yin (shadow) is the feminine embodiment of chi. It represents earth, night, the moon, dark, cool, calm, downwards motion, passivity, moisture, emptiness, heaviness. Yang (sunny) is chi's masculine component. It represents heaven, day, the sun, light, warm, upwards motion, activity, fullness, dryness, lightness. Yin and yang together describe the condition of life, which is in a state of constant change and transition. Something is never just yin or yang, but is in flux between the two extremes, and there is always a part of one in the other. This can be seen in the taiji, or yin/yang symbol, represented by the dynamic curve and contrasting dot that separates yin from yang. The line between the two is not straight, as transitions are never abrupt, but gradual, like a rising/falling curve. The dot reminds us that there is always some yin in yang, and yang in yin.

Although everything in the universe has both yin and yang qualities, some things will be primarily one or the other. This holds true in people's personality types and in their health. The goal is always to maintain an equal amount of both as too much yin or too much yang can have disastrous consequences, especially in health.

Chinese medical practitioners have devised methods to diagnose a person's energetic balance of yin and yang, and come up with treatment plans based on those results. See also: **Five Element Cycle, Taoism, Traditional Chinese Medicine.**

Yoga (Sanskrit yui, 'to unite, bind, yoke') An Indian spiritual philosophy that seeks to join or 'yoke' all aspects of a person – physical body with mind and spirit – to achieve a happy, balanced life and, ultimately, unite the self with the universal consciousness. Patanjali, the author of the texts **Yoga Sutras** upon which yoga is based, felt that it was 'the ability to direct and sustain mental activity without distraction'. In the West yoga is best known as a physical discipline and exercise system popular among celebrities and other fashionistas. Its original aim, however, was to escape the karmic cycle of cause and effect and reach **enlightenment.**

As far back as 3000 BC, references to yoga have been found in Indian historic documents and artefacts, although the *Yoga Sutras* were not written down until sometime between 200 BC and 200 AD. In this text, the guru Patanjali defined the eight limbs or **ashtangas** that made up yogic practice. If practitioners followed these eight limbs, they would develop the necessary level of discernment and clarity of perception necessary to achieve ultimate bliss.

The eight limbs are: **yama** (moral social conduct); **niyama** (moral individual conduct); **asana** (physical postures); **pranayama** (breath control); **pratyahara** (sense withdrawal); **dharana** (concentration); **dhyana** (meditation); and **samadhi** (self-realisation). Patanjali also listed the nine obstacles to successful yogic practice, which will sound very familiar: sickness; lack of mental effort; self-doubt; inattention; laziness or fatigue; over-indulgence or sensuality; false knowledge and misunderstanding; lack of concentration; and lack of perseverance.

There are many different ways of practising yoga, some which emphasise the physical aspects of the disciple over the spiritual. The **Bhagavad Gita** names 18 types, but the *Yoga Sutras* mention four distinctive 'paths' of yoga that are considered the most important: laya or **kundalini; mantra; hatha;** and **raja.** Over time, each of these paths has developed its own offshoots and schools of thought, but without a doubt the best-known and most popular in the West is hatha yoga, which focuses on the physical routines of the body over the development of the mind.

Yoga was first introduced to Western cultures during the height of the British Raj, when Queen Victoria brought yogis over to Britain to perform exotic yoga postures for her and her guests. Yoga's growth in the West, however, is due to the followers of **theosophy**, who translated in the late nineteenth/early twentieth century many of the Sanskrit and Hindu texts that underpin yoga's philosophy.

The eminent psychoanalyst **C.G. Jung** thought that yoga started to become popular in the West because of a disenchantment with formal religion and fascination for all things new. Whatever the reason, people of all ages at all levels of physical fitness now practise it. Benefits of yoga include increased mobility, stress reduction, relaxation, improved blood and breath circulation, improved overall physical fitness, increased self-confidence and a sense of well-being. See also: **Ayurveda**.

Yoga Sutras (Sanskrit *yui*, 'to unite, bind, yoke', + *sutra*, 'thread') A collection of 196 wise sayings by the guru Patanjali, written sometime between 200 BC and AD 200, which form the philosophical basis for the practice of **yoga**. Patanjali is an enigmatic, almost mythic figure about whom little is known, but his writings are now considered essential Hindu texts. In the *Sutras*, he details the eight steps or 'limbs' for the practice of **raja** (royal) yoga, which are used for all yoga styles, as well as the nine obstacles, which can commonly hamper your practice.

The *Sutras* are divided into four chapters, each covering a different area of yogic discipline. Patanjali supposedly wrote each section for a different disciple, each with a different personality, so the approach to the subject in each chapter varies.

The first section, 'contemplation', defines exactly what yoga is, and lists the obstacles you might encounter in practising it, as well as how to overcome these problems. The second chapter, 'method', explains the eight limbs (ashtangas) you need to utilise to concentrate the mind and attain yogic perfection. The third, 'exceptional faculties', describes the innate power of the mind when free from distractions, and the final chapter, 'serenity', outlines what a highest yogic master can achieve with his superbly concentrated mind.

Yoga, Ashtanga, also **Astanga** (Sanskrit *ashta*, 'eight', + *anga*, 'limb') An offshoot of **hatha yoga**, which seeks to increase body strength and mobility. 'Ashtanga' gets its name from the eightfold path set out in the *Yoga Sutras* and is a fast, athletic power-yoga first taught by Pattabhi Jois in Mysore and New York. Classes are structured to take the complete beginner carefully and thoroughly to increasing levels of attainment, through swift movement from one **asana** (yoga pose) to another. It is a physically intense, gymnastic, almost 'aerobic' form of yoga, and the one celebrities like Madonna and Gwyneth Paltrow practise.

Yoga, Bhakti (Sanskrit *bhaj*, 'to serve') One of the classic paths of yoga according to the **Yoga Sutras**. This is known as 'the yoga of devotion', both to others and to a power greater than ourselves. Because it emphasises mystical philosophy over physical discipline, it is not commonly practised in the West.

Yoga, Bikram An offshoot of **hatha yoga** developed by Indian healer Bikram Choudhury in the 1960s. After suffering a knee injury, Bikram was told he would never walk again. He refused to accept this and, after six months of intensive yoga, his knee completely healed. His recovery inspired him to formalise his method of yoga, which uses only 26 of the many thousands of **asanas**, or yoga postures, available. Bikram yoga is characterised by practice rooms of sweltering heat – as much as a sultry 40 degrees Centigrade. This heat allows the muscles, ligaments and joints to stretch without injury and aids the healing of existing injuries. It also promotes sweating, which flushes toxins from your system. Bikram yoga is considered a very challenging type of yoga, even for the fit, but many have used it to increase mobility and aid healing of old injuries about which conventional medicine could do nothing.

Yoga, Dhyana A meditative form of **yoga** mostly practised in Eastern cultures.

Yoga, Hatha (Sanskrit *Ha*, 'sun', + *Tha*, 'moon', or together 'power, forceful') One of the four main paths of **yoga** and the only form widely practised in the West. It is also known as the 'yoga of the body' because hatha emphasises the physical body over the mind's search for enlightenment. Traditionally this very physical discipline was regarded as preparation for the pursuit of **raja** (or royal) yoga, which seeks harmony of mind and body. Hatha is now practised for its own sake, particularly because Westerners (especially of Christian cultures) can gain the physical benefits of yoga without having to study and believe in its philosophy.

There are many different types or 'schools' of hatha yoga, each with a different emphasis on how you should perform the eight yogic disciplines, or **ashtangas**, with many of them named after the guru who devised them. Some of these are: **Iyengar**, **Sidda**, **Integral**, **Bikram**, **Sivananda**, Ananda, Anusara, Kripalu, Kali Ray TriYoga, Jiva Mukti, Svaroopa and Viniyoga.

Yoga, Integral A school of **hatha yoga** developed by guru Sri Aurobindo, which seeks to use the routines and feats of hatha to integrate the body and mind together to achieve 'self-integration'. The aim is to increase your levels of love, knowledge, wisdom, action and peace through physical movement and yogic discipline, and then you will be whole. You also chant **om** a lot.

Yoga, Iyengar Offshoot of **hatha yoga** developed by B.S.K. Iyengar and his students.

He wrote *Light on Yoga*, first published in 1966 but still one of most popular books ever written on the subject. In Iyengar yoga, the emphasis is on correct anatomical alignment, both in performing the **asanas**, or poses, and in performing **pranayama**, or breathing exercises. Iyengar constructed several unique props (wooden blocks, chairs, blankets and belts) to help his students in these movements. Once the asanas and pranayamas are mastered, work goes on in developing the other eight 'limbs' or **ashtanga** of yoga so that the mastery of body leads to the mastery of mind.

This school of yoga can best be distinguished from other yogic forms by three key elements: the *technique* of adjustments to align the body in correct poses and breathing; the exact *sequence* of how asanas and pranayamas are performed; and the *timing* or length of time spent in the postures and breathing exercises.

Yoga, Jnana A type of **yoga** that emphasises the intellect over physical disciplines. Jnana yoga seeks to gain knowledge and eliminate ignorance, and calls for an understanding of the sacred **Vedas**, notably the **Upanishads**, which contain a great number of esoteric doctrines. Jnana yoga's goal is *prajna*, transcendental wisdom through meditation and thought. Mainly practised in Eastern cultures.

Yoga, Karma (Sanskrit, 'action or work'). A type of **yoga** also known as 'the yoga of service in action', because it emphasises doing good for others as a remembrance of God and surrendering the rewards to God. Because it emphasises spiritual philosophy over physical discipline, it is not commonly practised in the West.

Yoga, Kriya A type of **yoga** that emphasises religious observance, purification and proper carrying through of ritual acts. It differs from **bhakti yoga** (the yoga of devotion) because there is more emphasis on physical practices and less on serving others. Kriya yoga focuses on three aspects: *tapas*, which shows how **asanas** (yoga poses) and **pranayama** (breath control) can help to remove physical or mental blocks or 'afflictions'; *svadhyaya*, the asking of questions and self-examination; and *isvarapranidhana*, the carrying out of actions that are not motivated by the prospect of a particular outcome. Mainly practised in Eastern cultures.

Yoga, Kundalini, also **Laya Yoga** (Sanskrit, 'the coil in the hair of the beloved') One of the classic paths of **yoga** according to the **Yoga Sutras**. This form of yoga is concerned with activating the power centres of the body, the **chakras**. It is also known as the yoga of 'latent spiritual awareness' because the goal is to arouse **kundalini**, the primal **psychic** force which sleeps like a coiled snake at the base of the spine. Once awakened, kundalini energy is directed up the main chakra channel of the spine, so that it may climb upwards and illuminate the brain, leading to enlightenment. Kundalini yoga is closely related to many **tantric** traditions, which seek ecstasy through religious and sexual practices.

Yoga, Laya see Kundalini Yoga

Yoga, Mantra, Nada (Sanskrit, 'uniting and holding') One of the four classic paths of **yoga** according to the **Yoga Sutras**, which uses sound – chants and mantras – to drive the mind into a higher state. Mantra yoga focuses on vibrations and radiations of life energy through sound. Like other therapies that use bells, drums and musical recordings to enhance health and healing processes, this type of yoga may affect the body via the endocrine system.

Yoga, Raja (Sanskrit, 'royal, king') One of the classic paths of yoga according to the **Yoga Sutras**, also known as the 'yoga of the mind'. Raja yoga is considered the highest form of yoga, whose practice ultimately leads to enlightenment. Raja yoga has as its goal to realise directly the absolute self by stilling the mind through concentrated meditative effort (via **asanas** and **pranayama** breathing exercises) so the light of the internal spirit can shine through.

Hatha yoga is often considered a precursor of raja yoga, because there must be absolute physical mastery of the body before mastery of the mind can take place. Raja yoga is mainly practised in Eastern cultures, especially India, with yogic masters ultimately achieving fantastic acts of control over their bodies, their abilities including **firewalking**, yogic flying and **levitation**.

Yoga, Sidda A spiritual school of **hatha yoga** brought to the West by Swami Muktananda. It teaches that all religions are equal and the only way to reach highest truth is to find the point at which all differences between religions disappear. Yoga disciplines can be used to reach this vanishing point, including chanting, contemplation and practising meditative **asanas**, or yoga postures.

Yoga, Sivananda Offshoot of **hatha yoga** developed by Swami Sivananda Sarawsati, and one of the largest schools of yoga in the world. Practitioners of this yogic style follow a set structure of classic **asanas** (poses), **pranayama** (breath control exercises) and relaxation.

Yoga, Tantric (Sanskrit, 'technique') A form of **yoga** that combines **tantric** practices with yogic disciplines. It is also known as 'the yoga of sexual polarity' because it seeks to balance male and female energies in the body, in a way that will ultimately lead to **enlightenment**. In tantric yoga, many of the practices are secret, and you only learn them through initiation by a **guru**. Study of tantric scriptures and the practices of tantric sexual ecstasies are followed, along with the more usual discipline of following the eight limbs or **ashtangas** of yoga. See also: **Kundalini, Tantric Sex**.

Yogananda, Paramahansa Modern pioneer of Eastern spiritual traditions in the West, and author of the 1946 book *Autobiography of a Yogi*, a book about the lives and powers of Hindu saints. After 56 years, the book is still in print and has been translated into over ten languages.

Yogis Practitioners of **yoga**. A male disciple is known as a yogi, and a female one a yogini. Advanced yogis have achieved great mental control over their bodies, and can exhibit almost **paranormal** abilities like **levitation**, **firewalking** or flying through the air. They are able to do this through manipulating their heart rate, blood pressure and respiration at will.

Yuga An epic measurement of time, according to **Hinduism**. Each yuga is of enormous length, and corresponds roughly to the 'ages of man' depicted in Greek and Roman mythology. There are four ages: *Krita Yuga*, the legendary Golden Age of gods and immortals; *Treta Yuga*, the Silver Age; *Dvapara Yuga*, the Bronze Age; and *Kali Yuga*, the Iron Age and the one we now find ourselves in. Each age represents a progressive decline away from the one before it, with our age characterised by quarrelling and hypocrisy. One day, when this world ends, we will return to the golden times of the Krita Yuga.

Yule (Old Norse *jul*, 'wheel') The **pagan** holiday of the midwinter **solstice**, celebrated on 22 December, whose customs and name have been assimilated into the Christian holiday of **Christmas**. Yule, and all of the different traditions associated with it, celebrates this as a time of death and rebirth. It is the shortest day of the year, when the sun appears to be dead, but the day also marks the 'birth' of its return journey.

The ancients, who each year feared the sun would disappear permanently, lit great bonfires and hung greenery about to encourage it to return. This 'festival of lights' was marked by copious feasting that took (and still takes) place as a magical gesture of faith, to convince the powers of nature to ensure there would be food in the spring, and a good harvest the following autumn. Yule is one of the eight **sabbats** (festival days) of the pagan year, combining Norse, Celtic, Mithraic, Greek and Roman traditions (especially of Saturnalia, held to honour the god Saturn and the winter solstice) into a glorious melange of feasting, play-acting, song and ritual.

Zakah, also **Zakat** (Arabic, 'purify'). One of the **five pillars of Islam**, which is an obligatory form of charity expected from every Muslim. It is mentioned in over 30 verses of the **Koran** as one of the ways to attain paradise in the afterlife. Muslims believe that all things belong to God and that wealth is held by men in trust for God. Because of this, man has a duty to share a percentage of his personal wealth with the less fortunate. By doing so, he 'purifies' his remaining possessions and encourages new growth by cutting back on that held previously. Each year, Muslims calculate their own zakah contributions individually and each contribution should equal out to $2\frac{1}{2}$ per cent of a person's capital.

Zarathustra, also **Zoroaster**, **Zor** A Persian prophet c. 600 BC, who founded the principles of the occult religion **Zoroastrianism**. His name in Greek was Zoroaster. As with many visionaries, he was in a mountain cave when the idea of Ahura Mazda, the one and only supreme being, came to him. In a land of multiple gods and deities, this was unusual. After that, Zarathustra preached the gospel of the one god fighting against evil. If you believed him, you were considered a follower of truth, or 'Asha'. If you did not, you were a follower of lies, or 'Druj'.

Unlike believers of **Christianity**, who hold that the world is inherently evil, Zarathustra felt the world was basically good, but had been corrupted by evil. Therefore, you had to choose which of two masters to serve in this world, and which decision you made determined where you would reside in the afterlife. Zarathustra felt that the **sun** was the living symbol of his one 'supreme being', which is why Zoroastrians pray to it each day.

Zazen   The practice of sitting meditation in Zen Buddhism, considered vital to let the inner Buddha nature within reveal itself. It is often referred to as 'just sitting', just 'being' rather than trying to 'become'. See also: **Zen Buddhism, Zen.**

Zeitgeist   (German *Zeit*, 'time', + *Geist*, 'spirit') A defining spirit of the age that epitomises the mood of a certain period of time or history. An example of this might be the images of jazz, cocktails and flappers which symbolise the spirit of the 1920s.

Psychoanalyst **Carl Jung** thought that this spirit could lead people to unconsciously form groups with a collective soul or **psyche**. The danger of this was that the dark underside of a group persona, the collective **shadow**, could form, with dangerous, disastrous consequences. As the shadow side of us represents that which we find most distasteful in ourselves, we find a way to cope with it by 'projecting' it onto another person or, in the case of a group persona, onto another group in society. Jung cited this as the reason why the Nazis formed a collective shadow, which they projected onto the Jewish people, whom they then saw as being worthless and evil.

Zen   (Japanese, 'meditation' from Sanskrit *dhyana*, via Chinese *ch'an*, 'meditation') Phrase for the Japanese school of Mahayana **Buddhism**. The original definition has expanded to refer to a general mindset encompassing such subjects as Japanese culture, archery, motorcycle maintenance, the Beat Poets, and a certain aesthetic of black and white, pure lines and open space. Zen also refers to a state of mind, where one tries to 'live in the moment', to calm restless thoughts by quiet **meditation** and deliberation on 'nothing'. A 'Zen awakening' occurs once a person realises that 'nothing' and 'now' constitute all there is, that what happens in the present is what life is, not future goals or past dreams; which is why a Zen Buddhist enjoins you to 'be here now'.

Zen Buddhism   A form of **Mahayana Buddhism** mainly practised in China, Japan and Korea, which considers **meditation** and intuition the keys to uncovering wisdom, compassion and, ultimately, **enlightenment**. Meditation helps followers of this tradition concentrate on living in the moment. Emphasis is given to the master and disciple relationship. Zen masters use **koans** and **mondos** to jolt the mindset of a disciple into **satori**. See also: **Buddhism, Zen.**

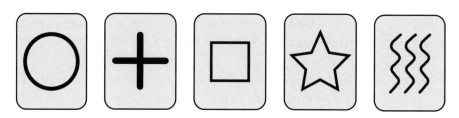

Zener cards

Zener Cards A pack of 25 cards devised in the 1920's and 1930's by Dr J.B. Rhine, for use in his experiments into **ESP** at Duke University in the United States. He named the pack after the psychologist Dr Karl Zener, who helped him develop the research project. There are five different card designs: square; star; circle; cross; and three wavy lines, with five of each design in a pack of Zener cards. The cards are shuffled and then turned over one by one by a 'sender', who sits in a different room from the 'percipient'. The goal is to record how many cards the percipient can correctly guess, merely by trying to 'tune in' to the sender's thoughts. The total of correct guesses or 'hits' is then compared to the number you might get correct by chance. The higher the number of hits, the higher your **psi** ability is considered to be.

Zero Balancing A form of **massage therapy** that concentrates on aligning body energies (called **life force, chi, prana**) with the body's physical structure. Zero balancing focuses very particularly on the skeletal system, and was designed by Dr Fritz Smith, an osteopath, acupuncturist and medical doctor, in 1973. He felt that there needed to be an **energy medicine** concentrating on our bones and joints, and developed zero balancing after years of study and casework.

Zero balancing addresses specific symptoms and a patient's concerns within a single session or short series of sessions. In a typical session, a client lies or sits comfortably while gentle traction and finger pressure are used at various places on the trunk, legs, neck and feet. Although the emphasis is on body structure, people often report a general sense of well-being after a treatment, and it frequently triggers a cathartic release of emotions after physical and mental trauma.

Zeus, also **Jupiter, Jove** The king of heaven and earth in Greek mythology, also known as the god of thunder and lightning. He was one of the sons of Chronos (Time) and Rhea (Earth) and was the ruling head of the Olympiad, the 12 chief gods and goddesses of Greek legend who lived on Mt Olympus. In Roman myth he is better known as Jove, or **Jupiter**.

Zodiac (Greek *zodiakos kyrklos*, 'circle of animals') The system astrologers use to mark out and name constellations in the sky that the sun, moon and other planets move through in a regular pattern. In Western astrology each band in the heavens is divided into 12 signs, each containing 30 degrees of longitude and acting as the barometer for various human traits, with each sign symbolised by an animal or mythical person or persons.

In order of their place on the wheel, the signs are: **Aries, Taurus, Gemini, Cancer, Leo, Virgo, Libra, Scorpio, Sagittarius, Capricorn, Aquarius** and **Pisces**. Your **horoscope** is a diagram of the heavens at the time of your birth. The sign you are born under is known as your **sun sign**, because, like the **sun** in the heavens, your horoscope's dominant characteristics determine who you are and will be in life. See also: **Astrology, Moon Signs**.

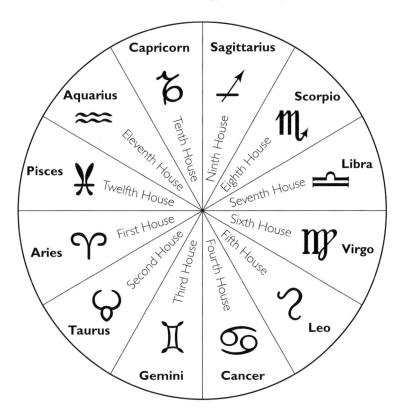

Zodiac wheel

Zohar, The, also **Zepher ha Zohar, Sepher ha Zohar** (Hebrew *Sepher ha Zohar*, 'Book of Splendour') The principle text and reference in the Jewish mystical tradition, the **Kabbalah**. The author of the Zohar is thought to be Spanish Kabbalist Moses de Leon, who wrote it sometime between AD 1280 and 1290. It explains the different rituals and studies to take on the **Tree of Life**, as well as containing commentary on the Jewish scriptures.

Zombie   (African Kongo *nzambi*, 'spirit of a dead person') A corpse that has been reanimated through a **voodoo** enchantment. Zombies have no will of their own, are usually speechless and act as slaves to their reanimator. One theory proposes that the legend of zombies may have arisen from someone held prisoner by a voodoo practitioner, who was drugged into a catatonic state by a cocktail of neurotoxins and psychotropic substances for the time of their internment.

Zor, Zoroaster   see Zarathustra

Zoroastrianism   Mystic religion based on the teachings of the ancient Persian prophet **Zarathustra** (known as Zoroaster in Greek).

Bibliography

Adams, Peter, *Homoeopathy*, Element Books, 1999

Alexander, Skye, *Magickal Astrology*, New Page Books, 2000

Allan, Tony, *Prophecies*, Duncan Baird Publishers, 2002

Applegate, Susan, 'Chiron: finding new horizons', *Prediction Magazine*, February 2003

Applegate, Susan, 'Mantras: the cosmic sound of words', *Prediction Magazine*, November 2001

Barefoot Doctor (Stephen Russell), *Barefoot Doctor's Handbook for the Urban Warrior*, Piatkus Books, 1998

Bartram, Thomas, *Bartram's Encyclopedia of Herbal Medicine*, Robinson, 1995

Batchelor, Martine, *First Directions: Zen*, Thorsons, 2001

Belle, Maureen L., *Gaiamancy: Creating Harmonious Environments*, White Doe Productions, 1999

Berry, Ruth, *Jung: A Beginner's Guide*, Hodder & Stoughton, 2000

Berry, Ruth, *Freud: A Beginner's Guide*, Hodder & Stoughton, 2000

Bloom, William, ed., *The Penguin Book of New Age and Holistic Writing*, Penguin Books, 2000

Bowes, Susan, *The Wiccan Handbook*, Godsfield Press, 2002

Budapest, Zsuzsanna, *The Holy Book of Women's Mysteries*, Wingbow Press, 1989

Bulfinch, Thomas, *Bulfinch's Mythology*, Avenel Books, 1978

Butler, Gillian and McManus, Freda, *Psychology: A Very Short Introduction*, Oxford University Press, 1998

Cainer, Jonathan, *Jonathan Cainer's Guide to the Zodiac*, Piatkus Books, 1997

Cainer, Jonathan and Rider, Carl, *The Psychic Explorer*, Piatkus Books, 1986

Campbell, Eileen and Brennan, J. H., *The Aquarian Guide to the New Age*, The Aquarian Press, 1990

Carlson, Ken, *Star Mana: The Healing Energies of Hawaii*, Starman Press, 1998

Chance, Jeremy, *First Directions: The Alexander Technique*, Thorsons, 2001

Charles, Liz, *A Practical Introduction to Homeopathy*, Caxton Editions, 2002

Chemelik, Stefan, *Chinese Herbal Secrets*, Newleaf/Gill & Macmillan, 1999

Clancy, John, 'Science or sorcery?' *Prediction Magazine*, April 2002

Clancy, John, 'Simply amazing', *Prediction Magazine*, June 2002

Coghill, Roger, *The Healing Energies of Light*, Gaia Books, 2000

Connelly, Ph.d., M.Ac., Dianne M., *Traditional Acupuncture: The Law of the Five Elements*, 5th edition, The Centre for Traditional Acupuncture, Inc., 1992

Conway, D. J., *Crystal Enchantments*, Piatkus Books, 2000

Conway, D. J., *Magickal Mystical Creatures*, 2nd edition, Llewellyn Publications, 2001

Coseschi, Paolo and Sneddon, Peta, *Healing with Osteopathy*, Gill & Macmillan, 1996

Cosman, Madeline Pelner, *Medieval Holidays and Festivals: A Calendar of Celebrations*, Piatkus Books, 1984

Cramer, Diane L., 'Simple health advice for your sign', *Horoscope Magazine*, September 2002

Dee, Jonathan, *Your Chinese Horoscope*, Silverdale Books, 2002

Dell, Linda Louisa, 'Lavenders blue', *Prediction Magazine*, November 2002

Djambazova, Veronica, 'Playing your cards right', *Prediction Magazine*, October 2001

Drury, Nevill, *The Dictionary of the Esoteric*, new edition, Watkins Publishing, 2002

Eason, Cassandra, *Every Woman a Witch*, Quantum, 1996

Eason, Cassandra, *Encyclopedia of Magic & Ancient Wisdom*, Piatkus Books, 2000

Eason, Cassandra, *A Complete Guide to Fairies and Magical Beings*, Piatkus Books, 2001

Eason, Cassandra, *The Complete Book of Women's Wisdom*, Piatkus Books, 2001

Eason, Cassandra, *10 Steps to Psychic Power*, Piatkus Books, 2002

Eden, Donna, *Energy Medicine*, Piatkus Books, 2000

Every Woman's Luck Book, Icon Books, 2002

Fenton-Smith, Paul, *Palmistry Revealed*, Heian International, Inc. 1996

Fitting, Lisa, *Nature's Wisdom*, Eyelevel Books, 2000

Fletcher, Joann, *The Egyptian Book of Living and Dying*, Duncan Baird Publishers, 2003

Franklin, Anna, 'Pathworking', *Prediction Magazine*, April 2002

Franklin, Anna, 'Shape-shifting', *Prediction Magazine*, July 2002

Fraser, Tara, *Yoga for You*, Duncan Baird Publishers, 2001

Gabay, J. Jonathan, *Reinvent Yourself*, Pearson Education Limited, 2002

Gerber, MD, Richard, *Vibrational Medicine for the 21st Century*, Piatkus Books, 2001

Gillett, Roy, *The Essence of Buddhism*, Caxton Editions, 2001

Haas MD, Elson M., *Staying Healthy with the Seasons*, Celestial Arts, 1981

Hamwee, John, *Zero Balancing: Touching the Energy of Bone*, Frances Lincoln, 1999

Hayward, Rick, 'The middle way', *Prediction Magazine*, January 2002

Hayward, Rick, 'Awakening the serpent', *Prediction Magazine*, June 2002

Herzberg, Eileen Inge, *Know Your Complementary Therapies*, Age Concern Books, 2001

Hicks, Angela, *The Five Laws of Healthy Living*, Thorsons, 1998

Hicks, Angela, *Principles of Chinese Medicine*, Thorsons, 1996

Hicks, Angela, *Healing Your Emotions*, Thorsons, 1999

Holford, Patrick, *The Optimum Nutrition Bible*, Piatkus Books, 1997

Kaptchuk, Ted J., *The Web that has no Weaver*, Rider Books 1983

Karcher, Stephen, *Total I Ching*, Little Brown, 2003

Khalsh, Guru Dharma Singh and O'Keeffe, Darryl, *Kundalini: The Essence of Yoga*, Gaia Books 2002

Kingston, Karen, *Creating Sacred Space with Feng Shui*, Piatkus Books, 1996

Knapp, Pia, 'Gaia: living earth', *Prediction Magazine*, May 2002

Konstant, Tina and Taylor, Morris, *Mental Space*, Pearsons Education Limited, 2002

Kwok, Man-Ho, translator and O'Brien, Joanne, ed., *Chinese Face and Hand Reading*, Piatkus Books, 1995

Lad, Vasant, *The Complete Book of Ayurvedic Home Remedies*, Piatkus Books, 1999

Lamont-Brown, Raymond, *Scottish Folklore*, Birlinn, 1996

Leith, Drew, 'The power of runes', *Kindred Spirit Magazine*, Issue 40, Autumn 1997

Lemesurier, Peter, *Nostradamus in the 21st Century*, Piatkus Books, 2000

Linn, Denise, *Space Clearing*, Ebury Press, 2000

MacKenzie, Vicki, ed., *Why Buddhism? Westerners in search of wisdom*, Thorsons, 2003

Mann, Felix, *The Meridians of Acupuncture*, Heinemann 1964

Matthews, John, *The Summer Solstice*, Godsfield Press, 2002

Matthews, John and Caitlin, *The Encyclopaedia of Celtic Wisdom*, Rider Books, 2001

McDermott, Ian and O'Connor, Joseph, *NLP and Health*, Thorsons, 2001

McIntyre, Anne, *The Complete Woman's Herbal*, Gaia Books, 1994

McKenzie, Eleanor and Mann, Niclaire, *Thai Bodywork*, Hamlyn Publishing, 2002

McNamara, Rita J., *Energetic Bodywork: Practical Techniques*, Samuel Weiser, Inc., 1986

Mehta, Narendra, *Indian Head Massage*, Thorsons, 1999

Miller, Gustavus Hindman, *10,000 Dreams Interpreted*, Element Books, 1996

Mole, Peter, *Acupuncture: Energy Balancing for Body, Mind and Spirit*, Element, 1992

Montgomery, Clifton, 'Hunt for the unicorn', *Prediction Magazine*, December 2001

Moorey, Teresa, *Paganism: A Beginner's Guide*, Hodder & Stoughton, 1999

Moorey, Teresa, 'Over the moon', *Prediction Magazine*, March 2002

Morningstar, Sally, *Ayurveda for Health and Well-Being*, Southwater/Anness Publishing Limited, 1999

Morrisson, Dorothy, *Yule: A Celebration of Light and Warmth*, Llewellyn Publications, 2000

Murray, Michael, N.D. and Pizzorno, Joseph, N.D., *Encyclopedia of Natural Medicine* 2nd edition, Prima Books, 1998

Newnham, David, 'Out of it', *Guardian Weekend Magazine*, 8 June, 2002

Nobel, Steve, 'Age of transition', *Prediction Magazine*, July 2002

Norman, Laura, *The Reflexology Handbook*, Piatkus Books, 1988

North, Lynne, 'Space clearing', *Prediction Magazine*, November 2002

Okawa, Ryuho, *The Essence of Buddha*, Little Brown, 2002

Olsen, Kristin, *The Encyclopaedia of Alternative Health Care*, Piatkus Books, 1989

Paterson, Jacqui, 'Past life regression: myth or magic?' *Real Magazine*, Issue 16, 2002

Patrick Mark, 'Everyday psychics', *Prediction Magazine*, September 2000

Phillips, Kathy, *The Spirit of Yoga*, Cassell and Co., 2001

Phillips, Sue, 'Peak experience', *Prediction Magazine*, August 2002

Randles, Jenny, *The Paranornal Source Book*, Piatkus Books, 1999

Roden, Shirlie, *Sound Healing*, Piatkus Books, 1999

Root-Bernstein, Robert and Michèle, *Honey, Mud, Maggots and other Medical Marvels*, Macmillian Press, 1997

Ross, Jeremy, *Acupuncture Point Combinations: Key to Clinical Success*, Churchill Livingstone, 1995

Rossman, M.D., Martin L., *Guided Imagery for Self-Healing*, H.J. Kramer and New World Library, 2000

Roud, S. and Simpson, J., *Oxford Dictionary of English Folklore*, Oxford University Press, 2000

Ryman, Danièle, *Danièle Ryman's Aromatherapy Bible*, new edition, Piatkus Books, 2002

Ryrie, Charlie, *The Healing Energies of Water*, Gaia Books, 1998

Sands, Helen Raphael, *Labyrinth: Pathway to Meditation and Healing*, Gaia Books, 2000

Sayre-Adams, Jean and Wright, Steve, *The Theory and Practice of Therapeutic Touch*, Churchill Livingstone, 1995

Schoen, Allen M., *Kindred Spirits*, Broadway Books, 2001

Senn, Bryan, *Drums of Terror: Voodoo in the Cinema*, Midnight Marquee Press, Inc., 1998

Shanghai College of Traditional Medicine, translated and edited by Bensky, Dan and O'Connor, John, *Acupuncture: A Comprehensive Text*, Eastland Press, 1981

Shine, Norman, *Numerology*, Simon and Schuster, 1994

Simpson, Liz, *The Healing Energies of Earth*, Gaia Books, 1999

Simpson, Liz, *Awaken Your Goddess*, Gaia Books, 2000

Sinclair, Charles, 'Grail quest', *Prediction Magazine*, April 2002

Smith, Jack, 'Romany ways', *Prediction Magazine*, October 2001

Stanway, Dr Penny, *LifeLight: Light and Colour for Health and Healing*, Gaia Books, 2001

Teal, Celeste, 'Chiron: the ancient healer in modern times', *Horoscope Magazine*, June 2002

The New Oxford Dictionary of English, Oxford University Press, 2002

Tobyn, Graeme, *Culpeper's Medicine*, Element Books, 1997

Tzu, Lao, translated by Mitchell, Stephen, *Tao Te Ching*, Frances Lincoln, 1999

Various contributors, *Cultural Diversity Guide*, Meridian Broadcasting Limited, 2001

Watson, Donald, *A Dictionary of Mind and Spirit*, André Deutsch, 1991

Webb, Karen, *First Directions: The Enneagram*, Thorsons, 2001

Webb, Simon, 'Dragon's breath', *Prediction Magazine*, November 2001

West, Peter, 'Chiron: the modern influence in your chart', *Prediction Magazine*, January 2003

Westbury, Virginia, 'Labyrinths: from ancient paths to modern art forms', *Spirituality and Health Magazine*, Autumn 2001

Wildish, Paul, *The Big Book of Ch'i*, Thorsons, 2000

Wildwood, Chrissie, *The Encyclopedia of Healing Plants*, Piatkus Books, 1998

Williamson, Marion, 'Believe your eyes', *Prediction Magazine*, August 2002

Williamson, Marion, 'Taking the plane', *Prediction Magazine*, September 2002

Williamson, Marion, 'Some like it hot', *Prediction Magazine*, October 2002

Williamson, Marion, 'Course review: massage in a bottle', *Prediction Magazine*, November 2002

Wills, Pauline, *Colour Healing*, Piatkus Books, 1999

Worsley, J.R., *Acupuncture: Is it for you?* Element, 1998

Zimmerman, J.E., *Dictionary of Classical Mythology*, Harper and Row, 1964

Internet references

Channel 4 Complementary Health Microsite
   www.Channel4.com/health/microsites/C/comp.medicine/
Encyclopedia Mythica
   www.pantheon.org/mythica.html
God-u-Like: An irreverent look at the faith industry
   www.godulike.co.uk
Jonathan Cainer Online
   stars.metawire.com
Jung Lexicon by Darryl Sharpe
   www.cgjungpage.org/jpintro.html
Occultopedia: An Encyclopedia of the Occult, The Unexplained,
   Myths and More...
   www.occultopedia.com
OCRT: Ontario Consultants on Religious Tolerance
   www.religioustolerance.org
Open Directory Project
   dmoz.org
Skeptics Dictionary by Robert Todd Carroll copyright 2002
   skepdic.com
Witch's Brew for All of Mother's Children
   www.witchs-brew.com

Index

Index